James William Wells

Exploring and Travelling Three Thousand Miles through Brazil

From Rio de Janeiro to Maranhão: Vol. 2

James William Wells

Exploring and Travelling Three Thousand Miles through Brazil
From Rio de Janeiro to Maranhão: Vol. 2

ISBN/EAN: 9783337211370

Printed in Europe, USA, Canada, Australia, Japan

Cover: Foto ©Andreas Hilbeck / pixelio.de

More available books at **www.hansebooks.com**

EXPLORING AND TRAVELLING

THREE THOUSAND MILES THROUGH BRAZIL

FROM RIO DE JANEIRO TO MARANHÃO

WITH AN APPENDIX CONTAINING STATISTICS AND OBSERVATIONS ON
CLIMATE, RAILWAYS, CENTRAL SUGAR FACTORIES, MINING, COM-
MERCE, AND FINANCE; THE PAST, PRESENT, AND FUTURE,
AND PHYSICAL GEOGRAPHY OF BRAZIL.

BY

JAMES W. WELLS,

M. INST. C.E., F.R.G.S.

*ILLUSTRATED WITH NUMEROUS REPRODUCTIONS OF THE AUTHOR'S
SKETCHES, AND ORIGINAL MAPS AND SECTIONS.*

IN TWO VOLUMES

VOL. II.

London

SAMPSON LOW, MARSTON, SEARLE, & RIVINGTON

CROWN BUILDINGS, 188, FLEET STREET

1886

LONDON:
PRINTED BY GILBERT AND RIVINGTON, LD.,
ST. JOHN'S HOUSE, CLERKENWELL ROAD, E.C.

CONTENTS.

CHAPTER I.

FROM JANUARIA TO MANGA DO ARMADOR.

PAGE

Our united troops—A pleasant ride in the forest—Fazenda de Mócambo—A Brazilian gentleman—Luxurious quarters—Produce in excess of demand—Cheap land—Invisible ladies—British weather—Evidences of cultivation—A cattle farm—A fortunate shelter—Rough fare—A sudden storm—Limestone hills—A varied country—Village of Jacaré—A river trader—Chaff—We astonish the natives—A détour—A trial to one's patience—Fantastic forms of limestone—A struggle amidst thorns, brambles, and swamps—A vaqueiro's house, grimy quarters—A musical disturbance—A wet morning, a wet day, and a flooded country—Hospitality refused—A refuge—A damp night's lodging—A goodnatured black—A welcome to sunshine again—Manga do Armador—Low type of inhabitants, a riverside Wapping—Effects of malaria—Probable future improvement in climate of River Valley 1

CHAPTER II.

FROM MANGA DO ARMADOR TO CARINHANHA.

Another wet march—Difficulties of passing flooded streams—Orchids—A varied vegetation—A jararaca-assu snake—A sensible woman—Generous and kind hosts—Valueless mutton—An industrious and contented man—Fazenda de Tabuá—Another ugly crossing—Cattle districts—Ponte de Lagoa—Mosquitos—A dreary night—Carousing black neighbours—Dismal squalor—A haunt of the demon sloth—The riverside road—The rising of the waters—The boundary of Minas Geraes and Bahia—The Rio Carinhanha—The city and its inhabitants—Secluded lives of the females—A long delay—Programme of explorations to be made—Climate—Idle lives—Improvidence—A vessel is chartered for a voyage down the river—Good-bye to old Tommy 18

CHAPTER III.

FROM CARINHANHA TO BARRA DO RIO GRANDE.

Departure from Carinhanha down the river—The Ajojo—Head winds—A mosquito-infested port—First night on the river—An early start—River etiquette—An impromptu sail—The shores of the river—The crew—Flooded lands—A sunset on the river—Great appetites of the crew—A misty morning—São Bom Jezus da Lapa—A curious rock—Who are we?—A hospitable padre—A riverside vicarage—A Brazilian Mecca—The crew ashore—Across country on a raft—The flood—A falling barometer—A squall—A dirty night—Mosquitos again—A night voyage—Sitio de Matto—Proposed capital of new province—The island of fear—Urubú—A sleepy city—A local magnate—The Brazilian student—A night ashore—A mountainous country—The Carnahuba palm—Bom Jardim—An excellent situation and healthy climate—Morro do Pará—An adventure—A bad lot—A geographical bootmaker—A dreamy night voyage—A riverside squatter—The war of the Guimaraẽs—Cidade da Barra 30

CHAPTER IV.

FROM BARRA DO RIO GRANDE TO BOQUEIRÃO.

Adeos—The yacht—Intruders—A swampy land—A night in a lagoon—A convenient "explorer's" bed—Water-lilies—Difficult navigation—Estreita da Serra—Hot weather—A toilsome progress—A river-scene—The splendid physique of the boatmen—Patient toilers—A tramp along the shore—An uncouth reception—A river blocked with fish—Slow travelling—On mule-back again—A jovial companion—Boqueirão—A picturesque situation—A possible future—A village schoolmaster—Indolence of the Boqueirãoenses—A pleasant evening—Navigation of the Rio Grande, etc. 58

CONTENTS.

CHAPTER V.

BOQUEIRÃO TO SANTA RITA.

My new troop—I pass for anti-Christo—The Rio Preto—New class of country—A park-like land—Marsh birds—A mid-day halt—An accident—Tamanduá—An exquisite evening scene—Rodrigues the tropeiro—Good times—A soap tree—Estreita—A contented and homely family—Gallinha d' Agua—A mandioca mill—A batuque dance—A missing mule—Countless butterflies—A prosperous people—Brazilian homes—Santa Rita—A hearty reception—Productions of Santa Rita—The street—Public officials—Various routes to Goyaz and the Tocantins—Dangers and difficulties threaten—Finding a strayed mule—The Santa Ritanas—A wet day in Santa Rita 73

CHAPTER VI.

FROM SANTA RITA TO FORMOSA.

Senhor Francisco—A medicinal plant for dropsy—Wooded lands—Peixe—Cattle-farmers—Donna Chiquinha and the Motucas—The Brazilian Tzetze—A cavalheiro d'industria—A successful gambler—A cold in the tropics—A rich soil—In the forest—A tired mule—Feroz attacked—Prompt revenge—Formosa—A friend in need—Intruders—A rainy season—The verdant village of Formosa—A pretty riverside—The tedium of delay—A prosperous farmer—Indolence of the natives—Doubtful ownership of land—The unknown Sapão—Preparations for entering wild districts—A cultivated valley—Death of Donna Chiquinha—A Brazilian wake—A Brazilian leather leggings—Rodrigue's temerity—Signs of fine weather—A morning's shooting 89

CHAPTER VII.

FROM FORMOSA TO THE MOUTH OF THE RIO SAPÃO.

Additions to my troop—Don Quixote—Forebodings of disaster—A wandering goldsmith—A cattle-farm—Approach to the Geraes—The Burity palm groves of the Sapão and its mouth—Santa Maria—Indian raids—The last houses—A charming situation—Prospects of adventure—Rodrigue's alarm—Difficulties of deciding upon a route—The Rio Sapão—José Grosso . 110

CHAPTER VIII.

FROM THE MOUTH TO THE SOURCE OF THE RIO SAPÃO.

The valley of the Sapão—No more roads—Signs of game—The morasses of the Burity groves—First night in the wilds—Sandstone hills of the Geraes—Picturesque country—Vampire bats—Runaway animals—The Geraes—Tree-lilies—Indications of saline earth—A glorious country for a ride—Macaws—A night alarm—A tapir—A glen of sylvan beauty—The Cabeça de Frade, a ground cactus—A grim solitude—A phosphorescent fungus, *flor de coco*—Construction of the fort—An escape from a centipede—Deer-stalking—Ant-hills and bees—Great quantities of honey—The Don reports signs of Indians—Daybreak in camp—Fording a morass—A novel method of deer-hunting—Indications of peccaries—A splendid climate—Lovely nights—Abundance of game—The swamp of the Nove Galhos—Head-quarters of the peccaries—An awkward situation—Peccaries *v.* dogs—An obstructed route—The valley again—Preparations to receive the enemy—The camp—The attack of the peccaries—A fierce onslaught—A wild, weird scene—An anxious moment—The retreat of the peccaries—The Don becomes deaf—The garrison reinforced—The battle renewed—Rodrigue trembles—A long night of excitement—The siege is raised after great loss by the enemy—Description of the peccaries—Corn in Egypt—Burity wine—A perplexing sight—A beautiful valley—The source of the Sapão—An interesting geographical discovery—Mysterious green grass—Pig-sticking—An ant-bear speared—The ant-bear described—Difficult travelling—Sufferings of the mules—An ascent—The lakes of the valley of the watershed—The equal altitude of flat-topped eminences—The watershed of the São Francisco and Tocantins—Denudation of the Western country—A grand country for cattle-breeding—A clump of Pindahibas 119

CHAPTER IX.

FROM THE SOURCE OF THE SAPÃO TO MATTO GRANDE.

Goyaz entered—Prairies—The gigantic fortress-like bluffs of the Chapada de Mangabeira—The Rio Diogo—Marching through solitudes—The roaring anaconda—The corn almost exhausted—Difficulty of following a route—Crossing the Corrego do Buraco do Diabo—A night-scene in camp—An uncertain route, and corn all gone—Strangers in sight—A council of war—A reconnaissance—The vegetation of the hill-tops—A world of brown grass—A puzzling prospect—Signs of distant habitations—The trail of the strangers—A Burity frond raft—On the track of the strangers—An exhilarating atmosphere—Healthy cattle—Arrival at a house—Peace or war?—A sturdy family of backwoodsmen—The strangers discovered—The outlawed Araujos—A kind and hospitable host—Anybody's land—The Sapão found to be a short cut to Goyaz—A lonely habitation—José do Matto Grande and his family—Escape from a long sojourn in a wilderness—A borderland farm—Arrival of my troop—A night under a roof again—An exploration and hunting party—A skirmish with the peccaries—Chased up a tree—A few exciting moments—The anaconda snakes of the marshes—Habits of the peccaries—Exploring the country 148

CHAPTER X.

FROM MATTO GRANDE TO PORTO FRANCO.

Isolated hills—Limestone formation—An undulating country—The Rio Somninho the source of the Sommo—Excellent cattle and grand grazing-'ands—Charming woods—Absence of fevers—Espirito Santo village—Top-boots from a snake-skin—A fine specimen skin—*Bicho de pé*—An independent village—A troublesome road—Boa Esperança—A *sertãoeijos* farm—An enterprising Brazilian—A night with *baratas* or cockroaches—A Brazilian pioneer—Dangers of river bathing—A tiresome ford—A stormy night under canvas—Bob escapes drowning—Hard work in crossing a stream—A rocky country—Vestiges of the old plateau—A rough bit of road—An adventure with a rattlesnake, and another with a huge stag—A party of travellers—The good-natured *Geralistas* of Jalapão—The barren *gerães*—Arrive at Porto Franco—The farm at Porto Franco—I become wearied with my travels—Dull times—Cattle-raising at Porto Franco—A wild plantation—Good treatment of slaves—Climate—Costliness of salt—Indians and missionaries—A raft is constructed—Good-bye to my followers—The crew of the raft . 169

CHAPTER XI.

FROM PORTO FRANCO DOWN THE RIO DO SOMNO TO THE TOCANTINS.

Adeosito Porto Franco—On the Rio do Somno—Our first pancada—Camp ashore—Indian cookery—A perilous prospect—A gusty evening—A jaguar's roar—Morning on the river—The banks of the Somno—Curious bees'-nest—Birds and animals of the river-side—Pancadas—Feroz, and his swimming powers—A wild cat shot—Cooking under difficulties—A rough night—Bad prospects—Approach to the rapids—Shooting the r. pids of "O Funil"—Imprisoned in the valley of the river—Grand scenery—Borne onwards in a rush of waters—A sudden and terrible spectacle—In the vortex of the Apertada Hora—A few breathless moments—On the rocks—A wild struggle—A narrow escape—Disappearance of the river—An unexpected outlet—Splendid behaviour of the crew—Loss and damage—A solitude —An in ersecting mountain range—An uncomfortable night—Signs of diamonds—Peccaries again—A cautious advance in the woods—Sent up a tree—Skirmishing—Pork for dinner—Patience, and obedience of Feroz—The wild banana—Monkeys —Life on the Somno—Bob's damp bed—A hot day—A squalid farm—The Rio Perdido—The shores filled with animal life—The lower Somno—Reach the Tocantins 192

CHAPTER XII.

FROM PEDRO AFFONSO TO CAROLINA DOWN THE RIO TOCANTINS.

Arrival at Pedro Affonso—An indifferent host—Too late for the last "bote"—The botes and traders of the Rio Tocantins—An old Indian settlement—Indian boys—The Montaria The new crew—Frae Rafael and his mission—The Coroado Indians—The country around the village—A tender craft—My tent is sacrificed—Adeos, Pedro Affonso—Cramped accommodation—Paddles of the Tocantins v. São Francisco—The shores of the Tocantins—A murderous rascal and his home—Persecution of the Indians and unpunished crimes of the interior of Brazil—Well-watered lands—Bico de Toucano and his resources—On the river Tocantins—A woeful loss—Uselessness of the inhabitants—Arrival at Carolina—Advised to abandon the voyage to Para—The city and its inhabitants—Disappointment in obtaining a troop for the journey overland—Scarcity of game —A hilly neighbourhood—Gold and copper districts—A church festival—A negro festival 214

CHAPTER XIII.

FROM CAROLINA TO CHAPADA.

Departure from Carolina—Poor means of land travelling in North Brazil—Chasing cattle—A complimentary escort—A merry camp—A hilly, elevated country—Picturesque hills—Angelino—An industrious negro—Castle Hill—A curious formation

—My fellow-traveller—A thinly-inhabited country—Rough tracks—In the woods in the darkness—A scramble in the dark—João Nogueiro—A copper region—Our wretched packhorses—Dewy nights in camp—A march on foot—Scarcity of game—A charming camp—A strange tree—The Serra da Cinta an important range—A mountain path—A rattlesnake—Misery of travelling with poor animals—A tiring tramp—A palm forest—Morro do Frade—Timidity of countrywomen—A welcome rest—An untidy farm—Good news: a fresh horse—Flat plains and deep valleys—In a butcher's shop for the night—Copper indications—Trezedellas—Arrive at Chapada . 237

CHAPTER XIV.

FROM CHAPADA, DOWN THE RIO GRAJAHU, TO VICTORIA ON THE RIO MEARIM.

A pleasant family—Chapada children—A rich copper region—The sessions at Chapada—Trade—A white Indian—We charter an *igarité*—A grand departure from Capada—Our new craft and its crew—The river Grajahu and its beauties—A camp by the forest—Howling monkeys—A quiet solitude—Mosquitos again—Animal life of the river-side—A mountain of whetstones—A hill of satin spar—A foul place—A night voyage—Snags—Buried alive—A night of torment—*Botes* of the river—In the forest—Ferocious fish; the *piranhas*—A race—A tortuous river—Morro do Oratorio—Fishing—Vegetation of the shores—Gammella Indians—First habitations since leaving Chapada—Hidden beauties—*Pium* sand-flies—Snags—An Indian anecdote—An exchange of compliments—The effect of a revolver—A morning mist—Torments of sand-flies—A day's journey to gain 600 yards—A useful parasite—An evening scene—A collision with a snag—Boarded by fire-ants—Amidst the bush in the darkness—A perfect inferno—Continual torments—The Director of Indians—Valuable natural productions of the forest—Indian village—Sobradinho and its tenants—A landslip—Itambeira Indians—Fever appears—A grand forest—Brown river-water—Untiring paddlers—An alligator and the *Piranhas*—A Penelope—A lost dinner—A dense bush—An Indian alarm—A noisy night with frogs—Dangers of a sleep on a sand-bank—Mournful tokens—The deadly climate of the river in certain seasons—More copper indications—A grand copper region—Ingativas—A diver bird—A farm abandoned through mosquitos—A long day's work—A weary night—Inhabited lands—Brilliant distinctness of tropical scenery—An industrious couple—*A capoeira de palmerias*—A haunted lake—The submerged lands of the mouth of the Grajahu—A steaming-hot locality—On the Rio Mearim—No land to camp on—A slow and fatiguing journey—Arrive at Victoria—Rough quarters 259

CHAPTER XV.

FROM VICTORIA TO MARANHÃO.

S. Antonio's day at Victoria—The town and its Padre—Good-bye to my companion—On to Arary—A bustling port—An influential trader—Portuguese hospitality—Passage booked to Maranhão—An evening thunder-storm—An unusual scene—A return from the wilderness—A gossip with a frank young lady—A marshy country—A considerable proprietor—The navigation of the lower river and its trade—A crowded craft—Kindness of mine host—Rough accommodation—A dreary scene—A tidal wave—A river steamer—In the bay of São Marcos—Land at Maranhão—A return to civilization—Difficulties in leaving the port—A helpless countryman and a kind and useful Brazilian official—On board the *Bahia*—An attack of fever at sea—Bob's disgust and departure to his home—Adieu to poor Feroz—Lost, stolen, or strayed . . . 297

APPENDIX A.—SURVEY OF THE RIOS PARAOPEBA AND UPPER RIO SÃO FRANCISCO 311

APPENDIX B.—EXPLORATION OF THE TOCANTINS—SÃO FRANCISCO WATERSHED; FROM CARINHANHA TO THE VALLEY OF THE PARANAN 313

APPENDIX C.—CLIMATE . . 316

APPENDIX D.—GOLD AND DIAMOND MINING . 325

APPENDIX E.—RAILWAYS . 332

APPENDIX F.—CENTRAL SUGAR FACTORIES . . 344

APPENDIX G.—THE PAST, PRESENT, AND FUTURE OF BRAZIL . 347

APPENDIX H.—THE PHYSICAL GEOGRAPHY OF BRAZIL . 359

LIST OF ILLUSTRATIONS AND MAPS.

                                                                                                   PAGE

The cave-church, village, and rock of São Bom Jezus da Lapa *Frontispiece*

An evening thunder-storm	1
A matutor on a chilly morning	18
The North Square, city of Carinhanha	26
Sailing down the Rio São Francisco	30
In the lagoons of the Rio Grande	58
Sunset on the Rio Grande	65
Marsh birds: the Jabiru-moleque stork, the Quem-quem, and the Jaçaná	73
The wooded valley of the Rio Preto, near Formosa	89
Buritirana and Burity palms and the Rio Preto at Santo Maria	110
A peccary "at bay"	119
The camp stormed by peccaries	134
Pig-sticking in Goyaz	140
An "indio manso" (a friendly Indian)	148
A night-scene in camp in the wilds of Goyaz	153
Sighting strangers in the wilderness	155
A narrow escape from drowning	169
The Morro do Munducuru	180
Departure from Porto Franco on the Rio do Somno	192
In the rapids of the Apertada Hora	203
On the Rio Tocantins	214
The city of Carolina, Rio Tocantins	231
A midnight festival at Carolina	236
Crossing the arid table-lands of Maranhão	237
Crossing the Serra da Cinta	250
The praça of the town of Chapada	257
Manoel the pilot	260
An Indian	277
A field of sugar-cane	297
The port of Arary, Rio Mearim	299

MAPS AND SECTONS.

	PAGE
Sketch map of route from the source of the Rio Sapão to the Rio Tocantins, and a section showing elevations of land	148
Sketch map of route from Carolina to Chapada, and a section showing elevations of land	237
Longitudinal section of formation level of railway in the valleys of the Rio Parñopeba and upper Rio São Francisco	311

General map of Route from Rio de Janeiro to Maranhão, showing configuration of surface of country, and a section showing elevation of land traversed.

A physical map of Brazil.

THREE THOUSAND MILES THROUGH BRAZIL.

CHAPTER I.

FROM JANUARIA TO MANGA DO ARMADOR.

Our united troops—A pleasant ride in the forest—Fazenda de Mocombo—A Brazilian gentleman—Luxurious quarters—Produce in excess of demand—Cheap land—Invisible ladies—British weather—Evidences of cultivation—A cattle farm—A fortunate shelter—Rough fare—A sudden storm—Limestone hills—A varied country—Village of Jacaré—A river trader—Chaff—We astonish the natives—A detour—A trial to one's patience—Fantastic forms of limestone—A struggle amidst thorns, brambles, and swamps—A vaqueiro's house, grimy quarters—A musical disturbance—A wet morning, a wet day, and a flooded country—Hospitality refused—A refuge—A damp night's lodging—A good-natured black—A welcome to sunshine again—Manga do Armador—Low type of inhabitants, a riverside Wapping—Effects of malaria—Probable future improvement in climate of River Valley.

January 23rd.—This morning our united troops made a goodly show as we defiled out of the city. Besides our three selves we had nine men, one boy, twenty-seven mules and horses, and three dogs, Feroz, Caranca, and Pequeno.

Soon after leaving the town, the road gradually leads away from the river-side, passing many habitations and long level tracts of inundated land, the openings in the low scrub being the only indications of the road; this extended for eight or nine miles, when the track entered a forest of splendid trees, where a, fairly good and broad waggon-road offered us a pleasant canter ahead of the mule-train.

Even the dogs, by their gambols and joyful barkings, seemed to appreciate the merits of a dry wide road in the pleasant shade.

The forest was singularly free from the usual dense undergrowth, and many charming glades and openings between the grand trees formed many scenes of sylvan beauty. Conspicuous amongst the trees were giant buttressed *gammeleira*, many of them wreathed in massive encircling *llianas*, such as the *monstera deliciosa*, and bedecked with brilliant flowering crimson *bromelias*. Delicate tree and other ferns, and *guariroba* and *jeribá* palms softened with their feathery foliage the dark outline of the massive trunks. *Cipos* or creepers hung in long pendent lines like the cordage of a ship, or formed graceful curves from tree to tree; numerous orchids, parasites, mosses, and lichens decorated the trunks and branches, to such an extent that almost every tree was a garden in itself.

At the end of twenty miles, the even ground of the forest changed to rolling hills of a more upland country that had been cleared of its primitive forest and turned into pasture-land.

We soon afterwards arrived at a substantial, two-storied fazenda, the Fazenda de Mocombo.[1] Along its wide front, extended on the first floor, a pleasantly shaded verandah where an old gentleman in a dressing-gown was seated in a rocking-chair; and on our requesting permission to speak with the proprietor, he replied, "*Sou seu criado*" (I am your servant), and further desired us to dismount and enter. We presented our cards and briefly explained our nationality and

---

[1] This place is indicated on maps as a village or small town. Not at all an uncommon mistake is it to thus misrepresent the most important estates as villages. Mocombo, like Quilombo, is a retreat of fugitive slaves.

purposes, and that our large troop would shortly arrive. The old gentleman courteously apologized for not rising from his chair, saying, " *Sou muito velho e doente* " (I am very old and ill); but, with a kindly smile, he expressed his pleasure to receive us, and all the poor accommodation of his house was at our disposition, clapped his hands, and directed his negros to take the animals and prepare for the rest of the troop.

Our worthy host was a Senhor Marcellino—I regret I have forgotten the rest ôf his name—a well-educated gentleman and representative of the class of educated Brazilian planters. I shall long remember and be grateful, not only for the personal comforts bestowed upon us, but for the genial courtesy and kindliness expressed by this kind old gentleman in every word and deed. That night we revelled in the almost forgotten luxuries of a well-appointed bedroom and a civilized table: to meet such a place as this in these backwoods is like finding a jewel in a dust-heap.

The verandah overlooked a prettily arranged flower and fruit garden in the front of the house, where we found many an European garden flower growing in great luxuriance. Beyond the garden, the ground stretched far away in great rolling grassy downs, dotted with many herds of browsing cattle; the tall straight trunks of a neighbouring forest and the blue outline of distant highlands completed the picture; by the side of the fazenda a clear stream of water murmured a monotone as it flowed amongst the stones of a pebbly bed, and created the pleasant music of the splash of the falling water of an adjoining water-wheel. In our pleasant circumstances, with what an appreciative mind a traveller can enjoy the peaceful surroundings of such a scene in the quiet of the evening, when the lights of the western sky assume the pearly greys and delicate azure tints of the short twilight of these regions, and the first chill mists of night appear in filmy clouds like snow-white wool.

Our host unfortunately had to retire early, but before doing so he told us in conversation that his family had occupied lands in and around Januaria for many generations, and had been planters in the good old mining and colonial times, when agricultural produce was scarce and very valuable and slaves were cheap ; now, he says, we are all planters or traders, and produce more than we can profitably dispose of; he further told us that he owned an adjoining estate of rich forest and pasture-land with a good house, fences, and farm buildings on it ; the area was very considerable—in fact, he hardly knew its extent ; for this he said he would accept 200*l.*, for there were many more sellers of land than buyers.

I know we all saw with regret the sun rise the next morning and necessitate our departure from the most comfortable quarters we had met with since leaving Taboleiro Grande. There were some female occupants of the fazenda, for we heard their voices, but they were as removed from sight as if they were the inmates of an Eastern harem.

As usual in many of the better order of fazendas in the country, we were only permitted to pay for the corn the animals had consumed, but I knew that some of the blacks would have a merry time after we had left; for it is rarely that these poor slaves in these country *engenhos* can obtain a few luxuries to soften their dreary lives. Unfortunately we were not enabled to get away so early as anticipated, for a sudden and violent downpour of rain prevented the loading of the mules for some hours, as it is always advisable in travelling not only to " keep your powder dry," but your baggage also.

Late in the morning, however, the united troop formed the order of march, and away we once more jog, jogged, splashing through the muddy road and turbulent little streams ; a drizzle still was falling, the sky was overcast with masses of piled up leaden-coloured clouds, and the vegetation dripped with moisture from every leaf as we again entered the sombre shade of forest.

A rainy day in Brazil seems to have much more depressing effects than even to a tourist in an out-of-the-way village, say in the west of Ireland, for in these tropical countries' one gets so accustomed to the glare and brightness of the sunshine, the brilliant skies, and foliage glistening in the fierce light, that whenever a day of the drizzling British climate occurs, down goes the thermometer, up goes one's liver, everything becomes damp, and chilly, and muddy, and every one looks pinched, cold, and disagreeable.

Here in the forest, as we ride along splashing in the mud, carefully drawing mackintoshes over every corner of our limbs, for the wet leaves of branches occasionally sweep our faces, and ornament our noses with drops of crystal water; detached clouds of mist glide like phantoms through the trees, and the drip, drip, drip of water is heard everywhere; then sometimes a mule, without apparent reason, would stampede off into the adjoining bush, jam and crush the baggage against the trees, the noise creates other stampedes and confusion of all the troop; all our careful arrangement of mackintoshes are no longer regarded as each of us struggles amongst the wet bushes to catch the recalcitrant mules, and reform the troop; of course, on such occasions it always rains harder, so on we go, wet, chilly and muddy, to an unknown camp.

In this forest-land, we passed in the lowlands many clearings of exhausted or existing cultivated plots of maize, beans, tobacco, cotton, castor-tree, and mandioca; the soil is exceedingly rich and well watered, and the country is admitted to be very salubrious, yet land can be obtained here in comparatively almost any quantity and quality, forest, grass, or scrub, for a mere bagatelle.

In the afternoon we emerged from the almost continual forest on to undulating hilly ground, grass-clad hills, and wooded, watered valleys, combining all the elements required for cattle-raising or agriculture in admirable combination. At about 3 p.m., after travelling about eighteen miles, we arrived at the currals and adobe houses of a fazenda nestling in the shade of great *gammelcira* trees and paddocks of fruit-trees: oranges, bananas, *papaw*, *ginipapos*, *jaboticabas*,

&c. The sky had cleared, and the sun's rays brightened up the scene, the place looked homely and prosperous, although to an English farmer's eyes it would have appeared very untidy.

On riding up to the door of the residence, a general stampede of all the female occupants took place; doors and window shutters were hurriedly closed and fastened as we approached. Some blacks engaged in yoking oxen to a bullock-cart informed us that the "senhor" was not at home, that his name was Marcellino de Sá, a breeder of cattle and manufacturer of *rapadura* (bricks of sugar), and that a short distance beyond was an empty house that we might occupy for the night.

Continuing our journey over more hills of grass and scrub, and streamlets and woods in the bottoms, we eventually crossed a stream 100 feet wide, flowing over a flat rocky bed, with banks of gravel, and ascended the rise of a hill on the opposite side, and there found our new quarters, quite a new large house with a tiled roof, adobe walls, shuttered windows, and the door standing invitingly open; truly we had no reason to regret Senhor Marcellino's absence, such quarters as these were to be duly appreciated in such weather as we might expect at night.

It was a lively and bustling scene, as mule after mule arrived and the process of unloading and carrying the baggage into the house went on; then man and horse stretched their stiffened limbs. Each of the mules as soon as relieved of its burdens, after a good sniff and examination of the ground, walks round the selected spot once, and then slowly goes down on its knees, and turns over on its back for a good roll in the sand.

Whilst the dinner was in process of preparation, my two companions and I adjourned to the stream at the bottom of the hill for a plunge and a swim in the pellucid water. The preparations for dinner were not made by a cook in a white blouse and cap, in a modern kitchen, but by black and muddy Bob; in a pail of water, beans, dry beef, and salt pork were indiscriminately soaked, and a little of the accompanying dirt extracted before being put in the saucepan or on the fire. The house was admirably situated, and commanded extensive views of well-diversified scenery all around; at the foot of the hill was the stream of clear water, clear even then in the rainy weather; beyond it in all directions appeared rolling hills, some clad with fine forests, others with grass or with low scrub between thickets of trees and groups of palms. Away to the west about ten or twelve miles, appeared the dark outline of an irregular range of elevated hills, forming probably the bluffs of the Western São Franciscan table-land.

As the sun set dark banks of clouds gathered over these heights, shadowing their blue outlines to dark purples and greys; as the clouds advanced the shadows extended over hill and dale, then slanting lines of pale grey appeared between clouds and hills, thunder crashed, and jagged lines of vivid light flashed, slight puffs of wind were occasionally felt, a distant hoarse murmur was heard, the clouds rapidly extended, enveloping earth and sky in a pall of grey mist, more and more puffs of wind, a few heavy drops of warm rain fell, then the leaves whirled in the air, palms and trees bowed, and with a hoarse cry the storm of wind and rain, and crashing thunder and vivid lightning was upon us. Thankful we were as we sat in the semi-darkness with door and window closed to have such a sanctuary. How the wind howled around, and the vivid flashes of lightning illumined the interior of the room, followed by terrific salvoes of heaven's artillery! Soon, the thunder became fainter and more distant, and the rain and wind ceased as suddenly as it commenced. On opening the door, behold a starry night and streamlets of water coursing madly down the hill; the thunder muttered in the distance, as the clouds and mist disappeared to the east, and the tropical squall was over.

It was not long after the crash of the storm had ceased

before the house echoed to the measured notes of its sleeping tenants.

January 25.—It was a welcome sound that awoke us with the first glimmer of daylight, the steady crunch of the mules enjoying their feed of corn. It is always a relief to find on awakening that no animals are missing.

Once more jog, jog, on the road to the north. It was twelve miles to Jacaré,[2] a small village situated on the banks of the river. We passed through a rough and varied district, forest and second-growth being the main features of the vegetation; on the way were many strange and weird hills of limestone rock, worn and chased by ages into towers and pinnacles and other fantastic forms, the interstices being filled with a variety of a huge blue cactus, and by other vegetation too numerous to specify. The road was alternately rugged from rocks and roots of trees, slippery from the rain, and soft and swampy in the hollows; we passed not more than a half-dozen roadside habitations on the way.

The *arraial* or hamlet of Jacaré consists simply of one street of scattered houses and huts facing the river, and contains about 300 souls; almost every habitation has its own compound in which grow many of the fruit and other trees common to the district. A wide straggling road largely overgrown with grass, forms the main thoroughfare; a few large trees grow on the river-banks, under the shade of which are discussed local politics and the crops, and form collectively the village ale-house and exchange mart for the transaction of business with the river-traders. A tumble-down old barn of a church is of course the indispensable adjunct to the village.

On riding up to the door of the most comfortable-looking house, the owner invited us to enter and partake of the inevitable coffee; then ensued the usual questions as to our business, ages, salaries, &c. In the meantime all the village

[2] Alligator.

gossips crowd round the door, the usual gaping, listless, idle group.

We heard that we should find ahead many habitations by the riverside, but that the road skirting the river was flooded, and it would be advisable to take a guide to show us through the woods around the hills of Itacaramby, a little further on. A halt was necessary to rest the animals and to shoe many of them after the rough ride of the morning.

A stroll through the village showed us the usual life of these riverside hamlets. A trader's *barca* was at the muddy *praia* surrounded by a number of brown and black women, chaffering with the pedlar for a cotton dress, needles, ribbons, flaming red or blue shawls, &c.; at the moment he was showing them, to their intense delight, a straw hat, trimmed with the brightest of ribbons and imitation flowers; they could not find the wherewithal to purchase it, and the hat was restored to its box, amidst the sighs and regrets of the women. "*Ai! Sta. Maria! Que chapeo bonito! Que coisa linda! Ai di mim, isto não é para pobres como nos.*" (Ah! Holy Mary! What a lovely hat! What a pretty thing! But, dear me, this is not for poor people like us.)

Hard by, under the shade of trees, another group of men were tinkling guitars, and shouting their impromptu songs, that we found were descriptive of the arrival of the *inglezes* (ourselves), their white skin, the great troop, the fat mules, our land far away where lived all the rich people and no poor ones, &c., &c., concluding each refrain with "*Olhe! as moças estão olhando*" (Look! the girls are watching you). The latter observation created a giggle amongst the dark *houris* of the *barca*, between whom and the songster ensued a mild form of banter.

A countryman with a horseload of beans and salted *surubim* was going from house to house to find a purchaser, a few cattle and pigs were browsing on the bush by the river-banks, a few loungers at the doorways, and half-clad women leaning in the windows, or working the old pillow lace, and the sounds of the shrill piping chant of the village school, completed the rest of the life of the village, as it appeared to us.

In front of the village extended the broad and turbid waters of the flooded river, bearing many a snag on its flowing surface, and excepting the *barca* at the *praia*, no other craft was visible, either up or down the grand mass of water.

During our perambulations we had been accompanied by all the *moleques*[3] of the village, who listened with astonished eyes and open mouth to our conversation with each other in English. I do not think a single object of our costume escaped their observation and remarks; they darted ahead and about us, like village boys at home around an arriving circus caravan.

Taking a guide with us, at 2 p.m. we filed out of the village into lower ground, inundated from the high water of the river; the flood extended for a long way inland, the bush and trees of the banks alone indicating their margins; for two miles we splashed through this pea-soup-looking water, when our guide led us off to the left, on to higher ground, and entered apparently a pathless forest; as he went on hacking with his *facão*,[4] a way through bush and briar, and we saw our long troop of mules with their projecting packs, and in front the pathless matted bramble, it certainly did appear puzzling how we were to get on. Upon asking our guide what was his object in plunging into this maze, he informed us that an elevated mass of rock we had perceived in front of us, and known as the Morro de Itacarambi, extended to the river's banks, and the road at its foot is only passable when the river is not flooded, and that somewhere in the forest there was a path that passed to the rear of these hills. A few of the men were called up with billhook and knife, to assist the guide to clear the way. Slowly we forged ahead, the ground in many places being treacherously soft and boggy, in which the animals sank, and were with difficulty extracted; the trailing vines and thorny bramble tore

[3] Coloured boys.   [4] Large wood-knife.

our clothes and faces, the animals got squeezed in between trees, or crushed against trunks of trees, and immediately a mule meets an obstacle to his progress he is at once seized with a frantic desire to go ahead with all his force ; result, something gives way and down come the packs, and away goes the mule into the midst of bramble and briar ; add to it all, a hot steamy fetid atmosphere, like that of a hot-house, foul exhalations from the swampy soil, and myriads of mosquitos. Verily it was a good trial to one's patience and philosophy.

After an hour of vexatious and laborious work we came alongside the precipitous walls of the Morro, towering above the woods in pinnacled and otherwise fantastic forms of limestone rock, worn by the weather of ages into strange and weird shapes like the ruins of old castles ; immense candelabra cactii in the hollows of the rock added their strange forms to the hobgoblin appearance of the place.

It was a queer scene to see us struggling and working our way in the close pestiferous heat, amongst the trees and vines of that grim solitude; but time and patience effect wonders, for in another hour we found the long-sought-for trail, but hardly better than the pathless jungle we had passed, for it was thickly obstructed by roots, quagmires, trunks of trees, creepers, and bramble ; however, it afforded us an indication that we were in the right direction, as the prospect of passing a night in such a locality would have been anything but pleasant. Four miles only, we afterwards were told, was the estimated distance through that tangled maze.

This Morro de Itacarambi is a strange feature of the country ; it is an elongated mass of limestone rising abruptly from a plain, for we had travelled around it inland from river-bank to river-bank, and all the way found the ground around it practically flat and swampy. It stands there a solitary remnant of the land that once filled the valley of the river, a grim vestige of bygone ages. The limestone hills on the road to Jacaré are precisely of a similar formation.

As the sun became low in the west we emerged once more into daylight and open space ; before us stretched a broad expanse of swamp, bounded on the east by a belt of forest that excluded a view of the river, and on the west by rising ground covered with cerrado scrub.

Learning that a cattle farm was at the further side of the swamp, about two miles distant, we pushed on our panting weary animals, splashing through the flooded land, and often floundering in the many quagmires; finally we reached the Sitio de Itacarambi, the outlying station of a cattle fazenda, and residence of a cow-herd (*vaqueiro*). It consisted merely of an open shed with a corner partitioned off by mud walls ; at the rear was the cattle curral, knee-deep in black fetid mud that extended to the floor of the open shed. All around outside the ground was marshy, wet, and muddy.

The *vaqueiro* willingly consented to shelter us for the night, his roof and dry floor being very acceptable in such a sloppy neighbourhood, albeit the odours of the mud of the curral were not those of Araby the bless'd. That night Bob had to "hurry up" with his messes, for our long day's ride of twenty-four miles had created appetites that an alderman would have envied.

After dinner as we enjoyed the fragrant weed, in the darkness rendered visible by the dim smokey light of a solitary lamp of cotton-wick placed in the shallow iron cup of castor-oil, and by the flickering light of a log-fire, we forgot the fatigues of the day, and the squalor around us, and one and all dropped off into dreamland ; unfortunately our slumbers were not to last long, for the house was soon after invaded by a number of carousing friends of our host, who noisily entered regardless of his sleeping guests; songs and dances were soon started, accompanied by a rub-a-dub-dub symphony on a drum, constructed out of the hollow trunk of a tree, on the extremities of which sheep-skins had been stretched. Many and hearty were the blessings we called down upon the strangers, and the air became blue with the observations ; finally, our host, noticing our restlessness (it evidently occurred to him for the first time that perhaps we might not appreciate the concert), blandly inquired · if the turmoil was inconvenient : the answer he received immediately cleared away all doubts. When he suggested to his friends that the *estrangeiros* (foreigners) perhaps might want to sleep, the rough, but good fellows immediately desisted, and calm and peace ensued.

January 26th.—This morning there was rain, steadily pouring rain and drifting clouds of mist and drizzle, that shrouded from view all distant objects and made the air damp and chilly. The men presented a benumbed appearance when they arrived with the mules from the adjoining pasture, their heads and shoulders carefully enveloped in their *ponchos*, but legs and feet bare, their faces were blanched and blue, and their teeth chattered with cold. No, their faces were not exactly blue, their brown complexions assumed more of a drab, or dirty yellow tinge ; dripping with wet, they looked like turkey-buzzards after a shower. They took very kindly to a dram of *cachaça*, tossing it off without a wink, with a sigh of satisfaction, and "*Ah! agora o bixo morreo!*" (Ah! now the *bixo* has died)—that awful insect that is always being killed, but only dies to again resuscitate, a veritable Phœnix amongst insects.

One by one the animals were led into the shed and loaded under cover. Breakfast over, and an extra ration of rum served out to the men to keep off the chills, away we filed off in the driving rain and flooded land.

Fortunately, we obtained a guide from amongst last night's visitors, otherwise it was very doubtful if we should have been able to find our way through the water that covered the land. All day we splashed through the water, always keeping by the river-banks, then all submerged. It rained all day; the sky overcast with grey clouds and leaden in its hues, the surrounding country all obscured in driving mist and rain, and the chilly, damp air, altogether formed anything but a conventional Brazilian picture.

The adjoining country is low-lying grass land, intersected

by bushes and occasional clumps of woods. The few poor huts we passed were flooded and deserted; water, water everywhere, and not a place to rest. In the afternoon the weather became worse, violent gusts of wind swept by and rain poured in torrents, accompanied by thunder and lightning; several deep holes of small streams had with great difficulty been crossed; in one case, the packs were unloaded in the wet and mire, and carried across on the men's backs, the animals swimming across; everything, man and baggage, was thoroughly soaked, but there was no alternative but to proceed; we might just as well have camped in a shallow lake as to have stayed there.

At 4 p.m. we sighted a *vaqueiro's* house on dry ground, called Poco de Lavagem, but the owner being away, the female occupants would neither appear nor answer to our summons, and remained silent and invisible behind the closed doors and windows. After a consultation it was decided to push on again, as higher ground was reported to be had further on. The pack-mules were with difficulty driven away from the inhospitable house, grunting as a mule will grunt when he is disgusted.

The rain still came down in torrents, and the water in places became so deep that the mules were almost swimming; we were in despair when we thought of our clothes, stores, &c., and saw the boxes and trunks continually dip into the water. Not a human being had been met the whole of the long day.

Fortunately, towards the late afternoon the waters shallowed, and at last, in the fading light of this gloomy day, dry ground was reached, and better still, a house with an open and empty *copial* (large open verandah) in the front of it. On knocking at the door it was found to be closed and fastened, and no one replied. We could not, however, stand upon ceremony, and hastily got the baggage under cover of the friendly roof.

How wet, cold and hungry we all were! with some difficulty wood was obtained from a thicket hard by, and there was soon a welcome fire burning, over which Bob soon prepared some dampers of *farinha* (*bejoo*) that stayed our ravenous hunger until the beans were ready; from 7 a.m. to 7 p.m. is a long day's ride through rain and flooded land all the way, without a halt for rest or refreshment.

In the evening the owner of the house, a black man, and his wife, a mulatto, arrived. We tendered our apologies for our occupation of his verandah (then well filled-up with ourselves, men, saddles, and baggage); he good-humouredly told us to make ourselves at home, and that his "house was at our orders." As we saw no more of him that night, perhaps he thought it just as well not to kick against the pricks; it would have required a good many owners to have turned us out into that dark wet night. We had to make ourselves as comfortable as the limited space afforded; we certainly had a sound thatch roof overhead, but from the open front and sides the driving moisture-laden wind blew upon us all night. Well-aired beds were not *de rigueur* that night.

Although I have mentioned the chilliness of the air, I found the thermometer registered 70° (F.) in the day, and 65° (F.) in the evening. It is really not the temperature that makes one feel cold; it is the excessive and penetrating dampness of the air, that seems to have a peculiar affinity to one's bones.

That night, after the mules had had a feed of corn, they were turned loose in the darkness to find a pasture for themselves, and early in the morning every one appeared in camp, waiting for another ration of maize, evidently having fared but poorly in the night; but corn, it is well known, constitutes the sum-total of a mule's earthly happiness.

On our host informing us that the Arraial da Manga do Amador was only four miles distant, we made an early breakfastless departure, in order to reach that place and rest the mules for the day, and dry our sopping effects.

A clear bright morning followed the wet of the previous day; how welcome was the sun again after such a day! and as we cantered along ahead of the mule-train we felt inclined to shout, like Massaniello, "Hail! smiling morn," for verily the distant hills, the foliage, and river were gilded and bright with the burnished rays of the morning sun; but as it ascended in the heavens, its heat eventually developed such a steam from the saturated ground, that the atmosphere became like a vapour-bath, the wind died away, and the temperature became close, hot, and stifling.

On the borders of pools of water, rapidly evaporating, myriads of butterflies covered the moist ground, rising in clouds as we rode through them, like a fall of variously-coloured snow; they were of many varieties, but the common brimstone colour predominated.

Manga do Amador was at last sighted, situated on high ground by the river-side.[5] On arrival we succeeded in obtaining a large and fairly-clean empty house, where, as soon as the troop arrived, the wet baggage was unpacked, and clothes and stores extended in the sunshine in a yard at the rear; such a cleaning and drying of clothes and persons, for we all felt such very way-worn travellers.

The village is built upon two elevations, eighty feet above the river, and consists of a dilapidated old church, and about fifty or sixty houses or ranchos occupied by the variously-coloured, mixed races of the country, *bodes*,[6] *cabras*,[7] *caboclos*,[8] and negros.

I did not see in the whole village any semblance to a white skin; even the more well-to-do indicated by their flat faces and lank black hair, their Indian origin; there seemed to be more than the usual apathy in this place, and scant of civility, they had barely energy enough to favour us with the usual inspection, or wearily turn their limp lounging forms towards us as we passed.

[5] It is eighty miles from Januaria by the river; the bluffs of the banks are thirty-four feet above ordinary water-level.

[6] *Bode*, a male goat, is a slang term for a mulatto.

[7] *Cabra*, a female goat, is a common name for any coloured individual, but only applied to the lower classes.

[8] *Caboclo*, a countryman, but the name infers generally an Indian origin.

There was a great predominance of ill-favoured mulatto and *caboclo* women, tricked out in all the coarse finery of country-embroidered chemises, many-coloured ribbons and gorgeously-coloured cotton-skirts; nearly all were tinkling guitars, and swinging in hammocks in their grass-thatched, mud-walled huts.

This place is a species of riverside Wapping, or Southsea of the olden time, and a favourite place of call for the *barqueiros* to have "a day ashore;" but there being no ships in port, perhaps accounted for the more than usual want of animation.

In all these riverside settlements a traveller cannot help noticing the emaciated frames and listless countenances of many of the inhabitants, due in a great measure to repeated attacks of *sezoës*, or *maleta*, as the intermittent fevers are variously termed. A wholesome life, and a few local efforts might probably prevent the development of the disease; but an utter neglect of all hygiene, poor diet, excess in drink and debauchery, late hours, and the squalor and filth of the habitations are a direct invitation of the sickness in a malarious district. As a proof that the fevers can be greatly avoided, it will be observed that all the wealthier classes are comparatively robust, and free from the complaint even in districts that have a bad name; there are, however, some localities, like the Upper São Francisco, that, in its present wild state, are simply untenable, no personal care or precaution being sufficient to guard against an attack of the endemical fevers.

The rich red earth of the river bluffs, and the many fine trees in the clumps of woodland that surrounded the village, indicate the excellence of the soil. When this grand natural highway of inland Brazil becomes developed by thrifty and energetic immigrants, what a paradise it must necessarily become; the fevers will disappear, as they have disappeared in many parts of the United States, by occupation and cultivation of the land.

CHAPTER II.

FROM MANGA DO ARMADOR TO CARINHANHA.

Another wet march—Difficulties of passing flooded streams—Orchids—A varied vegetation—A jararaca-assu snake—A sensible woman—Generous and kind hosts—Valueless mutton—An industrious and contented man—Fazenda de Tabuá—Another ugly crossing—Cattle districts—Ponte de Lagoa—Mosquitos—A dreary night—Carousing black neighbours—Dismal squalor—A haunt of the demon sloth—The riverside road—The rising of the waters—The boundary of Minas Geraes and Bahia—The Rio Carinhanha—The city and its inhabitants—Secluded lives of the females—A long delay—Programme of explorations to be made—Climate—Idle lives—Improvidence—A vessel is chartered for a voyage down the river—Good-bye to old Tommy.

A matuto on a chilly morning.

REFRESHED and reinvigorated after a day's lounge, the early morning saw us once more on the march, but gusts of wind and a heavy leaden sky gave indications of another wet march, and as we descended gradually from the wooded bluffs of the Manga to again flooded lowlands, the rain came down in violence, as though it had been reserving its force for us to fairly get under way.

At two miles out we came across an ugly swollen stream, showing only the bush-tops above water to indicate the neighbourhood of the banks. It had to be crossed, however, somehow. By searching, the men found a tree-trunk three feet under the rushing water, that served as a bridge for foot-travellers; a number of saplings were lashed together to serve as a long firm handrail, the ends being secured to the bush on each side of the stream; then ensued the wearisome work and delay of unpacking all the baggage and transporting it on the men's backs, the submerged trunk serving as a bridge; we were carried across in similar baggage fashion; then after one or two exceedingly narrow escapes from drowning, all the animals were safely swum across; all the time the rain poured down pitilessly.

On the other side of the stream the ground was higher and not flooded, and covered with a magnificent forest growth. I never saw so many orchids and other objects of interest as in this forest; especially noticeable was a grand vine bearing bright crimson passion flowers. One orchid, whose flowers I plucked, possessed a perfume like heliotrope. Often the only answer to any inquiries for local names of these plants is "*uma flor atoá*," or "*uma coisa atoá*," i.e. "a useless flower," or "a useless thing."[1]

One might easily have filled any number of pages in only attempting to describe the varied vegetation, the great quantities of variegated leaf plants,[2] the maze of tree-trunks, the coiling, festooned, all-embracing vines, the buttressed trees, trees tall and smooth as a scaffold-pole, or studded with spikes like the *mamma de porco*,[3] here where every tree or palm, or sapling, or vine is different to its neighbour, only a series of drawings, or a volume of description could really convey an idea of these woods.

On the road through this forest, the men killed a large *jararaca-assu*, five feet nine inches in length.

[1] A very good story was once told me of an English mining engineer, who came out to report upon a mining property in Brazil, and understanding nothing of Portuguese, he described, in his report, a certain species of rock as being known to the natives by the name of "*pedra atoá*," or, in other words, a useless good-for-nothing stone.

[2] *Xanthoxylon*, sp.

[3] *Caladium*, gen.

A mid-day halt was made during a cessation of the rain in a piece of open rolling hill-country by the side of a small swiftly flowing rivulet.

Long sheets of water bordered by cerrado, or grass, or clumps of wood, was the type of country traversed in the afternoon.

At 4 p.m. we arrived at a comparatively neat and bustling cattle-fazenda, situated on a gentle rise from the lowlands, and surrounded by *cerrado*. At the door of the house a neatly dressed young woman was standing, who, strange enough, did not run away on our approach.

On inquiring if we could obtain pasturage for the animals, she informed us that although her husband was not at the moment at home, she expected him to arrive shortly, and that we were quite welcome; there was good pasture close by, and would we dismount, enter, and take some coffee. Here was a change indeed! what varieties of people one meets in a day's march, and how difficult it is to generalize a nation by the individuals one becomes associated with, for here was a country-woman who fled not at sight of strangers.

Inside the house there were many indications of thrift and activity; the furniture was naturally plain and simple, yet there was an air of comfort rarely met with. We were shown into a large room with tables, chairs, and benches, and were told it was at our disposition; a neighbouring closed shed received the luggage, and the tent was raised for the men.

Seeing a number of sheep wandering about, I asked our hostess if we might purchase one.

"Purchase one of those useless animals? What for?"

I explained that we should duly appreciate their flesh for dinner.

"*Deos me livre*," she replied with astonishment, "what eat those *bixos*! why you may have a half-dozen if you like; but sell them we cannot, as they are valueless."[4]

[4] The country Brazilians have a curious antipathy to mutton that is

Whilst we were carefully superintending the grilling of kidneys and mutton-chops, our host arrived, a good-looking active young man of twenty-five or twenty six years of age, and as near a white man as the country-side can produce. He was very cheery and kind, and endeavoured to do all in his power to make us comfortable. He had excellent beds made up for us of sacks filled with leaves of the husks of maize, and that, I can assure any one, is not to be despised, especially when accompanied by rugs, pillows, and clean sheets.

Our host told us he had been married eight years, and was then twenty-six years old; he had inherited the lands from his father with a few slaves; he owned many herds of cattle and cultivated a *roça*; that he enjoyed excellent health, and with his wife and children he was, as he really appeared to be, perfectly happy and contented; he had enough to supply his simple requirements, and every year his stock was increasing. We chatted on until late in the evening, and our host and his wife were apparently so interested in our conversation that they were loth to leave us; we sat around a fire in the yard, some on chairs, some on logs, some on hides, and roasted sweet mandioca in the fire; the senhora eventually fetched her guitar, and favoured us with songs that, if rather high-pitched and nasal, were at least kindly meant. Our best thanks and kindest remembrances to the fazendeiro de Tabuá.

January 29th.—On leaving Tabuá the next morning we experienced again rough treatment by the weather, for as we entered a second growth of forest (forest bush and scrub), down came the rain again, and also in a short distance another ugly stream, the Riacho de Colindo, appeared as a bar to our progress; its steep slippery banks, and deep

simply incomprehensible; they themselves can give no reason, beyond the fact that they have never been accustomed to it. It is quite within the last twenty years that mutton can be obtained in the butchers' shops even in Rio de Janeiro. I remember that in Pernambuco in 1868 to 1873 the only mutton procurable was what could be obtained from the passing Royal Mail steamers.

swiftly flowing waters appeared almost impassable. After a long time and much difficulty a tall *jacarandá* sapling was felled, and hauled into a proper position across the flood, to serve as a *pinguella*,[5] and by its help, with time, labour, and patience, the opposite shore was finally reached with all the baggage.

Further on the country becomes more and more open, long stretches of grass sward and thin cerrado-covered hills appear, and frequent roadside habitations, chiefly small cattle-stations or herdsmen's huts, indicate a purely and simple cattle district.

Twenty-four miles of steady jogging found us at sunset at Ponte da Lagoa, a small *retiro* or cattle-station belonging to a neighbouring fazenda.

My companions and I were a long way ahead of the troop, the sky was becoming black with the massing of clouds of an approaching wet night, and the small hut of the *retiro*, temporarily crowded with odorous field-hands and their friends, afforded not the slightest shelter for our large party. It was level betting which arrived first, baggage or rain: it was almost dark before both arrived at the same time; it was a dead-heat between them. The two tents were hastily raised, but not before we were freely sprinkled and bespattered with mud; a small lean-to of boughs and grass was constructed for Bob's kitchen shelter. The wet grass and soil of the interior of the tents were not the most enviable places for repose, but in them, nevertheless, we had to lay our hides for beds, and make the most of circumstances. The air was extremely hot and stifling, and to our sorrow we soon found filled with torturing mosquitos, in such numbers that all thoughts of sleep were impossible.

Seeing that our black neighbours in the *retiro* were evidently equally tormented, by the clouds of cow-dung smoke issuing from their roof, I sent to beg a quantity, which they

---

[5] *Pinguella* is a common term used to express a tree or a log thrown across a stream for the use of foot-passengers.

willingly gave us from a store they had collected. We soon had this burning in and outside of the tents.

The smell, or the smoke, of burning cow-dung, is certainly most effective in driving off mosquitos—in fact, the most efficacious remedy used in Brazil; as soon, however, as the smoke ceases, the mosquitos return with reinforcements; consequently it is a choice between being half-suffocated with the fumes or of suffering the insects to inflict their worst. Whilst awake, we sneeze, cough, the eyes smart, and we rub our tingling bodies until sleep relieves us, then the fires expire, and the mosquitos recommence their attacks. What with the close hot steamy atmosphere, our fatigues, smoke, hard beds, and mosquitos, it was a long and weary night, and the morning found us in a feverish state of body and mind.

Our black friends had evidently determined to make a night of it, for we heard their guitars, voices, and the hand-clapping and shuffling of feet of the *batuque* dance all the night long.

January 30*th.*—The cool air of dawn, the morning coffee, and a bucket of water to a certain extent refreshed and cooled our feverish and smarting bodies.

The broad light of daylight revealed an abject scene of dreary discomfort in the hut of our neighbours, a smoke-begrimed, old and rotten rancho, the thatch decayed, and festering with age and damp, the whole almost tottering with decrepitude; logs, refuse and rubbish, rotten hides and rotten saddles, encumbered the interior and surroundings; rank grass and bush partially hid from view the wretched abode; the inhabitants appeared wan and sickly from their last night's debauchery, evidently having drunk heavily of the fiery *cachaça*, as most of them were yet "half-seas over." These are the conditions that promote and foster the intermittent fevers.[6]

---

[6] It is a false idea that the Brazilians have, of drinking inordinate quantities of raw spirit as a preventitive of ague. The custom only disturbs the constitutional functions, debilitates, and renders them more liable to the infection.

Near the hut was a poor weed-overgrown *roça;* where tall castor-oil-trees mingled their beautiful foliage with the tall stems of Indian corn, beans struggled for life with coarse weeds, grass and *samambaha* bracken; small plots of *manioc* were almost indistinguishable in the chaos of plants, decayed and broken fences, and all the other evidences of idleness and neglect. Gladly we departed from such a haunt of the demon sloth.

A steep descent by a zigzag, slippery path, knee-deep in mud, brought us to a foaming stream, fortunately not deep, and which we were enabled to ford with but a slight wetting to the baggage.

Four miles more of open country interspersed with hollows filled with brambley scrub and woods, brought us to the Corrego de Escuro, another similarly ugly place to what we had experienced on each of the last two days. Two or three hours of hard and anxious work, however, saw us again on the other side.

Beyond the Corrego de Escuro the road follows the crest of the river-banks for two or three miles, the adjoining land is extremely low, and away to our left the floods covered many miles of country. On our right were the turbid waters of the São Francisco; we were on a ridge with water on each side; the river was evidently rising, for in many places we could see the waters breaking down barriers and invading new areas; many parts of the road were already under water for considerable distances, the bushes being the only evidences of the existence of *terra firma* in the vast expanse of waters.

Another four miles brought us to higher ground and the Fazenda de Escuro, a small cattle-farm by the riverside. Pushing on over two more miles of flat, partially inundated land brought us to the Rio Carinhanha, where we leave the Province of Minas Geraes, in which we have so long been journeying, for that of Bahia on the other side of this river. Owing to the floods, neither banks, nor mouth of the river could be distinguished, only the tops of bushes indicated approximately its limits.

A ferry is provided at this place in the form of a large *ajojo*. My companions and I crossed over at once, leaving our train to follow. The water of the Carinhanha was beautifully clear, even in that time of rains, a fact that shows that its course traverses either a comparatively flat and sandy or a rocky country. The former is the case.

Two miles more by a perfectly flat plain with a lagoon in its centre, brought us at last to our destination. A few outlying scattered and thatched huts first indicate our approach to the town. Then the cemetery appears in sight, a square enclosure, surrounded by a neat whitewashed wall of adobe bricks, with a wooden gate and entrance; a little further on we pass up a sandy street lined with poor adobe houses and palm-thatched huts of wattle and dab, that leads us to the square, containing the town residences of the wealthier farmers of the neighbourhood, the houses of the district judge, priest, lawyer, doctor, public prosecutor, municipal judge, justice of the peace, and the principal traders of the city, the principal church, the gaol, and the municipal chambers. All this is suggestive of wealth and prosperity and fine buildings, but, alas! it is as deceptive as similar names would be in the first nucleus of a town in the Western States of the United States. There is not a single *sobrado* or two-storied house in the whole town, but the houses of the whiter and more well-to-do classes are exceptionally neat and clean. In front of them are raised brick pavements where, in rocking-chairs, the families assemble in the cool of the evening for coffee, chat, or a nasal song "*do amor*," accompanied by the tinkling notes of the wire strings of the native-made guitar.

The church is a plain whitewashed oblong edifice of brick, a roof of tiles, and tile-roofed open corridors run along each side of the building. The gaol is a huge birdcage of sticks and mud, and roofed with tiles, very old and very dilapidated; such a place of detention would amuse any ordinary civilized rough, but the few prisoners in the cage were apparently contented with their lot, and did not wish for a change, otherwise they doubtless would have moved ere this; they had plenty to eat, and from their friends outside could obtain tobacco, rum, guitars, go for a walk occasionally, and sleep the rest of their time away. What more could they do if they were free? Beyond the south square a street leads into the more plebian north square, that with a few more streets completes the little city, Cidade de Carinhanha.

We proceeded to visit, firstly, Mr. J. B——. Our delay was reduced to the minimum compatible with the necessity of the

The North Square, City of Carinhanha.

discussion of business and future movements. Mr. A. F—— was found located in the black and brown interior of an unwhitewashed, smoke-begrimed mud-hut, facing the birdcage-like gaol. We ourselves, with the assistance of Dr. João Lopes Rodrigues, usually known as Dr. Lopes, obtained each one a wretched shanty. Our friend is the gentleman Captain Burton met with seven years previously, at Malhada, and brought down with him in his "brig." With the Captain's permission, I will repeat his observations of this gentleman:—

"A white man walked in whilst we were sitting with Lieut. Loureiro, and astonished us by his civilized aspect, amongst all this Gente de Côr; he was introduced as Dr. (M.D.) João Lopes Rodrigues, who had graduated at Rio de Janeiro, and had settled at Carinhanha. No one had the indecency to ask him the reason why; he complained of the Prequiça do Sertão—the idleness of the wild country—and of stimulus being totally wanted, except when a stranger happens to pass, I have heard the same in Dublin society; possibly Dr. Rodrigues, like a certain Abyssinian traveller, found 'making up his mind' a severe and protracted process. He had suffered from the damp of the river valley, always cold-damp or hot-damp, so different from the dry air and sweet waters of the sandy table-lands on both sides of, and generally at short distances from, the river. He had none of the pretentious manner and address usually adopted by the Bahiano, who holds himself the cream of Brazilian cream, and he readily accepted a passage in the raft to his home, about two miles down stream."

And at Carinanha he further says: "Dr. Rodrigues led us to his house in the square, and offered us the luxuries of sofa and rocking-chair, wax candles, and a map of the war; moreover he gave me his photograph."

I had many opportunities of meeting the Doctor, and also Doctor José Marianno dos Campos, the Juiz de Direito, and other local officials, white men and apparently gentlemen, and can testify to their courteous manners and many little acts of kindness. One day we caught a glimpse of the wife of Doctor Lopes, certainly the only pretty face we had seen for a long time, and the only one perceptible in Carinhanha; but the Doctor, with all his polish, maintains the old Portuguese custom of secluding the female part of his household from the contact of strangers. What an awful life it must be for a young woman in these circumstances, no relief or change to the dull routine and monotony of her daily life, immured in the small rooms at rear of the house, that only look out upon a yard with a few fruit-trees and flowers.

Ten days we passed in this sleepy city, waiting for Mr. J. B—— to make up his mind and arrive at some determination of his next movements. Finally it was decided that he would personally examine the country between here and the Rio Tocantins, accompanied by Messrs. A. F—— and H. O——, Mr. H. G—— remaining at Carinhanha until his return. I received instructions to go to the mouth of the Rio Grande, and proceed up that river, cross the divide, and descend the Rio do Somno, and the Tocantins, and afterwards to find my way to Bahia on the coast.

The days passed very slowly and monotonously, the weather was hot and sultry, sometimes reaching 92° in the shade in the day-time, yet there appeared to be no sickness, although the greater part of the inhabitants appeared to be without occupation, sleeping and lounging in the day-time, and playing the guitar, singing, dancing, and drinking *cachaça* at night. It would appear strange at first to imagine how these people manage to subsist; the reason of so much loafing is, that after a few days' work in the fields or on the river, either in cultivating the ground, in fishing, or by petty trading, the men manage to gather a little cash, and then return to the town, where they idle away their time in drink and debauchery until their means are exhausted and they are forced to again return to a little more work. No provision is made for old age or sickness, or large families, for when either of these contingencies occur, the men take to begging like ducks to water, and accost you with " Alms, for the love of God, for a poor old man—or for a poor sick man—or for a poor father burdened with a numerous family," &c., as the various circumstances may be. It is rare that they are refused a copper, if it is, the refusal is always accompanied by a touch of the hat and a *perdoe*[7] (pardon), an exculpatory reply that is meant to excuse not so much a disinclination to confer the alms for the sake of the beggar, but for " the love of God," in whose name it has been requested.

We divided our time in taking walks in the town and adjoining country, in visiting the *Gente graúdo*,[8] in chatting

---

[7] Pronounce *pear-doy-ee*.

[8] This expression is used to signify people of importance. The words

Good-bye to "Tommy." 29

with the customerless shopkeepers, or sketching, writing, or discussing our future journeys.

Having at last received my final instructions, an *ajoojo*, belonging to one of the storekeepers, was chartered to take me to the Rio Grande for the sum of 274$ 000, this amount included the wages of pilot and two boatmen, and provisions for same, for about a week's journey, that cost per day about four times the price of the fares of the Royal Mail steamers for a similar period.

I had now to part with poor old "Tommy," my ancient and much bantered grey mule, that had carried me safely, without any mishap, for two years of constant work. It was like parting with an old friend. I was very fond of the animal, and had done my best to win his affection, but corn was ever his soul-absorbing thought.

The rest of my troop I handed over to my companions for their journey by land to the Tocantins.[9]

literally mean "matured people," consequently the expression combines both age, position, or wealth.

[9] A brief summary of their exploration will be found in Appendix B, at the end of this volume.

CHAPTER III.

FROM CARINHANHA TO BARRA DO RIO GRANDE.

Departure from Carinhanha down the river—The Ajojo—Head winds—A mosquito-infested port—First night on the river—An early start—River etiquette—An impromptu sail—The shores of the river—The crew—Flooded lands—A sunset on the river—Great appetites of the crew—A misty morning—São Bom Jezus da Lapa—A curious rock—Who are we?—A hospitable padre—A riverside vicarage—A Brazilian Mecca—The crew ashore—Across country on a raft—The flood—A falling barometer—A squall—A dirty night—Mosquitos again—A night voyage—Sitio de Matto—Proposed capital of new province—The island of fear—Urubú—A sleepy city—A local magnate—The Brazilian student—A night ashore—A mountainous country—The Carnahuba palm—Bom Jardim—An excellent situation and healthy climate—Morro do Pará—An adventure—A bad lot—A geographical bootmaker—A dreamy night voyage—A riverside squatter—The war of the Guimaraes—Cidade de Barra.

ACCOMPANIED by my companions, and Dr. Lopes and others of the *Gente graúda*, I proceeded to the muddy shore, where our final *adeos* were made in good hearty English handshaking with my old companions, and embraces with my Brazilian friends.

As we paddled down the strong current of the still flooded river, the group on the bank became smaller and smaller as the distance increased, and faint shouts were heard of " Good-bye, old fellow," "Good luck to you," &c., and from Mr. J. B., "Whatever you do, take care of the aneroids, the an-e-roids."

I now had an opportunity of looking around me in my new condition. As familiar memories occurred of the jog, jog of the mules, and how hard the seat of the saddle used to become towards the afternoon, and the cramped stiffened limbs, I must confess that my first sensations were extremely pleasurable, as we glided smoothly along by the river-banks, topped sometimes by forest or bush, sometimes by roças. The craft consisted of two native cedar-wood canoes, or dug-outs, about thirty feet long, placed two feet apart, forming a sort of pontoon by means of a number of saplings placed close together athwart the canoes for about two-thirds of their length, making a comparatively even deck, the extremities of the canoes were uncovered; the quarter-deck was occupied by the poop, or state room, a gipsy-like hut of bamboos and other pliable sticks, bent in the form of a half-hoop, other sticks laid longitudinally and lashed to the hoops received a palm-leaf thatch, covered by raw hides, each one of the saloon extremities was open and unprotected. The state room was sufficiently high to receive my baggage and a bed of hide and rugs spread upon fragrant grass, over which hung suspended a mosquito-net; forwards in the foc'sel my man Bob (who yet accompanied me with the dog Feroz), was arranging his kitchen, a half-tub of earth, on which were spread the materials for a fire for the inevitable beans (*feijões*), around him were the packed tent, saddles, bridles, *batterie de cuisine*, and stores for the voyage.

Ahead in the bows, the two paddlers were hard at work against a strong northerly breeze that was then springing up, and yelling at the tops of their voices as they stood up and worked the long heavy paddles. "*Adeos, Carinhanha! Adeos! Adeos, Mariquinha minha bemzinha!*"[1]

In the afternoon the wind increased and as the craft com-

---

[1] Good-bye, Carinhanha! Good-bye! Good-bye, little Mary, my darling.

menced to "put her nose into it" and take in water over her bows from the short chopping waves, we were obliged to run along close in shore.

The strong head-wind, even with the current in our favour, prevented making much headway, consequently at sunset, we found ourselves only ten miles out, and the wind blowing up-stream in strong fitful gusts, forced us to seek refuge from a dirty night in a little cove, where we made fast and landed for wood; but we had not been there long before an ominous high note, "*pee-e-njen-njen*," indicated the approach of mosquitos, and, truly, in a few moments, we were surrounded by a perfect roar of myriads of the insects. How they made us move about, and vengefully smite ourselves on face, neck, hands, arms, and legs; how we capered and blessed. The enemy were too many for us, and sink or swim, we pushed off into the darkening boisterous night, taking many of the mosquitos as passengers.

Half an hour later found us again anchored alongside a sandbank, against which the waves of the river rolled like a little sea, and made the craft pitch freely, but it rode the water fairly, and if we sunk in the night it would be in shallow water. Out in this open roadstead the wind blew so strong and cold and damp, that the rugs were very acceptable.

The movement of the raft, the sounds of the ripple and wash of the water alongside, the broad open expanse of the flowing river, faintly shimmering in the pale light of the starry night, the hurtling of the wind amongst the trees on shore, the splash of fish, and the murmur of the men's voices, created a scene of novelty and of strangeness.

February 11.—The men were up and paddling long before the sun, or I, had risen. The noise of getting under way awoke me, but the sight of dense mists on the river, and the comparative comfort of my couch, and the knowledge that there was no mule to mount, made one feel like a city clerk on a Sunday, when he realizes that there is no necessity to get up in the darkness and cold of a winter's morning, and be in the city at 9 a.m.

The wind had dropped, and the morning sun rose with splendour and rapidly dissipated the chilly mists. The craft followed the full force of the mid-stream, and the paddlers worked with a will, shouting their river-songs, and slanging a passing *barca*, whose polemen were chaffing and ridiculing our plebeian *ajojo*.[2] Right and left of us extended the banks of the river, capped by bush or thin belts of forest, behind which extend long stretches of shallow lagoons. On the west bank the ground is perceptibly higher, and high bluffs frequently appear, topped by habitations or small farms.

The east bank is lower and flatter, and presents more the appearance of the recedence of the waters, whereas the other side appears as though it is being continually undermined by the river. I especially noticed this peculiarity during the rest of the voyage, and also on the upper river; naturally, there are many exceptions to this rule, even to the reverse, but altogether that is undoubtedly the general appearance. Can it be the effect of the rotation of the earth on its axis upon this long length of waters flowing almost on a meridian from south to north?

A fair wind from the south springing up, I conceived the idea of rigging up a sail. Taking from my trunks some sheets, now long out of use, Bob was instructed to sew them together; a mast and spar were obtained from the forest, and in due time, to the great delight of the crew, a lug-sail was hoisted, and the wind being fresh and fair, it succeeded excellently, and sent the water foaming by the bows. I believe this was the first sail that had been spread on those waters, for so said the pilot. There is no feasible reason why this

---

[2] It is customary to all the river craft—*barcas, ajojos* and large canoes—to carry a large tin speaking-trumpet, in order that the two latter may salute the two former in passing, which is then promptly responded. If it is not done, as on the above occasion, a storm of opprobrium and foul language, or ridicule, emanates from the crew of the *barcas* as a protest against the breach of river etiquette.

river should not be navigated by sailing craft, other than that the boatmen, for generations, have become habituated to the pole and paddle, and, like all customs in Brazil, it is almost impossible to make any change.[3]

We pass by an ever-varying scenery on shore, sometimes an extensive sheet of water, showing where the river has submerged its margin and extended for miles inland, a sheet of yellow water dotted with bushes and trees, or where the tops of fences, surrounded by trees, show an inundated *roça*, or high perpendicular banks and bluffs of red and white sandy clay, were miniature slips sometimes occur, and slide down with a thud and splash into the undermining river; these high bluffs are topped by forest, or with little clearings, and straw-thatched, mud-walled huts, whose inhabitants, whenever they appear, are duly chaffed by the irrepressible crew; the pilot, yawning a formidable opening, mildly expostulates, and tells them to "*ter modo*" (to have manners, i.e., behave themselves).

At eleven o'clock, the craft passed Barreiros, a small hamlet on the right bank, forty miles from Carinhanha.

At sunset we reached Palma, a solitary house on the west bank, sixty-eight miles from Carinhanha. The occupants were in hourly expectation of the waters rising still higher, and overflowing the banks and flooding them out. A large canoe was moored close by, in which they had embarked their few poor goods and chattels, all ready for a retreat.

The wind had died away at 3 p.m., when the sail was furled. As the *ajojo* laid alongside the grassy edge of the bank, the waters almost flush with the surface of the soil, the scene was remarkably charming; there was not a speck of cloud to mar the soft blues and pearls of the evening sky, not a ripple ruffled the smooth surface of the water, that reflected like a looking-glass the graduated half-tones of the

---

[3] The danger of capsizing from sudden gusts of wind from S.E. to N.W., *redemonhos* or *pés de vento*, is the usual excuse given for not using sails. Ignorance of their use is probably the truer reason.

sky; across the picture stretched the long dark outline of the opposite shore; the smoke of our fire curled upwards, a spiral column of blue; the lines of the *ajojo* in the foreground formed a bold outline of dark shade against the soft masses of light beyond it. In the elements of the picture there was nothing exceptional; a raft, a broad sheet of water, a long narrow line of forested banks, and the sky; it was simply a picture of wonderful colours and graduated tones.

Another picture of a more material character was to see the boatmen seat themselves around a huge basin of boiled *feijão, toucinho,* and *farinha*; they take the mess with their fingers, squeeze it into little balls, and swallow it with a gulp, much the same as a dog does any tit-bit. I mentally cubed up the quantity originally in the bowl, and divided it by the number of consumers. The result arrived at was far in excess of what I had imagined to be the capacity of the human stomach.[4] About a gill of *cachaça* was then swallowed in the same pill-like way, then their cigarettes lighted, those men were happy, and ready for work.

Mosquitos arrived as darkness came on, but although many an occasional slap and anathema was heard, the men were soon asleep.

My craft was not a first-class ship like Captain Burton's brig *Eliza*. Mine could not aspire to be anything but a lugger, neither was my state-room so roomy, or upholstered so richly and conveniently as that celebrated brig's. My space was more limited, and, after the unaccustomed want of exercise all day, great is one's wakefulness and long are the evenings; but the mosquitos settled the question, whether I should perambulate the bank or retire to my narrow quarters, by driving me to the friendly shelter of the mosquito-net.

[4] M. Halfield, who must have had a considerable experience of these boatmen during his survey of the river, states that their powers of consumption are four times those of an ordinary land-labourer, and those are sufficiently vast.

February 12.—Thanks to the mosquitos' and a fine night, the lugger stood out to sea in the early hours of morning. The atmosphere was not cold, but a moist fresh air came up-stream, and made one feel chilly and damp.

The river was so high that long stretches of the banks, miles in extent, were under water, and in many places the flood rushed inland like a mill-race; the higher banks were almost everywhere capped by many huts and small farms.

Soon after mid-day we sailed into the port of the Thauma-turgical São Bom Jesus de Lapa, at the base of a huge rock that rears itself above the flat surrounding country; it is twenty-eight miles from Palma, and ninety-six from Carinhanha. The craft passed over the submerged banks, fences, *roças*, and bush, and anchored in a partly flooded street leading to the village, that is situated on higher ground, above all flood levels.

The first appearance of this huge limestone rock, that rises so abruptly from a flat flooded plain, is very striking. A perpendicular wall of rock, about 180 feet high and 150 yards wide, faces the river, and extends inland for more or less 600 yards; its face is seamed with the action of weather of untold ages, grey and hoary with time and lichens. Its summit bristles with pinnacles, sharp pointed rocks, and detached blocks. In the holes and crannies, blue *munducaru* candelabra-like cactus, and other varieties, form characteristic and quaint features, very similar to the vegetation on the limestone rocks passed on the road north of Carinhanha. Two openings in the river front form entrances to a cave, that has been utilized as a church, and forms one of the holiest of the holies of the São Francisco regions.

Some of the *povo* (people) now approached us, and inquired, "*O que é que tem para negociar?*" (What have you got to trade?) Our reply that we had nothing to sell, and did not wish to purchase anything, as usual created astonishment. Their looks evidently expressed an unuttered inquiry of "Well, who and what can you be then?" But my request

Frontispiece to Vol. II.   THE CAVE-CHURCH, ROCK, AND VILLAGE OF SÃO BOM JESUS DA LAPA.   See Vol. II. p. 36.

to be directed to the residence of the Padre somewhat reassured them, and they willingly showed the way.

The principal *venda* and dry-goods store constituted the rectory, and there at home in his shop, I found the Padre, Senor F—— de F——, a tall, gaunt-limbed, last-week shaved, forty-year-old son of Portugal, dressed in *ceroulas*,[5] not very white cotton shirt, and a faded coloured-print dressing-gown; his bare feet dragged about a pair of slip-shod clattering wooden *tamancos*, or clogs. He looked at my card that I handed to him, turned it over, held it up to the light, said "*Nao entendo*" (I do not understand it), and handed it back to me, saying he would not deprive me of it. When, however, I tendered a request to see the celebrated church and cave, he brightened up, and replied, "*Pois nao*" (certainly), "but enter and have some dinner first; it is just ready."

I at once took kindly to that clerical Portugee, and entering his sanctum behind his odorous store, he proceeded to clear out a pig, some fowls, some black and whitey-brown naked children, and black and whitey-brown women; he dusted a very dusty stool, and cleared a space on a table littered with miscellaneous articles.

"Don't make any ceremony," said he; "sit down and be at your ease."

A greasy, garlic-flavoured repast, accompanied by a bottle of *restillo*, duly appeared, followed by coffee. Afterwards we proceeded to the cave.[6]

A sharp ramp, paved with limestone flags, leads from the street up the side of the face of the cliff, and terminates in a flight of limestone steps. This brought us to a landing in front of the opening to the cave, paved with square tiles, and sur-

---

[5] Drawers.
[6] This vicarge must be a rather desirable living, for the predecessor of the present vicar retired to Portugal with a respectable fortune, and I was told that mine host arrived here "*pé no chão*," i e. barefooted, but since then he has remitted considerable sums to his native town.

rounded by a balustrade and six pillars of whitewashed limestone. The entrance is closed by double doors, opened by means of a ponderous key my host carried. A few paces brought us within the sacred precincts of the cave, that turns sharply to the right, parallel with the face of the rock, so that the second opening that is noticeable from the outside serves to admit daylight through its glazed window on to the altar at the further extremity of the cave. The dingy cave is about 100 feet long by twenty to twenty-five feet high, and varies in width from thirty to fifty feet. Over the altar the stone roof is faced by arched panels of wood moulded painted and gilded. On the wall above the altar is the tawdrily-painted but miraculous crucifix of São Bom Jezus da Lapa ; below it is a figure of the Virgin and child. There are also two minor altars in niches, one on each side, with figures of saints of minor local importance. A massive silver lamp hangs from the roof in front of the altar.

With the further exception of a wooden balustrade enclosure near the entrance for the use of a choir, and the whitewashed rock walls, all the rest of the cave is as Nature constructed it. On one side of the cave are suspended numerous wax models of arms, legs, heads, feet, breasts, &c., that represent the wonderfully miraculous cures of accidents and diseases made by the saint. Many framed certificates and descriptions testify to miracles that could not be modelled.

This cave is the Mecca of the São Francisco: it is holy throughout ; the soil of the floor, the dust of the wall, possess extraordinary virtues, and are used as specifics for most of the ills that flesh is heir to. No boats pass the shrine without leaving an offering, and the country people make long and distant pilgrimages to propitiate the favour of the saint, or to return thanks for imaginary conferred blessings.

Tradition states that a woman in search of a missing child had found him leaning out of the window of the cave so far that he fell out, and would have been dashed to pieces, but fortunately she had time to ejaculate, "*Nosso Senhor da Lapa me ajude!*" (Our Lord of the cave help me!). The child alighted as lightly as a descending hydraulic lift when the conductor pulls the rope.

The saint is remarkably well provided for, being the owner of several fazendas and numerous fat slaves. I was directed where to place my gift to the church, which was temporarily taken possession of by my guide.

A walk through the hamlet showed that it has considerably increased in size and importance since Captain Burton visited it, as the greater part of the thatched huts were new, and several more were in process of construction. The Padre stated that the population comprised about 1500 souls, but I imagine that half that quantity would be an outside number.

There were numerous little vendas and "grog" shops, evidently showing that at Festival time high jinks are played here, as undoubtedly is the case. There is comparatively little business done except with the passing boatmen, who would not dare to pass the shrine without a visit, a gift, and frequently a carousal in the village, in honour of the saint.

After our walk we discussed a bottle of English pale ale in the Padre's bar-parlour, and I parted from my, if rather uncouth and grubby, yet kind-hearted and good-natured clerical friend.

On arriving at the boat, I there found only Manoel, the piloto, looking very glum.

"Where are the men?" I inquire.

"Oh! they have been to see Nosso Senhor, and they will be sure to get *bebido* (drunk)."

"How can that make them *bebido?*"

"Why, they will go to the village and drink *manipocira*."[7]

"Well, go and hunt them up."

In a few minutes he returned with the crew and Bob in his charge. An odour of cachaça, frequent eructations, and

[7] *Manipocira*, a local slang term for *cachaça*.

imbecilic smiles evidenced their potations; however, they were quiet and could keep their legs, so we prepared to pole off.

At that moment a *moleque* came alongside with a box on his head; he hurried up, and handed me the contents, six bottles of pale ale, saying "*É o Senhor Padre, que mandou*" (It is the Senhor Padre that sent it). It was very kind, but I could not spare time to return to thank him, so I sent him a note expressing ("*à la Brasilien*") "my great estimation of his noble character."

It was laborious work beating out to an offing against the strong currents, and tree, hut, bush, and fence obstructed water, but one does not "cross country" on a raft every day.

The ground at the base of the rock receives the full force of the current of the river, and forms a little bay and eddy. It is a popular belief on the upper river, that any present to the saint that is there thrown into the stream, will be carried down and landed at the Lapa. The position of the bay and its eddies may well retain for a long time any floating matter, that superstition would easily attribute to the saint's miraculous influence and powers of attraction.

For some distance down the river the margins were indicated by a perfect archipelago of islands, on which were many roças and habitations, many of the latter deserted on account of the floods.

The barometer showed signs of an approaching "temporal" (squall), and I informed the piloto that the instrument indicated bad weather, and directed him to find a safe port of refuge. He expressed his astonishment thereat by saying, "*O que bixinho! De veras estes inglezes tem coisas exquisitas. Ai meo Deos.*" (O what a creature! Truly these English have strange things! Ah! meo Deos). It was fully two miles down-stream before we found ourselves in a little cove, formed by the mouth of a stream, with a roça on each of its banks.

The atmosphere was hot and sultry, and the sky was rapidly becoming overcast with densely-black clouds, and all the indications of a wild night. Mosquitos also found us out, and bit and stung us with the extra venom they appear to possess before a storm; but we could not venture out into the darkening waters in the face of the coming storm. A sudden and violent gust of wind from the north, a few big drops of rain, a crash of thunder, followed by a vivid flash—a pause—an intense stillness—the darkness blacker—from downstream a mass of grey mist and cloud advances, and envelopes and blots from the view the banks and river. Suddenly, with a howl, the wind and rain strike us with such force that our craft rolls violently. How the wind screamed, and the rain beat pitilessly; the thunder crashed in grand volumes of sound; truly, in the gathering darkness of night, it was a pandemonium.

The ruddy flickering light of the camp-fire on a bank under the lee of some trees, the dark figures of the men passing to and fro, added to the weirdness of the scene of gloom and hurly-burly. But the mosquitos, although every gust of wind blew them away, returned in dense clouds. There was nothing weird about that; one can enjoy, even if in discomfort, a properly-developed storm and its accompanying turmoil and majesty of sound and force; but mosquitos disturb one's meditations so, and on that particular night I would back the most Christian and peaceably-disposed human being to develop such energy and vengeance in his slaps that he previously was unaware existed in his constitution, let alone expressing himself in forcible language, even to naughty and prohibited words. The Portuguese language is relieving up to a certain point; but its expressions become monotonous to an Englishman by constant repetition, and hard expressive Anglo-Saxon is necessary to meet the continued torments of such a night of mosquitos. As to the mosquito-net, it seemed more like a trap to keep them in, rather than fulfil its purpose of keeping them out.

The full violence of the storm soon exhausted itself, but the night still continued too "dirty" to allow us to venture to sea; it was only in the early hours of morning, with chilled feet, smarting limbs, and heated aching head, that we were enabled with safety to sail away.

What a relief to get away from those diabolical insects, and breathe the fresh but damp air of the early dark misty morning.

I turned in, oblivious of banks, or shoals, or scenery, feeling an all-absorbing sense of satisfaction that my torment was over. It is a pity Dante did not know the São Francisco in the rainy season, as a circle of everlasting mosquitos would have been much more tantalizing than his ovens and other pleasant inventions for "making things hot" for poor humanity.

Captain Burton should congratulate himself upon having chosen another season of the year, whereby he avoided the horrible nights of misery we had to undergo, forcing us on more than one occasion to travel all night, and take our chance of snags in the starlighted waters; otherwise those night-voyages were delightful, drifting lazily down the stream, turning slowly round and round in mid-channel, awake and watchful for hidden dangers, for a collision with, or grounding upon, any submerged obstacle, would probably have canted the raft, filled the canoes with water, and then to the bottom, or take our chance of a long long swim in the hurrying flood to the distant shore. However, fortune and weather favoured us; and truly pleasant it was to lay extended in the stern of one of the canoes, and listen to the pilot's yarns of the river traditions, a continuous monotone, accompanied by the voices of the men singing the river-songs, the ripple and swash of the waters, and the sough of the passing breeze; and the dimly-seen distant horizon, partially obscured by flitting clouds of mist under the dark vault of the star-studded night; the cool damp air, the surrounding stillness and darkness, created an indefinable charm, that, with a fillip of danger to give it piquancy, rendered sleep not only undesirable, but unsought for.

In the early morning we passed Sitio de Matto, a small village of scattered houses built on the summit of a high bluff; this is one of the sites for the capital of the long-proposed new Province of São Francisco; the other sites proposed are Januaria, Bom Jardim, Urubú, Cidade de Barra, Xique-Xique, and Joázeiro.

From its central position, high elevation, and other circumstances, Bom Jardim presents the most favourable features. Cidade de Barra is commercially well situated, but its low situation, subject to great inundations, should prohibit its selection; but its powerful and influential son, the Conservative Senator, the Barão de Cotegipe, Manoel Mauricio Vanderley, probably exercises his power to prevent the formation of the new province, unless his native town is made the capital. It is now many years since this project was first mooted, and even now, at the time this volume is being written, nothing has yet been decided.

The "*Ilha de Medo*" (Island of Fear), passed this morning, is an historical reminiscence of colonial times; the piloto told me that tradition says it and the adjoining country was formerly occupied by a race of Indians,[8] who levied tribute upon, or massacred, all passing travellers, like the old German Barons of the Middle Ages. Now there are only peaceful roças, and anything but warlike inhabitants.

During the morning I shot two beautiful white herons (*garcias*), and on the banks I noticed several spoonbills, a not uncommon bird here.

In the afternoon, about 5 p.m., we reached Urubú, a town of some 3000 inhabitants and three churches. The town lays back from the river, separated from it by a low, marshy plain, then all but inundated. A gentle rise brings one to the Rua da Conceição, a long street parallel to the river; some of the houses are fairly good and even pretentious, and

[8] The Tupinamba Indians, now extinct.

certainly the best yet seen on the riverside; the other habitations comprise the usual adobe houses, palm-frond huts, railed compounds and rude gardens. The long silent streets were almost as quiet as the "City" on a Sunday, but my advent was the signal for the expected appearance at doors and windows of giggling women and silent lounging men; boys and girls rushed here and there to get a better view, like boys in London at sight of a crowd, and rushing along inquire "what's up."

On entering a venda, my appearance created as much commotion amongst the town politicians there assembled, as if I had been a tame elephant, or similar curiosity. The Juiz de Direito and Delegado were at their fazendas, but I was shown a "*casa nobre*" close by as the residence of the Senhor Commandante Coronel, and informed in a *sotto voce* voice that he was "*uma pessoa graúda*," "*muito rico*" and "*muito importante*." I resolved to "*comprimentar*" this evidently "big man" of the town. Accordingly I entered his open entrance-door and clapped my hands.

A nasal voice responded, "*Quem é?*" (Who is it?)

"*Seu criado*" (Your servant), I reply, in orthodox fashion.

Again is the unknown nasal voice heard, "*Quem é?*"

This time I reply, "*Gente de fora*" (meaning really a stranger).

A slipshod old negro woman, nationally half-undressed, opened the door and blinked at me half-scowlingly, half-wonderingly.

"*O Senhor Coronel, esta em casa?*" (Is the Senor Colonel at home?) I inquire.

"*'N'hor sim.*"[9]

"Tell him that '*um homen de fora*' (a stranger) wishes to see him."

I awaited patiently in the brick-paved entrance for some minutes, until a stentorian voice calls out from the summit of some stairs, "*Quem é?*"

I reply, "*De fora*."

---

[9] Abbreviation of *senhor sim*, or *sim senhor*—yes, sir. Pronounce *een-yór-see*.

"*Suba*" (come up), is the reply of the voice.

I ascend the stairs and meet a robust, middle-aged, white man, a Brazilian gentleman in appearance. I inquire if I have the honour of addressing the "*Coronel.*"

"Your servant," is the reply, accompanied with a bow.

I hand my card, and briefly explain that, being a foreigner and a passing traveller, I had taken the opportunity of calling upon one of the most distinguished residents of the "*beira de Rio*" (river-side).

He put up a *pince-nez* and looked at my card, and eyed my travel-stained appearance from head to foot.

"Come in and join us at dinner; we are just sitting down."

I apologized for my rough appearance.

"*Nao faça ceremonia*" (do not stand upon ceremony) is the hospitable answer, and immediately I am ushered into the presence of his family circle.

I found myself once again in civilized society; a good-looking white girl of twenty years, dressed in white muslin, her black hair decorated with the sweet *angelico* (Cape jessamine), received me courteously; two young *medicos* from Bahia lately "*formado*" (graduated), more superciliously. My rough appearance and the plebeian *ajôjo*, of whose arrival they had doubtless already heard, did not constitute, in their estimation, the dignity compatible with a "*doutor.*"[10] After a while

---

[10] Young Brazil, as a student, often passes a wild dissipated life like any other students, but when he obtains his degree and assumes his gown he becomes at once "*um homen serio*" (a respectable serious member of society), and a great advocate of form and ceremony, chimney-pots, and black frockcoats, &c. I remember in after years, when I was carrying out the works for the Dom Pedro Segundo Railway in Rio de Janeiro, I had designed some extensive warehouses of brick, for which I was anxious to utilize some excellent bricks manufactured in the neighbourhood, but as good bricklayers were scarce, I had to go to work myself, with coat off and shirt-sleeves rolled up, to initiate unskilled workmen into good bricklayers. I noticed that my young assistants, newly fledged, or "*formado*" Brazilian engineers, evidently thought that I had lost caste by such manual labour; they promptly dropped the *senhor doutor*, and I became thenceforward simply *Senhor Wess*.

however, their assumed artificial gloss wore off, and they became more amiable, and finally offered me "Best Bristol Bird's-eye" tobacco. The "*Coronel*" was evidently satisfied with my respectability, as he insisted upon my remaining at his house for the night. Thoughts of the mosquitos and the prevailing damp dews of night did not require much pressing to induce me to accept his hospitality. A hammock was placed at my disposal, but when I turned in, I found I had made no grand exchange, for mosquitos were plentiful, and in a hammock, whatever position one may assume, there must necessarily be some protuberant part of the body over which the mosquitos have "grand old times," the thickness of the hammock-cloth, a sheet and *pyjamas* are trifling obstacles to their prospecting operations. In such conditions one feels afterwards as if he had been swathed in a mustard poultice.

I learned afterwards that the "*Coronel*" is accredited with the possession of a hundred contos of reis (say 10,000*l*.), a rarely-met-with capital in the inland provinces of Brazil, which one can quite understand, as the possessor of such a sum would most likely find his way to more luxurious centres, where at least some value can be reaped by the benefits (questionable, if you like) of the civilized coast cities.

February 14.—The country side bordering the river to-day presented a considerable change to the upper river-side, for here the land shows quite a rugged mountainous appearance. Down-stream, the valley winds its way in serpentine curves between projecting buttresses of hills that appear in the distance to dovetail into each other. On either hand are seen hills upon hills; some, long unbroken ridges covered with cerrado; others, huge rounded hills covered with forest; so elevated, indeed, is the land, that it reminded me of the mountainous coast between Cape Frio and Rio de Janeiro. The day was most brilliant and hot, the thermometer registering 88° under the awning of the state-room. Not a breath of air ruffled the glassy surface of the water, it was like moving over a sheet of quicksilver. We passed many places where the banks were high and far better adapted for townships than most of the existing settlements. I noticed for the first time the wonderfully useful Carnahuba palm (*Copernicia cerifera* of Martius) ; probably there is no other product of the vegetable kingdom that offers such a variety of useful purposes as this elegant palm. Although this tree, like most other Brazilian products, has been fully noticed and described by many travellers, I cannot but help mentioning some of its qualities.

It resists intense and protracted droughts, and is always green and vigorous ; it produces an equivalent to sarsaparilla ; a nutritious vegetable, like cabbage ; wine ; vinegar ; a saccharine substance ; a starch, resembling and equivalent to sago ; other substances resemble, or by processes are made to substitute, maizena, coffee, cork, wax, salt, alkali, and cocoanut milk ; and from its various materials are manufactured, wax-candles, soap, mats, hats, musical instruments, water-tubes, pumps, ropes and cords, stakes for fences, timber for joists, rafters and other materials for building purposes, strong and light fibres which acquire a beautiful lustre, and in times of great drought it has supplied food for the starving inhabitants. This palm is justly considered the most valuable production of the Sertão.

Late in the afternoon we arrived at Bom Jardim, 200 miles from Carinhanha, where I landed amongst a little fleet of canoes, ajojos, and barcas. The *arrial* or village is admirably situated on the summit of high ground that slopes to the water's edge, and consists of a long street parallel to the course of the river, on one side the rear of the houses faces the water, and their railed and fenced-in compounds extend to the river-banks. The lower portions were then flooded from the then unusually high water. The highest flood known only slightly submerged the south end of the street.

A young friend of the "*Coronel*" at Urubú, to whom I had given a lift to this place, introduced me to the village schoolmaster, who kindly offered me a vacant room in his house to sling my hammock and perhaps escape the mosquitos.

A pleasant breeze was blowing and made my stroll through the village the more enjoyable after the cramped space of the *ajojo*, and the close heat of the long day. It is a bright little place, the houses are gay with colour, and each one has its own garden of fruit-trees and flowers ; the people appeared to be more industrious and prosperous, and looked much healthier than is usually the case on the river-side.

The distant possibility of the Bahia Central Railway making its terminus here, unlimited space for building, higher ground in the neighbourhood for those requiring a change of climate, admirable facilities for river-side wharves, a central position for the trade of the interior, and its comparatively healthy climate, all point to a probable flourishing future for Bom Jardim.

We were away before the first glimmer of dawn, paddling down mid-stream in the misty damp air of early morning.

All this morning the scenery we passed through was exceptionally charming, especially the fine range of hills, called the Serra de Pinxahyn, and its many ramifications, all densely wooded, and offering excellent localities for healthy settlements.

A long journey of sixty-four miles brought us at sunset to Morro de Pará, a small poverty ague-stricken hamlet of about twenty houses, situated at the base of a large solitary hill. The houses are built of adobe and thatched with carnahuba palm-leaves. The place looked dark and dreary, and from its low swampy situation, arose a close fetid atmosphere, clouds of mosquitos, and the rank smell peculiar to rotting vegetation, altogether very suggestive of malaria and chills, but having landed I determined to inspect the place.

On passing by an open rancho, where a number of men were playing cards, I was invited to join their circle ; at the same time, in a half-maudlin state, they advanced towards me and insisted upon a loving embrace. " *Venha ca, Senhor*

Branco, e jogar um tiquinho com marimpó" (Come here, Senhor Whiteman, and play a little at *marimpó*). I confessed my ignorance, but in vain ; I was surrounded by my convivial friends, who were considerably " screwed," and as I attempted to proceed onwards, a leering brawny mulatto, clad in a coarse shirt, drawers, and leather hat, placed himself in my way. Whilst hesitating whether to show my revolver, or trip-up my lurching opponent, and possibly have a struggle in the darkness with the unknown inhabitants, or else to make a dash for the *ajojo,* some 500 yards away—a grizzled, grey-bearded light mulatto man joined the group, now loudly vociferating that " I was going to study *marimpó*." The stranger took in the situation at a glance, and beckoning to me to follow, partly by persuasion, coaxing, and a little firm force, succeeded in extricating me from the circle of carousers, odorous with coarse spirits and the *catinga de negro ;* probably no harm was intended by them, but the drunken countryman (*matuto*) is at best a reckless dangerous fellow.

My companion told me that they were an idle set of gamblers and horse-stealers, who made this place their headquarters, and advised me to get away at once as they were intoxicated and reckless, and might at any moment regret having allowed my departure. My good friend told me he was a " shoemaker by trade," and owned a roça close by, which served to support his family, otherwise he would gladly leave this den of thieves ; he further informed me that he was very fond of *geographia,* and, really, the old fellow possessed a limited and crude idea of other lands besides his own rarely possessed even by better educated men in the country.

I found the *ajojo* rolling on the wavelets beating on the shore, caused by a fresh breeze from the south, and the men heaping imprecations on the myriads of mosquitos that surrounded them. Being a fine moonlight night, we pushed off into mid-stream and hoisted sail.

The voyage in the cool of the night, and on the sparkling

moonlit waters, was really enjoyable; such a change from the muddy, fetid banks of Morro de Para, and its rowdy village. The wind bore us along gaily and made the water ripple as the heavy craft rode over the waves. The men seemed to feel the soothing influence of the scene, for they sang in low voices many of their river songs, one expressing how his absence was deplored by the fair ones of up and down river, and that he was only "humbugged" by the mother of his especial darling.

> Rio arriba e rio abaixo,
> Todo o mundo me chorou,
> Só foi a mae de minha benzinha,
> Que me enganou.

After a time the men dropped off to sleep, all but the pilot, who kept a watchful look-out for snags. I did not turn in until the early morning, for although this kind of voyaging at night is very pleasant, yet our fragile craft was not safe enough to turn in regardless of a possible spill.

February 16.—By daybreak it was found that we had travelled twenty-four miles in the night, although in the last few hours the wind had dropped, and we had then simply drifted down stream with the current. Soon after daybreak we landed at a river-side cattle-station, to procure milk, eggs, fowls, and vegetables. The owner, a huge creole negro *vaqueiro* (herdsman), received us with blunt heartiness, and at once provided me with five bottles of milk and some two dozen eggs and some sweet potatoes, for which he would receive no payment, except " *uma pingazinha para matar o bixo* " (a little " tot " of *cachaça* to kill the worm). His home was a bright little place, the adobe-walled hut, thatched with palm-leaves, was in good repair, and its interior neat and tidy; it nestled amidst orange and lemon-trees, bananas, and the rich vegetation of the river-side; in front of the hut, a level well swept area of dark red soil extended to the edge of the, here, lofty banks, beyond which spread out the broad sky reflected expanse of the noble river. His darkie wife and grown-up children were comfortably clad and looked clean, cheerful, and healthy. Pigs, goats, turkeys, fowls, horses, and cattle, in an adjoining paddock, added to the homeliness of the place. The few fowls I bought were very cheap, 320 reis each (about 8*d*.).

The river-side in this district is well populated; the banks show many labourers' huts and farm buildings, many of the latter look neat and clean, but all are of the simplest and plainest construction.

There are many tales extant of this river-side, tales of the old colonial times, and of family feuds and battles. At Urubú, many years ago, a terrible struggle occurred between two brothers, the Guimaraês, causing quite a civil war, in which the greater part of the inhabitants joined one side or the other. The town of Urubú itself was besieged, the churches and other buildings yet present the bullet-marks and other traces of the struggle. It became eventually a Kilkenny cat business, for the two brothers exterminated not only all their family, their father, mother, sisters, and other brothers, but were themselves eventually destroyed. As many as 2000 combatants are reported to have taken part in some of the battles. For a long time it created a great anarchy, and was only finally stopped by the government sending troops to quell the disturbance. It is spoken of as the *Guerra dos Guimaraês* (the war of the Guimaraês).[1]

Towards mid-day, after passing by flat and low-lying country, consisting of dense bush and cerrado, and long stretches of flooded swamps, we sighted in the north-east the Serra do Gentiho running north and south, and soon after-

[1] This district of Urubú, Xique-xique, and Joazeiro, has ever been one of the most turbulent centres of Brazil, a political volcano, and now in the present year, 1886, the lower reaches of the river are infested with bandits, who levy contributions upon all passing river-craft, so much so, that much of the traffic between Barrā, and Joazeiro, has been stopped. Police were sent to maintain order, but the officer in command considered it advisable to keep out of danger by remaining in the towns. But it will probably soon again resume its generally peaceful state.

wards the towers and roofs of the churches, and the white and many-coloured houses of the Cidade de Barra.

At the landing-place, quite a busy noisy scene existed; there were large and small *barcas, ajojos,* and canoes from both up and down the river, and *burity*-frond rafts (*balsas*) from the Rio Grande, some anchored, some on the muddy shore. The shore was strewn with old canoes, defunct *balsas*, rubbish, offal, logs of timber, &c., black *urubus* and gaunt black pigs feasted on the garbage and refuse of the city, freely strewed about the odorous mud. Black washerwomen, with their ample skirts tucked up, stood in the water belabouring their washing with sticks, or banged it upon flat slabs, or else stood with their hands on their hips chaffing the boatmen of the various craft. Men were squabbling on shore, or singing as they discharged cargoes from *barcas* and *ajojos*, others stood about driving bargains, and loafers squatted on the logs, or leaned against anything that would support them.

The landing-place, like most of these riverside settlements, is the exchange-mart for the transaction of most local business. On each side of the Porto the walled compounds of houses back on to the banks; in front is a small open square, containing a few stores, facing the river.

On landing and picking my way amidst the garbage and mud, and up a gentle ramp of hard clay and sand, I found myself a stranger, and without any useful letters of introduction, in the city of Barra do Rio Grande.[2]

From the little square in which I found myself, streets lead away right and left, parallel to the banks of the river. On the left, the street consists of the open shops and stores of various trades and vendas; on the right, the houses are chiefly private dwellings; this latter part terminates in a large open square, containing the more superior houses, and the new great unfinished church, out of all proportion to the city, and

[2] It was created a *villa* (town) by *resolucão regia* (royal resolution) on the 1st of December, 1752, and became *cidade* (city) by *lei Provincial* (Provincial law) on the 16th of June, 1873.

that, as Captain Burton justly says, makes the city appear like an annexe to its matrix.

There being no signs of a *hospedaria* or 'otel anywhere, I wended my way to a dry-goods store in front of the Porto to make inquiries. I found there a pleasant-looking Portuguese, reposing on his counter, and killing time by killing flies. He could not direct me to any place where I might find accommodation, but kindly took pity upon my homeless state, and frankly offered me the hospitality of his abode; and learning that he was a bachelor, and there being no fear of dreadful Brazilian *enfans terribles*, I gladly accepted his kind offer.

In taking a walk through the city, it presents but a mean appearance; the streets are long irregular and sandy, there are a few pretentious houses with glazed windows, and front walls faced with Portuguese glazed square tiles, and a brick *trottoir*, where the inmates place their rocking-chairs in the cool of the evening to enjoy its pleasant temperature, or receive a visit from a neighbour; but the greater part of the houses are of white or colour-washed adobe walls; others in the suburbs are more homely still, mere huts of sticks plastered with clay, and roofs of grass.

In the compounds of the houses are many fruit and flower trees, both much subjected to the destructive ravages of the great leaf-carrying Sauba ant;[3] near the north square, and at the west end of the city, the bush and trees mingle with the houses and border the thoroughfare; otherwise, the sandy dust of the streets, the glare of the white houses and walls make one's eyes blink with the blaze of reflected light.

There is considerable movement in the streets, but confined to pedestrians, for rarely is seen a bullock-cart; carriages are as absent from this city as in any negro hamlet in the centre of Africa. Among the wayfarers, black brown and yellow complexions predominate; the whites are chiefly the traders

[3] *Œcodoma cephalotes.*

of the river, the planters, shopkeepers, and the local public officials, and their families.

The ground occupied by the city is practically flat, and is situated on the obtuse angle formed by the junction of the Rio Grande with the Rio São Francisco, and as it is only seventeen to twenty-four feet above ordinary low-water mark of the river, and as extraordinary floods have risen to thirty-six feet above that level, it may easily be conceived what disastrous consequences an inundation of twelve to eighteen feet of water over the whole of the city must bring; and how it must necessarily prohibit any great development of this otherwise admirably situated city, that commands the exit of 480 miles of free river navigation of the Rio Grande and its tributaries, besides a considerable carrying trade on the Rio São Francisco.

During the days ensuing my arrival, I prosecuted inquiries as to my intended route and means of travelling that resulted in forming the acquaintance of the local authorities and notables, all, without exception, polished well-educated Brazilian gentlemen: especially must I *destacar* (stake out), as a Brazilian would say, Dr. Firmino Lopes de Castro the Municipal Judge and the editor of the *Echo do Rio Sao Francisco* (a small weekly of two sheets); Dr. Antonio Pereira de Castro, the Public Prosecutor; Capitão Francisco Antonio Barbosa, a trader; and my kind host, Senhor Emilio Souza Rodrigues; all of whom rendered me invaluable assistance in procuring information and means of travelling, but of the Rio do Somno and Carolina no one could tell me anything; they were not only *terras incognitas*, but the very names were unknown.

Capitão Barbosa, who had already made several journeys to Goyaz by the valleys of the Rios Grande and Preto, recommended to me a certain Rodrigues as an experienced muleteer, and who would contract to take me anywhere. This individual, who lived on the opposite side of the river, was sent for and negotiations entered into.

He was a tall full-bearded white man, with a good-looking and pleasant, if rather simple face. He said he could calculate the distance to the Tocantins, although he had never been there, nor ever heard of the Somno, or Carolina; yet he closed a bargain with me to provide mules and men, sufficient to transport myself and my effects to Carolina, for 350$000 (then about 35*l.*), provisions to be provided by myself. The bargain was closed, but it was ten days after my arrival before he could collect his animals and I could get away.

In the meantime, many agreeable days were passed in the pleasant society of my new acquaintances, and before my departure a day's shooting was arranged. Not then having a gun, I purchased in the city a light thin tube of Belgian manufacture, about the size of a large revolver barrel; it was light and handy, and as it could only be charged with a small quantity of powder and shot, it was not likely to burst, or perhaps do any harm to any flying game.

One day, with the first glimpse of daylight, our party assembled, eight guns in all, to go for a cockney's day's shooting, to shoot what we might find. A walk of four miles over sandy and grassy plains, and by green marshes bordered by reeds, bushes, and palms, brought us to the wide flat shallow morass that surrounds the city and extends from the Rio Grande to the São Francisco, where we separated. The marshes were full of brilliant dragon-flies darting from reed to reed, or poising in mid-air, and noisy with the screamers and other aquatic birds common to lakes and swamps in Brazil, but they were all very wild and difficult to approach, and having no dogs, we failed to secure the results of many of the shots. Probably the "sport" would have disgusted a genuine sportsman, for there was not a decent gun amongst the whole party. Each one stalked his game by creeping among the reeds and bush, and invariably bagged his bird whilst it was swimming or wading, and generally even waited for it to remain still.

It was very hot work, the sun poured down its rays upon

the shadeless flats, and glimmered fiercely upon steaming lakes and swamps, and many of my companions, unused to much outdoor exercise, were thoroughly tired out when we assembled at eleven o'clock under a grove of trees to breakfast. There our attendants had put up hammocks and prepared a welcome repast. Everyone soon reduced his clothing to a minimum quantity, and several collapsed into hammocks, or on the grass, thoroughly prostrated with fatigue. We were accompanied by an amusing character, a harmless lunatic, calling himself "General Barbosa;" he had once been an influential trader in the city, but meeting with disastrous losses, the consequent trouble shattered his reason. Otherwise he was a hale robust old man, full of fun, and extremely amusing; his weakness was in imagining himself some great and wealthy personage, and in making gifts to his friends of fabulous sums. He was a great favourite with the townspeople, and charitably well cared for by them.

Later on, a few more hours were spent in perambulating the marshy lands—on my part more for the sake of exercise and of being familiar with the districts, than for the poor sport.

Our total bag amounted to nine *mareccas* (wild duck), five *caruhunas* (grey herons), six *quem-quem* and four *jaçanas* (screamers and *jaçana parras*), eight *pombas* (pigeons), and three *soccós* (bitterns); thirty-five birds all told.

The city is reported to contain a population of 4000 to 5000 inhabitants, and judging by its extent I should say it has quite the latter number. It carries on a considerable import trade of articles of local consumption from the Rio Grande districts, and exports thence in return the merchandise it receives from Bahia, and its position enables it to command a considerable carrying trade up and down the river; but there is very little exportation to the coast of national produce, as the long overland journey to Bahia is too expensive, and its cost leaves little or no margin for profit to the producer.

During my ten days' stay in this place, much rain fell, generally at night, in the form of squalls and thunder-showers, after days of close, sultry heat. The thermometer ranged from 80° to 86° in the daytime, falling to 76° at night.

When Rodrigues announced his readiness to depart, I learned that an empty *barca* was returning up the Rio Grande, and so took the opportunity to charter it, in order to make personal observations of the river.

CHAPTER IV.

FROM BARRA DO RIO GRANDE TO BOQUEIRÃO.

Adeos—The yacht—Intruders—A swampy land—A night in a lagoon—A convenient "explorer's" bed—Water-lilies—Difficult navigation—Estreita da Serra—Hot weather—A toilsome progress—A river-scene—The splendid physique of the boatmen—Patient toilers—A tramp along the shore—An uncouth reception—A river blocked with fish—Slow travelling—On mule-back again—A jovial companion—Boqueirão—A picturesque situation—A possible future—A village schoolmaster—Indolence of the Boqueirãoenses—A pleasant evening—Navigation of the Rio Grande, etc.

February 26.—Many of my kind friends in this little city of kind people assembled to wish me "*boa viagem*," and give me a final embrace and a pat on the back. "*Adeos, Amigos! Adeos, Senhor Doutor!*" The polemen shout "*Vum emborer*" (*vamos embora*, "let us be off") as we glide from amidst the other craft and the floating rubbish of the shore.

The men impel the *barca* slowly along amidst the numerous river-craft and keep close in shore out of the strong current of the stream. We pass by the river-front walls of the yards and gardens (many are flooded) of the houses of the water-street. Scores of black washerwomen stand in the water and chatter, giggle, and make loud observations as we pass onwards. Little naked pot-bellied piccaninies skylark in the muddy water like veritable tadpoles.

My yacht, (called the *Villa Pastoura*,) to my satisfaction, offers a much better accommodation than the plebeian *ajojo* and its cramped space. Although far inferior to some of the large gaudily-painted *barcas* of the Rio São Francisco, yet it contains a roomy saloon six feet wide, nine feet long, and six feet high, with shuttered windows at the sides, and doors at each end. The sides and ends are constructed of boards, and the curved roof thatched with *carnahuba* palm-leaves. Forwards of the cabin the *barca* is undecked, excepting the narrow tramp-way that extends from stem to stern, where the men pace with slow and laborious strides as they pole the boat up-stream; it requires sharp work to haul up the poles at the end of the tramp, hasten back to the bows and get the poles again thrust against the bottom of the river, for the current is so strong that headway is easily lost.

Shortly after starting, the *barca* was poled alongside the shore, where a coloured man and a woman came aboard carrying a guitar and a bundle, and straightway proceeding to my cabin, seated themselves, without uttering a word, or a by-your-leave, on my bed, and began to make themselves comfortable. I had seen in my travels one or two cases of unmitigated impertinence, but none equal to this. I called the *piloto* and inquired of him if I had not chartered the *barca* for myself.

"*Sim Senhor*," he replied.

"What do you mean, then, by allowing these people to thus intrude themselves in my cabin? Send them away."

"*Nao fazem mal*" (They won't do any harm); "they are only passengers going up the river."

It required some rough words and some hot ones before the skipper could be convinced that I really objected to share the cabin with other passengers, without at least being consulted.

With assumed innocence, he remarked, "You certainly

paid so much money for the hire of the *barca*, but how can it matter to you how much you pay, the *barca* is empty, and you cannot fill it all up yourself, therefore what difference can it make to you, if I earn a few more milreis by taking a few more passengers?"

The male passenger now offered to retire, but pleaded for a lift by saying, "Ah! Senhor Capitão, have pity on a poor man and his wife, who are anxious to get back to their family and their roça; the rice is all ripe and wants collecting, and the floods will soon destroy it all; we will be very quiet, and keep in the bows of the *barca*, and you shall not be inconvenienced."

The man had a fairly honest face, and as they were only going a few leagues, I consented to their occupying the bows. This matter had not been long settled, and we had proceeded but a short distance on our way, before a canoe came alongside, and the crew assisted two negro-women to come aboard, who also marched straight into my cabin; despite the flowers in their wool, their smart cotton skirts, gaudy shawls, and embroidered chemises, they were neither young, fair, nor good-looking, and as they had evidently been running to catch the *barca*, they were hot and perspiring, and emitted such an odour as only two stout negro ladies can produce in favourable conditions.

Another angry discussion with the *piloto* naturally ensued, wherein I demanded to be put ashore, for I would proceed no further; excuses, promises, apologies he tried in vain, and finally, the odorous ladies had to return to their canoe, freely expressing their opinion that I was "*o diabo*," and "*um homen brabo e de mau genio*" (the devil, and a fierce and evil-disposed man). Eventually the city is left behind, but the progress of the yacht is miserably slow; on many occasions the polemen fail to reach the bottom with their poles, owing to the depth of water even close in shore, where they have to hold on to the bushes of the submerged banks that often sweep the roof of the cabin.

As far as one can discern, the adjoining lands appear to be a low-lying level plain, covered with low dense bush, and occasional patches of open country with many shallow lagoons. We now leave the strong current of the river, pass over the submerged banks and enter one of these lagoons, where the shallow water, and the imperceptible current permits good progress to be made for some time, until the lagoon narrows to a narrow tortuous channel, thickly obstructed by bushes, that require the use of axe and billhook to clear the way.

These lagoons, at this season of the year (February) when the river is in flood, follow the course of the Rio Grande for many miles, and also communicate with the Rio São Francisco at the rear of the city of Barra, making its situation practically an island.

At 6 p.m. the *barca* is hauled alongside the swampy margins of another lagoon, surrounded by low bushes, and anchored for the night. What a place to pass the night in! The land shows hardly any perceptible rise from the water; its sandy surface is littered with the rotting twigs and fallen leaves of the bushes, and saturated by a late extension of the waters of the lagoon; a hot humid air arises from the sodden soil laden with pestiferous miasma and the musty odour of decaying vegetation.

At 8 p.m. the thermometer registered 88° in the cabin. In such a situation and atmosphere mosquitos were naturally plentiful, but the mosquito-net gave relief from one torment at least, but the cabin was very suggestive of a vapour bath.

I now found the benefit of a portable camp-bed I had had made in Barra, which is so exceptionally convenient that I will describe it for the benefit of future travellers.

Two light cedar-wood boxes were made, each twenty-seven inches long, sixteen inches wide, eighteen inches high (the cedar-wood is preferable, as it is strong and light, and its odour keeps away white ants and other insects); over the whole of the boxes a raw wet bullock-skin was tacked, which, as soon as it dries, greatly strengthens the trunks, and renders them impervious to water. At the two upper front corners of each box, iron sockets were screwed to receive the iron hooks at the ends of the bars of wood that form the side of the bed. The bars of wood are each two inches wide, two and a half inches deep, and forty-six inches long; hooks were screwed to the top ends of the bars, which are hooked into the sockets at corners of boxes. A piece of good stout canvas is tacked along the outer side of one bar, pulled tight over the upper side, and secured by tacks to the outer side of the other bar. The bed is then complete. The bars can be removed at once with the canvas, and rolled up, forming a parcel forty-six inches long and about five inches diameter, to which may be added rugs, mackintosh sheet, and an air-pillow, or these latter articles may be stowed in the trunks. As the locks should be on the sides of the trunks that face each other, it is evident that the boxes cannot be opened without turning out the occupier of the bed. A ring is also screwed to the ends of each box, through which is passed a stout raw ox-hide rope; that passing under the boxes the looped ends serve to suspend the trunks to the pack-saddle.

The next morning the first lights of dawn found us again working a way amongst the bushes, where the branches spring in our faces and knock off hats, and the brambles scratch the flesh of the bare chests and arms of the pole-men; it is the funniest of navigation. The story of the celebrated American flat-bottomed boats that are reported to be able to cross country on a dewy morning, appears feasible, when one looks around on this occasion and sees the dense bush on every side, as though we were carrying a boat through a flooded wood of huge gooseberry-bushes and other similar vegetation.

It was not before 9 a m. that *Villa Pastoura* emerged from the bush into the open waters of the Rio Grande, where, in addition to the strong current of the stream, another difficulty was encountered, for the whole width of the river, about 500 feet, was covered with a dense impenetrable mass of floating water-lilies, called *golfoés*, and bearing numerous beautiful light-mauve-coloured flowers; the mass was being carried along with the current, and extended as far up and down the river as the range of vision permitted; the dense mass crushed against the sides of the *barca*, and drove it again into the bush, to which we held on for upwards of half an hour; no abatement, however, being perceptible in the quantity or force of the drifting vegetation, we were obliged to again take to the bush and lagoons.

One hour's more laborious work amongst the trees found us in a long lagoon of open water, up which the brawny polemen sent the *Villa* flying.

In all these margins of lakes and swamps there is hardly any animal life to be seen, even small birds are rarely sighted; it is a huge silent watery solitude.

At the end of the lagoon the *barca* again entered the river, where the plants were yet numerous, but more in the form of detached floating islands that permitted of a passage by keeping close in shore, where even so, the *barca* received many a scrunch when the plants piled up in masses around the bows, and obliged us to make fast with might and main to the bushes of the banks. As yet no banks or dry land were perceptible from the river; only the tops of the bushes indicated the whereabouts of the submerged margins of the stream, but about six miles ahead a blue line of hills was visible, with a dip in the centre through which the river passes, called *Estreita da Serra* (the strait of the Serra).

Towards evening a few banks of higher ground appeared above the waters, and at sunset the *barca* was hove to for the night at Porto da Fazenda de Serrote, a little cove and the landing-place of a neighbouring farm, and twenty miles from Barra.

During the night a few mosquitos serenaded us with

their little bagpipes, but nowhere in those flooded lands were they so troublesome as on the Rio São Francisco.

The day had been very oppressively hot, 88° in the shade; in the evening the temperature dropped to 80° at 8 p.m., still quite warm enough.

It was hard laborious work next morning poling up stream; the water-lilies still floated by in immense quantities, and often and often quite barred our progress. It was not until breakfast time, 9 a.m., that the Serra noticed in the afternoon of the previous day was reached.

The open window of the saloon formed a frame to a picture of the scene outside. There, on the bosom of the river, float the broad flat expanse of pale dull green leaves, and the delicate mauve-coloured flowers of the drifting masses of water-lilies, here and there dotted with the dark red-brown *jacanas*, screaming like a kitten, and whose light bodies and widely-expanded long toes enable them to easily run over the surface of the floating vegetation in their quest of food. Down the centre of the revolving masses of plants the strong current of the stream had formed a channel of open water, that glitters in the sunlight like a streak of burnished gold. Long lines of thick bushes indicate the margins of the stream; at their rear many carnahuba palms, singly and in groups, rear up their spiral stems, often covered with bromelias, ferns, and climbing parasitic vines. Their fan-like leaves rustle and scintillate with many a brilliant gleam, and sparkle as the passing breeze sweeps by. Further inland a ridge of hills forms the background; their gullies, their grassy summits, and bush and boulder-strewn sides are minutely delineated in the full glare of the morning sun, the light azure sky and its dazzling white clouds.

The open door shows a picture of a more prosaic character, an untidy dirty but picturesque scene. Reclining in the bows are the four semi-nude figures of the copper-coloured stalwart boatmen, eating their breakfast from one common huge bowl of beans, rice, and dried beef. They are splendidly made fellows, and their slightest movement shows the play of wiry muscles in arms and chest; the sun beats on their naked bodies as heedlessly as upon the water. Near the entrance to the doorway, on the floor of the *barca*, my cook is preparing my matutinal repast over a fire made upon a half-barrel of sand; by his side are the third-class passengers (the couple who came aboard at Barra), also preparing some mystic messes for themselves; the piloto is squatting on his heels in the trampway fishing, but not a bite rewards him.

Sunset on the Rio Grande.

The rest of the day was consumed in poling slowly up stream, until the water became so deep that no bottom could be found, that necessitated another long and toilsome struggle through the bush to a lagoon, and a halt for the night; the temperature was then pleasant, 78°, and mosquitos absent. The day's voyage consisted of nine miles only.

The noise of bushes scraping the cabin, as we toiled again through bush, awakened me the next morning; although not more than about 200 yards in extent, it was fully two hours before we were out of the jungle and again on the river, at last comparatively free from the water lilies.

In all this toilsome voyage, struggling against ever-recurring difficulties, requiring great and continued labour to overcome them, I could not but help a feeling of admiration for the captain and crew, as they toiled long and patiently at their arduous work; from stewey morn to stewey eve they laboured, yet, no matter how difficult the obstacle, or great the disappointment caused by the current in the river carrying away the craft, and losing the results of heavy work, not a murmur was heard, not a "satanism" uttered, they worked with the patience of ants. Evidently they had long been accustomed to the labour and its trials, and accepted their worries as inevitable, and to be borne with that patience that all troubles should be met with.

At breakfast time we stopped at Curral das Egoas, the port of a small fazenda a little inland; here our third-class passengers left us, and hearing that a path accompanied the river-side to another small farm, four miles away, I determined to walk the intervening distance, and went ashore with Bob and Feroz.

It was pleasant to thus stretch one's cramped limbs, but a deep light sandy soil made walking very heavy work. The path leads through the shadeless low bushes on the fetid margins of lagoons. It was natural to expect to find some duck or other aquatic birds in these little-frequented places, but all the way not a feather was sighted. These inundated sandy lands are but great dreary solitudes of bush and swamps, where the air is close hot and laden with exhalations; the vegetation is even uninteresting, no flowers or ferns vary the monotony of the thorny bushes and scrub, there are no parasites or *llianas*, that contribute so much by their beauty to render impressive any scene in the wilderness, no matter how distant or unfrequented it may be.

Finally, we reached Caiçara, our destination, a small house with adobe walls and thatched roof, with a *curral*, or cattle-pen, adjoining. Some women at the door had sighted our approach, and at once fled indoors. Consequently, when we arrived, we found doors and windows closed and barred. I suppose that my sun helmet stamps me at once as a stranger and a doubtful party.

An Uncouth Reception.

Whilst we were seated by the river-side, awaiting the approach of the *barca*, two leather-clad men approached us from the house, and came shyly forward. Bob asked them if they had any fishing-lines and hooks. They made no reply, and only gazed stolidly and silently at him. On his repeating his question, they, still glaring at first one, then the other of us, abstractedly replied, "*Nao entendo sua falla*," (I don't understand your talk.)

To gain the confidence of the lower type of Brazilian peasant, it is necessary to address them in their own patois and local expressions, for even a native like Bob, from a distant province, is liable to be treated as a strange being, even though the various provincialisms are very slightly different one to the other. Bob laughed at them, and called them "*gente bruto*" (rough ignorant people). They remained for some time silently wonderingly gazing at us, and making no reply to our questions or observations. I do not suppose any African traveller ever met such uncouth boorishness amongst the wild negros of Africa.

After a long period of steadfast staring, our visitors retired as silently as they came, and the *barca* soon after arrived.

Two more miles up the river, to another little port called Barreiros, terminated the day.

The evening was spent in fishing, and a few welcome fish were caught, a little shower of rain apparently making them take the bait, for I had tried several times before on the voyage, but had not succeeded in obtaining even a nibble.

The *piloto* gravely informed me that in the Rio das Ondas, an affluent of the upper Rio Grande, the fish at times become so plentiful that they impede navigation to such an extent that it is difficult for a canoe to make headway. It is curious to remark, in all parts of Brazil, how, if any particular locality has a reputation for anything, for gold, diamonds, fevers, game, &c., its merits, or demerits, will be spread abroad, and immensely magnified and distorted, and travellers must accept all information of distant parts with a liberal discount for such exaggeration. How many a time have I been misled about the *mooeenta carssar* (*muita caça*, heaps of game), of various places, and have gone over the ground with a gun, only to return with an insignificant bag.

At night the thermometer registered 85° F., and mosquitos were on the war-path.

March 2.—Temperature at sunrise 81°. I continued my walk along the river-side path in the early morning; the soil is everywhere sandy, but much firmer than on the previous day's walk. The country shows the same tame appearance, bushes, thorny scrub and lagoons. On the way I managed to bag a brace of *mareccas*, small handsome wild duck, and a *gallinha-d'agoa* (coot). A very few poor straw huts with their little *roças* occasionally border the roadside.

The rest of the day passed hotly and slowly, the run of the yacht being only ten miles, although the men worked well and patiently.

The land still shows much the same character, but it is more elevated, and consequently less inundated. The halt for the night was at Porteira, a small river-side house, forty miles from Barra.

March 3.—I was awakened this morning by the *piloto* informing me that Rodrigues and the troop were on the other side of the river; this was good news indeed, and I joyfully left the Villa Pastura. I cannot recommend a cruise up the Rio Grande in flood time as a means of relaxation from the worries of business; in fact, if the tourist is not well provided with an ample stock of patience, he had better secure some comfortable quarters in a lunatic asylum against his return.

I found with Rodrigues, Capitão Francisco Antonio Barbosa, who was on a trading expedition to Goyaz, with a large troop of pack-mules carrying his wares. He will proceed up the valley of the Rio Grande, cross the divide, and then on to Palma and the Upper Tocantins, where he exchanges his goods for hides, and for the gold, and gold-dust, found in those regions.

Leaving my baggage with the Villa Pastura, to be carried on to the mouth of the Rio Preto, I rode on with the Capitão and my troop.

It was quite a treat to be once again across my old pigskin, and to feel myself once more jog, jog; I felt I had got back to real work and business once more.

The Capitão was an excellent companion, full of anecdotes and fun; his round jovial face is sunburnt and bearded, and pleasant to see, his laugh is hearty, and bluff and boisterous is his manner. He is a powerfully-built fellow, but, despite his joviality, there is a sharp twinkle in his eyes that makes one feel instinctively that it would be better to have him as a friend rather than a foe, and that any business transactions had better be avoided. He carried in one of his holsters a wonderful twenty-chamber revolver, that he was very proud of, an old weapon of Belgian manufacture.

About mid-day we reached Boqueirão,[1] a small hamlet of twenty-five wattle and dab huts and houses, surrounded by bush and a few fine trees. The place is very picturesquely situated at the base of a range of hills that intersect the course of the Rio Grande. The extremities of the hills terminate on each side of the river in easy slopes to the edge of the stream; the adjoining margins of the river are flat grassy swards, but slightly raised above the level of the water. The surface of the serra is comparatively regular, and thinly covered with woods, but in places appear huge boulders of rock, a compact gneiss, veined with crystals and white quartz.

These hills, about 300 or 400 feet above the river, constitute a continuation of the watershed of the Rio Preto and the Paranagua district in the north, and extend to the hilly country below Bom Jardim on the Rio São Francisco.

The inhabitants of the hamlet are extremely poor, and

[1] *Boqueirão*, a gap or pass in a mountain-range.

appear to be greatly debilitated by the effects of intermittent fevers or *maleta*, evidently mainly fostered by their poor diet and idle dissolute lives. Yet, despite its possible insalubrity, the admirable situation at the junction of the navigable streams, Rios Grande and Preto, must necessarily, in the course of time, have a commercial value. However distant its future may be, a time will be when its waters will be covered with vessels and its hill-sides echo to the sound of the passing steamers. The banks could easily furnish natural wharves, for deep quiet water is always found alongside, and the stream is 400 feet wide.

The Capitão took me to the only decent house in the place, that of the schoolmaster, Senhor Rezende, a good-looking white youth from Bahia, but whose slight figure and melancholy depressed appearance, formed a great contrast to the jovial burly Capitão. The inevitable hammocks were soon brought in and suspended, and served both as chairs, sofa, or bed. After a short stay and breakfast, the Capitão continued his journey to the distant Tocantins, where, in crossing the arid table-lands of the watershed of the São Francisco-Tocantins, he will have to travel for days over waterless sandy wastes, probably the most arid section of any part of Brazil. The *barca* arrived soon after sunset.

Senhor Rezende was not exhilarating company. He said he had been misinformed in Bahia, or at least, like most of the Brazilians on the coast, he had no conception whatever of the nature and character of the " Far West " of Brazil. He received a small pittance from Government for teaching the children of the neighbourhood; his pupils were sallow wizened listless-eyed white and whitey-brown children of nine to twelve years. He said it was absolutely impossible to obtain fresh meat unless he purchased a calf or an ox, for his neighbours would not, or could not, share the cost with him, and he alone could not afford it. It is not surprising that the young fellow was melancholy and depressed; he had spent his little all in the expenses of the journey from

BOQUEIRÃO AND ITS INHABITANTS.

Bahia, and saw no gleam of hope for better things in the future before him; his neighbours were rude uneducated *matutos*, they have no ambition, no "go" in them, no will or desire for anything but to sleep away their days and pass their nights in singing, dancing, and revelry. Money, they rarely see, to some, it is almost unknown; their food is farinha and river-fish, varied with beans, pumpkins, yams, and sweet potatoes; possibly a vegetarian may consider this excellent food for the tropics, but it is not suited to a malarious climate, for experience shows that an absence of nitrogenous food, such as toucinho, generates a lowering of the vitality and prepares the body for readily absorbing malaria.[2]

Inhabitants of any country like these of Boqueirão are as useless as if they did not exist, they have nothing to sell, or means for purchase; their little labour is expended in raising a few vegetables, fishing, and in building a poor hut, barely sufficient to accommodate them; it is never repaired, and when the rain comes in in one part of the roof, the hammock is moved to another corner, until finally, when the hut decays and collapses in spite of props, another one is built alongside it. The women make the few cotton garments of the men, that, like the huts, are never repaired, and are worn until the rags will no longer hold together. Yet withal, they are the most independent of all peoples, proud of their right to do nothing, and they do it most effectually.

From the Barra to the town of Campo Largo on the Rio Grande there is 180 miles of perfectly free navigation, absolutely devoid of obstacles, the average velocity is $1\frac{6}{10}$ mile per hour, minimum depth eleven feet in the dries. At Campo Largo the stream is 325 feet wide. Beyond this place the stream is navigable for yet eighty miles to the village of Limoeira, but it is troublesome in some of the bends of the river where small rapids occur. Above Limoeira rocks commence,

---

[2] The natives, especially the poorer classes, are much more subject to the intermittent fevers in Brazil than newly-arrived Europeans.

and not even canoes can pass in some places. Its feeders are the Rio Preto, more or less navigable for 128 miles as far as Formosa; the Rio Branco, with thirty-seven miles to Jacaré; and the Rio das Ondas, with eight miles; consequently, the Rio Grande and its feeders contain 433 miles of navigable streams.[3]

Between Boqueirão and the Barra the land forms a wide flat sandy and swampy plain, where the soil is so very poor, that only coarse hardy varieties of thorns and bush are able to withstand the droughts of the dry seasons; in the rains this area is subject to widely-extending inundations. It must consequently long remain an untenanted waste. There are few inhabitants in this district, and those only occupy the occasional high grounds near the river. I was told that, away from the river, the inland districts are practically uninhabited and pathless.

[3] These notes are taken from surveys made by M. Halfield.

CHAPTER V.

BOQUEIRÃO TO SANTA RITA.

My new troop—I pass as anti-Christo—The Rio Preto—New class of country—A park-like land—Marsh birds—A mid-day halt—An accident—Tamanduá—An exquisite evening scene—Rodrigues the tropeiro—Good times—A soap tree—Estreita—A contented and homely family—Gallinha d'Agua—A mandioca mill—A batuque dance—A missing mule—Countless butterflies—A prosperous people—Brazilian homes—Santa Rita—A hearty reception—Productions of Santa Rita—The street—Public officials—Various routes to Goyaz and the Tocantins—Dangers and difficulties threaten—Finding a strayed mule—The Santa Ritanas—A wet day in Santa Rita.

Jabiru-moleque stork.

SOME hours of the next morning were consumed in arranging and distributing the baggage between the pack-mules, altering and overhauling the harness, replacing missing shoes of the animals, and carefully preparing for the journey, and a little before mid-day we got away.

The party consisted of myself, Rodrigues the *tropeiro*, and Bob the cook, all mounted on mules; two negro lads accompanied on foot to drive the four baggage-mules, and my dog Feroz and Rodrigues' mongrel Ferro, completed the troop, and of course the monkey, Donna Chiquinha, who took up her accustomed place on the top of my mule's head, holding on with her hands to his long ears. The mule could not understand it at first, but he soon reconciled himself to the situation.

The mules were small but strong active little animals. One carried the tent, another my two trunks and portable bed, the others carried the provisions, a few clothes of Rodrigues and of the men, the cooking utensils, and a few tins of powder and shot.

Rodrigues told me of an amusing incident that occurred when he passed Caiçara, where I had waited for the arrival of the *barca* on the 1st inst. He had stopped at the house to ask for a drink of milk, but as the tenants were all vigorously *rezando* (praying in a chanting voice), he inquired what they were praying for, as it was not a day usually devoted to church purposes; he was informed that a strange white man and a coloured man had passed there that day, and that the white man, who looked like Anti-Christo, was coming into the country to make slaves of the people, and that they were praying to the Nossa Senhora of something or other to protect them from the *diabo* and all his machinations. Thus I found I had been ungenerously mistaken for the "old gentleman," though what I may have inadvertently done to induce them to form that idea, was utterly beyond my comprehension.

Within a mile of Boqueirão is the mouth of the Rio Preto (Black River), evidently so called from the dark appearance of the water which, nevertheless, is perfectly clear and sweet; it is a slow-flowing deep stream, about 150 to 200 feet wide. As soon as we entered the valley of the Rio Preto, the appearance of the country became vastly different to the low lands of the lower Rio Grande; it seemed as though the gap in the hills at Boqueirão constituted an entrance to another land. The surface is yet level and sandy, and shows occasional scattered shallow pools of water, but the ground is covered with a delightfully soft green sward; there is an utter absence of scrub, and detached groups of trees and palms, encircled with beds of arums, and other flowers, dot the surface of the grass and create quite a park-like appearance. The river meanders in serpentine curves through lawn-like grounds, its waters almost flush with the grass; no tangled bush or wild bramble are visible to mar with their rank growth the neat and clean-looking scene, that looks as though it is under the careful charge of gardeners, so fresh and free from disorder does it appear; even the pools of water have an appearance of artificial lakelets.

Away to the right, about a mile or a little more, appear the ridges of the Boqueirão range of hills, that gradually recede from sight as we advance up the valley, otherwise the land appears in all directions to be practically flat.

Animal life is also abundant. Parrots and hawks screamed, flocks of parroquets chattered noisily as they flew in clouds from one clump of trees to another, and as we rode on over the level firm sand and soft sward, many other birds came in sight, such as pearly-grey ring-doves, brown wood-pigeons, and numerous small brown ground-doves (*rolas*), and in some of the pretty lakes and on their margins of grass, reeds, and aquatic plants, there were plenty of water-fowl, *mareccas* (small wild duck), *gallinhas d'agoa* (almost similar to the Leicestershire moor-hen, *Gallinula Chloropus*), numerous grey and black-striped *quem-quem*, emitting a kitten-like cry, and the common screaming *jaçana* (*Parra Jaçana*), common to all the swamps of Brazil. I noticed also a fine *soccó boi* (bittern),[1] standing in the water with its long neck stowed away between its shoulders, and occasionally uttering boom-like notes. We soon had a capital bag of doves and ducks, sufficient for dinner and breakfast for all hands.

At two p.m., as the heat of the sun was very great, and the mules were not yet in proper training, a halt was made by the banks of the Rio Preto; a lawn-like flat sward bordered the water's edge, ornamented by groups of slender *Burityrana*

[1] Ardea exilis (?).

palms, mirroring their graceful outlines of stems and foliage in the smooth clear dark water, and the surrounding vegetation still consisted of the scattered dense clumps of trees. A plunge and swim in the cool water was particularly enjoyable, but in coming out, I met with a disaster by striking my knee against the spines of the submerged trunk of a tree; the pain for several moments was very sharp from the effects of the venomous thorn, my knee rapidly swelled, but an outward application of *cachaça* partially allayed it, and eventually I was enabled to jog on again, albeit with a stiff and aching joint.

At six p.m. we reached Tamanduá, a new house by the riverside, thirteen miles from Boqueirão. The proprietor welcomed us warmly, brought coffee and milk, and gave us a spare room.

As the shades of evening approach, the scenery near the little farm becomes exquisitely soft and charming. Around us, and extending from the borders of the rippling river to far away, is a broad expanse of bright green meadow land, dotted here and there with gleaming lakelets, some bordered by many flowering aquatic plants, others by groves of stately trees and delicate palms; other flower-encircled thickets form isolated groups out in the open plain, or on the margins of the river mirror their forms in the warm sky-reflected waters and form with their foliage a tracery against the clear cloudless sky, dark blue in the east, a pearly grey in the west; great shadows steal softly across the warm toned grassland and glistening waters, birds twitter their "good night," or harsh screams sound from the lakes, as some water fowl rise and wend their way homewards with heavy flight; a sweetly odorous and gentle breeze softly rustles and sways the plumes of the palms whose burnished leaves shimmer and flash with the scintillations of diamonds in the last golden rays of departing day. What colours there were, and how vain to attempt to convey them by words to those who have not had the privilege of witnessing the delicate opal tints of a soft tropical sunset.

March 5.—Although we were all up by daybreak, it was

nearly eight a.m. before the march was continued, Rodrigues all the meanwhile nagging at his lads for their dilatoriness, and calling them sons of various animals. He might have saved himself the trouble, however, for they paid not the slightest attention to his " Billingsgate," and chatted and laughed, and otherwise joked with the most imperturbable good humour, that made the old man furious and yellow with disturbed spleen. He is rather a nervous irritable old fellow, and I am afraid I shall have trouble with him if we meet with any difficulties in our march through Goyaz, for it is no use worrying over trifles in a journey through Brazil. " *Paciença* " is the motto for all travellers, and even residents, in this land of ever-recurring vexations.

The ground travelled over that morning still continued to present its flat and park-like appearance. The road tracks were of firm dry sand, and so entirely free from obstacles, that travelling was quite enjoyable. On the way some more ducks and doves were bagged, to supply an excellent breakfast at the mid-day halt.

After a ride of twelve miles, we rested on a mossy bank under the spreading branches of a huge mimosa by the riverside ; a welcome rest, as my leg had become very stiff and painful, otherwise such pleasant picnic scenes were delightful. Such " real good times " are not often to be met with in roughing it in Brazil. We had everything a traveller could desire ! fresh water alongside the road, fine weather, excellent ground to travel upon, pasturage for the animals, plenty of birds on the way, and fish in the river.

The river is generally bordered by great numbers of large trees. One variety produces a fruit like the prickly pod of the castor-oil plant ; another supplies a large brown round fruit, about the size of a large apple ; the first yields more oil than the castor-oil plant, and the latter [2] makes excellent vegetable soap.

A long hot but pleasant ride in the afternoon, through

---

[2] *Sapindus saponaria.* One tree will produce several bushels of fruit that contains a great quantity of saponaceous matter.

a houseless open flat country, by small belts of woods and by many lakes of crystal water, found us by sunset at Estreita, thirty-six miles from Boqueirão, a small cattle station by the side of a picturesque wood, and close to the river. The farmer, a simple-looking leather-clad man, offered us a spare room, and supplied us with milk, eggs, cheeses, and fowls. He told me he had never been anywhere except to the neighbouring town of Santa Rita, twenty-eight miles further on, and that journey he only made once a year. He had no conception of the outside world; to him Santa Rita was the beau ideal of a grand city. He was industrious and well-to-do, contented, and consequently probably as happy as any mortal can expect to be in this vale of tears. His wife was a buxom hearty *parda* (a light-brown mulatto), and the mother of seven strapping boys, all clad in leather suits, and who assisted their father in his work of cattle raising. It was really a picture of rural felicity; how different to the wretched people of the lower Rio Grande, yet not one member of the family had the faintest conception of the alphabet. The old man said his father got along very well without reading or writing, and so had he and his old woman, and he did not see why his sons should bother about it.

To bring ambition and discontent into such a household would be an unpardonable wrong. Like all these countrymen, good, bad, or indifferent, these also were highly religious, after their manner. Many gaudily-coloured prints of saints were nailed to the whitewashed walls, and at one end of their principal room was a gaudily-dressed doll, with an enormous crown of tinsel on its head, and representing a "Nossa Senhora" of something. Around the image hung several strips of narrow coloured ribbon that had been blessed by the padre of Santa Rita, and served as specifics against most diseases, including even the *diabo* and all his works.

March 6.—The morning's ride cut off a long bend of the river of six or eight miles, and although we thus left the immediate margins of the stream, the country still showed the same features common to this valley. Occasionally through some of the more open lands on our right, glimpses could be obtained of the distant highlands of the divide of this valley and the sources of the rivers of the Paranagua basin, in the Province of Piauhy.

At sunset we reached another farm at Gallinha d'Agua, fifty-six miles from Boqueirão. The place was charged with the unpleasant odours peculiar to a mandioca mill and drying-pan, and generated by the process of extracting the prussic acid contained in the roots. The smell, like that of coarse rancid butter, served to attract a goodly army of bloodthirsty mosquitos. We therefore sought and found a sweeter camping-site a little further on, in a grassy well-watered glade.

In the evening the sounds of the thrum-thrum of a *viola* (banjo) coming from the farm close by, made an irresistible attraction to the men, who promptly disappeared from camp. Later on, Rodrigues and I wended our way to the place of revelry, where we discovered our men hard at work in dancing with the male inmates of the farm, while the females crowded the doorways and peered over each other at the dancers. On our arrival they giggled like any country lasses, and after a whispered consultation they made a noisy stampede indoors.

These dances have already been described, with the accompanying wild songs, sung in high-pitched notes, rapidly uttered, the monotonous thrum-thrum of the *violas*, and the regular beat of the shuffling or stamping feet. But we wanted the men to be fresh for work the next day, so they had to stop their "*divertimento*" and go to bed in the odorous mosquito-infested open shed of the mill, but their hides are tough, and I believe that mosquitos die poisoned when they bite a perspiring negro.

March 7.—Our intentions were good to get away early, but alas! when the lads arrived, they stated that two mules could not be found. Rodrigues, after screaming out a volley of imprecations, and calling the boys "*Cobras d' infirno*," &c., mounted a mule and went in search of the missing ones. Long hours passed by in waiting for him until about midday, when he returned, looking very much dejected. He could find no news of the lost animals, and was afraid that they had been stolen, as a noted horse-stealer, João da Cruz, had passed by on the previous day.

Tired of the delay of waiting, I pushed on to Santa Rita, sixteen miles away, accompanied by Bob and one baggage-mule.

That afternoon's ride showed a change in the character of the country, for the land is more undulating and more wooded, with numerous little streams and shallow lakes in the hollows. Each of these little streams and lakes was the resort of clouds of countless butterflies, that dotted the ground like the daisies of spring; at our approach they rose from the ground in great swarms, fluttering and flashing their varied colours of dark-blue, light-blue, brown, pink, vermillion, yellow and white. The waters of the lakes were also teeming and noisy with numerous water-fowl common to Brazilian marshes, all of which I have already mentioned in previous chapters. Many farms and habitations were passed on the way, Boa Vista, Boca de Catinga, and others, all evidencing a certain air of Brazilian rural prosperity and comfort.

The word comfort must, however, be considered relatively, for, from an English point of view, such a desirable quality rarely exists amongst the Brazilians, either on the coast or in the interior, their greatest idea of comfort being to revel in extreme *déshabillé*, dressed in an old dressing-gown (the older it is the better), drawers, and slippers down-at-heel, and swing in a hammock or a rocking-chair in a verandah; around dust and disorder may reign supreme and unregarded; to be able to "*ficar a seu gosto*" (to be as you like) is the desideratum; (and yet there is latent wisdom in such a taste, for the stiff harness of grim propriety and respectability will sometimes make a "raw" on those of us who have been privileged to breathe the pure and untrammelled atmosphere of unconventionality, in places far beyond the reach of Mrs. Grundy and chimney-pot hats). I do not apply these remarks so much to the fanciful dwellings of the rich classes of the principal coast towns, where one so often finds a combination of luxury and bad taste; I refer especially to farmers and similar classes of the interior, to them "cosyness," "snugness," are unexplainable terms, and with the word "home" no words exist in their language to really correspond to them.

The first indication of the approach to the town of Santa Rita is a mud-walled cemetery by the side of a shallow lagoon; over its entrance gateway some rude attempts at stone ornamentation appear; then the large edifice of the big new church of "*Rosario de Santa Rita*" comes into view, that brings us to a long wide tortuous grass-grown sandy street, lined by houses of various sizes and forms, some of wattle and dab, others are more pretentious in whitewashed walls, coloured doors and windows, and tiled roofs.

On inquiring for the residence of the *Promotor Publico* (public prosecutor), Dr. Louis Baptista de Souza, to whom I had brought letters of introduction from my friends at Barra, I was directed to one of the neatest houses, where I found this gentleman asleep in a hammock, clad in a dressing-gown and slippers. On his awakening and finding me apologizing for an apparent intrusion—(I had been shown into the room by a negro lad)—he incontinently disappeared with a "*com licensa*" and my letter into an adjoining apartment. Soon, however, he returned, dressed in the latest "*modo da Bahia*," black coat and vest, white trousers, shirt, collar, and patent shoes; truly it was an unexpected vision in this semi-barbarous *sertão*. He received me with a smile and a hearty welcome, and ordered my trunks into an adjoining bedroom. His address was like that of most educated Brazilians, when they choose to assume it, courteous and genial; he was a good-looking young white man, about twenty-six years of age, his clear oval face, fine dark eyes, well-formed features, and heavy black moustache were good enough to serve for a typical hero of a three-volume novel. His brother, Senhor Francisco, soon after arrived, and made himself equally "chummey." My coat and riding-boots were soon removed by orders from my new friends, and their temporarily-assumed war-paint was soon re-exchanged for dressing-gowns and slippers; the same comfortable garments were brought for my use, a hammock was slung for me, a *refresco* of cachaça, lemon, sugar, and water was mixed for me, and I was directed to "*ficar a meo gosto*" (to be as I liked), and told "*a casa está a seos ordens*" (the house is at your orders), and that they hoped I should not be in a hurry to leave.

Thus lounging in our respective hammocks, we chatted of our friends in Cidade de Barra, my intended journey, its purpose, and the best means of acquiring information about it.

Truly it was a pleasant lounge after the fatigues of the journey, and to meet such pleasant fellows, and such a frank welcome was very gratifying. A bath, and then a dinner, with once again a white tablecloth, made one feel quite a Christian.

The town consists of one long street of houses and huts, (parallel with the course of the river,) and a few scattered huts in its rear on the land side. The church, like nearly all others in the Sertão, was commenced many years ago on a too pretentious scale, both in size and style, and, as a natural consequence, its completion is prevented through want of funds.

It is a big bare ugly structure, ninety-six feet by sixty feet. Its walls are built of unplastered rubble, its roof of tiles, its floor of brick, and its tawdry altar is resplendent with tinsel, gilt, and gaudy cloths. Although it is consecrated, and services are held within its precincts every Sunday and Saint's-day, it will probably be many many years before it is finished, and long may it be, for such wasteful expenditure cannot be otherwise than reprehensible in such a poverty-stricken country where so much is required for the common weal.

The town is situated at a considerable distance from the river, and separated from it by an extensive low marshy flat, crossed by a canal that leads from the river to alongside the rear of the gardens of the houses on the south side of the street.

Alongside the natural quays of the canal were two *barcas* and three *balsas* (rafts) loading with beans, maize, hides, and *rapadura*, for exportation to Cidade de Barra. The presence of these craft was good enough proof of the navigability of the Rio Preto thus far.

The *piloto* of one of the *barcas* said that he had brought his cargo chiefly from Formosa, up-stream, a length of the river that is fairly navigable, except in the dries, where a few *pancadas* (small rapids) appear in places below that village.

The neighbourhood produces hides, dried beef, maize, beans, rice, *rapadura* (compressed sugar bricks), and farinha, but cattle-breeding is the chief occupation.

There are a few fairly-stocked stores in the town, where one meets Tennant's ale, Huntley and Palmer's biscuits, Swedish matches, pyretic saline, American and French patent medicines, Birmingham and Sheffield hardware, Staffordshire china ware, and Manchester's goods, the latter's cotton prints and shawls being gorgeous with the brightest colours the printer can use, and the prints thick with starch and of the poorest materials.

Although there is an appearance of comparative prosperity in the little town, its streets are as dull as a small English provincial town on a rainy day. As I glance down the long street I see only a pack-horse waiting hopeless and dejected at a venda door for its master; another is coming up the street with a load of bananas, maize, and rude native earthenware water-jugs, followed by its brown master in cotton shirt, drawers, and straw hat ; two or three negro women in bright red or blue shawls, gossiping at doorways ; a few male loungers at other doors ; a few starving mongrels and a stray porker ; a few heads leaning out of the windows, and a few women squatting on doorsteps making the pillow-lace.

What a place of despair this must be for any educated man to pass the best days of his life in, men like my friends and the Juiz de Direito and other public officials, men who have no hobby to occupy their attention, no interest in the surrounding country, either as botanists, zoologists, geologists, or artists ; no books or periodicals, and very little work to do. Their lives are chiefly passed in their hammocks, sleeping, smoking, chatting ; their diversions are riding, a little shooting, backgammon, &c. ; their official occupations, even with all the Brazilian "red tape," occupy but a mere fraction of their time. Fortunately for them, their early associations and dispositions enable them to bear with equanimity a life that, to an active European, would be intolerable.

I called upon the Juiz de Direito,[3] Dr. D——, to whom I delivered a letter of introduction. I found this gentleman *en déshabillé*, of course in a hammock, slung in a brick-paved front room furnished with a cane sofa and the inevitable two cane chairs placed at right angles to it at each extremity, a small rug in front of the sofa, china spittoons on the floor, a few more cane chairs, two tables, a few glass vases, and a small library of legal and French works. The doctor was evidently suffering from the depressing influences of his monotonous life, for he wearily raised himself, and yawningly requested me to be seated and be *"a seu gosto"* whilst he perused my letter. "Sim Senhor ! anything I can do for you will be a pleasure ; I am at your orders." Having said which he relapsed again into weariness and his hammock, evidently thinking he had done all that was necessary. In reply to my various inquiries for information on various

[3] The judge of the county sessions.

matters, he only yawned dismally, and said he knew nothing about them, but suggested one or two men in the town who might inform me. I thought it best to relieve the doctor of my disturbing presence and troublesome uninteresting queries, so bid him *adeos*. His *adeos* was uttered with an evident sigh of relief at my departure.

Eventually, by the aid of my two friends, I was enabled to glean the following. A track leads from Sta. Rita to Carolina, through the provinces of Maranhão and Piauhy, but is rarely travelled over, and is full of difficulties. At twenty-eight to thirty miles from the town it ascends the precipitous slopes of a table-land, known as the Serra do Tipy (the division of the valley of the Rio Preto and that of the rivers of Piauhy), a branch of which extends in the form of a ridge to Boqueirão, near the mouth of the Rio Preto. This table-land forms part of the Brazilian north-eastern watershed.

A certain Lieut. Moraes, long ago conceived the idea of forming a canal between the Rio Preto and the rivers of the Parangual basin, with the object of diminishing the effects of the great droughts that often occur in the northern provinces, where the Government have lately spent some £20,000 in abortive attempts to construct great reservoirs in Ceara. The cost of throwing the Rio Preto over the dividing serras would probably be sufficient to buy up all Ceara.

There is a good road up the Rio Preto, and also up the Rio Grande, but beyond their sources there is a precipitous descent to the lower lands in the province of Goyaz. In both cases there is reported to be a waterless *travessia*[1] across barren sandy *geraes*, or table-lands, for two days' journey. The Rio do Sapão, a tributary of the Preto, was unexplored, and the whereabouts of the Rio do Somno was unknown. Not to fatigue the reader with my reasonings, eventually I came to the conclusion that the Sapão would not only

---

[1] This word is derived from *travessa*, a passage, and is used in Brazil to designate a journey of one or more days over arid lands, devoid of water or pasture.

possibly give me a good pass into Goyaz, but be a straighter direction, and would probably lead into the valley of the Somno, and this route I determined to explore.

Wandering and hostile *tapuias* [5] (Indians), were reported to frequent that neighbourhood, and at various times had made attacks on the homesteads on the borders of the unexplored districts. When my determination was known to my informants, I was strongly dissuaded from undertaking what they called a perilous enterprise, unless accompanied by a large armed escort and a baggage-train of provisions and water, otherwise I must perish. My informants poured forth a veritable chorus of the many dangers and risks I must necessarily incur. *Tapuias brabas* (wild Indians), *Quilombos* (outlaws and runaway slaves), *Bixos* (jaguars and vast herds of fierce peccaries), *Sucurihus* (the enormous Brazilian anaconda boa), starvation, fevers, and impenetrable forest, or impassable prairies, mountains, and swamps. I confess it was about as complete an epitome of all the possible dangers a traveller could possibly incur in Brazil. As, however, my informants had no actual knowledge on which to base their fears, the districts being utterly unknown, these inconveniences evidently only existed in the usual fervid imagination that the Brazilian countryman is so fond of forming of unfamiliar places.

In the afternoon Rodrigues arrived with the truant mules and the rest of the troop. He had had a long and weary *caça* (hunt) for them in the little-populated country, and only late on the next day had found them, sixteen miles to the rear of the camp, grazing with a number of mares.

It is only by patiently following the tracks of a runaway in an open country, that there is any chance of finding it, and for this work a skilled *tropeiro* is wonderfully apt, in following a sign here and there, in recognizing some peculiar size or form of the hoofs of the missing one, or in detecting

---

[5] The word "tapuia" is the name of one of the chief races of the aboriginal Indians.

the almost invisible tracks across low grass, they almost possess the wonderful gifts of Indians for this purpose.

A stroll in the evening showed the street a little more lively, for many families were seated in chairs on the *calçado* (brick pavement), in front of their houses, to whom my friends severally introduced me. I was always kindly received, coffee and sweets being, of course, always served,—I was really impregnated with coffee that night.—Most of the men had heard all about me already—name, age, salary, business, married or otherwise—and for such matters as they were not informed upon, they drew upon their imagination, my salary was the favourite point of discussion, which I was repeatedly called upon to settle definitely, it was evidently inexplicable to them why I evaded the question; my reticence was put down as one of the strange freaks of those *inglezes*. The garrulous old ladies took kinder to me when I informed them that we had churches in our country and that I was a *Christão* and not a *pagão*. As to the younger ladies, many of whom were very pretty and even white, they were unapproachable; a shy look, a whisper to her nearest female friend, and a convulsive giggle, was the invariable response to my observations. On one occasion one of the girls was told by her father to "*canta um pouco*" (sing a little). Mariquinha, of course, at once dutifully obeyed, and fetched her *viola* (banjo), and favoured us with a most ear-piercing high nasal treble *canta a moda*, that was listened to by her friends and neighbours with lively gratification. Imagine such a girl with "Caudle lecture power"—it made one shudder with suicidal thoughts.

March 9.—The next morning heavy black clouds obscured the sun and sky, a sultry heat and a low moaning wind betokened a heavy wet day, and soon after sunrise big drops fell, followed by a rush of cold wind, a crash of thunder, and the rain at once attended strictly to its duties; long and hard it rained until the afternoon, when it terminated in occasional showers. If the town presented a dull lifeless appearance in the bright sunshine, imagine what a deserted village it must have appeared on a pouring wet day, not a soul was visible in the flooded streets, doors and windows were nearly all closed, the open stores alone showing a human being, shivering with the damp air, and the cigarette-smoking store-keeper leaning with elbows on his counter, staring vacantly into the street.

CHAPTER VI.

FROM SANTA RITA TO FORMOSA.

Senhor Francisco—A medicinal plant for dropsy—Wooded lands—Peixe—Cattle-farmers—Donna Chiquinha and the Motucas—The Brazilian Tzetze—A cavalheiro d' industria—A successful gambler—A cold in the tropics—A rich soil—In the forest—A tired mule—Feroz attacked—Prompt revenge—Formosa—A friend in need—Intruders—A rainy season—The verdant village of Formosa—A pretty riverside—The tedium of delay—A prosperous farmer—Indolence of the natives—Doubtful ownership of land—The unknown Sapão—Preparations for entering wild districts—A cultivated valley—Death of Donna Chiquinha—A Brazilian wake—A Brazilian leather leggings—Rodrigues' temerity—Signs of fine weather—A morning's shooting.

The wooded valley of the Rio Preto, near Formosa.

March 10.—Rain again in the morning prevented a departure before mid-day. Senhor Francisco accompanied me, as he had some business to transact up the river.

After leaving Santa Rita, the country assumes a totally different appearance to what it shows on the other side of the town. The ground is more undulating, and the soil, red clay, is much more fertile, and covered with extensive second-growth woods, showing occasionally some fine timber.

I was pointed out a *cipo* or vine, (known by the name of *Costella de Gállinha*,) as a wonderful specific for the treatment of certain forms of dropsy; there are also great quantities of wild *herva doce* (aniseed).

During the ride the river often came into view; its current was perceptibly stronger, but not sufficient to prohibit navigation. Towards evening the track passed over more level and swampier ground, and at sunset the camp was pitched by the side of large marsh, or rather, low lands flooded from the previous rain. Close by was a straw hut, the only habitation we had passed on the road, although many tracks branched off to various farms and habitations situated more inland from the river.

March 11.—A long day's ride through a long shady solitude of woods, hills, and dales, and through many a swollen rivulet, brought us at night to Peixe, a small collection of five habitations.

The next day's ride was through a similar country, but a little more open. Camped at night at Morrinho, 124 miles from Boqueirão.

Although the soil of these districts is excellent, agriculture is almost *nil*, cattle-breeding being the favourite occupation. But these woodland pastures are subject to a great pest in the form of the Brazilian *tzetze*, the Motuca fly;[1] the cattle herd together in a close group for mutual tail-brushing during daylight, and only at night, when the flies disappear, are they enabled to graze; the fly draws blood wherever it bites; our mules' ears, necks, and haunches were covered with the flies, and beads of blood appeared wherever they settled. My mule was very fortunate in having Donna Chiquinha, the monkey, on his head, for it afforded her evident enjoyment to smash the flies wherever they settled within her reach; it was quite amusing to watch her, sometimes she would take a hitch with her prehensile tail round one of the mule's ears and lower herself down and clear off the flies from cheeks and

[1] *Hadrus lepidotus.*

nostrils, and then climb over on to the other side for a similar purpose; the mule seemed to appreciate her kindness, for he would always keep the ear to which she was suspended perfectly erect, so as to assist her as much as possible; there was evidently a friendship established between the two animals. Fortunately for ourselves, the flies do not appear to attack human beings, otherwise we should have had a bad time. In appearance they somewhat resemble a common house-fly, only the bodies are black and a little larger, and the extremities of the wings appear as though clipped off with a pair of scissors.

Soon after camping, a white man arrived with a troop of horses; he was mounted on a splendid mule, jingling with small silver bells attached to the harness that was freely covered with silver mounts. He dashed up to our camp at a fast *skippado*, and pulled up suddenly *cavalheiro* fashion, by forcing his spirited animal on its haunches. He was a wild handsome-looking fellow, a beau-ideal of a *cavalheiro*. A broad Panama hat rakishly cocked aside, shaded a keen sunburnt oval white face with aquiline nose, long straight black eyebrows, large dark eyes flashing with devilry, a small firm mouth covered by a jet-black moustache, a small trimmed black beard, and small ears, and long wavy black hair set off his small well-poised head; around his neck hung a blue poncho, with one fold thrown over his shoulder, sufficient to show his lithe active figure. Coat, trousers, and shirt of European cut and texture, long yellow boots with huge silver spurs, a heavily-mounted riding-whip, silver-mounted pistols in his holsters, saddle-cloth of jaguar-skin. Verily! one of Captain Mayne Reid's villains come to life; it is a pity he had a plain coat, for I missed the conventional crimson sash, the braided jacket and vest, the wide fringed trousers, and the other "fixings." Naturally I could not do otherwise than invite such a *distincto pessoa* to *ápear* (dismount) and *entrar* my tent. He dismounted at once, and advanced with a free and easy air and outstretched hand.

My dog was evidently suspicious of him, for after a good smell at his legs he gave a low angry growl, as Feroz only utters when he has biting business in view; he was gently admonished by a kick to behave himself and at once laid himself down, but kept one eye on our visitor, and ominously wagged his tail.

The stranger stated that he came to *comprimentar* (compliment) fellow-travellers; we mutually bow, and I invite him to our rough fare then being placed on the dining-table, i.e. one of my trunks. We were all hungry, and no more words or compliments were wasted until after the cloth, no, the plates were removed, and the wine (*cachaça*) was brought upon the table, and cigarettes produced and lighted; then the stranger opened with a fire of questions of the usual inquisitive character, and barely waiting for replies, proceeded to inform us of his own affairs. He had travelled from the Villa de Palma on the Tocantins, which he stated was 360 miles away, he had come down the valley of the Rio Preto, and was returning to his native place, Joazeiro on the lower São Francisco, about another 360 miles. His ostensible purpose in visiting Palma had been to purchase horses; but, as he said with a laugh, "the *povo* (people) there, fortunately, happened to be very fond of *jogo* (gambling), and as I play a little, I have got my horses for nothing, and also cleaned out all the money in the neighbourhood, about six *contos* of reis (600*l.*)." As I looked at his keen devil-me-care face, and his lithe sinewy limbs, I thought the poor deluded countrymen would have small chances with such a palpable sharper, and meet a foe ready for a quarrel. "Have you made many journeys like this?" I inquire. "Oh! that's my *vida* (my life), I go wherever there are horses and money, and remain until they are mine." "Had many quarrels?" "*Muito*" (lots). "Killed any one?" "*Algumos*" (some). "Let us have a little *jogosinho* (small play), just to *passar o tempo*" (to pass the time), said he. "My friend, I have neither *contos* of reis, nor horses to lose, neither do I wish to be included in your *algumos*."

Making all due allowance for braggadocio, this fellow was evidently a successful professional gambler, or in other words, sharper, and his life must necessarily have led him into many a quarrel; when on such occasions, it is like the old California times, who is smartest, kills, but instead of the revolver, here it is the *faca de ponta* (dagger).

Probably there was a good deal of truth in his candid avowal, of having had many quarrels with fatal terminations, as gambling and "*amor*" are some of the chief causes of the frequent use of the knife in Brazil; where, in the interior especially, a man is no more condemned socially by his countrymen for killing, than he would be in England if he had horsewhipped an enemy. Yet, with all this lax morality, probably there is no safer country on the globe than Brazil for a traveller, if he only has common courtesy, and avoids wine, intrigues, politics, and gambling. Being among Brazilians, it becomes necessary to judge their failings more from their point of view rather than by an English standard. Doubtless, the conscience of the *cavalheiro* is as easy as an Indian's after scalping an enemy.

Before leaving, the *cavalheiro* confirmed the reports I had received in Santa Rita, as to the sharp ascent from Goyaz to the highlands of the divide; he further told me he had travelled nine days without passing a single habitation, but had met everywhere plenty of game, deer, peccaries, tapirs, jaguars, perdix, &c. No water is found on the table-lands, only in the valleys. At last our friend got up, and bid us *Adeos*, and *Boa viagem*.

March 13.—This morning Senhor Francisco left me for another direction. The *cavalheiro* again visited us early, but I excused myself on the plea of a bad feverish cold, and he went his way.

I got up with a really bad cold that was not improved by a wet morning, a cold anywhere is not agreeable, but in the tropics it is always especially unpleasant and aggravated, and often productive of intermittent fever.

All that day we traversed magnificent hilly forest-land,

land that would produce luxuriantly all tropical growths. Sugar-cane yields a crop, year by year, without replanting, for ten years or more. The river flows through a deep narrow valley, winding in and out between precipitous wooded hills, whose sides slope down to the water's edge, covered with dense forest. Some of these forested valleys were exceedingly picturesque: the blue-sky-reflected surface of the river winds round the bases of the dark verdure-clad slopes, where the trees are each one different to its neighbour, and some rear up above their fellows, and spread out like a huge umbrella of dark green foliage; tall buff pale-grey blue and brown trunks, straight as a scaffold-pole, show up clearly against the dark shady background of tangled vines and foliage; the silver-leaved and tall slender stemmed *Imbauba*, the purple or golden *Bigonia* the *Pau d'Arco*, are conspicuous, both by their numbers and colours; trees that form the most striking features of all the forests from Rio de Janeiro to thus far.

I halted for a moment to gaze through an opening in the forest, like through a frame of leaves, upon the brilliant sunlit waters of the river deep down in the curving valley, the bright glare contrasting so strongly with the deep shade of the interior of the forest, murmuring with the steady hum of insects; such as the high notes of steely-blue mosquitos, the buzz of bees or of a blundering beetle charging blindly against a tree, and the droning whistle of many *cigarros*, all mingling melodiously with the faint gurgle of the river as it sweeps by the pendent branches of trees, and where a blue kingfisher darts like a flashing jewel into the water from an outstretched withered branch, covered by crimson-flowering bromelias, climbing ferns, orchids, mosses, and hanging ropes of vines, swinging in the gentle breeze a nest of the *japim* bird.[2] A shrill ear-piercing *cigarro* close by suddenly startles one like the sudden escape of steam from an engine, and brings one's eyes to the surrounding maze of huge buttressed trunks spotted with lichens

[2] *Cassicus icteronotus.*

and mosses; the vines, tangled, hanging like ropes, festooned, coiled on the ground, or throttling the trunks like huge snakes; the myrtle-like bushes; the tall slender saplings struggling upwards to the sunlight; giant tree-ferns and slender palms; the fluttering butterflies like specks of scarlet in the shadowy light, the faint mingled odour of spice, moss, and damp decaying leaves. It is all the same forest one sees everywhere, only varied in its details, as it varies at every step.

The voices of the men urging on the mules up the root-encumbered ascent, awakes one from a dreamy mood. "*O! Diamante!*" "*O! Baroneza!*" "*Ora! mula do diabo.*" The latter exclamation is uttered as a mule struggles amidst the holes or a network of roots in the narrow path. As the animals arrive, their panting heaving sides, distended nostrils, and flanks streaming with sweat, show the effects of the climb up the sharp ascent obstructed with the deep cavities washed out of the interstices between the roots of trees, great and small, that so thickly encumber the path.

The mule loaded with the tent is almost done up, as is evident by its trembling panting limbs, drooping head, and the limp ears, no longer erect, or turned smartly to front or rear at every passing sound. Rodrigues observes, "*Quasi cansou*" (it is nearly done up).

The load and pack were removed, and placed on Bob's riding-mule, and thus released of its burden the animal was enabled to continue the journey.

In the afternoon we reached Formosa in a sharp shower of rain. Our arrival created a great commotion in this backwoods village. Pigs squealed, dogs yelped and barked, and men, women, and children rushed to doors and windows for a good stare. Feroz, who was quietly trotting by my side, received a warm reception from dozens of mongrel curs, and as I rode up to a house, they all set upon him with yelps and barks, but not wishing to have any disturbance with any owner of these curs, I called to Feroz "*deita*" (lie down), and the good dog immediately laid down with his head between his paws silent and as contemptuous of the curs that were biting and worrying him, as though they were so many flies. He had, however, one eye fixed appealingly on me, evidently waiting for permission to go for them. I called to the people of the house to call off the dogs, but they merely looked at me, whispered to one another, and made no reply; so row or no row, I uttered the patiently waited-for word "*pega*" (seize 'em). In an instant Feroz was on his legs,—scrunch,—a leap,—another scrunch, and two curs lay on their broken backs gasping; the others, with tails well stowed away, with wild yelps, were off up and down the street, where, when at a safe distance, they barked defiance.

Feroz, his stump of a tail erect and motionless, showed a contemptuous indifference to his enemies and to his fallen foes, who were both in a bad way. "*O que cachorro! O que cachorro brabo!*" (O what a dog! O what a fierce dog) I heard the people say, partly in admiration, partly in surprise.

I eventually met the sub-delegado, Senhor José Moreira de Cunha e Souza, a pleasant honest-looking ruddy-faced nearly white man. My business and my desire for a house for a day or two was briefly explained; he expressed great astonishment at the object of my journey and the proposed route, but kindly offered any advice or assistance I might require. "First," said he, "let me get you a house; mine is empty now, as my family is at the farm, and you can occupy it as long as you please; and let me tell you at once that you must not expect to get away so soon as you anticipate, as we are now going to have the fortnight's heavy rain, that always occurs in the latter half of this month, and the country beyond here will be impassable; besides, you are *muito constipado e tem febre* (feverish cold); you must be treated before you go on."

The kind old man then conducted me to the best house in the village, one with wattle and dab walls and a tile roof, doors and shuttered windows. The floors are of mother earth, the rough mud walls are unplastered and unwhitewashed, and the woodwork is all unpainted. Above the unceiled rooms, as usual, appear the rafters and tiles of the roof. There are five large rooms in the house and commodious open sheds in the compound. If not attractive in its appearance, it had the merits of being commodious and dry.

After inducting me to this establishment, Senhor José left us to return to his farm across the water, after promising to meet again and consult upon future proceedings.

I now set to work to doctor my cold; but, alas! a figure appears lounging in the window, another at the door; another and another comes, and soon doors and windows are blocked; the *povo* (people) outside tiptoe over each other's shoulder to get a peep at the "*estrangeiro*," "*homen de fora*," "*pagão*," "*doutor*," "*branco*," "*inglez*," "*bixo*," as I am variously termed.[3] I inwardly groan at the well-known infliction, and call Rodrigues, and request him to take a bottle or two of *cachaça*, thank the *povo* for their complimentary visit, and explain to them that I am *incommodado* (unwell), and require to be quiet and *descansar* (rest). This was said in a back room, as the front room was filled by the curious lounging crowd, squatting on their heels, smoking and freely expectorating from profound depths, eyeing my traps, and handling what they could lay hands upon, discussing in whispers their opinions of the make and nature of the various odds and ends. Rodrigues departed on his mission, and I listened to sundry "Ah's!" smacking of lips, coughs and expectoration, and mutterings of "*O que cachaça boa e forte!*" (what strong good *cachaça*); and a shuffle of feet as my visitors all quietly retired.

On returning to the front room a broom is evidently necessary to remove the vestiges of the visit, for the floor is an unpleasant sight. Eventually each of the four front windows became again filled by lounging occupants, leaning

---

[3] "Foreigner," "a man from beyond their district," "pagan," 'doctor," "white," "Englishman," "*bixo*." This latter means any living thing.

with arms folded on the window-sill, and chins firmly resting on their wrists; their fixed eyes glare on my every movement, until I put the room in semi-darkness by gently closing the shutters in their faces with a *com licensa* (allow me.)

All that night the wind blew fiercely, accompanied by a driving rain, that made the air chilly (70 F.) and damp.

The next morning broke with a dull leaden sky; the wind had ceased, but the rain came down in long straight lines; for three days and nights this weather lasted with only a few minutes' intermission. The damp seemed to pervade everything; the trees dripped with moisture, rivulets formed in the street, pools of water collected in the rooms from holes in the roof, and when the wind blew, a fine mist was blown about inside through the open joints of the tiles; clothes, rugs, provisions, everything became damp and even wet, and a young forest of blue fungus rapidly accumulated on boots, saddles, and harness. To cure a cold under these conditions was no easy task, but Rodrigues made some herb decoctions, and with a few doses of quinine I was fairly well on the third day, when a little welcome sunshine appeared that soon, however, generated a close hot steamy atmosphere.

I then took a walk through the village. It consists of two irregular streets, parallel to each other; the houses are of the usual wattle and dab, and the birdcage-like huts of upright poles placed near together, with a ridge roof of thatch. The one or two rooms at the rear part of the huts are divided by wattle or mud walls, or by plaited palm-leaf partitions; chairs or tables are rarely seen, their places are filled by a few logs or a plain bench, and a miscellaneous litter of hammocks, hides, earthen pots, pillows for the pillow-lace, the *pilão*, or big pestle for pounding coffee or maize, stray sticks, cheap weak guns, and various rubbish. Many of the fronts of the huts are all open, and there one sees the women, smoking, squatting on the ground, and working the pillow-lace; the men asleep in hammocks, and naked brown pot-bellied children swarming everywhere in company with gaunt pigs and gaunter mongrel dogs, and a few fowls and turkeys complete the family circle.

The street opposite to mine is very wide, and contains the church, a plain old building in fair order, and shows a date 1790; therefore this is evidently not a new settlement. The streets are densely overgrown with bush, so thickly in some places as to obscure the sight of the houses from the opposite side; paths wind in and out amongst the weeds and bushes in all directions, and as there are apparently no carts or wheeled vehicles, the absence of a cleared thoroughfare is of no consequence.

Vegetation seems to take possession of Formosa, in front, in rear, and round about each house; in every nook and cranny grow thick bush and large trees, the roofs are masses of shrubs, each compound has some fruit, such as bananas, oranges, *mamão* (papaw), guava, and figs, and the castor-oil plant is in almost every one. The soil, consisting of a dark red earth, is exceedingly rich, as the surrounding verdure plainly shows.

The river Preto, about 100 yards from the village, is a beautiful clear stream, flowing over a pebbly bed, bordered by gently rising slopes of soft sward shaded by clumps of trees and palms, large and small. There I found an *ajojo* loading up *rapadura* sugar and *cachaça* from the sub-delegado's farm, for sale in Santa Rita. A walk along the grassy margins of the river showed many a pretty scene, constantly varying from forest to detached thickets of trees bush and open lawn-like ground; many varieties of small birds chirrupped a welcome to the sunshine, and the fussy little brown *João de Barra* fluttered his wings as he rapidly uttered his *tremolo* whistle; the water rippled placidly by, and bathed the foliage of many a drooping bush, and the roots of many a tree. What a paradise this place might be made in the hands of a thrifty people, a people contented to live on the results of reasonable labours. But vast sums must be spent in not only opening communications with the coast but the intervening country must be also populated before this district can be profitably utilized, as its merits deserve.

Black clouds now appearing, I hurried home just in time to escape the prelude to another three days' constant rain. The time passed very slowly; no books or papers to read; every book, periodical, and newspaper that I possessed had been carefully perused, even every advertisement in the newspapers, many more than a year old. My only resource was sketching; without that I felt that in this abode of indolence I should begin to be like the inhabitants, take to a hammock, and sleep my time away. It is strange how the feeling creeps on one, how the desire to do nothing grows upon one in such circumstances as I was placed; it was only by assuming my mackintosh, top-boots, &c., and taking a walk through the mud and rain that the feeling could be resisted.

A day or two of fine weather eventually occurred, that I took advantage of to visit the sub-delegado, the only industrious man in the place. Taking Rodrigues with me, we crossed the river in a very cranky canoe (the only ferry), and had a most enjoyable walk through forest and small plantations to the farm of Senhor José, about three miles from the village. I found the ruddy robust old man of sixty-five years at home; he was glad to see me, and gave me a hearty shake of the hand.

His home is situated in a long wide valley all under cultivation; sugar-cane, mandioca, maize, beans, coffee, bananas, and the castor-plant, everything grows most luxuriantly. As for the coffee-trees, I never saw any better in the coffee districts of Rio de Janeiro.

He works very hard undoubtedly, yet his home is but an abode of muddle and discomfort. A small thatched house of mud walls provides a minimum sleeping accommodation for himself and family; the bare interior contains only a few beds, hammocks, and benches. Outside, in several open sheds, is passed the daily life; a long table and benches in one constitutes the common room for meals, a kitchen is in another. In other sheds are the rude wood-roller cane-mill, the open pans for drying farinha, the *monjolo* or maize-crusher, the barns and store-houses. A pen for cattle and an enclosed wilderness of fruits and flowers form the outskirts of the buildings. And scattered everywhere is harness for cattle and horses, goads, saddles, hides, guns, sacks, pestles for coffee—anywhere and everywhere, a place for nothing nowhere. Yet it must be remembered that such untidiness is a national habit, and what to a foreigner appears chaos and discomfort, is here so much evidence of prosperity.

The old man had no children and only three slaves; extra labour he hired at 320 reis (8*d.*) per day with food. He cannot spare the time to take his produce to the market at Santa Rita, except on rare occasions, and is obliged to sell it to traders who come to Formosa, who make as much profit by their petty trading as he does by his hard work. He much regrets that there is not some cheaper and more rapid communication with Cidade de Barra, for there prices are three times higher than at Formosa. At present there is no prospect of any great results for his labours, beyond competency, contentment, and independence.

He spoke in bitter terms of the indolence of the Formosanas, for only absolute want drives them to do a little work, that is stopped as soon as they have laid in a stock of dried beef, farinha, *cachaça*, and maybe a new piece of cotton for their women; then no inducement will make them give up the hammock in the day, and the viola, dance, and *cachaça* at night. He further told me, that when a penniless young man, he had passed through Formosa, and noticing the fertility of the soil, he had then determined to "squat" there, and single-handed and without resources or money he had turned the originally forest-clad valley, little by little, by forty years of constant labour, into its now flourishing state of cultivation. He was reticent as to how he obtained the land; probably there was no owner, and he had no legal right to it, as, however, no one disputed his possession, he became virtually the proprietor.

He was much troubled with the persecution of bixos of various kinds: jaguars destroyed his cattle on the campos, and deer, capivaras, tapir, peccaries, foxes, pacas (spotted cavy), and cotia (agouti) frequently inflicted great damage to his crops in the valley.

Friend José, thrown upon his own resources at an early age, has had to combine within himself the many trades and occupations of general farmer, carpenter, blacksmith, farrier, butcher, police-agent, &c. He further told me that, owing to his prosperity, he had drawn upon himself the envy, hatred, and malice of that village of skulkers, Formosa.

There were a good number of women about his house, old and young, ugly and good-looking, black, brown, yellow, and nearly white. I am sadly afraid that his code of morality would not be acceptable to Mrs. Grundy; that respectable lady would hold up her hand aghast. The old man invited us to his dinner—a liberal supply of soup, fish, venison, beans, sweet mandioca, and sweet potatoes, followed by sweets, and the inevitable *pinga* of *cachaça*, and then coffee. It was all greasy and garlicky, and the surroundings were dirty, dusty, and untidy; but long ago I had overcome any qualms on those points.

He could give me no information about the Somno, as he had never heard of it by name; and knew very little about the Sapão, except that it was reported to be infested with Indians, jaguars, fevers, &c.—the usual Brazilian supposition of all unexplored parts. One thing, he said, you must provide against, not only hunger for yourselves, but for your mules also because if you come across any *capim agreste crua* (tall rank coarse and matted old prairie-grass, the growth of years), you will not only have a difficulty to force your way through it, but the mules will probably find nothing to eat except a few bushes by the streams, and you won't always find streams. It will be necessary to take two more mules loaded with maize, and pig-skins for carrying water.

The two extra mules the good old fellow offered to hire for thirty milreis for the journey (about 3*l*.). He also suggested the advisability of taking with me some one who had had experience of the wilds of Goyaz, and said he would send a certain Antonio de Lapa to see me, a man who had travelled over and traded in all parts of Goyaz, a great *caçador* (hunter), and who had on several occasions commanded expeditions against the Indians—in fact, a Brazilian "Leather-leggings." He also promised to send a young Cherente Indian, a young fellow he had brought up from boyhood, who had been captured some years ago in one of the border skirmishes' with the Indians, and who had already accompanied Antonio on several of his journeys.

It was only within the last few years that the Indians had ceased to be troublesome; before that time all outlying habitations, even in that neighbourhood, were exceedingly perilous abodes. Now the Gentihos were all relegated to the Sapão, the mysterious haunt of all the dangers to be found in Brazil, at least according to report.

The sun was about turning in for the night as we finished our talking and prepared to depart, but Senhor José would not hear of our walking back, and insisted on my taking his favourite horse, a grand *skippador*, and also one for Rodrigues, sending a boy at the same time to bring them back.

It was as well we rode, for by the time we reached Formosa, it was again raining heavily. On arriving home, I was very much distressed to find Dona Chiquinha very ill, and apparently suffering from an attack of ague. Bob had wrapped her up in a *poncho*, and laid her in front of the fire, where she shivered and trembled violently. The poor monkey had been ailing for some days, and had already received a dose of castor oil. Poor Dona, she was so intensely cold that in her efforts to get warm, several times she would have burnt herself in getting too near the blaze. We did our best for her, but she died in my arms that evening, and gave me an intelligent look as she made a faint attempt at a final bass *coo-hu-oo*. Poor Dona, I shall miss her greatly, for she had been my daily companion in all my journeys from the Upper São Francisco, and had wiled away many a long hour of solitude with her tricks.

About midnight, I was awakened by most unearthly noises, and the glare of lights in the street. On going to the door, I found nearly all the women of the village collected near a house close by, some crying, others screaming their loudest, others singing a wild dirge, and all the dogs and cocks of the village barking and crowing.

It was a Brazilian wake, for I learned that a man had died in an adjoining hut that night. I had been asked on one occasion to see him, for I, being a *doutor*, it was evident that I must necessarily be a *medico*, and notwithstanding my protestations to the contrary, I had to go.

The sick man was suffering from an acute inflammation of the liver. High fever, jaundiced skin, cough, vomiting, great pain in the region of the liver aggravated by pressure breathing or coughing and extending to the top of the right shoulder. I could do nothing but apply hot-water flannels that momentarily relieved the pain, but otherwise, I was powerless to help the poor man, who was far beyond the help of my polycrest, "Cockle's pills." There were no medicines in the village, consequently he could only be treated with native herbs and simples, and die.

The lights emanated from flaming torches carried by the women and some men. The screams, wailing, and monotonous droning of the dirge, the moving figures in the flickering smoky glare, the open hut, where the corpse lay exposed to view, on a trestle bed, made an indescribably weird scene. The widow could be seen wildly throwing about her arms, screaming violently, tearing her hair, calling, "*Ai! Jezus! Ai! meo Deos! Ai! santissima Virgem!*" &c., and otherwise conducting herself like a person bereft of her senses. The clamour and noises continued unceasingly.

I noticed the agony of woe was fed and supported by

liberal and frequent libations of *cachaça*, it was almost funny to see at times a brown woman—her long Indian hair all dishevelled, her chemise all awry, her eyes bleared and watery with excitement and drink—take a good pull at the *cachaça* bottle, give a grunt of satisfaction, wash her mouth out with water, and eject it through the interstices of her filed teeth; then pull herself together, and go to business again, by throwing back her head, and opening her mouth for the proper development of a series of ear-splitting howls. The music was evidently distributed in parts, for the widow and near relations performed the screams, others the howls, and the rest the dirges; few men were present, and even those did did not participate in the concert.

About 3 p.m. a procession of men approached with a rough well-worn second-hand coffin, evidently representing the duties of a hearse. In front of it a huge rough wood crucifix was carried, and each man bore a lighted taper. Not much time or ceremony was wasted in placing the body in the coffin, for in a few minutes the whole procession returned with it to the church, accompanied by all the women, who had apparently reserved their lungs for this, the finale; they whirled about, threw their arms in the air, and screamed their hardest like dancing dervishes, while the men tramped on quietly, now joining in the dirge. It was indeed a strange scene in the darkness of night, to see the moving train of flickering lights, flaring torches, and wild excited women, and hear the unearthly noises. There was no priest to perform the burial service, and the body was simply taken out of the coffin, cast into a hole in the ground in the cemetery, and the earth quickly stamped down.

Occasionally the priest from Santa Rita visits the place, to marry, baptize, or to read a mass for those who have died since his last visit.

A comparatively blissful quiet night then ensued, broken only by the crowing of all the cocks, and the barking of all the mongrels of the village.

Several wet days again followed. Slow indeed the time passed, the rain was so heavy and continuous that I was almost a prisoner in the house; sketching was my only relief to the monotony.

Neighbours, however, favoured me with calls, who all told terrible tales of the Sapão, of hunting, and of Indian raids.

Within a few years, in the neighbouring district of Paranagua, huts had been sacked, the men killed, and the women and children carried into captivity, yet from what I could glean it appeared to be only retaliation for inflicted wrongs, as the Indians, especially the boys, are considered lawful prey for any one to capture, kill, or make a slave of.

It is the old old story of all the border-lands: of aborigines and whites in all the backwoods of the old and new world.

Amongst my visitors came the celebrated Antonio da Lapa, evidently a character. A man of two yards of broad square-shouldered but skinny humanity, about fifty years old, dried and burnt up with perpetual exposure; his head is small and cocoa-nut in shape, but bright small black eyes peer from under his shaggy brows; his face is gaunt and thin, and his mouth and chin are covered with a small grizzled beard and moustache, the latter brown with snuff. His garments comprise hat, coat, and tight trousers of soft tanned deer-skin, and a striped blue cotton shirt; on his bare feet are strapped a pair of huge rusty spurs, a long knife is in his girdle, and in his hands is a long small-barrelled flint-lock gun of antique make: truly he looked a Brazilian Don Quixote, as he stood before me in an easy attitude, with his claw-like hands clasped together over his gun.

"*Então, Senhor Antonio, quer me accompanhar ao outro mundo*" (Well, Antonio, do you want to accompany me to the other world)? "*Onde V'nce quizer*" (Wherever you wish), he replies. The old leather-leggings certainly has a business-like appearance for the Geraes, but I look doubtingly at that wonderful gun of his, and say, "You are not going to take that thing, are you?" "This," he says, holding up the ancient gas-pipe with sparkling eyes; "Ah! see what we will do with it, why there is not another gun like it anywhere." That I was ready to admit, but its merits looked more than doubtful. We then discussed terms of association. He was to accompany the troop and make himself generally useful, and remain until his services should be no longer required, for twenty milreis per month (2*l*.), and his food. I gave him instructions at once to purchase a fat bullock and turn it into jerked beef as soon as there was any sunny weather. He directed Rodrigues and his men how to make ball and shot cartridges for their gas-pipes. "We shall have plenty of sport," he said, with a chuckle, "*indios, porcos e veados*" (Indians, pigs, and deer), "and maybe jaguars." Rodrigues did not at all look happy at these remarks, and the many yarns the villagers had told him were having their due effect upon him. Later on, he came to me and said, "Senhor Doutor, I am a *tropeiro*, and do not mind travelling anywhere where there is a road, but to go into these wild *geraes* to starve, or get lost, or maybe fight Indians, jaguars, pigs, and all other kinds of devilry. *Não Senhor, V'ou me embora* (I will be off)." I appealed to his sense of justice, that in having made a contract he must fulfil it. I appealed to his dignity, his courage, his patriotism, his sense of honour, &c., &c., but all in vain, the old man said he must return to his family, with the old old story, that his wife was sick, or his mother might die, and that the beans, or the rice, or the maize in the roça wanted gathering. As a last resource, I tried another tack; "Well, Mr. Senhor Rodrigues, if you want to return, you must return alone, I shall not pay you one *vintem*, and I shall get the *sub-delegado* to send your mules and men on with me, and if you resist, you will be locked up." It was only a threat, as I could not have seized his animals, but it served my purpose, for he said, after thinking some time, "Well, do as you please, good-bye my poor little ones, my wife, and my house, that I shall never see again."

The rain continued with slight intermissions until April

3rd, when a clear bright sunny morning and a cloudless sky, at last indicated that the rain of the season was over.

In the meantime Senhor José had been to see me, and I had returned his visit early one morning in order to get some shooting. We left his home amidst pouring rain, and started for his roça, taking with us some dozen mongrel curs, all especially half starved for the occasion. On arriving near the adjoining woods the dogs were turned loose, and a very short time afterwards their voices indicated that they had struck a trail. We had stowed ourselves meanwhile behind some bushes bordering an exit from the woods, and soon afterwards a beautiful gazelle-like Matirio deer came bounding out into the more open plantations. The animal stopped one moment, with foreleg upraised, extended ear, and expanded nostril, evidently scenting our presence; the sounds of the approaching dogs impelled her forwards again—crack!—and the delicate creature falls forwards, shot by José. A *cotia*[4] (*agouti*) follows with long kangaroo-like leaps; this falls an easy prize. The dogs then strike off in another direction and finally emerge from the woods some distance away, in pursuit of some animal we cannot distinguish; whatever it is, it is making for the little stream in the centre of the valley. "*Vamos, doutor*," cries José, and bounds off with the activity of a young man, crashing through scattered clumps of cane, jumping logs, now in a hole of mud, now dodging the branches of the castor-plants, onwards and downwards, down a steep slope to the stream; the dogs meanwhile baying loudly and coming towards us. Suddenly the old man stops and fires; "There she goes," he calls out, and points at a *paca* swimming in the water. At this moment a huge snout appears as the dogs come in sight, it is but for a moment, for it suddenly dives. "*O bixo do diabo*," exclaims José, as he witnesses the diving animal (a *capivara*, the farmers' pest), and having reloaded, away we both start in pursuit, the dogs now with us. It is

---

[4] *Clenodactylus brasiliensis*, Blainville.

a funny idea of sport; the rain is coming down heavily, we are covered with burrs and mud, and scratched by brambles, but nevertheless we slip down steep slopes, and wriggle through bushes, just in time to get simultaneously long shots at the *capivara* then in shallow water; it is evidently wounded, but retreats into the adjoining bushes, where he is followed by the dogs, and where we find him at bay with his haunches freely bleeding but showing a gallant front to the dogs, who have cut off his retreat; two shots from my revolver end the chase. It had been sharp quick work, and we had had a capital run, if one may so term it. The bag comprised a deer, an *agouti*, two spotted *cavies*, and a *capivara*. The *capivara* is hardly eatable, for it has a gland that must be cut out immediately after death; otherwise, the flesh has a strong musky flavour, and even under the most favourable circumstances, it yet retains an unpleasant taste. Farmers destroy them unmercifully, as they inflict great damage in the roças. The rest of the bag were all delicacies for the table, especially the *cavy* (*paca*), than which there is no better flesh when young and well prepared.

On other occasions when I braved the weather in my walks, I found many birds in some of the flooded hollows of the country, beautiful white herons,[5] large ducks,[6] and the usual birds common to the swamps and lakes of Brazil.

[5] *Ardea candidissima.*   [6] *Anas moschata.*

CHAPTER VII.

FROM FORMOSA TO THE MOUTH OF THE RIO SAPÃO.

Additions to my troop—Don Quixote—Forebodings of disaster—A wandering goldsmith—A cattle-farm—Approach to the Geraes—The Burity palm groves of the Sapão and its mouth—Santa Maria—Indian raids—The last houses—A charming situation—Prospects of adventure—Rodrigues' alarm—Difficulties of deciding upon a route—The Rio Sapão—José Grosso.

The Rio Preto at Santa Maria.

AT last, once more we move on again, and bid adieu to Formosa, glad indeed to escape out of that woe-begone collection of wretched hovels, especially after the long and vexatious delay of twenty-two days of weary, dreary waiting for a cessation of the continual rains, and then, finally, making the preparations for the journey into the surrounding unknown country, such as drying and salting beef for provisions, for which purpose the sun is indispensable. My troop now consisted of Rodrigues and Bob mounted on mules, Antonio da Lapa on horseback, and Serga, Roberto and Archanjo on foot, four mules carrying the baggage, and two others loaded with maize, and the two dogs. My good friend, the *sub-delegado*, never failed to impress me with his opinion that it would be madness to think of venturing into the wilds of the Sapão without such a valiant hunter and Indian fighter as Antonio, one who so well knew the devilries of the *tapuias*. As I looked at this specimen of a Brazilian "Leather-leggings," his horse, arms, and accoutrements, well, he did look funny, and not quite up to my idea of what a captain of my escort should be. His horse, an old mottled grey, is pensive and somnolent; his knees are largely developed, and have a perceptible cant forward, his ribs are countable, his mane is stubby and uncombed, his eyes are heavy with sleep, there is a general air of depression about the beast that, if it indicates an absence of vice, shows that it is no fiery steed. His rider, a fit Don Quixote for such an evident Rozinante, appears much the same as described on his first visit to me, with the addition of an old frayed blue *capote* fastened to his saddle.

The Cherente Indian, "Trascuhyn" by name, who came on one occasion to see me, at the last moment failed to appear, and we went without him.

All the village had assembled to witness our departure, amongst them my kind old friend, the *sub-delegado*. They bade us "*Adeos!*[1] *Até a volta! Até a outra vista!*" &c. To which we duly reply, "*Se Deos quizer.*"[2] At the same time many croaked dismal forebodings of peril and danger by Indians, hunger and thirst, fevers, jaguars, and wild pigs that they thought we were so foolishly going to meet. Rodrigues paled visably, and gladly would have returned, were it not that he knew he would not in that case be paid anything for the hire of his mules and men.

This day's journey was only fourteen miles, as it was found necessary to stop and give the jerked beef a little more of the sun.

[1] Adieu! Until you return. Until we see you again.
[2] If God wills it.

The country passed through was hilly, well watered in the bottoms and richly wooded, habitations were few and far between. We accompanied the river almost all the way, the adjoining land was often flat, and afforded good travelling, although we had to cross many a marsh, and wade through small lakes. Very little animal life was to be seen except a few water-fowl.

The valley gives one the appearance of having been excavated out of the adjoining plains, for although for a short distance, say one to three hundred yards, the land is slightly undulating and hilly, an ascent or examination of the more distant and higher elevations show their summits to be level and extending far away to the horizon, an arid *agreste* grass prairie.

Early in the afternoon we arrived at the Fazenda de Vão, belonging to a Major Antonio de Miranda, consisting of a few large birdcage-looking huts, with all the paraphernalia of a *fazendeiro de gado* (cattle-breeder). At this place a wandering Italian journeyman goldsmith was staying. He told me he had been in Brazil six years, and had travelled over a great section of the empire; but, as might be expected, such a rolling stone had gathered but little moss; certainly that was not the place to expect to meet a goldsmith in, where his prospects of doing a roaring trade in these moneyless districts must be very small indeed.

My comfortable tent was put up, and the night passed pleasantly; the temperature was delightful, and mosquitos were absent. Feroz's sudden onslaughts on to the too inquisitive wandering pigs of the farm, alone disturbing the quiet of the night.

The next morning the animals were fortunately found where they were expected to be, and a good start made, and I rode on ahead with Don Quixote. The country now began to show signs of an approach to the Geraes, changing from the wooded lands of Formosa to what is known as *cerrado fechado*, that is, thick, scrubby vegetation, with often many patches of tall rank *agreste* grass, thorny bramble, prickly dwarf palms and thick bushes between the trees; still the soil was in many places rich, and admirable pasturage could easily be obtained, yet, during the morning's ride, away from the narrow path we travelled, no signs of life or cultivation, met our view; no sound was heard but the rippling of the water of the river and the rustle of the passing breeze; even birds were rarely seen. About mid-day we reached a small farm, fazenda or retiro, as the small farms are more generally called, and known as Matto Grosso, twenty-eight miles from Formosa. There Rodrigues made his mid-day halt to rest the animals and breakfast, although it wanted but four miles to the day's destination, the mouth of the Sapão. After a hasty breakfast, Don Quixote and I rode on to the mysterious Sapão, where all our perils were supposed to commence. At every mile we passed, the country became more and more open, and on arrival at the mouth of the Sapão, we found a most decided change. As far as we could see up the valley of the Sapão, both banks appeared fringed by narrow belts of Burity palms, eighty feet high, the first time that I had seen these beautiful palms in such quantities,[3] in fact they form the characteristic feature of the country about to be entered, and will be more fully mentioned later on. By the side of the Burity groves, the land is flat and often swampy for small distances away from the stream, and then rises in gentle *cerrado* or grass-covered slopes, to the often almost perpendicular slopes of the adjoining table-lands. These slopes, when viewed from the river valley, give the appearance of a range of hills, whereas they are really the walls of the denuded table-lands: their flat-topped summits extend in a level plain to wherever may be the next valley.

At the junction of the Sapão with the Rio Preto, are a few houses, known as Sta. Maria, the last habitations we

[3] The few scattered examples that one meets with in the swamps of Minas, bear no comparison to these beautiful groves.

shall see for many days; they form really an outpost on the borders of the unknown. Many of the houses are rudely fortified by thick walls of sun-dried bricks, loopholed for musketry firing, and roofed with two layers of palm-leaf thatch, between which is laid a thick and substantial layer of clay, as a protection against a possible firing of the grass covering by fiery arrows on occasions of attack.

Although it was then some years since the *tapuias* (Cherentes and Coroados) visited the neighbourhood, the inhabitants still pass an uncomfortable life of suspense and expectation, and the women and children venture but short distances from their houses. This place has been in times past, the scene of many an Indian raid, and skirmishes with loss on both sides; and many a head of cattle have the ravagers carried away with them, and occasionally some women or children, who disappeared into the then wilds of Goyaz, never to return.[4] I suggested to my "Leather-leggings" that those

---

[4] Gardner, the naturalist, passed through Santa Maria in the year 1838, on his way from Ceara, through Goyaz, to Rio de Janeiro. His descriptions of this place, written nearly fifty years ago, are quite applicable to the present times, so few changes having meanwhile occurred. He mentions how the people were even then scared out of their lives by the dread of Indian attacks, as the following extracts from his work will show:—

"We were not far from the house on which the outrage I have before mentioned was committed by the Indians. The attack was made during the day, while the men were absent in the fields, and after burning the house and killing three women, they carried off two children. The people at Santa Maria informed me that they lived in constant dread of the Indians, and that they had serious intentions of removing to a more populous district. These Indians live generally at a considerable distance to the north-west, and are known as Cherentes. It is supposed this attack originated in consequence of one of the Indians having been fired at and wounded by mistake, who, in revenge, had, with the assistance of his countrymen, committed the outrage above mentioned."

. . . .

"The stories he told of the Indians alarmed my party very much, and I was in consequence obliged to get all my arms put in order, so as to make as formidable an appearance as possible."

. . . .

"The country people have all a dread of this wild and uninhabited

would have been good occasions to exercise his redoubtable powers. He beamed on me a sickly smile, and after recounting what I am afraid was many an imaginary conflict he had had with the Indians, he observed that to go after a retreating horde of *tapuias* retiring with their spoil, would necessitate a larger number of men than would be possible to collect in the districts. "How about our little troop then?" I inquired.

"Ah!" said he, solemnly, and raising his hat, "God only knows if we shall ever return."

Fortunately for myself, I had already had so varied an experience of the powers of imagination of the Brazilian countrymen of the dangers and evils of distant districts, that I had become thoroughly sceptical of all they told me. Not so, unfortunately, was my tropeiro, Rodrigues, he literally quaked with fear when he heard these wonderful stories.

Up to this point I found the Rio Preto navigable for light draught craft, drawing say three feet of water. The width varies from 100 to 200 feet, the average velocity of the river is about two miles per hour; in a few bends there are a few insignificant rapids, but against which a small steamer could easily make head-way.[5]

track (the road up the Rio Preto from Santa Maria), and before entering it I was often asked if I was not afraid to do so, with so few attendants. Their own fear is, I believe, greatly owing to their own cowardice, a very common feeling in all parts of the country I have visited."

. . . .

But Mr. Gardner made a great mistake with reference to the course of the Rio Preto when he stated "the Rio Preto falls into the Rio São Francisco, a little above Villa da Barra," for this river, as my journey has shown, enters the Rio Grande at Boqueirão.

[5] The following shallows and strong currents are the chief impediments to the navigation of the Rio Preto.

Atoleiro	55 kilometers	below Formosa.
Porto Raso	37 ,,	,, ,,
Marimbondo	21 ,,	,, ,,
Jatobá	12 ,,	,, ,,
Raposa	7 ,,	,, ,,
Vão da Batalha	16 ,,	above ,,
Vão do Angico	19 ,,	,, ,,

The situation of Sta. Maria is very picturesque. The black but clear waters of the river flow almost on a level with the soft grass sward of the banks, that are dotted here and there by clumps of Pindahybas, Burityranas, Burity palms, and bamboos. The atmosphere is clear as crystal, an exhilarating breeze blows fresh and cool, and with the bright blue sky and verdant landscape of rolling grassy hills, and the neighbouring rich red slopes of the table-lands, the place forms altogether a charming locality for a residence, and with the admirable pasturage, quite explains how the people have remained here despite its Indian inconveniences, which I confess I must realize to appreciate.[6]

A little before dark, Rodrigues and the troop joined us, when we crossed the Sapão by transporting the baggage in a canoe, swimming the animals across the stream and then bivouacked for the night.

In the evening we received a visit from the local magnates. It was quite amusing to see their long faces, expressive of a holy horror at our temerity, and they soon added another item to the already formidable list of woes to come, namely, vampire bats, that were said to exist in such numbers in a part of the valley of the Sapão, about sixteen miles away, that it is there impossible for any animal to live through the night. This was almost too much for Rodrigues, for when, in addition to so many possible personal dangers, there was a further possibility of losing his mules, the very idea made him desperate, and he at once declared he would go no further.

It was only by alternate threats of imprisonment by the sub-delegado at Formosa, and coaxing him, and finally

Vão de Capyvara . . . 21 kilometers above Formosa.
Vão do Brejo Grande . . 31 ,, ,, ,,

Of these Porto Raso is the shallowest, but even in the dry season its canal has a minimum depth of four feet.

[6] The aneroids indicated 1752 feet above the sea and 420 feet above the Rio São Francisco at Cidade da Barra.

promising to pay him for any animal he might lose, that I at last succeeded in pacifying him. Poor Rodrigues, I am afraid his dreams that night were a nightmare of jaguars, Indians, wild pigs, bats, anacondas, fugitive slaves, and bleached skeletons.

Although the route by the Rio Sapão was not embodied in my instructions, the Rio do Somno clearly was. Yet up to the present point, I had not been able to obtain the slightest information as to its whereabouts; as, however, a road accompanies the Rio do Preto, and thence passes into Goyaz, passing travellers would certainly have mentioned in Formosa or Sta. Rita this river Somno in the tales of their travels, if it existed in their line of route.

At Sta. Maria, I gleaned that the western slopes of the watershed of the São Francisco and Tocantins are exceedingly precipitous, or as my informant told me, that when any one looks down from the summits towards the lowlands in Goyaz, the depth is so great that the distant landscape appears *azul* (blue). I did not, however, believe that my informant had ever been there, yet, as in that direction there is apparently no Somno, and the divide is possibly very precipitous, I determined to at least try the Sapão, especially as its apparent course seemed to meet my views of what my general direction should be.

The Rio Sapão, at its junction with the Rio Preto, is a slow-flowing stream, about fifty feet wide and twelve feet deep, and if it extends any distance with this quantity and depth of water, and with easy gradients, its course will only require a little straightening to make a good natural canal, but I am afraid that this century will not see the execution, or even necessity, of such a work, for there are so many fertile lands near the coast, yet to be developed, before these central districts are likely to be inhabited and cultivated as they should be.

Amongst my visitors was a strong, well-built, honest-looking fellow, José Grosso by name; he had travelled a good deal in Goyaz, and Piauhy, and, on one occasion, had alone explored the mysterious Sapão for thirty miles. He willingly accepted an invitation to join my party. Rodrigues looked at him in wonderment, as a fool about to unnecessarily incur a great risk. I was glad to have José, as until then, my man Bob was the only man whom I could rely upon in any emergency.

CHAPTER VIII.

FROM THE MOUTH TO THE SOURCE OF THE RIO SAPÃO.

The valley of the Sapão—No more roads—Signs of game—The morasses of the Burity groves—First night in the wilds—Sandstone hills of the Geraes—Picturesque country—Vampire bats—Runaway animals—The Geraes—Tree-lilies—Indications of saline earth—A glorious country for a ride—Macaws—A night alarm—A tapir—A glen of sylvan beauty—The Cabeca de Frade, a ground cactus—A grim solitude—A phosphorescent fungus, flor de coco—Construction of the fort—An escape from a centipede—Deer-stalking—Ant-hills and bees—Great quantities of honey—The Don reports signs of Indians—Daybreak in camp—Fording a morass—A novel method of deer-hunting—Indications of peccaries—A splendid climate—Lovely nights—Abundance of game—The swamp of the Nove Galhos—Head-quarters of the peccaries—An awkward situation—Peccaries v. dogs—An obstructed route—The valley again—Preparations to receive the enemy—The camp—The attack of the peccaries—A fierce onslaught—A wild, weird scene—An anxious moment—The retreat of the peccaries—The Don becomes deaf—The garrison reinforced—The battle renewed—Rodrigues trembles—A long night of excitement—The siege is raised after great loss by the enemy—Description of the peccaries—Corn in Egypt—Burity wine—A perplexing sight—A beautiful valley—The source of the Sapão—An interesting geographical discovery—Mysterious green grass—Pig-sticking—An ant-bear speared—The ant-bear described—Difficult travelling—Sufferings of the mules—An ascent—The lakes of the valley of the watershed—The equal altitude of flat-topped eminences—The watershed of the São Francisco and Tocantins—Denudation of the Western country—A grand country for cattle-breeding—A clump of Pindahibas.

An enraged peccary.

April 6.—A lovely morning, like Devonshire Dartmoor on an early summer day, found us all ready for a start, but we were delayed a few hours for José Grosso, who eventually arrived.

We had travelled but a few miles up the south bank of the Sapão, when it became evident that all habitations had ceased; there were no more tracks, and the grass in the bottom lands was so tall and rank that it was very difficult to force our way through it, and now the tracks of many animals became hourly more frequent; already I had noticed the spoor of the jaguar, the *guará* or red-wolf, tapir, capyvara, deer, peccaries, and other animals.

In all my travels hitherto in Brazil, I had never seen such apparently happy hunting-grounds. Rodrigues duly quaked at the signs. After a march of ten miles, we came across a long depression that extended from the table-lands to the Sapão, and down the centre of it, we reluctantly sighted long avenues of Buritys, pleasant to view certainly as a picturesque sight, but much "cussed" by a traveller.

These palms invariably grow in boggy land, and when found thus in the form of avenues, they indicate the presence of a deep morass, across which a horse or mule cannot pass without danger and difficulty. On this occasion, in searching for a passage, a pole was easily driven six feet into the soft black soil, so we gave up the attempt and went two or three miles out of our way to get round the line of the palms that intersected our line of march at right angles.

This place, known as *Brejão* (a large swamp), is a celebrated place for the bats, so we pushed on for four miles more, and arrived at sunset at what José called *Brejo de Lama* (mud swamp), where we pitched our camp amidst the tall grass of its margins.

During this day's march in this, my first experience of the purely and simply Brazilian wilds, I experienced a degree of exhilaration and enjoyment I had not known for a long time, I attributed the feeling to the effects of the wonderfully pure healthy atmosphere, the brightness of the open country, and the prevailing cool fresh breezes, and perhaps very largely to an excellent state of health.

The most striking features of the valley are the many glades, or rather avenues of Buritys, that grow almost invariably in a straight line, the distances between the palms are naturally irregular, but the long, straight avenues make them appear as though they were planted by the hand of man.

The adjoining morasses that fill up the width of the depressions, usually from 100 to 200 yards wide, are covered with a bright green but coarse wiry grass, unfit even for mules to graze upon, it is very acrid rough and hard, and soon creates sores upon the gums of the animals.

On each side of the river, from a few hundred yards to one to two miles' distance, the slopes, or walls of the enclosing table-land rise up in cliffs of variously-coloured sandstones, furrowed by deep ravines that are often filled with bush; the appearance of these walls, variegated with the many colours of their formation (reds, buffs, yellows, whites, and greys), in contrast with the bright blue sky, the bright green grass and palm avenues of the swamps, and the tawny brown yellow of the cerrado-covered surfaces of the undulating hills of the valley,—all, hills, cliffs, and marshes, glowing in the fierce sunshine, and droning with that hum of insects peculiar to marshes steaming under a tropical sun, formed such pictures of grand compositions of colours as would make any artist's heart rejoice.

After despatching a frugal dinner of dried beef (*carne secca*) and beans, and giving the mules their rations of corn, they were turned loose to obtain what pasture they could find from the young shoots of bamboos, of which there were many clumps near. Every one then assumed a recumbent position on hides on the ground, or in hammocks slung to the trees. Rodrigues as usual, entertained us with his fears of troubles and dangers to come, until we all dozed off under the roof of the bright starry sky.

At daybreak we breakfasted whilst the men went in search of the animals. After a long delay, they return and report four animals are missing (and those that they had found were freely punctured with the bites of the bats) : there was no remedy but to again send off the men to hunt for them and patience.

Hour after hour passed, yet neither men nor animals arrived. How hot and weary it was, thus idly waiting in the shadeless sunlight, for the trees were so sparely scattered, and so thinly clad with foliage, that shade there was none. It was not until 2.30 that the men returned with the animals, and 3 p.m. before we got away; the wretched animals had gone back in the night to Sta. Maria, with the probable intention of continuing their homeward journey, evidently disgusted with their poor pasture.

That day we did not accomplish more than six miles, and camped for the night by the side of a morass, to which the men gave the name of *Brejo de Lontra* (Otter Swamp) owing to one of these animals paying our camp a visit. The dogs gave chase, but the otter took refuge in the waters of the marsh.

The next morning, during the usual delay in getting the animals fed and harnessed, José and I climbed the cliffs of the table-land, whence, perceiving that the river makes a considerable bend, I determined to get the troop on to the highlands, and thus shorten the way.

After some time and trouble we found an easy ascent for the animals, and proceeded on our journey in what to me was another new world, "The Geraes of Goyaz." Far as could be discerned the land extends flat as a table, not the slightest undulation is perceptible; the sandy loose soil is sparely covered with tufts of grey-green thin wiry grass, a few gnarled and distorted cork-trees, and great numbers of the strange tree-lily (*Vellozia*) or Canella d'Ema, blooming with beautiful mauve-coloured flowers at the end of each branch; in form the plant resembles a candelabra, but in composition, to no production of the vegetable world; the branches and stem consist as it were of a number of deep cups, placed one within the other, strung upon a hard and tough pithy stem that runs through the centre. (There is a very good dried specimen in the British Museum.) This plant is peculiarly characteristic of these *geraes*, or *taboleiros*, as they are variously termed. Gardner mentions the same plant in the *taboleiros* of Diamantina, Piauhy, and Goyaz.[1]

These *geraes* are a glorious place for a gallop, and in their exhilarating atmosphere one feels radiant with crude health that however develops such an appetite, and perhaps a drinketite, that in the solitude of the far-extending pathless plain he experiences an imaginary mirage of pleasant English country road-side inns, and conjures up visions of the good things to be found therein.

On the ascent of the table-land I noticed one or two salt-licks, showing numerous traces of various animals. If this saline earth could be utilized, it would prove immensely valuable, for salt is relatively the most costly article of consumption of the interior of Brazil, the greater part of it being transported at great labour and expense from the sea-coast. Rio de Janeiro is mainly supplied from the Canary Islands, and forwards the salt to the distant interiors of Minas Geraes and Goyaz.

Numerous pairs of macaws passed us flying, and made the wilderness resound with their loud discordant screeches. These birds are particularly fond of the fruit of the Burity, and a salt-lick is a great attraction to them; they delight also in rolling themselves in the sand, for which purpose the streams and *geraes* of this district are adapted.

But excepting these birds, there is nothing else to break the grim solitude and silence of these wilds, and although there are certainly plenty of indications of game, hitherto I had not been able to see any. But José and Don Quixote craved my patience for a little longer.

---

[1] There are several known and described species of this strange plant, but the largest size hitherto known does not attain a greater height than four to five feet, whereas those of the Sapão varied from the small young plant to fully matured ones of eight or nine feet high.

Our camp that night was pitched in an open grass-land where the rank coarse grass was inconveniently high and suggestive of an ambuscade, so at least Rodrigues remarked. In the comparative absence of pasture for the animals, I now appreciated the wisdom of the advice I received at Formosa to bring the two loads of maize.

Around the camp-fire in the evening, I thought Don Quixote would fairly have brought poor Rodrigues into a delirium of fright with his anecdotes of the district; even stolid José added his quota to the agony of the poor man.

Late in the evening we were aroused by the dogs starting off with loud barks into the surrounding darkness; this was enough for Rodrigues, he wildly arose and shouted, "*As armas, rapaziadas, as armas, as tapuias, ai! Meo Deos! vou morrer*" (To arms, boys, to arms, the Indians, ah! *Meo Deos!* I shall die),—discharged his gun wildly in the darkness, and of course created a great confusion amongst his own men, who all did the same before we could prevent them. Expostulation was vain, until José delivered a well-planted kick, that brought the timorous man to his senses.

The dogs eventually returned, and in the morning we found the tracks of a tapir that had passed near the camp and caused the alarm. Rodrigues looked foolish and crestfallen, and I hoped the absurd lesson would be beneficial; he was well laughed at, and that has more effect on these people than any reprimands.

April 8th.—A happy start was made this morning early, and eventually we covered twenty-four miles; the route went principally over the *geracs*, and occasionally we had to descend and cross some of the many tributaries of the Sapão, either marsh or rivulets.

One stream, which we baptized Riacho do Salto, after a pretty waterfall in its course, was a gem of sylvan beauty. A bubbling stream of purest water, tumbling over lichen and moss-covered boulders, through a little paradise of some of the most beautiful vegetation of the tropics, tree-ferns, and clumps of arborescent grasses, palms of many kinds, orchids, and bromelias in full flower, mossy banks, and many varieties of ferns, the whole gracefully festooned by lianas and vines, and to give further brilliancy, myriads of bright butterflies, and several humming-birds added their flashing colours to the bright and picturesque surroundings.

We rested here at mid-day; even my companions, who had no more appreciation of the beauties of nature than is usually found wanting in the Brazilian countryman, even they expressed it as "*muita bonita*" (very pretty), and men and animals had a good bath before again proceeding.

The rest of the day's march showed the usual features of the *geraes*, except that ground-palms, and a ground-cactus, *cabeça de frade*,[2] became more frequent, the latter inconveniently so for the men on foot. It is like the top of a ball, about nine or twelve inches in diameter, ribbed like a melon, and raised above the ground only an inch or two; its surface is thickly covered with long and strong spines, and as it is difficult to notice amongst the tufts of grass, it is very dangerous; fortunately the men were cautious, and met no accident. Cattle and horses are said to be very fond of its fleshy interior, and soon learn to tread down the spines with their hoofs.

Late in the afternoon we camped by the side of a wood near the Sapão, to whose neighbourhood we had again descended in quest of water for the camp.

The locality was very grim and solitary; near us a thick wood cast its shadows over the hollow in which we were camped; tall rank grass covered the ground; the Sapão flowed sluggishly by without a gurgle, looking as it wound its way between its groves of Buritys, like a veritable black Styx. Right and left of it, in the now much narrowed valley, reared up high above us the dark outline of the slopes of the taboleiros, whose deep shadows added to the murkiness of the locality; the men's voices almost became

[2] *Melocactus* or *Echinocactus*.

painful in the intense stillness and silence. The men with bated breath said, "*Que lugar feia*" (what an ugly place), and dubbed it *brejo escuro* (the dark swamp).

Amidst the surrounding darkness of the night there was noticeable a large pale-blue light, and on going to examine what it might arise from, I found it to be a phosphorescent fungus growing upon the base of a dwarf palm. It is known as the *flor de coco* (*Fungus phosphoricus*).

At this camp we built a *trincheira*[3] of the saddles and baggage by piling them up in the form of a hollow square, an excellent defence against the peccaries or other enemies. Arms were loaded, cartridges served out, and watches arranged for the night.

As we lay on the ground around the fire, some on hides or cloaks, the bright light on one side, and behind and all around the black shadows of night, I thought what excellent targets we should make for any wandering *tapuias*. The night, however, passed uneventfully, without even a bark from the dogs.

During the night, feeling something wriggling in my boot, I made a sleepy movement, and the insect, whatever it was, moved out. In the morning, in rolling up my rug, a huge centipede was found coiled up in the folds. I expect it was the visitor to my leg; if so, I had a fortunate escape from its poisonous claws.

This morning the indispensable leather water-bottle was missing; that caused another delay whilst two men returned over yesterday's trail to find it.

I availed myself of the opportunity to go with the Don on the *geraes* in quest of some change of diet, leaving José Grosso in charge of the camp.

After a short but sharp scramble up the face of the nearest cliffs, we arrived at the summit, where the flat expanse of the *geraes* opened out to our view. Almost the first objects we discerned were a buck and doe, and as the little wind was

[3] Literally, a trench.

towards us, they had not yet perceived our presence. We worked our way through the tall grass until within easy range, and easily bagged our game; at the same time, Antonio pointed to me the antlers of a numerous herd scampering off through the grass. However, we were not on a hunting expedition, and were contented with our prey, a small species of deer, almost gazelles in the appearance of their delicate proportions, beautiful heads and bright full beaming eyes; they are known as the *galheiro* and *campeira*,[1] the buck and doe of the campos or plains. Small as the deer were, mine at least soon became an increasing load as we staggered back to camp, perspiring under the already hot sun, and stumbling amongst the boulders and tall grass of the descent, where we were away from the pleasant breeze. I thought of the glory of marching into camp with my bag, but every moment that gazelle apparently became heavier, and I had to give up my gratification and send a man to fetch it.

That day's march was up the valley, as the table-lands did not offer any means of ascent for the animals; a notable feature of the day was the great number of ant-hills, four to six or seven feet high, constructed of clay originally by a species of white ant, but then occupied—certainly one out of every three—by the *abelha de cupim* (bee of the white ants). These bees had turned the ants out of their quarters and domiciled themselves in their place. Without exaggeration I believe many tons of honey could be collected from these mounds; in one hill alone we extracted sufficient to satisfy the appetites of every one—even the mules had their share. The honey is found in little compact balls of delicate black wax, about one and a half inch in diameter; each ball is separate and distinct from its neighbour, and the honey is most excellent in flavour. The bees of course flew about us, but were perfectly harmless; they are small and black, not much bigger than a house-fly; the mystery is how they can conquer and drive off the white ants; perhaps many a battle

[1] *Mazama campestris?*

was fought before they gave up possession; however, the bees were evidently masters of the situation. Several dozens of the mounds were examined, and more than a third were occupied by the bees, but only on two or three occasions was the same mound found occupied jointly by the bees and ants.

The land passed over this day, was alternately the low marshy land immediately adjoining the river, or the gently undulating thin cerrado-covered hills separating it from the slopes of the table-land ; but many a wearisome détour had to be made round the *burity* swamps that continually intersected the route.

Later in the afternoon we arrived at a stream flowing from apparently a long way in the *geraes*, where we camped. This stream we called Riberão do Veado, in commemoration of our excellent dinner of roast venison ; the flesh was very palatable, and formed an agreeable change to our diet.

After dinner Antonio called me aside, and gave me the unpleasant news that Indians were in the neighbourhood ; he came to that conclusion by noticing a bees'-nest that had been taken, and had also seen the footprints of Indians. I asked him why he did not show me at the time ; he replied that he did not want to frighten me then, but thought afterwards he had better tell me. I had a good suspicion that the old Don was trying on me the effects of his imagination. I took council with José, who looked grave and thought it might be so, but did not believe it. I had to tell the old Don that if he tried any practical jokes of that kind, I would dock a meal or two. He swore by all the saints that he was speaking the truth. We made our usual preparations, but the night passed happily without incident.

April 10.—With what a sense of relief a traveller in these *geraes* awakes in the morning, and finds all his animals in camp munching their corn ; and after the damp dewy night, with beard and rugs ringing wet with the heavy night-dews, how acceptable is the hot coffee in the early twilight, when the ground is wet, and grass and foliage jewelled with dew-drops, and light puffy clouds of mist here and there veil the views of grass-land and shrub, and curl in drifting wreaths amidst the noble colonnades of the *buritys*. It is very nice to read about, is this camping out in the open; but the feeling in the morning on awakening is grubbiness, damp-ness, and soreness. But, next to the coffee, is the enjoyment of a good bath, and this the Riberão afforded to perfection—glorious cool clear water, pellucid as air.

We ascended the Riberão for a mile or two, until we found a crossing, and then struck across the flat *geraes* parallel with the course of the Sapão. At mid-day we crossed another stream, or rather *burityzal;* although the ground was soft, a passage was made by spreading in a line on the swamp the raw-hide covers of the pack-saddles, over which we drove the animals at a run. As it was necessary to make occasional observations in the Sapão valley, our course was again directed towards the river.

During the day we bagged three more deer. On one occasion I tried an experiment that I had seen Antonio prac-tise, namely in enveloping myself from head to foot in my cloak, and advancing boldly towards a herd of deer. They gazed at me for some time in startled wonderment, and actually approached me. I was taking a steady aim with my revolver, when Feroz and Pensamento dashed past me after the game; of course the herd was off like the wind, and the dogs soon returned, evidently wondering where the deer had disappeared to.

I rode on ahead with the Don, leaving our track clearly marked in the tall grass. On the way we killed two more deer, and might have secured others, but it would have been mere slaughter, as we had sufficient for our requirements for some days.

About mid-day we struck the head-springs of a *burityzal* running into the Sapão. There we awaited the troop, that soon arrived, halted, and breakfasted. We found plenty of signs of peccaries, so much so that I began to credit their existence; the grass was worn into many paths by their feet, and pools of water were still disturbed where they had apparently only lately revelled. This we christened Brejo do Diogo.

The Don and I again pushed on ahead, this time over a clear open sandy campos, very thinly covered with scattered tufts of thin wiry grass, and occasionally a few *canella d'ema* trees, and *cabeça de frade cactii*. We rode on for about six miles, and saw ahead a long valley extending from the *geraes* into the Sapão, and so thickly studded with *burity* palms that it was evident there would be no alternative but to ascend its course until a crossing could be found, for in these *burityzals* the width and depth of the morass is always in proportion to the density of growth of the palms; the closer they are together, the more impassable is the swamp. I calculated we were then five miles from the Sapão, and it would have been no use to descend the *burityzal*, as the likelihood of a crossing lower down is always less.

We eventually camped by the side of this swamp.

In that clear and healthy atmosphere and daily exercise we were fortunately all in excellent health; and our fare, although of the roughest kind, was never more enjoyed by any foxhunter after a good day's run after the hounds. Those evenings, never shall I forget them, as we reposed on the ground by the camp-fire on hides or rugs, and listened to the stories of the Don under the clear starlit heavens, and the pure cool atmosphere. As none of the anticipated evils had yet appeared, the men were becoming more reconciled, excepting of course, Rodrigues, who I believe imagined that every tree on the horizon was a prowling Indian in search of his blood.

We were off soon after daybreak; I rode on up the valley ahead with the Don and Bob, in quest of a crossing. We had ridden but a short distance, when we saw that at last we had reached the happy hunting-grounds we had heard so much of. First we sighted a few deer, then, further on, they became

ABUNDANCE OF GAME. 131

quite numerous. Suddenly the Don excitedly called my attention to two small black animals scampering across the low grass of the marsh ahead. "*Porcos! porcos!*" said he; the peccaries, however, soon disappeared out of sight. About 500 yards from us was a herd of seven deer; the Don could stay no longer; he said he must have a shot. This time, after enveloping his head in a red handkerchief, he crawled towards the animals on his hands and knees, bobbing his head up and down as he advanced. A fine buck left his family to inquire into the nature of his strange visitor. I saw the Don take aim with that wonderful gun of his, a puff of blue smoke arose from the neighbourhood of his shoulder, and then another from the muzzle of his gun, and the graceful animal fell. Bob and I afterwards went after another herd, but we could not get within range; the news was evidently spreading amongst the deer that a "chiel" was amongst them.

We eventually came across the traces of all the animals to be found in these regions, even jaguars and ant-bears.

We had to travel quite seven miles from our camp before we found any possible crossing of the swamp, so wide and deep was the morass; in fact, we had to go to the source of the water at the foot of the scarped hills of the table-land, where we found a meeting of no less than nine different morasses, each one complete with its avenue of palms. What a wonderful scene it was!

It became necessary to round every one of these branches, for we were down in the deep narrow valley, where the slopes of the table-land surrounded us like a wall, up which there was no visible ascent. The tall rank grass was also littered with boulders of sandstone and short gnarled and distorted cork-trees; it was a toilsome march for both men and animals, but there, certainly must be the headquarters of all the peccaries of the region, for everywhere the ground was furrowed and rooted up, the grass trodden down in long lanes, the pools of water turbid from their wallowing, and the place odorous as a rank pigsty; and yet, strange to say, not a pig was to be seen, fortunately for us; for in such an inconvenient place an attack from these vicious animals in the numbers they could evidently collect would have enabled them to take us at great disadvantage.

We pushed on the animals to get out of this pig-set man-trap, and eventually got clear of the labyrinth on the further side of the last feeder of the main morass, and, after some difficulty, found an ascent on to the *geraes*, where we made a bee-line to the Sapão across the flats.

During the passage of the swamps the Don said,—

"Ah! Senhor Doctor, what a shame to leave such a lovely place; if you and I were only here to-night, what fun we would have with the peccaries; but, patience, they will make us a visit to-night because of the trail of the dogs."

But neither time nor place would permit of carrying out the Don's desires, as there was neither water nor pasture for the animals. The Don's remark about the peccaries paying us a visit is owing to a popular belief that these animals, when in considerable numbers, will follow a dog's trail for many miles, and attack and kill him. In fact, it is customary with the hunters to imitate the barking of a dog to attract the attention of the pigs, and induce them to collect together and make an attack; when, the hunters being safely ensconced in trees, the game is perfectly safe, as the men have only to shoot what they require.

The ground traversed that afternoon was not so free from bush as we had hitherto found, being in many places thickly covered with dense cerrado (abounding in immense quantities of the indiarubber-producing Mangaba-tree), where progress was very slow and difficult, and required the free use of our wood-knives. After a long and wearisome march, we reached the valley of the Sapão again, quite eight miles from the peccaries' haunt.

I found the river valley presented much the same characteristics as we had found lower down. For the purposes of a railway it is admirable; the gradients are practically

PREPARATIONS TO RECEIVE THE ENEMY. 133

level, and the only works of art required would be in crossing the many *burity* swamps that intersect the route, and these, although numerous, are narrow.

Even the Rio Sapão itself could doubtless be made into a good canal, in the absence of a railway, for there is plenty of water, and the ground offers great facilities for straightening its course.

Especial care was taken in preparing the camp that night. The Don and José superintended the operation of constructing the fort, the sides of which were further protected by spreading over them the hides used for covering the packs of the mules. Bush was also cut to make up and enlarge the defences, and a strong stake was driven into the ground inside the fort for the purpose of securing the dogs in case the peccaries arrived. The camp was made on the borders of a clump of trees, to which we were enabled to sling the hammocks, no one caring to sleep on terra firma that night, but two of the men who were unprovided with hammocks spread their hides on the ground inside the fort.

After dinner, of course, peccaries formed the sole subject of conversation, but hour after hour went by, yet no signs of their presence appeared; and, after arranging the watches for the night, we turned in, and with the fatigues of the day I was soon asleep.

It appeared to me, however, that I had barely closed my eyes, when I felt my hammock violently shaken. It was the Don awakening me, saying, "Wake up, here are the *porcos*, we are going to have some fun." The first peculiarity that struck me was the prevalence of the odour of old pigsties. I sat up, looked around and listened. The pitchy blackness of night surrounded us, but the fire burning brightly, sent its flickering light upon the tree-trunks, the foliage, and the hammocks; two men were in the fort with gun and knife in hand, and the dogs tied to their stake were with difficulty kept quiet, and vented their excitement in deep growls. As I listened it became evident that we were surrounded by some animals, for in many directions was heard in the stillness of night, the sound of bodies moving through the bush, twigs snapping, grass rustling, &c. It was a moment of suspense, but not for long; for suddenly, from all around us, came a blood-curdling sound of the simultaneous snapping of teeth from vast numbers of the enemy, followed by the appearance of a crowd of charging black animals, rushing with wonderful speed towards a common centre, the fort. We in the hammocks each lighted a coil of wax tapers that were prepared ready for the occasion. And what a scene ensued! the fire was rapidly scattered, and partly extinguished; under and around us was a seething mass of black peccaries, barely distinguishable in the dim light, but all pushing and struggling to the front; the men in the fort had discharged their weapons, and were hard at work hacking and thrusting at the peccaries as they endeavoured to swarm up the smooth surface of the hides that covered the sides of the fort. The men in the hammocks, after discharging their guns, reached down and slashed with their knives at the swarming animals below them. The attack was more like the wild reckless bravery of the Arabs of the Soudan, for as pig after pig fell squealing and disabled, scores more struggled for his place. The faint light of the tapers and the partly extinguished fire served but to dimly illuminate the elements of the strange noisy wildly weird scene; the trunks of the surrounding trees and their foliage; the swinging hammocks with their occupants reaching downwards, cutting and thrusting with their long gleaming knives; the dim figures of the men in the *trincheria*, repelling with shouts and thrusts the swarming enemy; the wild rushing charging forms of the black bodies of the peccaries, as in great numbers they threw themselves against the fort, regardless of being struck down one after the other, and always impelled forwards by those in the rear struggling to the front, others made ineffectual attempts to reach our hammocks or viciously gashed the trees that gave us support; the extremely disagreeable and nauseous odours

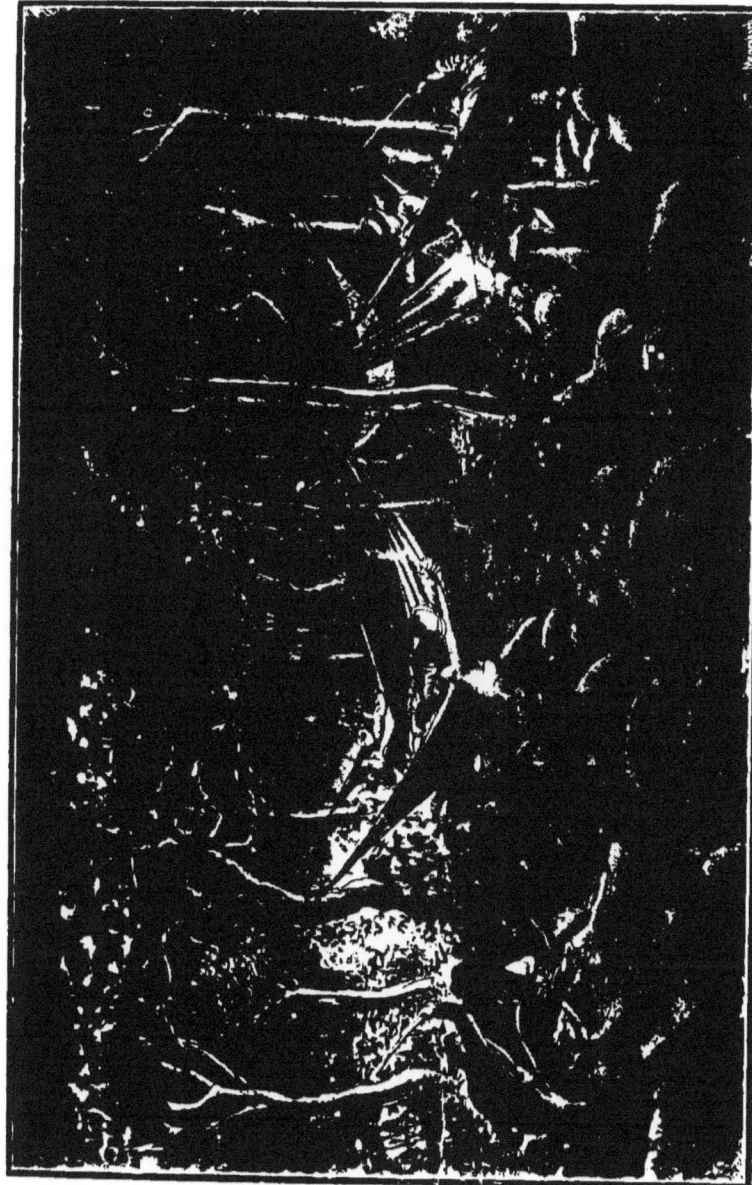

THE CAMP STORMED BY PECCARIES.

Vol. II. p. 134.

of the animals, their snapping of teeth like musketry file-firing, the reports of the firearms, the shouts of the men, the howling and barking of the dogs, and the dim light, created an indescribably strange and exciting scene. Every bullet of my revolver took effect. I shouted to the men to reserve their fire, and fire volleys, but it was like talking in a gale of wind at sea.

In spite of all efforts, still the battle raged. The animals appeared to be in immense numbers, for as far as the faint light would permit, the ground was seen covered with their moving bodies, rushing, struggling, the strongest beating down the weakest, grunting, squealing, and snapping their teeth; and noticeable above everything was the abominable exhalations from their bodies, an odour like a combination of rank butter and garlic.

I was getting anxious not only for my baggage, but for the men behind the fort, who had to cut and thrust like madmen; the excitement was intense. The strong raw hides were ripped up as though slashed with a sharp knife, and the bags of beans and farinha were freely streaming their contents on the ground from innumerable rippings from the keen sharp tusks.

Although we in the hammocks were quite safe, the fort was trembling; many of the saddles and bags had been displaced by the sheer pressure of the enemy. Our few miserable firearms appeared to have no more effect than so many popguns, although the ground was becoming strewn with the bodies of the slain and disabled. At last I succeeded in getting the men in the hammocks to fire volleys at a given place, and after a time this appeared to have an effect, for as suddenly as the attack commenced, so it ceased; and the animals withdrew simultaneously and in silence.

The Don (his voice chuckling with glee) called to us to get ready again as they would probably return. "Ah!" said he to me in a low voice, "what a splendid time we are having!" I thought, however, of the men in the fort, one of whom was stanching blood from his wrist. I told the Don to go and reinforce them; but suddenly the Don became very deaf; he was very snug in his hammock and really could not hear me; but José, like a good fellow, got out, ran for the fort, jumped in, and helped the men to make good the damages. We could still hear the pigs in the bush, and presently, without a moment's warning, we again heard that diabolical crash of teeth from a complete circle around us, followed immediately by another wild charge, and the battle was again renewed with all its hurly-burly; but then, after the first flush of excitement we became cooler, and José in the fort was a host in himself; this attack was of much shorter duration, and the enemy once more suddenly retreated. In the pause that ensued I thought of Rodrigues, as it then occurred to me that I had not hitherto noticed him; his hammock was quite still, and its edges drawn together over his body that formed a round ball-like protuberance in the centre. I saw it all, and could picture the poor terror-stricken man, coiled up, with blanched face and bated breath and making himself as small as possible. The men in the fort had behaved very pluckily.

Six or seven other attacks eventually followed, but each one became weaker, and the intervals between of longer duration. The eventful night seemed interminable, and finally it was not until near daybreak that we heard the last grunt.

At the first lights of grey dawn José proposed to reconnoitre, and went off for the purpose. At first he proceeded very gingerly from tree to tree. I proposed to myself to go also, but just at that moment I had a fellow-feeling for the Don's deafness, and thought what a comfortable place a hammock was, and that really I could do no good; and further I remembered that generals should always occupy high commanding positions; everyone was chary of moving from their places of security.

José soon afterwards returned, and reported that the enemy had finally withdrawn.

Thoughts of the horses and mules then occurred to us, and we anxiously awaited their arrival, for they had acquired the habit of appearing in camp of their own accord in the early morning for their matutinal feed of corn. Thankfully I saw three or four soon after arrive, but two men had to go for the others, that were fortunately found browsing on a plentiful supply of the shoots of young bamboos. Happily the animals had been pasturing in a direction opposite to that from whence the peccaries came, otherwise there would have been a stampede.

Almost the first thing the men did after the final retreat of the peccaries was to slash the skin on the top of the loins of the defunct enemy, and extract the gland that creates the disgusting odour peculiar to these animals; for if not extracted soon after death, it taints the flesh to such an extent as to render it uneatable except by Indians, who do not object to any flavour, and eat all their animal food cooked on the same principle as an European cook prepares a woodcock. There were twenty-seven dead pigs found in and about the camp, and also several wounded, to whom it was necessary to give the *coup de grâce*. The wounds were mostly from the knives and small axes, but a very considerable number of the wounded must have got away to recover, or linger unfortunately in pain.

Six of the plumpest were selected for drying and salting, the preparations for which, and also to repair the damages done to the bags of provisions, delayed our departure for some time.

An examination of these animals showed them to be a species of peccary resembling that known as the *Dicotyles labiatus*, but an essential difference was noticeable in the absence of the white lips that give the name to that species; our enemies had black snouts and dark lips, otherwise they corresponded in other points.

They had four incisors on the upper jaw, and six molars on each side above and below; while the tusks, although smaller than a pig's, are much finer and sharper, inclined slightly backwards, and closely overlap each other. Some of the bodies of the animals measured thirty-six inches in length. They are more slender in build than the common pig, and covered with long stiff bristles, coloured with alternate rings of grey, light-brown, and black. These colours vary with the size and age of the animals, and as either one predominates, they cause the animal to appear either brown, grey, or black; the largest we found was almost entirely black, whereas the smallest had quite a brown appearance. During the battle I could not help noticing the apparent method of their movements, as though they were led by chiefs. It appears that their mode of attack on such an occasion as they favoured us with, is to surround in silence, by a complete circle, the object to be stormed; when, at a given signal, a simultaneous snapping of teeth takes place, followed by a general converging rush to the centre, whereby the largest and strongest reach the front first, and the smallest bring up the rear; their retreat is carried out on an equally methodical system. There is a small red species known by the Guarany name of *caëitatu*;[5] our friends are known by the Brazilian cognomen of *queixadas*, or *porcos de matto*. From what I had witnessed during the past night, I can quite understand how these courageous animals in large numbers are capable of surrounding and destroying a powerful jaguar; and if my dog Feroz had fallen amongst them, he would doubtless have made a brave fight, but he would not have had the slightest chance of escape, and fortunately for us the ropes of the hammocks did not break, as hammock-strings will sometimes do at untoward moments, otherwise I should not be here to tell this tale.

But now, from the camp fire, comes the odour of roast peccary, for parts of them were already cooking for breakfast, and emitting a vastly more acceptable odour to what they did when alive. When ready, it is needless to say that, after the long night and in the keen dewy morning air, how appre-

[5] *Dicotyles torquatos.*

ciated were our visitors even without apple sauce, for then there was not the slightest trace of the objectionable odour.

We marched up the valley of the Sapão, now a narrow sluggish stream of beautifully clear but dark water, flowing almost on a level with the adjoining grass-lands, fringed with thin belts or avenues of the *buritys*.[6] The stream, although deep, eight to ten feet, was not more than ten or twelve feet wide; we were evidently nearing its source.[7]

We had not travelled more than a mile from our camp, when we topped a slight ridge that intersected our route, and which had hitherto hidden the view of the upper valley. On arriving at this point a most perplexing view met my gaze, for instead of finding the valley narrowing, as it had done hitherto, it opened out into a hollow basin about two miles wide and three miles long, and nearly surrounded by hills, or rather the bluffs of the *geraes*.

The greater part of the area of this depression is occupied by a marshy lake fringed by thousands and thousands of *buritys*. The water is evidently not deep, as scattered clumps of reeds, and grass, and palms could be seen growing over the whole of its surface. Beyond the immediate margins of this shallow lake the ground is covered with *buritys*, some in groups, some in pairs, some in long straight avenues. The whole of this valley is, with the exception of a few breaks, surrounded by the picturesquely-coloured sandstone bluffs of the *geraes*.

There was a bright blue sky overhead, flecked with fleecy white clouds sufficient to throw passing shadows over the

---

[6] On many occasions the men had cut down some of these palms, and as the trunks lay prostrate had hollowed out a hole about eight inches square; this speedily fills with a nearly transparent liquor, and makes a most refreshing drink, resembling very much the milk of green cocoanuts, but much sweeter. From this the natives make the celebrated *vinho de burity* by allowing it to stand and ferment. It is then a strong intoxicating beverage, and much prized by the Indians. Thus the name of this palm—*Mauritia vinefera*.

[7] The scene of last night's adventure I called Batalha (Battle).

landscape; green in the grass of the marshes, blue in the sky-reflected lake, golden brown over all the higher lands that are covered with the accumulated growth of ages of grass, and further varied by the many rich tints of the precipitous slopes of the enclosing scarped bluffs of the highlands—truly it was a grand combination of colour and form, and what a profound solitude!

In the N.W. and S.W. directions two openings appear where the land, more or less level with the swamp, forms a clear horizon against the blue sky. These two openings are

Pig-sticking in Goyaz (*see page* 150).

separated by a range of flat-topped hills, with perpendicular sides and a base of the natural slope of earth. These hills are remarkable in their appearance, and resemble a huge Titanic fortress.

I determined to explore the apparent exit of the waters of the lake from the two openings in the aforesaid N.W. and S.W. directions, for which purpose it was apparently necessary to go round three-fourths of the entire circumference of the swamps and lakes ahead of us.

The Sapão here loses its character of a river flowing between clearly defined banks, as its waters and lines of *buritys* gradually spread and mingle with those of the broad swampy lake, where the palms no longer appear in the form of avenues, but in dense and broad scattered clumps, whose growth indicates the almost impassable nature of a great morass.

We travelled on, skirting as near as possible the course of the Sapão, for it occurred to me that if this lake drained to the west by the S.W. and N.W. openings, I had made a very interesting geographical discovery, namely, *that the whole of the vast territory forming the N.E. section of Brazil is practically an island*, as any water flowing to the west must necessarily eventually join the Tocantins.

On the way I noticed a little hillock surrounded by swamp and covered with *green* grass, whereas *all* similar ground was covered with the brown and densely matted grass of the growth of ages. The Don, observing my looks, came up to me with a mysterious look, and said, " *É gente! seja quem fôr, são quilombeiros oú tapuias*" (Whatever it may be, it is people, fugitive slaves or Indians). Certainly this patch of green grass on high ground was mysterious; we looked around but could see no other indications of humanity, so pressed on with the march.

As several peccaries had crossed our path lately, José and the Don cut three long straight bamboos; to the ends of each we fastened our sharp-pointed knives, for the purpose of pig-sticking. But the first use we had for our lances was for a different animal; our dogs had suddenly disappeared into the tall grass, barking loudly, and a few moments afterwards a huge ant-bear[8] came rolling out into the open semi-marsh

---

[8] The great *tamandua-bandeira* of the Brazilians, the *tamanoir* of Buffon (*Myrmecophaga jubata*). This animal measured—head, sixteen inches; back, four feet; tail, four feet; total length about nine feet four inches. It was the finest specimen I had seen. Its peculiar motion in running is owing to its necessity of having to double up its huge hawkbeak-like claws, and run on the outer upper portion of the fore-feet, that gives it a motion very similar to what a man would appear like if he had to double up his fists and walk on all fours, using the tops of his wrists

land, followed by the dogs; it went at a good pace, but with most extraordinary and ludicrous movements. It became then very interesting to watch the sagacity of the dogs, as they hung well on to his rear, trying to seize only the tail of the animal, and keeping well out of reach of his powerful fore-legs armed with tremendous claws. The dogs, however, were evidently losing their caution and getting closer, and the cumbersome beast had already made some particularly rapid blows in attempting to rip the dogs. Fearing a possible disaster to my faithful Feroz, we galloped on, but it is amazing the speed these cumbersome ant-bears can develop. We had to put our animals to their sharpest paces to come up with the quarry, when we had the opportunity of fleshing our lances. The bear died hard, lying on its back and striking out with its fore-legs. The men cut off portions of the flesh to eat, but when afterwards prepared, I found it too strongly flavoured with formic acid to be agreeable, and the dogs refused it.

It then occurred to me that the incident of the discovery by the Don of the robbery of a bees'-nest some days ago, might possibly be explained by it having been taken by an ant-bear, and not by a prowling stranger as he supposed.

instead of his hands. This animal is totally devoid of teeth; its mouth is a small slit at the end of an elongated snout; the head is long and slender, and quite out of proportion to the other massive parts of its body; the eyes are small, and the tongue, long cylindrical and protractile, is lubricated with a gummy saliva, specially adapting it for insect food. The immense muscular development of the huge fore-legs, each armed with four formidable hook-like claws, enables it with facility to destroy the strongly-built sun-dried clay hillocks of the termites, or white ants. The hair of the head is short and close, but over the rest of the body it is long coarse, and shaggy, especially on the top of the neck and back. The colour of the head is a mixture of grey and brown, the upper part of the body is deep brown and silvery white. What principally distinguishes this species from the smaller one, the *tamandua* (*Myrmecophaga tamandua*), is a broad black band, bordered on each side with a similar one of a white or light greyish-brown colour; commencing on the chest it passes obliquely over each shoulder, where it terminates in a point. These bands have originated the term *bandeira*, a flag.

Although the appearance of this great valley looked so charming and so easy for travelling, we found it very toilsome; the flat ground near the borders of the great lake, only covered with scattered tufts of short thin grass, looked very pleasant, but we found it to consist almost entirely of quagmires, that in some places extend to the base of the enclosing highlands. Many a time we had to try the expedient of driving the animals over the hides laid on the wet grass, to prevent them being engulfed in the swamp; to avoid the swamps there was no alternative but to force our way through the tall matted grass of the higher ground at the base of the surrounding cliffs.

On the way we came across several peccaries, singly and in pairs, but the rough nature of the ground would not permit a chase. We saved our spears for more open lands.

The mules showed signs of their hard work, the want of pasture, and the roughness of the route especially, for their chests, faces, and fore-legs were quite denuded of hair, in continually forcing their way through the tall grass. Close by a thicket of *pindaiba* palms and young bamboos I pitched camp, with the purpose of resting men and animals, and of ascending an adjoining bluff to reconnoitre.

I took the Don with me, though he pulled a wry face at the prospect of the climb. He would have become deaf again, I know, but he saw it was no use, so brought his scaffold-pole of a gun with him and off we went.

After a short but severe climb we reached the top. Looking down as I did upon the great valley, it naturally presented a different appearance to the distant view in the morning. It is not one large swampy lake, as it at first appeared, but a number of large and small lakes of water connected by channels or divided by strips of dry land. The exertion of the ascent was rewarded, for it enabled me to distinguish a probable short cut across the valley, for on the opposite side of the thicket of *pindaibas*, where the camp was pitched, was a natural and apparently dry causeway, leading to the opposite side of the valley, and dividing the lakes into two distinct sets. There did not appear to be a bush or tree in the whole valley, excepting the vegetation peculiar to the swamps, *pindaibas* and *buritys;* all the dry land was covered with the matted dry brown grass *agreste crua*, as it is termed. The opposite side of the valley is shut in by the range of fortress-like hills, that terminate abruptly at their north and south extremities. The summit of this range appeared to be on the same level as where I stood, as did also the hills to the right and to the left, and behind me the *geraes* stretched far away, flat as a table. The whole formation of these valleys could be easily understood.

The summit of this wide far extending Chapada da Mangabeira, the watershed of the São Francisco and Tocantins, is most probably a relic of a great plateau that perhaps once extended from the table-lands of Bahia, east of the São Francisco to the Western highlands of the Tocantins, in Goyaz. As, however, the lower waters of this latter river have not been dammed up to the extent caused to the Rio São Francisco by the rocks of the Paulo Affonso falls, the level of the Tocantins is much lower than this river, consequently the Western drainage from the watershed is sharper than the Eastern, and thus is seen as soon as the divide is passed, the evidences of great denudations that have not only scooped out the valleys of streams, but have lowered the whole surface of the land, excepting where here and there a few isolated flat-topped hills remain to indicate its former level.[9]

Away to my right I saw the neighbourhood of our last night's adventure, and looking down upon the panorama of the valley I comprehended what immense détours we had made that day, having travelled perhaps sixteen miles while making only four in a straight line.

[9] In a paper on a "Sketch of the Physical Geography of Brazil," read by me before the Royal Geographical Society on the 8th February, 1886, I described the apparent denudations that have so evidently occurred in this and many parts of Brazil. See Appendix H.

In these pathless wilds it is all very well to determine a given direction, the difficulty is to follow it through the many obstacles in the form of swamps, or tangled grass.

After the descent we went on foot to examine the causeway, where we found the land dry, and the grass beaten down in many tracks either by man or quadruped, most probably the latter, as we had seen many moving bodies in the distance, that my glass led me to believe to be either *tapirs* or *capyvaras*.

If the dry grass of this valley was annually consumed by fire, what a grand cattle-raising district it would be, for this *agreste* when burnt every year affords very good pasture; it is only when it is very old that it becomes hard and acrid, and more resembles canebrake than grass.

The clump of *pindaibas* near our camp looked like an ornamental piece of shrubbery in a tropical meadow. It formed almost a complete oval in area, in the centre were *buritys*, and around them the graceful *pindaibas;* at their base a mass of ferns and flowering shrubs that made the borders of the clump clearly defined amidst the flat marshy land surrounding it.

April 13.—This morning the thermometer registered 68°, a degree of temperature that in these latitudes creates quite a sensation of chilliness, especially if one has passed the night sleeping in the open air.

With the exception of a false alarm from Rodrigues, the night passed placidly and without incident. This camp we named Pindaibas.

Early in the morning we wended our way across the natural causeway observed yesterday, and reached the opposite side of the valley where I halted the troop, and then rode on with the Don towards the south-west opening of the basin.

Numerous tracks of wild animals, especially peccaries, were met with, and a few deer were sighted a long way off. The south-west opening proved to be really a drainage of the south section of the lakes, where the overflow issues in the form of a considerable rivulet, and flows towards the south-west of Goyaz.

After rounding the extreme south corner of the cliffs on the right, we came suddenly within sight of a vast panorama of far extending low undulating hills, covered as far as the eye could perceive with the brown grass of the growth of ages. About ten miles away to the west and south-west are a range of hills; some are isolated and resemble martello towers perched upon a rounded sloping base, others form lines of irregularly-shaped hills.

The course of the valley of the stream by which we were standing, disappeared far away to the S.S.W. As I calculated upon going W. to N.W., this direction did not suit my purpose.[1]

The drop of the land from where we stood to the ground below us is very abrupt and considerable, and I could, to a certain extent, comprehend the motives that induced my informant in Sta. Maria to tell me that the lower ground beyond the source of the Rio Preto became blue with the great depth; for here a faintly blue and transparent haze covered the landscape that gave it an exaggerated appearance of depth and distance. The stream beside me was flowing at a rapid pace, and lower down it became a series of falls and rapids.

Whilst looking about us, a few peccaries emerged from some *burity* groves on to the comparatively open ground where we were. Such an opportunity was not to be neglected, and away we charged upon the valiant animals. They awaited our approach for a moment, until we neared them, when, after hesitating whether they should charge us or not, they snapped their tusks together with sharp clicks, wheeled, and fled. We had a glorious run over the sandy ground, only sparely covered with tufts of thin wiry grass, and finally

---

[1] This stream, I afterwards judged, must be the source of the Rio Novo, that when it joins a Rio Preto, constitutes one of the main feeders of the Rio do Somno. This Rio Preto is entirely distinct from the stream that the Rio Sapão enters.

succeeded in spearing two of the peccaries that apparently disdained to run away at a rapid pace.

I now returned to camp, and thence we all marched on to the northern end of the hills to the north-west opening of the valley.

There again another view of the solitudes of Goyaz appeared, but being from a different point of observation, the view presented other features. At this, the before mentioned north-west outlet of Varjem Bonita, it proved as I anticipated, the western exit of the northern group of lakes and swamps of the valley, and thus completed the circle of waters around the north-east portion of Brazil; for as the Sapão is the easterly drainage, and this new stream flowing to the west must necessarily find its way to the Tocantins, even if it is not one of the sources of the Rio do Somno.

The new river travelled with a rapid current and many falls for less than half a mile, and there the surface of the country fell rapidly in extensive round, rolling hills. We stopped here for breakfast, named the camp Bom Successo (Good Success) after the very satisfactory termination of my labours so far. The stream my men named Rio Diogo.

I could not, under the circumstances, but celebrate the event by uncorking my last bottle of Bass's bitter beer, and leave the empty bottle stuck upon a pole, a sign of British occupation.

The highest elevation of the waters of the divide above the city of Barra do Rio Grande was found to be 778 feet, and 2090 feet above the sea-level. The distance by road is approximately 330 miles, but as the course of the rivers is very much more sinuous and consequently longer, their mean gradient should not be more than two feet four inches per mile; and as there is not one waterfall in their whole extent, the possibility of future navigation, and the actual existence of favourable conditions for a line of easy gradients can easily be comprehended.

CHAPTER IX.

FROM THE SOURCE OF THE SAPÃO TO MATTO GRANDE.

Goyaz entered—Prairies—The gigantic fortress-like bluffs of the Chapada de Mangabeira—The Rio Diogo—Marching through solitudes—The roaring anaconda—The corn almost exhausted—Difficulty of following a route—Crossing the Corrego do Buraco do Diabo—A night-scene in camp—An uncertain route, and corn all gone—Strangers in sight—A council of war—A reconnoissance—The vegetation of the hill-tops—A world of brown grass—A puzzling prospect—Signs of distant habitations—The trail of the strangers—A Burity frond raft—On the track of the strangers—An exhilarating atmosphere—Healthy cattle—Arrival at a house—Peace or war?—A sturdy family of backwoodsmen — The strangers discovered — The outlawed Araujos—A kind and hospitable host—Anybody's land—The Sapão found to be a short cut to Goyaz—A lonely habitation—José do Matto Grande and his family—Escape from a long sojourn in a wilderness—A borderland farm—Arrival of my troop—A night under a roof again—An exploration and hunting party—A skirmish with the peccaries—Chased up a tree—A few exciting moments—The anaconda snakes of the marshes—Habits of the peccaries—Exploring the country.

An "indio manso."

April 15th.—Having thus passed the divide of the São Francisco and Tocantins basins, we had consequently entered the Province of Goyaz. The summit of

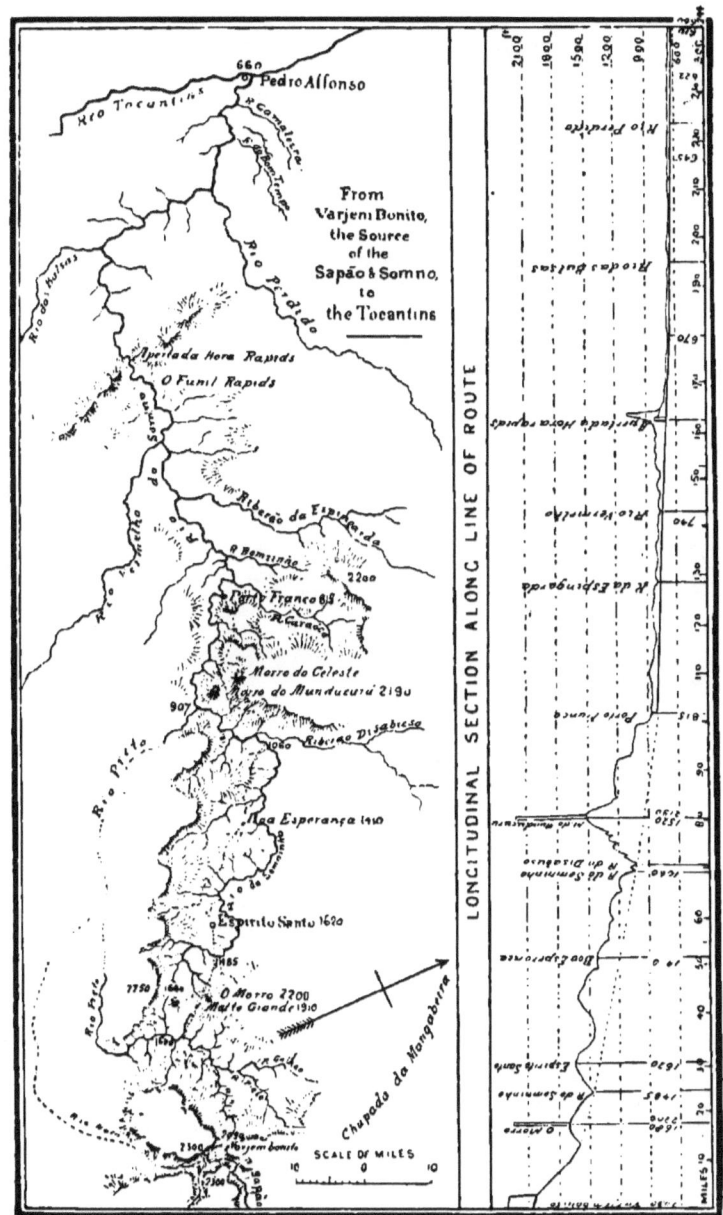

ROUTE MAP—VARJEM BONITO TO THE TOCANTINS.

the flat-topped cliffs that surround the Varjem Bonita,¹ are about 2300 feet above the sea.

The configuration of the land now before us presents immense distinctions to what we had lately travelled over. From the summit of a long rounded hill of tall grass, we see behind us, the western limits and bluffs of the Chapada da Mangabeira,² that long, wide, sandy, flat, treeless table-land, that extends from the neighbouring boundaries of Maranhão and Goyaz, and stretches in an undulating direction almost due south, to the line of mountain ranges of true upheaved strata in Southern Goyaz. The appearance of these bluffs is extraordinarily strange. Every few miles along their fronts great gaps appear, that mark the existence of springs and waters flowing to the west. The summits of the bluffs form a series of parallel levels, as though they had been jack-planed and rolled; the upper face of the cliffs are perpendicular walls, rising from the natural earth slopes formed by the accumulation of the fallen sandstone disintegrated by time and weather. They have the appearance, at a distance, of long lines of gigantic fortresses, commanding the vast areas below and in front of them, of the rolling brown grass hills and winding *burity* palm-grove valleys, and, further to the west, of tall isolated martello-tower-looking hills, or small groups of other flat-topped hills, like outlying forts of the main chain of fortifications.

We followed all day the descending course of the Rio Diogo, by forcing a way through the tall rank grass that everywhere covers the undulating hills.

It is a lovely country, and the air is superb and delightfully cool and fresh; there is no stagnant water, nor rotting vegetation, nor mosquitos, nor pests of any kind. The breeze sweeps over the billowy surface of the grass like over a ripe field of corn; it is all so bright and clear that one feels aglow with health and animation.

As the train of nine mules, two horses, and three men on foot, wend their way in single file through the tangled grass

---

¹ Beautiful lowland. ² The "Flats of the *mangaba* tree."

by the margins of the avenues of palms, the unaccustomed appearance and noise of the troop disturb the many denizens of the groves, great purple or crimson and gold macaws[3] protest, with loud harsh shrieks, against our intrusion of their domains, green parrots, and the lovely golden head *jandaias*[4] also screech and chatter; occasionally a low hoarse roar is heard amidst the morass at the base of the palms, said to come from the great sucurihus or anacondas; a deer sometimes bounds away ahead of us, or the grass often vibrates with the rush of a peccary scampering away; then, if the grass is not too high, some of us leave the ranks, lance in hand, for a chase. The active animals generally escape, but we have many an exciting run, greatly to the delight of the dogs, and occasionally succeed in fleshing our spears.

Often are seen, in some of the green marshy valleys, herds of the small campos deer, that are not by any means so tame as those of the Sapão, and long before we can get within range they are off, a fact that makes me think we are not far from inhabited districts.

The numerous groves of *buritys* with their deep morasses that so continually obstruct the route, give much trouble to cross or to go round, and treble or quadruple the distances, that is especially annoying, for I am anxious about the mules, that are in a most woeful condition. The pasture has been so very bad, and contains so little nutriment that they become very fatigued with the great labour of forcing a way through the grass, and their chests and fore-legs are denuded of hair, and the skin of many of them is scarified and bleeding from the cuts of the hard and often cane-brake-like grass. In some places this is five or six feet high, a dense tangle of matted canes, in others it is only two or three feet in height. The corn is nearly exhausted, and only sufficient for one, or at most two, days' rations. It was most fortunate that it had been brought, otherwise the troop could not possibly have travelled so far without it.

[3] *Ara ararauna.*   [4] *Tangynathus*, sp.

A Brazilian mule, hardy and strong as it is, is, without its corn, about as useful as a locomotive without fuel.

In travelling through an open country like this, it would appear comparatively easy to follow a wished-for direction; on foot, yes, but not with a troop of pack-mules For instance, I want to go west or north-west; I see in those directions groups of hills on the horizon, some eight or ten miles away, and instead of the Rio Diogo flowing in that direction, several small streams join it, flowing from the west and north-west, and the Rio itself takes a course to the S.S.W., and in the pitiable condition of the animals I dare not take them away from at least the neighbourhood of water on to perhaps, waterless arid highlands. Consequently, I resolved to follow the course of the Rio Diogo for at least a day or two. A short distance on, the Rio Diogo joins a more considerable stream, that flows from a northerly source. We continued to follow the course of these united waters.

Late in the afternoon a stream, most inconvenient for passing, barred our way; it enters the now deep swift waters of the Rio Diogo on our right, bordered by high banks and belts of thick woods, that could only be passed after much labour and risk. The stream in front of us is small in volume, tumbling over rocks and boulders at the bottom of a deep gulley with precipitous sides, full of *atoleiros* (springs and quagmires). José rode a long way up the margins of its course to find a passage, but only returned as the sun sank below the horizon. He reported that up above, the stream opened out into a wide impassable Burityzal, that apparently extended miles away to the cliffs of the table-lands; there was absolutely no pasture near us except the leaves of bushes, but on the other side there were some bamboos and a thin cerrado. For the sake of the animals, it was necessary to get them on the other side of the stream at all hazards.

One mule is led down the steep slope, where he soon sinks in the soft morass and struggles and plunges furiously, snorting with terror, his eyes distended and nostrils quivering; with a final effort he rears himself out of the bog, but only to slip and fall; away he rolls down the sharp descent, pack and all, and lands upon his back amongst the rocks below; the men follow, and relieve the poor beast of his pack, when he staggers to his feet, and, after several struggles and failures, he finally reaches the top of the bank on the opposite side.

All the rest of the mules had to be unloaded, and the baggage carried to the other side on the men's heads, for the area of a man's foot will carry his weight over places where the small hoof of a mule would inextricably sink.

It proved a very troublesome and difficult task to get the rest of the animals across the gorge, but, after many a struggle and tumble, with the help of hides laid on the worst places, down which they slipped on their haunches, we finally succeeded in landing them on the other side, bruised, shaken, and trembling in every limb, but otherwise unhurt.

The camp fire had been lighted in the meantime, and a quantity of young bamboo shoots collected for fodder for the poor famished animals. The men unanimously baptized the stream, *Corrego do Buraco do Diabo*.

It was 7.30 p.m. before we had everything stowed for the night, and ourselves seated around the fire discussing roast peccary and the prospects of the next day's discoveries, or a night visit from the peccaries, or *tapuias*. Nothing, however, could be finer than the lovely moonlight night, with a temperature of 70°, and an absence of any torturing insects or other pests. The camp was pitched amongst the trees of a thin cerrado, hard by the deep dell of a small feeder of the *Corrego do Buraco do Diabo*. It was a picturesque scene in the obscurity of night, for the blaze of the fire throws strong flashes of light on the trees, the hammocks, the fort, the grass, and the moving figures of the men, one of whom is roasting a leg of *peccary* on a spit before the fire for breakfast, another is giving the mules their last feed of corn, another struggles up the grotto with a saucepan of water for the beans, another is cleaning a pig we had speared on the march, Antonio puffs his cigarette

and relates his yarns, (the other men are away hobbling
some of the mules), I sit upon my box bed and wonder when I
shall be out of these wilds. Dark shadows are around us, the
darkness of night out in unknown wilds, that one can so easily
people with possible objectionable visitors, a vague feeling
of uncannyness creeps over one, like what I remember feeling
as a child for a certain dark closet in the old home. Overhead
the new moon plays hide and seek with occasional masses of
clouds, or breaks out in a clear bright sky as they roll on-

A night-scene in camp in the wilds of Goyaz.

wards, making the details of the distant landscape clear and
definable in the cold light. Strange sounds, peculiar to the
night, strike with startling suddenness on the quiet of the
camp, hushing the murmur of conversation, and making all
listen with overstrung nerves until the noise of the fall of a
crumbling ember of the fire recalls our wandering faculties,
or Antonio softly says, "*Não he nada, he' algum bixo*" (It is
nothing, it is some bicho or other). But if Feroz gives a
low growl, it is curious to see the keen attention, how weapons

are grasped, and heads raised in listening attitudes. One acquires this way a peculiarly light sleep. I could then sleep well all through the night anywhere and anyhow, and get up fresh in the morning, and yet it seemed as though I had heard every sound and noticed every movement that had taken place throughout the night, even to every time the man on watch replenished the fire, or raised the lid of the pot to see how the beans were cooking. But the presence of my excellent watch dog, "Feroz," was ever a source of security against surprise. It would be difficult for any being to approach the camp, and not find him alert and ready with his deep warning growl.

April 16 dawns upon us a clear bright morning, as free from mist as the mid-day, but several of the mules are missing, having probably strayed away in search of pasture. The men follow their tracks easily through the tall grass of the hills, but it requires a long tramp to find them, and it is ten o'clock before we can get away.

It is a queer feeling with which one leaves a camp in these unknown wilds to go out in the wide wilderness, with failing animals, exhausted stores of corn, and the rivers flowing in a course at right angles to the desired direction. About mid-day we topped the summit of a long hill, and sighted a wonderful array of long avenues of *buritys*, extending far away in the hollows of wide shallow valleys, enclosed by great undulating brown grass hills and the fortress-like hills of the Chapada da Mangabeira in the background.

Whilst we halted a moment to gaze about us, Antonio, who had very keen vision, suddenly ejaculated, "*Olha la! gente, gente, lá estão elles*" (Look there! people, people, there they are), and directed my attention to a couple of black specks on the brow of a distant hill. On applying my glasses, I made out two horsemen, quite motionless, and apparently watching our movements. Rodrigues soon joined us, and discovering the cause of our inquiring looks, at once became very excited, shouting to the men, "To arms, boys, to arms; the Indians, get ready the cartridges."

"Hold your tongue, and do not be stupid," quietly observed José in reply.

Meanwhile the two strangers, evidently not liking our appearance, rode away and soon disappeared from view. A council of war was held, and the general opinion was that

Sighting strangers in the wilderness—The fortress-like hills of the Chapada da Mangabeira—Burity palm groves and grassy savannahs.

they were "*quilombeiros*," or part of a band of fugitive slaves under the command of a certain Araujo (a kind of Brazilian Rob Roy), who was supposed to have his headquarters somewhere in these districts. I could not but help thinking that they were hunters from some near settlement, and proposed to follow their tracks, although the intervening marshes would necessitate an enormous détour, but as the course they took in going away would be likely to intersect our route, I determined to continue the journey, and so as to strike, then follow their tracks.

In the late afternoon we found some fair pasturage on a

hill-side that had evidently been burnt not very long ago, and close to a lofty isolated eminence. I pitched camp to rest and feed the animals, whilst I went on foot, accompanied by Antonio, to climb the hill and prospect the views.

The ascent was long and toilsome, through high matted grass and rugged ground, covered with boulders of a coarse variously-coloured sandstone, showing occasional veins of quartz, of white and of clear varieties, all strongly tinged yellowish-red with oxide of iron. On the summit of the hill we found an area about an acre in extent, perfectly flat, in places riven by ravines; the surface was grown over with vegetation similar to what we found on the table-lands, i.e. tufts of thin wiry grass, dwarf-ground palms, small *Mangabeira* and *cajew* trees, *Vellozias* and various scattered small bushes, and the sweetly perfumed white flowers of the *Spiranthera odoratissima*, all so different to the *agreste*-covered hills below us, as though we had ascended into another country.

Looking around us, was like looking upon a sea of huge mountainous waves of brown grass, far and near the same brown hue appeared, broken only by lines of *burity* palms and long narrow winding threads of woods in the more distant valleys, and the bluffs of the Chapada to the east; a long wide valley trended away to the south, the course of the Rio Diogo, a direction that considerably puzzled me; to the south-west a long ridge shut off an exit that way, and to the west and north-west other ridges and isolated hills apparently precluded the possibility of drainage to the Tocantins in those directions, but amongst these higher lands of the N.W., I could make out some green hills, evidently *queimados*; and what is this I see amongst such a vestige of human life? Yes, it is—a veritable column of smoke, but miles away, in a N.N.W. direction. Antonio, as usual, commenced croaking about *tapuias* and *quilombos*, but I resolved that if we did not come across the tracks of the strangers, I would proceed the next morning in the direction of the green grass and the burning matter.

After taking the bearings of the position of the smoke, and making a sketch plan of the intervening lands, we descended the hill, but instead of returning to camp, we crossed a stream and went onwards beyond it, to examine for traces of the strangers.

Our efforts were rewarded, for we came across the trail of two horsemen travelling west ; we followed their tracks for about a mile to alongside the banks of the Rio Diogo, on the opposite side of which was a small raft moored to some bushes.

"It is an Indian's raft," said Antonio on seeing it.

"Friend Antonio, if you utter another word about the *tapuias*, I will cut off your rations of *manipocira*,"[5] I replied, quite nauseated with the constant repetition of this bugbear.

The raft consisted of bundles of the long dried leaf-stems of the *burity* palms, laid in two layers transversely, one upon the other. The horsemen, probably those we had sighted in the morning, had evidently forded the river by the aid of the raft, for the prints of horses' hoofs and bare feet were distinctly visible in the sand of the shore. We returned to camp, and preparations were made to leave the animals, baggage, and some men there the next day, and then to proceed on foot to explore the green lands of the northwest.

Accordingly the next morning, taking with me Antonio and my special man Bob, and looking well to arms, with haversacks of provisions, water-bottles, and compass, we set out on foot on our exploration of the district of the mysterious smoke José Grosso was left in charge of the men and the camp, for Rodrigues was so scared that he was absolutely useless for the purpose.

We reached the river, where Bob plunged into the water, swam across, and returned poling the raft. On the other side we found a well-defined track, that we followed for a

---

[5] *Manipocira* is a term occasionally used to express a *mata bixo*, or a dram of *cachaça*.

long time without sighting anything except brown grass, *buritys*, and a few birds, amongst the latter some gorgeous gold and blue macaws (*Araras*). The ground was dry and sandy, in many places so soft and deep, that walking was hard work, yet what different effects the exercise produced to the moist clammy state that one gets into in the woods, for here on these breezy hills the sun and fresh dry air seem to absorb all perspiration, and despite the scorching rays of the sun, one feels lithe and springy, and equal to any exertion.

At last, after some couple of hours' tramp, we crossed a pretty little rivulet of clear water, (that like all the streams of these districts, flows over a rocky bed of hard coarse-grained sandstone), traversed a belt of forest and emerged on to a long gentle ascent all covered with the green grass of a *queimado*, and oh! welcome sight, a few cattle browsing on its summit; there must be somebody at home somewhere hereabouts. The cattle looked at us inquisitively for a few moments, then threw up their heels and scampered away. They were black in colour, and appeared to be in capital condition as near as we could judge from the distance; their horns were so enormous, and gave them such a ferocious appearance, that their retreat was not objected to.

About a mile further on, after passing a small roça in a clearing amidst the woods of a narrow valley, we reached a large birdcage-looking house of sticks and grass-thatched roof. A man who was standing in the doorway gazed wonderingly at us for a moment, and probably not liking the strange appearance of my helmet, at once retired within the house, from whence he soon reappeared with six tall brown-skinned men, each one armed with a gun.

I halted and called, "*Ó de casa,*" (Oh! house ahoy.)

"*Ó de fóra! É de paz ou guerra?*" (Without there! is it peace or war?) comes the reply.

"*Amigos e Christoẽs*"[6] (Friends and Christians) I answer.

[6] *Christoẽs* is a term generally applied to inhabitants of Indian districts

"*Pode chegar,*" (You can approach), the oldest man responded. All, however, handled their weapons and looked at us with evident surprise, but as we were only three in number and advanced with guns shouldered, their alarm quickly subsided.

I saw before me a group of a finer set of men than I had met with anywhere in Brazil. In front of them stood an elderly man, about sixty years of age, considerably over six feet in height, muscular broad-shouldered and deeply sunburnt, his square jaws were partly covered by beard and moustache, short wiry and grey, his nose was aquiline, his brows were heavy, and shaded keen piercing eyes, and altogether, he was a model of sinewy strength. His face wore an expression of curiosity and indecision, but it was that of a frank honest manly fellow; the other men, apparently his sons, were all tall we l-knit brown-skinned fellows, from about twenty to thirty-two years of age. All, father and sons, were clad alike in suits of tanned deerskin, hats, coats, vests, and trousers; their feet were bare, and their bodies shirtless.

I tendered a brief explanation of my presence in these wilds, and that I had left the rest of the troop in camp. The old man at once gave me a hearty welcome, slung up hammocks, and called his wife, a hale old browny dame, who had apparently retired to some inner room pending the inquiries of our mysterious selves.

During the conversation that ensued, I learned that the two horsemen we had sighted yesterday, and whose tracks we had followed, were two of the young men before us, who had been on a shooting excursion amongst the hills, and when they saw our rather large troop in those districts, (that they well knew were roadless,) they were considerably puzzled to account for our appearance, and, the distance being so great, they could only distinguish a large mounted party, and believing us to be some wandering *quilombeiros* or *Araujos*,

in Goyaz to indicate Brazilians; the aborigines being known as *tapuias*, *gentihos*, or *indios*.

they had ridden home as quickly as possible to inform their father that the *Araujos* were out on the war-path [7] and had consequently determined to remain at home that day, and scout for information on the next.

The sons now offered to go and fetch my troop, but, remembering the fright that Rodrigues would fall into at the sight of strangers, and probably fire at them first and make inquiries afterwards, I sent back Antonio with them, mine host kindly providing him with a horse for that purpose.

The old dame brings us gourds of milk, with farinha and coffee served up in smaller gourds. Cigarettes are lighted, my black bottle of cachaça is passed round to my hosts, who take a hearty pull at it, with a catching of the breath, and a sigh of gratification at such unusual luxury, "Ah! it is strong! good cachaça!"

A well-earned lounge in a hammock is now appreciated, and in a long and animated conversation we exchange our respective experiences, from which I glean the following. The neighbourhood, known as Jalapão, has not been colonized more than five or six years by the Christoũs, immigrants chiefly from the neighbouring province of Piauhy, who were attracted by the excellent pasture-lands of the hills, and the fertile soil of many of the valleys, and who have acquired, by the right of occupation only, the ownership of their lands, where possession is practically the ten points of the law.

About twenty miles in a N.W. direction is a small village

---

[7] These *Araujos* are the bogeys of these borderlands; whether they actually exist is more than doubtful. Story says that some years ago a certain *Araujo*, (who was celebrated in the Sertão for his numerous crimes,) finding that inconvenient inquiries were being made for him by the police authorities of the country towns, disappeared to the wilds of these districts, where he was supposed to have joined a retreat of fugitive slaves (*quilombeiros*); that certain outlying farms had been ruthlessly attacked and plundered by the bands under the leadership of the outlaw, and their tenants murdered with great brutality. This is the general report, but I failed to trace any of the alleged circumstances either to time or locality, neither could the supposed existence of the stronghold of the *Araujos* be traced to any particular neighbourhood.

known as Espirito Santo, and beyond it are a few cattle-farms.

A trail passes through Espirito Santo from Piauhy towards Natividade, in the south of Goyaz, and is the only road that exists in the country between the Chapada da Mangabeira and the Tocantins.

The only articles of export of the district are a few herds of cattle, that are driven to Paranagual, in Piauhy, or from thence to Santa Rita do Rio Preto, and are bartered for such articles of necessity as the district does not produce, guns, salt, powder and shot, cottons, knives, axes, bill-hooks, &c.

My route up the Sapão will open out a much shorter journey to Sta. Rita than the roundabout way through Piauhy, for, like the inhabitants of the Rio Preto, these had peopled the mysterious valley of the Sapão with such a variety of perils and dangers that the people preferred to go round by Piauhy rather than organize an exploring party and test its imagined dangers and difficulties.

The old man immensely exaggerated what he called "*a couragem do Senhor Doutor*" in traversing the Sapão with so small a party.

Certainly, if a very small fraction of the expected dangers had been met with, my exploration would probably have ended in disaster, but as I met with no marauding Indians or *quilombeiros*, nor prowling *onças*, nor pathless forests, nor malignant fevers, and only a skirmish with the peccaries, it was really not worth mentioning.

The old dame said she passed a very nervous life of suspense, for all her sons and her husband sometimes left her alone for days whilst they were away on a hunting expedition, and as her father and brother had been killed by an Indian raid on their home in Piauhy, she was never free from anxiety and memories of the terrible scenes of her young life.

Although this Jalapão is surrounded by immense tracks of unexplored lands, and tribes of Coroados are known to exist on the head-waters of the Rio do Manoel Alvos, within 100 miles, and semi-civilized tribes of Cherentes inhabit the banks of the Tocantins, there appears to be no fear amongst the males of *indios brabos* (wild Indians).

Senhor José do Matto Grande,[8] the name of my host (his surname being the title of his home), apparently spends a free, happy and independent life with his huge sons, who are really, in their manner and simplicity, only overgrown boys; and pleasing it is to see the respect and attention they pay to their parents.

Their *roça* in the woods, the game of the campos, and their herds of cattle, provide them with all their simple requirements—their house, food, and clothes. Were it not for salt, guns, powder and shot, they would be absolutely independent of the outer world; they are active, energetic and healthy, and in their habits are fairly clean; their only vices, an occasional cigarette or a dram of cachaça when they can get it, for it is fortunately in these districts scarce and dear.

I further learned that the river we had been latterly accompanying, and which the Rio Diogo had joined, is known as the Rio Preto, whose source is amongst the Chapadas of the Mangabeira, in a low valley somewhat similar to, and north of, that of the source of the Sapão, and that a little beyond it, streams flow towards the great navigable Paranáhyba.

If I had followed the sinuosities of the Rio Preto, it would have taken me into a pathless wilderness of almost impassable thick *capim agreste*, but would eventually have brought me, by a long détour, to its junction with the Rio do Somninho below Espirito Santo. Such a route would probably have kept me a week or a fortnight in the wilderness battling with the difficulties of progress, the tall grass, the many marshy streams and *buritysals*, and belts of woods, during which time the animals must certainly have failed.

[8] Joseph of the great forest, or thick woods.

A Borderland Farm.

The very thought of it made me stretch out my limbs in the comfortable *rêde* (hammock), with a feeling of intense satisfaction that I was so well out of it, and in the hands of such good people.

The walls of their house are built of strong upright *pindahiba* poles, placed close together; the door and window-frames are roughly-squared timbers; the roof is grass thatch, and the three rooms inside are formed by partitions of other upright poles; the kitchen is under an open shed, merely roofed over, where a few boulders of stone constitute the kitchen range, and a few earthenware pots, tin plates, spoons and gourds, the *batterie de cuisine*. In front of the house a fence of *pindahiba*[9] sticks encloses a clean-swept yard and a thatched hut that serves as a barn for storing the crops of beans, maize, rice, mandioca, yams, coffee, cotton, castor oil, beans, pumpkins and sweet potatoes, all of which are produced in their *roça*.

Many of the sticks of the *pindahiba* fence had taken root, and developed vigorous branches, although several of them had been put in the ground upside down.

An adjoining open shed contains the stove for drying farinha, and a rude pair of wood rollers, turned by hand by means of levers, for crushing cane and making a little *rapadura*. Running about at their own sweet wills are four pert tame *porcos de matto*, a gold and blue and a dark purple *arara*, three green parrots, a monkey, a score or so of fowls, a few pigs, goats, and some dogs, all with the exception of the latter perfectly tame, and the *araras* and parrots were excellent talkers.

In due time my troop arrived, and José extended to all a noisy welcome. Later on he invited all of us, master and man, to join a liberal dinner, that he and the old dame had prepared for us. It was a rough dinner-party, both guests and table appointments, but it was marked by a good temper, enormous appetites, and a thorough appreciation of the good

[9] *Xylopia sericea*.

things before us, and of the frank genial kindness of our hospitable hosts. In the evening the tent was pitched to accommodate my men, and all turned in early, each glad to be free from the watchful nights and anxieties of the past days.

The next morning, accompanied by José as a guide, I started to explore the surrounding districts, map out a rough plan of the course of the waters, and take barometrical observations. As the mules were considerably exhausted and required a rest, he kindly provided horses, and suggested that we should at the same time make a shooting-party. All his sons and my men were anxious to join, except Rodrigues, who with his two men remained behind to keep the old dame company. As we might possibly camp out, *ponchos* and bags of provisions were taken with us.

The horses were strong fresh and in good condition, but so wild and frisky, that care was required to prevent saddles becoming too suddenly unoccupied. Yet how enjoyable was that canter over the even surface of the rolling hills of short grass! how fresh and pure was the wonderfully clear air! so cool and exhilarating, and how strangely clear and minutely defined appeared even the most distant outlines of the horizon, free from the slightest trace of haze!

In the distant east and south-east appeared the ramparts of the outlying spurs of the strange-looking flat-topped table-lands of the Chapadas, showing even at a great distance the innumerable tints of their formation, and their steep scarped faces, furrowed by deep perpendicular clefts worn by the rains and weather of ages. Between us and these bluffs was a vast expanse of hills and vales, brown in the distance, green in the foreground; long winding lines of dark forest or avenues of *burity* groves filled the hollows; in all directions were scattered eminences of more flat-topped hills, some forming ranges, others isolated, others in groups, their furrowed perpendicular walls grandly picturesque in their beautiful tints.

We wended our way towards a part of the Rio Preto considerably below where we had crossed on the previous day, at the foot of a fall known as Cachoeira do Firmino. The sloping banks were so full of springs and quagmires, that great difficulty was experienced in descending them. The margins of the stream were free from woods, and on the adjoining land only a few *buritys* appeared in the boggy soil of the hollow, and a little *cerrado* here and there dotted the hill-slopes with its gnarled trees. The bed of the stream is limestone.

A little further on, in a wide shallow depression, was our host's favourite hunting-ground (where he had often found considerable quantities of peccaries), an immense *burityzal* that extended apparently from the Chapadas to the Rio Preto.

We halted at José's request and listened, and soon distinctly heard the grunt of the *porcos* amongst the *buritys*, where they feed on the fruits of the palms that form their favourite food.

Leaving the horses fastened to the trees of a thin *cerrado* that covered the sloping ground of the borders of the swamps, and haversacks, *ponchos*, and other *impedimenta*, suspended to the branches, we advanced to the attack.

I confessed to a feeling of trepidation and a certain bumping of the heart as we were about to leave the borders of the convenient trees so easy and apparently purposely constructed for a human retreat from the peccaries, but at that moment, a troop of some dozen of them emerged from the jungle of the swamp out into the open marshy land, and disappeared into the adjoining tall grass.

Three of the sons of José, with Antonio, Bob, and José Grosso, started at a run to cut off their retreat, and soon disappeared amidst the tall grass a little lower down the hill. After a few moments of suspense, we heard reports of guns and shouts to us to look out; at the same time another troop of peccaries appeared on the open marshes and followed the tracks of the others. The grass became agitated by the movements of the animals, and they soon afterwards entered the more open ground of the *cerrado* where we were waiting, pursued by the five men; we all fired, but as the range was long, there was not much execution. The animals, about forty in number, then suddenly halted and faced their pursuers with vicious little stampings of feet and snapping of teeth, and suddenly charged down upon the men and upon ourselves. Never was such gymnastic agility displayed as in the way that each of us rushed for, and scurried up, the nearest trees, many dropping their guns or knives in their hurry.

José and his sons were the coolest, especially the old man, who, perhaps a little too stiff for climbing, calmly placed his back against a tree, clasped it behind him with his left hand, and leaning forward in a semi-stooping posture, with his long *facão* at the ready, awaited the furious charge.

How gallantly they come sweeping along with their muzzles well down, but within a few feet of our trees they suddenly halt, and snapping their tusks, make short plunging charges. I had found a comfortable perch up a short gnarled tree, and taking careful aim at the peccaries near me, I knocked over three of them in five shots from my revolver.

They were charging José's legs at close quarters, but his long keen sharp-pointed knife flashes quickly as he rapidly delivers cuts and thrusts with telling effect. The other men, safely ensconced in the trees, have made good shots, but before any of us can reload the peccaries scamper away. All of us quickly descend from our perches and rush after the retreating animals, loading our guns as we run, but our brave foes suddenly halt and face us with a look of defiance and again make a gallant charge. How ignominious we appeared as we in our turn beat a hurried retreat to the nearest trees, where, not having time or finding conveniences for a climb, we were forced to imitate José's example and face the enemy with knives; but the peccaries after a momentary pause, dash onwards and disappear amidst the tall grass of the borders of the swamps, cross the marshes, and enter the jungle of the *buritys*.

Although the whole thing happened within a few moments, there were quite enough elements of danger to spice the sport, for, if in making our retreat, any of us had stumbled and fallen, the consequences must have been serious, if not fatal. I prefer the pig-sticking on mule-back with our extemporized spears. We gave the *coup de grâce* to the wounded, but many got away only partially damaged. We found our bag amounted to ten pigs, all in excellent condition.

As José and his sons were anxious for another tussle, we proceeded up the valley, and soon saw here and there a solitary grunter outside the growth of palms and aquatic vegetation of the swamps; and frequent grunts, heard amidst the groves, indicated the presence of considerable numbers of our foes.

A little further on, a spit of firm land only covered with short grass extended to near the groves, but no one cared to venture there so far from the friendly sanctuary of the trees, and possibly meet a huge anaconda coiled up in the swamp.[1]

José Grosso and one of our host's sons now returned to remain with the animals, whilst we proceeded a little further on in quest of a stray peccary. We walked about a mile, but

---

[1] These *barityzals* are the haunts of huge anacondas, of such a size that I hesitate to mention—certainly longer than I have ever heard of any species of snake in any part of the globe. José assured me that he had lost not only one but several bullocks on different occasions when the cattle had waded into the swamps to drink water, where he afterwards found only their heads and horns. I quote his story as he told me. I can give credence to him as he did not appear to be a man given to exaggeration, but not having personally seen a snake swallow a bullock, I cannot ask my readers to believe what I have only heard of, although I may feel disposed to credit it myself. José told me he had killed some scores, but had never utilized their tough skins for any purpose, although riding-boots are made from them in Espirito Santo. He also stated that these boas will sometimes utter a peculiar low, roaring noise in response to the reports of firearms. That I am disposed to credit, as I had myself on several occasions heard low, hoarse sounds emanate from the groves as we passed by.

found not what we hoped for, but on returning, some peccaries were seen straying towards the hills in twos or threes, homeward-bound to their lairs in the dells and grottos of the sources of streams at the foot of the bluffs of the Chapadas. We worked our way amidst the trees, and eventually obtained a few long shots, and succeeded in bagging two more.

It became a question whether we should pursue our journey to enable me to take my notes, and camp out and have another probable night-attack of peccaries, or return to Matto Grande. I thought a night of peace and quietness preferable, although perhaps very unsportsmanlike, and so we wended our way homewards.

It is rather unusual that these peccaries make such a brave fight in daylight, but it was chiefly owing to their accidentally finding themselves in such considerable numbers on this occasion, as they are commonly scattered over their feeding-grounds in very small parties during the day, and return to a common haunt at night, whence they sally out in immense numbers upon any foe that trespasses upon their neighbourhood, like when they tracked our dogs in the Sapão.

I spent the next day in taking observations of the surrounding neighbourhood, when, men and animals being reinvigorated with rest, I proceeded the day afterwards, on to Espirito Santo, taking my host with me as a guide.

I was naturally desirous to remunerate him on leaving, but he energetically protested against receiving any money, saying, " what was the good of it to him in those wilds ?" but he would accept with pleasure powder, shot, and salt, and right gladly I gave him all I could spare, and it made his heart rejoice at such a goodly supply.

CHAPTER X.

FROM MATTO GRANDE TO PORTO FRANCO.

Isolated hills—Limestone formation—An undulating country—The Rio Somninho the source of the Somno—Excellent cattle and grand grazing-lands—Charming woods—Absence of fevers—Espirito Santo village—Top-boots from a snake-skin—A fine specimen skin—*Bicho de pé*—An independent village—A troublesome road—Boa Esperança—A *sertãoejos* farm—An enterprising Brazilian—A night with *baratas* or cockroaches—A Brazilian pioneer—Dangers of river bathing—A tiresome ford—A stormy night under canvas—Bob escapes drowning—Hard work in crossing a stream—A rocky country—Vestiges of the old plateau—A rough bit of road—An adventure with a rattlesnake, and another with a huge stag—A party of travellers—The good-natured Geralistas of Jalapão—The barren *geraes*—Arrive at Porto Franco—The farm at Porto Franco—I become wearied with my travels—Dull times—Cattle-raising at Porto Franco—A wild plantation—Good treatment of slaves—Climate—Costliness of salt—Indians and missionaries—A raft is constructed—Good-bye to my followers—The crew of the raft.

Bob's escapade.

AFTER proceeding a few miles on our way, we passed near a high, solitary, flat topped hill, locally known as O Morro, a hill that forms a prominent landmark when seen from the exit of the valley of the Sapão. The face of this hill shows three different formations; the upper appears to be a limestone rock similar to what I had found in the streams, the middle a species of red sandstone, and below it is a stiff white gritty marly clay. The strata is practically horizontal, as far as I could judge.

The track was very fair, passing over gentle slopes, and winding round the heads of *burityzals* and wooded streams. At about six miles from Espirito Santo we crossed the Rio do Somninho, a stream of crystal water about thirty feet wide. It eventually joins the Rio Novo, when the united streams constitute the Rio do Somno, the bourne of my exploration.

We passed several herds of cattle belonging to my kind host José; they appeared fat and healthy. I must say that in all my peregrinations through Brazil I have never seen a district so admirably adapted for cattle-raising, for although the soil of the hills is almost all sandy, with a subsoil of clay upon rocks, yet the grass appears fresh and vigorous where it has been subjected to the annual burnings, and the best proof of its good qualities is the excellent condition of the cattle. Another advantage that this district possesses is that there is scarcely a square mile that is not watered by a running stream, or moistened by the springs of marshes, and the numerous strips of forests in the larger valleys indicate a soil good enough for any agricultural produce, as the luxuriant *roças* of José testify.

These belts of forests are wonderfully beautiful, for they contain many of the most delicate vegetable productions of the country, such a variety of palms, such grand tree-ferns, such festoons and hanging lines of flowers, like the *maracaja* or indigenous passion-flower, many varieties of convolvuli, and many species of flowers that I am utterly ignorant of; and the parasites, bromelias, the brilliantly-coloured wild pine-apples (*gravatas*), many varieties of variegated coloured leaf plants, splendid arums, and the great lobated leaves of the grand vine *Monstera deliciosa*, with its dropping lines of pendent aerial roots.. There is, moreover, an absence of rotting vegetation and of thick underwood, no faint malarious smells, no mosquitos or insect pests of any kind. The very swamps themselves are perfectly healthy, for they are unlike the marshes of the São Francisco, created by the overflow of a river, and then left to stagnate. Here they are caused by perpetually running springs of water, and are, moreover, freely exposed to the fresh breezes that continually and uninterruptedly sweep over these exposed hills and wide valleys. Truly it is a lovely country, and were it not so far away from the outer world, it would be a grand place for cattle-breeding and for immigration; as it is, so it will remain for probably many generations to come, until the United States become overpopulated, and perhaps the interior of Africa is all colonized, and a railway reaches this fair and beautiful land.

April 20.—Arrived at the little isolated hamlet of Espirito Santo, consisting of some twenty wattle and dab huts situated amidst a luxuriant vegetation of fine trees and thick bush.

Senhor José rode to the open door of a small house, where a shoemaker was cutting up the tanned skin of a huge *Sucurihu* or *Sucuriuba* boa. He laid down his work as his friend José approached, and saluted him with,—

"*Como tem passado compadre, é a comadre, é os meninos?*" ("How have you fared gossip, and the old lady, and the boys?")

When we entered the house I noticed with surprise the magnitude of the snake-skin that was being made into riding-boots, and expressed a desire to purchase it.

"This is nothing, it is only a baby," the shoemaker observed in reply to my expressions of wonder.

Yet tanned as it was, and necessarily much shrunk from its original dimensions, it measured three feet one inch wide, that would represent a diameter of say about a foot, and what was left of it measured nineteen feet six inches in length, but considerable pieces had already been cut off from each end. The shoemaker assured me that it was formerly twenty-five feet six inches long, and he confirmed the assertions made by Senhor José of the enormous size that these boas occasionally attain,[1] he readily sold me the remains of the skin for two milreis.

I obtained the use of a small empty hut, very smoky and smelly, where we remained the night and took away with us on the next morning a good supply of *chigoes* or jiggers,[2] that put a stop to all river bathing for a day or two, unless in unavoidable river crossings.[3]

Our arrival had created an evident sensation in the village; first all the boys and girls came running along, then sleepy yawning men followed lazily, women left off spinning cotton, or ceased to search each other's habitat of the "pulex capital." The whole village, all *compadres* or *comadres* of José, soon surrounded us, and brown grimy hands were stretched out for a limp handshake, not a grip or a squeeze, for the cold damp hands just flabbily touch one like a contact with a frog, or the fin of a fish; but I was short of provisions and had to be chummy. I chummed accordingly with grand results, for dried beef, fowls, *toucinho*, *farinha*, vegetables, eggs, and honey were plentifully supplied, and many of them were offered as presents.

The village is almost a self-supporting community, for very little is imported from the outer world, and nothing whatever exported. It is quite without any legal or police authorities, and the people govern themselves, a little *imperium in imperio*, yet the shoemaker told me that rarely any disturbances occur, and the people are peaceful and quiet,

---

[1] This great boa is variously known to naturalists as the *Eunectes murinus*; the *boa anaconda* of Daudin; the *boa murina* of Mart. It is the *culebra d'agua* of the Orinoco, and the *cobra de viado* of Pernambuco. Its Indian name expresses a roaring beast, owing to its sibilant powers. The word is composed of "*sucu*," a beast, and "*curu*," a snorter or roarer.

[2] *Pulex penetrans*.

[3] It is a common practice all over Brazil to fill the orifice made in the skin by the larvæ of these insects with limewash, to cause it to dry and heal, for if the wound is wetted, erysipelas or disorders of the skin will most probably ensue.

although there are one or two criminals amongst them who are "wanted" elsewhere.

As soon as the first flush of the excitement of our arrival was over, the villagers speedily relapsed into their ordinary semi-somnolent state, and returned each one to his or her hut, where they were soon afterwards seen recumbent in hammocks or on grass mats, in attitudes expressive of complete prostration. Probably, as slumber occupies so large a portion of their time, it leaves them few opportunities for quarrelling, even if energy necessary for such exertion was not wanting. The contrast between my stalwart friend José, his tall sons, and these limp boneless villagers, was very striking, and only shows that this climate is not necessarily debilitating to any one possessed of the most ordinary quantum of determination and moral strength of mind.

On observing a considerable preponderance of the numbers of women over the males, and remarking upon it, I learned that a considerable number of men had gone to some districts in the neighbourhood of Natividade, near the shores of the upper Tocantins, where a new discovery had been made of considerable deposits of alluvial gold. I could learn no more except that there was *muito ouro* (lots of gold); but the unusual fact of these sleepy people developing such unexpected energy and enterprise in making a mild "rush" for it, should indicate a certain amount of truth in the story.

This Natividade is one of the centres of the old mining operations of the early Portuguese colonists, a race of adventurous spirits who spread themselves over Minas Geraes, Goyaz, and Matto Grosso, in search of gold, like a swarm of ants. Gardner passed through Natividade in 1838, and describes in his book the even then terribly decadent state of the old town, and the vestiges of great alluvial washings long since abandoned. Probably the district would well repay prospecting by a mining expert, for although the old miners did their work effectually, they rarely attempted in those dark ages to wrestle with obstacles that can now be easily combated with the skill and appliances of the present day.

The next morning, José and his sons returned to their home in the wilderness, and we proceeded on our way.

We travelled twenty miles this day, arriving in the afternoon at a fazenda known as Boa Esperanza.[1] The way was full of difficulties, for several streams and many marshy valleys had to be passed. In some of the bogs the animals would sink almost to their girths, and in their struggles would often land their packs or their rider in the mud of the quagmires. No damage however occurred, and loud laughs and much joking saluted the luckless wight as he emerged all plastered with mud, or from a ducking in the water of the bogs. One stream flowing from some flat-topped hills on our left, gave us considerable trouble, for the water was deep and the current strong: no canoe was near nor any materials at hand for constructing a raft; the animals were swum across, and the baggage carried over in many trips on a rough litter borne on the heads of four men, for the water in some places reached their chins, and it required their united strength and very great exertion to keep their legs under their burden.

Boa Esperanza, the fazenda of the Senhor Capitão Fortunato d'Oliveira Mascarenhas, is quite a large establishment for these wilds, and very novel in its appearance, for all the several buildings were quite new and looked fresh and bright, and the materials used in the construction, the light yellow-ochre-coloured sticks of *pindahybas* and the dark bronze-green leaves of *piassava* palms, that served as thatch for the roof, and plaited, as a covering to the walls, created a most pleasant appearance, and harmonized with the surrounding landscape of green rolling hills, here and there dotted with groves of *buritys*, and the always beautiful thickets of *pindahybas*. Not a nail, a squared timber, a particle of clay, or a cord was

[1] Good hope.

used in any part of the structures, everything was provided by the produce of the woods.

The *capitão*, a hearty jovial well-built handsome white man, about sixty years old, received me with a bluff loud-voiced cheery welcome, that made one feel at once like an old acquaintance. After seeing the baggage stored in a rancho he had built expressly for the use of passing travellers, and the animals duly attended to, he showed me over his establishment. He must certainly be a hard-working fellow, for he had only settled in this district within the past twelve-month, and had certainly done wonders in this time. He had built a large and commodious hut, store-houses, slaves' quarters, and other outbuildings, put up a rough cane-mill, a still, fenced in a large curral for cattle and cleared a large tract of ground that showed luxuriant crops of miscellaneous produce. His household comprised his wife, two daughters, three adult sons, and three adult negro slaves, who appeared well treated and happy in their fate.

He expressed himself quite contented with the prospects of his enterprise, and hoped to be very successful; he can find a fair market for his cattle in Piauhy at 3*l*. a head, a low price certainly, but he appeared to consider it remunerative.

On retiring for the night to my quarters in a little room in the travellers' rancho, there appeared a pest that I had little calculated upon meeting in such a place; the light had not been long extinguished before strange rustling sounds were heard amidst the palm-leaves of the walls, and soon after it became evident that a considerable number of very respectably-sized insects were establishing a Newmarket on my rugs. On striking a light, to my great disgust, I perceived that the place was swarming with myriads of offensive-smelling *baratas* (huge cockroaches about two to two and a half inches long). It was raining heavily outside, and the men's quarters were also infested. Strong observations were freely bestowed upon the absent jovial Capitão, for we might have avoided such an infliction by occupying the tent, had we known of the prevalence of these repulsive insects, but seeing no other remedy, I rolled myself in my rug, and left the vile odorous insects to their own good will. In the morning, when I told the Capitão of the nuisance, he laughed heartily, and suggested that the taste of an Englishman must have been a great attraction to the *baratas*, for he had never known so few in his quarters; after all, he said, "*elles não fazem mal, são muito innocentes*" (they will not do any harm, they are very innocent). "Well! how about their *catinga?*" (odour). "Oh! one gets accustomed to that."

I found my baggage swarming with the disgusting insects, and it required several days before we could finally get the trunks and boxes free of them.

The Capitão, and a neighbour, a Tenente Militão (who had arrived during the previous evening, and who had been the prime mover in colonizing this Jalapão district), accompanied us a part of the way to show the road to the Riberão, the first of another series of troublesome streams that we had to cross this day, where there was no remedy but to unpack everything, swim the animals, and send one's clothes and all the baggage across on the men's heads, and swim across ourselves. But these Goyanno rivers, especially of these *geraes*, are reputed to be so well provided with strange and venomous tenants, that one cannot help a certain feeling of qualmishness in taking a header, for there are *jacarés* (alligators), electric eels, *piranhas* (a very ferocious but small fish), and finally, a certain *Aranha d'Agua* (literally water-spider), that I have been curious to see, but had hitherto failed; according to the descriptions, it is a species of sting-ray, that frequents the river-bottoms near the shore, and any one stepping upon it, treads upon a long spine that projects several inches from near the end of its tail, the wound causes great agony and often partial paralysis of the leg. I was much cautioned against it by the Tenente.

Three more similar portages we had to make on other

minor streams, and at twelve miles out the tracks led us again across the Somninho, there a considerable flooded stream about 120 feet in width. The water rushed along at a good pace where, at this the best fording-place, the depth was too great for the men to wade across. As it was yet early, it was determined to reach the other side that day, as Antonio thought we might make a raft and ferry over; accordingly the baggage was piled on the ground, and the men sent off with the animals to collect bundles of the fallen dry fronds of the *buritys* in any burityzals of the neighbourhood. In an hour they returned with the animals well loaded, and then set to work to construct a raft; the long stalks, six to eight feet long, exceedingly light and buoyant, were tied with *cipós* or vines into bundles about a foot in diameter, some half dozen of the bundles were laid together and lashed between some stout saplings, another layer of bundles was then placed transversely upon and well secured to the first, and the raft was complete: it was then duly launched and loaded with the baggage, and two men swam off with it; the current carried them some 600 feet down-stream before they could gain the opposite shore, covered with dense bushes and trees, where they had to hew a pathway through the bushes with their knives. After the baggage was safely landed, the heavy raft had to be dragged up-stream so as to fetch the landing-place again; this operation had to be repeated many times, then the animals were swum across, two of them being nearly carried down-stream to some rapids not far distant, and were only saved by sheer good-luck, in getting entangled in some projecting roots.

The sun was low before the tedious operation was completed, black clouds were gathering, thunder muttering, and the air was close and sultry, all indications of a coming bad night. We had so far been favoured with fine weather, that a continuance of such luck could not be expected, especially as April is a showery time, and the next month usually brings very heavy rains.

The tent was unpacked, trenches dug around it, and all made snug for the night. The poor tent, so rarely used, had often been the subject of much grumbling by Joaquim, who said that its weight was ruining his animals; but that night when the rain came down in torrents, when the winds howled and blew in fierce gusts, the thunder crashed and the lightning flashed, as it only does in the tropics, when withal the tent stood firm and we were all dry and snug within its welcome shelter; then no one complained of the much maligned tent that night.

The next morning appeared dark with black clouds, and the ground wet and soddened with yet heavy rain; the change, after such a continuance of brilliant mornings as we had experienced for so long, was dreary enough, and the difficulty of making a fire and preparing breakfast produced many a *diabo de chuva* from Bob, but the sight of the then much more flooded Somninho, a roaring impassable stream, made me congratulate myself that I had crossed it the previous day.

About 10 a.m. the rain ceased, and we soon after got under way, but only to go little more than a mile before we came across another turbulent stream, the Riberão do Disabuso, wide and shallow, but flowing swiftly over masses of rocks.

Bob stripped, and entered the river to try the ford; after a little wading he suddenly sank into a hole and was carried off his feet, and to our horror, was swept away down the stream amongst the jagged boulders, and soon disappeared out of sight around a bend of the river. We rushed down the riverside to render any possible help, but the banks were so wooded that we could not easily get near the water; we scrambled through the bushes, trees, and vines, and finally reached the top of the bank where, on looking eagerly down the stream, I was pleased to see my old follower seated on a rock and rubbing his shoulder. In reply to our shouts, he stood up and waved his hand, jumped into the water again, reached the opposite bank, and soon was seen running along, laughing heartily and showing his filed white teeth, as though it had been all a good joke. Fortunately for him he had been accustomed to rivers from a child, having been brought up on the banks of the Abacté, in Minas Geraes, where he worked as a *garimpeiro* [5] and diver.

He collected a quantity of stout *cipós* from a thicket hard by (he had taken his knife with him, slung to his waist by a string), and with these he formed a long strong rope, one end he secured to a tree on the bank, and then he entered the water with the coil, gradually uncoiling it as he proceeded; the water was not above his waist the greater part of the width of the stream until he neared the deep hole near our side, where he cautiously proceeded up-stream and found a shallower passage, and finally arrived in safety amongst us. His shoulder was bleeding and much contused, and he was altogether much bruised and knocked about, but not seriously hurt. A well-earned extra ration of *cachaça*, applied inwardly and externally, considerably soothed his ruffled feelings. With much trouble and exertion, the baggage was transported, but the animals gave much trouble; one was taken across at a time, two men assisting each one by holding well on to the halters. The *cipó* rope greatly facilitated the process, in fact it could not have been done without, so strong was the current.

Several other minor streams had to be passed further on with more or less difficulty, and late in the afternoon we left the grassy undulating country we had been so long accustomed to, and entered on rapidly rising and rugged rocky ground, covered with the gnarled trees and bush of cerrados, the approach to two lofty flat-topped hills about three miles apart, separated by a wide deep wooded defile, whose slopes were scattered with boulders large and small.

The hill on the right is known as the Morro do Celeste, that on our left as the Morro do Boté, or Morro do Munducuru, as it is variously termed; both hills are rich in colour, and

[5] A man employed in searching for diamonds.

fringed on their summits with bushes; a deep Indian red is the prevailing colour of the precipitous sides, rugged and worn into deep cavities, pinnacles, turrets, and buttresses.

The Morro do Boté is apparently so named from a rough resemblance to a boat turned bottom upwards. Near its southern extremity, a huge crevice appears like a great slit, the end that is thus divided heels over very much out of the perpendicular, and ready at any moment to form a great landslip.

The Morro do Bote or Munducuru.

It struck me at once that these hills are probably the vestiges of the high table-lands that once extended, (in continuation of the Chapada da Mangabeira,) over the whole of this valley of the Tocantins, and that the pending landslip of the Morro do Boté is an example of the vast denudation that has taken place, and is still going on.

The Somninho passes about two miles to the south of the hill in a deep valley, beyond which appear other flat-topped hills.

The road passes close to the eastern extremity of the Morro do Boté, where the grand perpendicular walls, like monstrous cliffs, rear up 500 or 600 feet above us, appearing ready to fall and crush us pigmies with thousands of tons of the rocks that look so hoary and weather-beaten, and showing an infinitude of colours all darkened with the effects of time, except in a few places where small slips have recently occurred, there the colours are lighter, and the divisions of strata are clearly defined. The lower part forms a natural slope of sand, rocks, and clay, covered with giant cacti, gnarled trees, dwarf bushes, and huge masses of stones. Some of the rocks that so freely cumber the surface of the ground are coarse granulated sandstones, white red and brown, showing occasionally veins of white quartz; amongst others are a few pieces of amygdaloid rocks, and masses of conglomerate or pudding stones.

After passing these venerable monuments of a primitive age, the track becomes a most diabolical bit of road, springs everywhere ooze from the ground, and form deep little valleys of bogs between ridges of rocks and loose stones, thickly overgrown with tall blue cacti, thorny bramble, and gnarled trees; we slipped down the slopes, got stuck in the morasses, scrambled up the ridges, and rolled gaily amidst the scattered rocks like a ship at sea, and faces and clothes were scratched and torn by the innumerable spines and thorns that so freely crowd the narrow path.

I gave up the attempt to ride at last, and went on on foot ahead, cutting a staff on the way to help a jump over many pools of stagnant water. Some distance ahead of the troop, as I was walking slowly down a slippery descent of mossy rocks and clay, a movement amidst the grass by the side of me attracted my attention, and on stopping a moment, the whirr of a rattle-snake's rattle kindly informed me of its proximity. I remained quiet, and the *bixo* slowly emerged on to the open track, when I administered with my staff, what one of my old comrades, would, under the circumstances have called a "slomicking oncer," and then carried away the rattle of nine rings as a trophy.

About half an hour afterwards, another adventure occurred. I had considerably outstripped the troop, and had passed the rugged broken ground, and was slowly ascending the slope of a grassy glade surrounded by trees: a stiff breeze was blowing towards me, and making the trees and leaves rustle briskly. As I topped the slight eminence, I was brought suddenly face to face with a huge stag, at the distance of about twenty paces, so unexpectedly that we were probably equally astonished; the animal gave a start and a bound, and then stood still, startled, yet looking at me apparently undecided whether to charge or retreat. I had my heavy revolver ready immediately, and at the first shot I wounded him, he stumbled for a moment and then lowered his splendid antlers for a charge, but a second and a third shot brought him effectually to the ground. It is not the first time that my revolver has killed a deer, but I certainly did not expect to do so in these districts, where all game must necessarily be very wild. The men behind, on hearing the shots, came up at a run, and told me that the stag is known as the *Sussuapara*, "*um bixo brabo é bixo atôa*" (a fierce and useless animal), and that its flesh is perfectly unpalatable on account of its strong *catinga*. I carried away its six-pronged antlers, that measured thirty inches from tip to tip, and about thirty-six inches in length. The animal stood four feet high from its haunch to the ground, and measured four feet six inches from muzzle to tail, its body was covered with long, coarse, tawny hair; it is a strongly built animal, of an exceedingly different type to the ordinary small gazelle-like deer one usually meets with in Brazil, and is the largest known species of the deer family on the South American continent.

Quite late in the afternoon, near the woods of a shallow depression of the land known as Brejo do Celeste, we met a party of mounted travellers, consisting of an elderly white man, two younger men and three females, with several black attendants on foot driving pack animals. As strangers on the road are rarely seen in these districts, the elderly man halted and inquired who we were, and whither bound; on my replying to Porto Franco, he informed me that he was the proprietor of that fazenda, a Senhor Capitão João Rodrigues de Nogueira,[6] and on his way to Piauhy with part of his family. I briefly acquainted him with the nature of my business, and he was good enough to write a hurried note to his sons at Porto Franco, to give me every attention and help. As it was getting late, and we were about to encamp, I offered the accommodation of my tent, but he declined it, as he hoped to reach a small farm near; we parted with mutual wishes for *Boa viagem* (a good journey, and God accompany you, and God permit that you may be fortunate).

Certainly these Geralistas of Jalapão are extremely kind to me, and as a stranger and a traveller I cannot but help feeling a strong sense of gratitude to them for their frank hospitality and an appreciation of their kindly natures.

We pitched camp there and raised the tent; the night passed by quietly, but with several showers of rain.

After leaving the Brejo do Celeste we struck across a comparatively flat stretch of barren Geraes, or *campos*, for about eight miles of deep sandy soil, dotted with sparse dwarf vegetation, such as scattered tufts of grass, dwarf *piassaba* palms, cactus, and a few bushes. At the end of these eight miles there is a sharp descent to a deep wide valley, known as *O baixão* (the great lowland), where we found the first habitation since leaving Boa Esperança, consisting of a grass hut and a small *roça*, owned by a negro and his family, who regaled us with milk and roasted *aipim*.

A slight ascent, and a ride of four miles over another flat campos, brought us to the edge of the highlands that enclose the great hollow wherein is situated Porto Franco. We descended, or rather scrambled down the precipitous slopes of

[6] Captain John Roderick of Walnut-tree.

the table-land by a rough path, steep and stony, and finally arrived at our destination.

Like all the other farms of Jalapão, the fazenda do Porto Franco is also quite a modern place, but rather substantially constructed, with adobe walls and tiled roofs, and a broad open verandah that extends along the front of the residence.

The captain must be well-to-do, for the numerous scattered huts, small outhouses and barns, the large cattle currals, and a goodly number of retainers indicated quite a large establishment; the wonder is, how profitable results can be obtained by any means of cattle-breeding or farming, so far from a market, and that of Piauhy only a poor and limited one.

A hearty welcome was bestowed upon us, as all strangers would similarly receive at this lonely place, for there are no more habitations between it and the banks of the Tocantins, and a passing stranger must really be a godsend. Doubtless the tenants have been from an early age accustomed to such solitudes, yet, even so, a fresh face must be as grateful a sight to them as it was to Robinson Crusoe.

With a sigh of relief I dismounted for the last time from the mule that had carried me so far, and so well, for another chapter of my travels and experiences had ended, as there terminated for a time my journeys by land.

The room I was shown into was very plain and homely, very homely indeed; bare earthen walls and floor, bare benches and bare tables, and not by any means a superabundance of the latter two items. The tenants were of varying tones of brown and "yaller," and their faces and cotton clothes would have been all the better for a good wash; yet, after their fashion, they were extremely kind, and showed a thorough goodwill to provide creature-comforts. A very smutty black girl from the kitchen brought coffee, a *moleque* brought sugar-cane chopped into conveniently eatable pieces, mine host produced his best *restillo*, with sugar and lemons and water.

But despite the goodwill of my friends, I was not happy

with the prospect of a day or two of delay, in making preparations for the journey down the river. I had then been so long on my peregrinations, that occasionally the weariness and monotony of the life produced an intense craving to get back again to the outer world, and at least hear what was there going on and making its history, for I had been without any European news or letters for four months. Captain Burton, in the *early* part of his journeys in Brazil, expatiates on the glories of solitude, and says, "How unhappy is the traveller, who, like St. Hilaire, is ever bemoaning the want of 'society,' of conversation; and who, 'reduced to the society of his plants,' consoles himself only by hoping to see the end of his journey! '*Une monotonie sans égale, une solitude profonde; rien qui pût me distraire un instant de mon ennui.*' This, too, from a naturalist. . . . '*Je finis par me désespérer à force d'ennui, et je ne pus m'empêcher de maudire les voyages.*' One understands the portrait which he draws of himself, veiled, with parasol to ward off the sun, and a twig to switch away the ticks. It suggests a scientific Mr. Ledbury." As my defective nature would not permit me to appreciate the captain's love of solitude, and not possessing the advantage of the monsieur's scientific lore, my long sojourn amongst the Matutos and *Sertanejos* began to produce its effects. It had lasted so long that I could heartily sympathize with the monsieur's want of a sight of civilized humanity, even with all its defects and conventionalities. Even the captain, at the termination of his journey, breathed a gentle sigh of relief, and said, "My task is done. I won its reward, and the strength passed away from me."

I passed a day at Porto Franco, verily one of the dullest corners of God's earth, and to which, in comparison, an English country village on a rainy day is a place of wild excitement. It rained a good Brazilian rain, but I made a few excursions on foot in the neighbourhood, and put my notes in order; that enabled me to get through the time, otherwise a few days' life there would probably have reduced one to a state of imbecility, or to the normal quiescent state of the country people.

It is probably a merciful dispensation of Providence, that these people do develop such a power of sleeping to fill up the void of doing nothing. Mine hosts were uneducated untravelled country folk, kind affable and exceedingly hospitable certainly, but an hour's conversation soon exhausts their little stock of information, and when they weary of pumping me, their awful yawns express their inanition, and a desire to *descansar* (rest a little) in their hammocks. Their occupations are those connected with stock-raising (about 2000 head of cattle belong to the fazenda), and in cultivating a small plot of ground to supply their principal provisions. Every year, the cattle are collected, and the calves and heifers branded with the stamp of the fazenda, a certain number of bullocks are driven to the market-towns of Piauhy, 200 or 500 miles away, where they only realize 3*l*. or 4*l*. per head. A certain number are also slaughtered, and the meat, made into dried beef, is sent with the hides, down the Rio do Somno on a *burity* raft, to Pedro Affonso, a small village on the Tocantins, at the mouth of the first-named river, where they are sold to the traders descending the Tocantins to Para. The raft is abandoned on reaching its destination, and the men return by land. The two men who undertake these journeys I have engaged to take me down the river.

In the neighbourhood there is little to interest one. The land is low and forms a considerable hollow in the surrounding higher lands that enclose it with sharp precipitous slopes. The soil is a light sandy loam, thinly covered with tufts of grass, small bushes, dwarf palms, ground cacti (*cabeça de frade*), and occasionally a few scattered clumps of woods or a grove of *buritis*. It is about 400 feet below the valley of the source of the Sapão, and is less exposed to the fresh breezes that sweep those highlands so uninterruptedly, and no longer is experienced the wonderfully exhilarating atmosphere peculiar to those districts.

The *roça* of the fazenda, is situated in a clearing of the woods on the borders of the river, about a mile away. There, cotton, coffee, sugar-cane, beans, mandioca, castor-plant, maize, yams, sweet potatoes, all grow in great luxuriance, but in the wildest confusion, a perfect wilderness, for little more is done than to roughly clear the ground, burn the felled trees and bushes, and plant in the rudest form the various seeds and cuttings of the different vegetables that are left undisturbed until they mature. The charred blackened stumps, the scattered boulders of stone, the wild extraneous growth of weeds (*samambaia* the Brazilian bracken, canebrake, brambles and grasses), that grow everywhere amidst the vegetables, and the roughly-constructed fences, and the surrounding tangled woods, present an aspect of peculiar dreariness, neglect, and untidy cultivation ; just so much is done as is only absolutely necessary and no more. But in such wild *roças*, and in the enclosing forest, there is plenty of interesting matter for the botanist, the naturalist, and the entomologist, in the marvellous growth of a varied vegetation, in the many birds, butterflies, and beetles, and the capyvaras, tapirs, cotias, pacas and coatis that create such great depredations, and destroy far more than they consume, a source of perpetual worry to the fazendeiro.

Although there are some dozen men on the farm, sons, or slaves, of the Capitão, their labour is badly and ineffectively utilized. During my stay, I did not see any one man do a fair day's work ; the slaves do pretty much as they like, they do not roll in the lap of luxury, certainly, but they are leniently, even kindly treated, and many a poor labourer at home would envy their lot. The whitey-brown and black women appear to do the most work, in cleaning by hand and spinning cotton, in weaving a rough cloth, in pounding maize or castor beans, or making farinha or *rapadura*, and even work in the fields when necessary.

The climate of this Jalapão district is certainly healthy, it is dry and hot on the plateaus and hills, but always tempered with cool fresh breezes; in the low wooded valleys the heat is naturally more humid. The temperature ranges during the year from 76° to 88° in the daytime, and from 70° to 78° at night. I have not of course been able to verify this personally, but from what I have noticed, and from information received, I calculate these are the approximate ranges. There are no endemic fevers or diseases, *sezoēs* and *maletas*, that is, remittent and intermittent fevers, very rarely occur. There are comparatively no mosquitos, carrapatos, sand-flies, nor other insect pests, except in the *roças* and woods, where a few ants, mosquitos and carrapatos are occasionally met with.

I am told, however, that jaguars and the great anacondas, (*sucurihus*) are the causes of considerable loss amongst the cattle, and the hunting of these destroyers, and of the deer and *perdiz* (partridges) that abound in these districts, forms the chief recreation and change in the monotonous existence of these people.

The rainy months are October, November, December, January, February, and May; April is showery, March, June, July, August, and September are dry.

Salt is the great want of these inland districts, it has to be brought from the Rio São Francisco through Piauhy, or from the coast, and is naturally exceedingly expensive, and forms the chief item of expense on the cattle-farms. It is the great necessity and article of traffic all over the inhabited interior of Brazil. The Don Pedro II. Railway alone carries yearly into the interior about 19,000 tons.

Although this Jalapão is so very thinly inhabited, and in spite of the many stories and rumours I had heard to the contrary, I could glean no evidence of the existence of the aborigines in a wild state in its neighbourhood; such as there are, are *aldeado* or settled in villages, under the care of Italian missionary monks, and designated as *indios mansos*[7] in contradistinction to *indios brabos*.[8] There is a village of the Coroado

[7] Tame Indians   [8] Wild Indians.

on the borders of the Manoel Alves Pequeno, about 100 miles to the north west, another of Caraújos near the source of the Manoel Alves Grande, about sixty miles to the north, and another of Cherentes on the Rio Ipíâbánha, seventy miles to the south of the mouth of the Rio do Somno.

On the morning of the second day my crew of two men, Jacinto and Jesuino, arrived, and set about collecting materials for constructing a raft; on the same day my troop and followers, José Grosso, Antonio and Roberto, with the two mules of Snr. José, returned by the Sapão, which will soon be utilized as a short cut from Santa Rita to these districts, but Rodrigues had not recovered from his numerous scares, and preferred to return to the Barra do Rio Grande by a long *détour* through the inhabited districts of Parnagua in Piauhy, rather than by the more direct route down the Sapão. He said, "No, sir! I do not want to know any more of that wild country, not for anything, *Deos* deliver me. In a white folk's land, yes sirree, I am disposed to travel where you will, but not in those wilds of the *diabo*." Poor Rodrigues, he was an honest straightforward fellow, but an arrant coward. Although my contract with him was to take me on to Carolina on the Tocantins for a stipulated sum, this sum I now paid him, $350,000 (say 35*l*.), with a gratu'ty of another $50,000, that after all was a low price for the use and services of three men and seven mules, for a journey of 460 miles, (or rather 500, including *détours*), that occupied two months, besides the time expended in returning; for allowing one milreis (two shillings) per day for each man and one for each animal, it would amount to $500,000. In Minas Geraes five and even sometimes ten milreis per day is the hire of an ordinary mule.

My especial attendant, Bob, remained with me, and agreed to accompany me to the coast. I can only say that I parted with my other followers with regret, for never could a traveller desire a set of men more patient in all trials and difficulties, more willing, and obliging, and respectful, than these good fellows. Rodrigues' timidity was a weakness, but it only created a laugh at his expense.

The two new raftmen, (*balseiros*), were two young men, about twenty-five years of age, over six feet in height, broad-shouldered and deep-chested powerful fellows, their colour a clear dark olive, their hair, long black and slightly curly, their faces were hairless; and their features sharp and prominent, and different both to the negro, or the common South American Indian type. They set about their work in a quiet methodical sort of way, were very quiet in their manner, and somewhat disposed to surliness.

The raft was finally constructed and ready; but on going aboard the clumsy heavy craft, it oscillated considerably with my weight, and I began to doubt what it would do under the weight of crew and cargo, there was much fear that Plimsoll's load-line would disappear. To test its stability, all the baggage and provisions were stowed aboard, and then the crew were called to make a trial trip. When all were aboard, its surface was level with the water, and it rolled very unpleasantly with our movements; however, we poled off for the trial, but a few yards were sufficient to prove its crankiness, even Jacinto, who had hitherto warranted its powers of carrying, called out, " Jesuino! Jesuino! Let's get back at once! I can do nothing with this *bixo*. I won't go in it, not for anything." After a sharp struggle with the current we reached the shore again.

The raft had to be dismantled, and reconstructed with another layer of bundles of *burity* leaf-stems, that will make the third. There was no going away that day, as horses had to be arranged to go a few miles to fetch the extra leaf-stems required. The men worked well, and late in the evening another larger raft (eight feet by twelve) was finished, and in the morning when we loaded it with cargo and crew it was fairly steady.

A kind of gipsy tent (five feet by seven feet) was then made, by bending into a series of semi-circular arches a number of

Pindahiba sticks, secured in position by horizontal rows of bamboos, one foot apart, the whole was then thatched with palm-leaves, and finally covered with dried raw hides: this shelter formed my home for several days. The steering capacities of the craft were of course *nil*, and although there were many awkward bits of water before us, the guidance of the cumbersome craft must depend upon the strength and activity of the polemen.

The worst place we shall have to face is the *Apertada Hora* (the narrowed hour, i.e. an hour of danger), where, at this season of the year, the prospects of a successful, or a disastrous passage, are about equal. This rapid, I am told, rushes with great force over and amongst innumerable rocks, between shoreless walls of perpendicular cliffs: when the river is flooded, the rocks are submerged, and when the water is low they are high above the current, and in either case the descent can be effected with comparative safety, but when the river is only half-flooded, the danger is very great, and the rapid well-nigh impassable, owing to the absence of any defined channel, and the difficulty of discerning the position of the rocks. As the river may be in any one of these conditions when we face the *Apertada Hora*, the meanwhile, will be a rather anxious time until we are out of the peril.

Departure from Porto Franco, on the Rio do Somno, Goyaz.

CHAPTER XI.

FROM PORTO FRANCO DOWN THE RIO DO SOMNO TO THE TOCANTINS.

Adeos to Porto Franco—On the Rio do Somno—Our first pancada—Camp ashore—Indian cookery—A perilous prospect—A gusty evening—A jaguar's roar—Morning on the river—The banks of the Somno—Curious bees'-nest—Birds and animals of the river-side—Pancadas—Feroz, and his swimming powers—A wild cat, shot—Cooking under difficulties—A rough night—Bad prospects—Approach to the rapids—Shooting the rapids of "O Funil"—Imprisoned in the valley of the river—Grand scenery—Borne onwards in a rush of waters—A sudden and terrible spectacle—In the vortex of the Apertada Hora—A few breathless moments—On the rocks—A wild struggle—A narrow escape—Disappearance of the river—An unexpected outlet—Splendid behaviour of the crew—Loss and damage—A solitude—An intersecting mountain range—An uncomfortable night—Signs of diamonds—Peccaries again—A cautious advance in the woods—Sent up a tree—Skirmishing—Pork for dinner—Patience and obedience of Feroz—The wild banana—Monkeys—Life on the Somno—Bob's damp bed—A hot day—A squalid farm—The Rio Perdido—The shores filled with animal life—The lower Somno—Reach the Tocantins.

April 25.—When ready for an early start in the morning, the crew recollected that they had to wash their clothes, and so delayed the departure for an hour. At last all was ready, and the people of the fazenda, Senhor Joaquim, and the other sons of Capitão Rodrigues, a Senhor Manoel da Fonseca Galvao, and the men, women, and children of the farm, lined the banks and cheered us heartily ; for a *balsa* voyage down the Somno, was an event in their uneventful lives, and doubly so when made by a stranger.

We pole out into the current and soon glide away from the little crowd on the bank, who send us cheer after cheer, and their shouts of " *Boa viagem*," and " *Adeos! até a volta !* " or " *até outra vista !* " (Good-bye ! until you return ! or, we see you again !) grow fainter and fainter as we drift onwards and disappear round a bend of the river. Good-bye, my friends, you have treated the *estrangeiro* with your rough frank hospitality, and although you may be careless and indolent, you are certainly kind and genuine ; your motto should be " sufficient for the day are the necessities thereof."

Once again on a river, gliding softly over the gently-rippling waters, for the raft is poled out to the middle of the stream, and we drift along at about two or three miles per hour.

The Somno, is here not generally more than 240 or 300 feet wide, but in some of the bends it widens out to 350 to 400 feet. Its depth is very variable ; in some places it is twenty feet, in others only five or six feet. The water is beautifully clear and transparent, and the scenery of the banks is inexpressibly charming. In many places they rise up into lofty many-coloured cliffs of sandstone, topped with forest and veiled with trailing flowering vines. In other places, the campos extends to ruddy banks and white sandy shores, in long slopes of greensward. In the shadowed pools of water at the bends, the lovely banks are mirrored as in a looking-glass.

A few miles below Porto Franco we passed our first *pancada*, (as a rush of water over the shallows is locally termed,) where we sped along amidst the wavelets that made our craft dance again, and swept past black pointed rocks, cleverly avoided by the exertions of the men, who displayed great physical strength, cool nerve, and a rapid comprehension of the circumstances; they handled their long twenty-four feet poles like light fishing-rods, giving a thrust here, a thrust there at the rocks, and so avoided the Scyllas and Charybdis on either side, and gained the peaceful waters ahead. They were a few moments of mild excitement, just enough to make one's eyes sparkle, and cause one to hold well on to the roof of the state-room.

It is certainly a novel feeling after the late continuous daily journeys on mule-back, to find oneself dreamily reclining on the raft, dabbling in the rippling water, and watching the ever-changing banks flit by like the changes of a cosmorama; it is all so idle, and yet so pleasant; but there is quite enough occupation to watch the bearings of the course, calculate the distance, and sketch in the position of the many streams and rivulets, that join the river on either side, and also to sound the depth as we drift along.

We have to make an early halt, for the percussion-caps of our only gun have been left at Porto Franco, and Jacinto must return overland to fetch them.

We haul-to for the night in a snug little cove, by the side of a beach of silvery white sand. On the top of the bank, there is only the meagre vegetation of the campos, that stretches far away in great earth-waves of grass, dotted occasionally with a few gnarled distorted trees and a little dwarf bush. Some space is cleared in the grass, the heavy tent is with difficulty dragged up the bank and raised (for the afternoon shows signs of a dirty night); wood is collected, and a brisk fire made, and a plunge and swim in the clear waters of the stream is enjoyed, even with the chance of meeting *aranhas d'aqua*, electric eels, piranhas, alligators, and other *bixos*.

Afterwards, some fishing-tackle is prepared and baited, and a few excellent fish are soon caught, and then cooked by Jesuino in Indian fashion. A hole, some six inches deep, is scraped out in the sand, the fish are cleaned,[1] wrapped in the aromatic leaves of *sassafraz*,[2] placed in the hole, and covered with sand. A fire is then made above it, and the fish, fresh and delicate, are, like the Egyptians, left to "stew in their own juice," and right good is the result.

The clouds thicken and darken as night comes on apace, and soon great gusts of wind test the tent-pegs, then down comes the rain in sheets of water. The raft is well secured, and we adjourn to the hospitable, but bare shelter of the tent, its only appointments being a few hides laid on the ground, and a castor-oil lamp suspended to the tent-pole. As we sip our coffee and enjoy a whiff, Jesuino recounts some of the yarns of the early settlers, and thus an hour or two of the long evening is wiled away. A good deal of the chat turns upon the Apertada Hora rapids, and the prospects of its good or bad conditions, for Jesuino had always gone down the river in the rainy, or in the dry, season, and in the irregular weather of April, it is apparently a "toss up" whether we shall come to grief, or get through with even damage, but, as Jesuino put it, with the fatalism of a Turk, "*Se Deos quizer, escaparemos senão morreremos*" (If God wills it, we shall escape; if not, we shall die). That was a very dubious prospect, but I consoled myself by making due allowances for the proverbial Brazilian exaggeration of dangers.

Now, how the wind howls and shakes the tent, making the canvas flap with loud reports, and outside, where the rain has long since extinguished the fire, a dense blackness prevails, and the night is noisy with sounds of rustling leaves and creaking trunks and branches. Certainly the air of a picnic, with which we commenced the evening, is no more, and I find that without the usual daily exercise, the hide on the ground seems to discover more angles and corners than usual in one's body.

About ten o'clock we were awakened by a low growl

[1] The Indians do not previously clean the fish, but I thought it as well to do so.   [2] *Nectandra cymbarum*.

from Feroz. At first we heard nothing but the drip drip from the trees (for the storm had passed away); then was unmistakably heard the distant roar of a jaguar. Feroz growled again and made a bolt for the tent door, but was caught just in time and chained up, otherwise he would have gone boldly to the fight, and then there would have been an end to my dog. My revolver was my only fire-arm, as Jacinto had not yet returned with the percussion-caps, and I must confess that it is not pleasant to feel that only a fold of canvas shields one from a prowling jaguar, going about seeking whom he may devour. Happily, the next roars became more and more distant, and finally were heard no more, but the incident banished sleep, and made the night long and weary.[3] I finally left the woodeny hide, crept down to the raft and crawled into the less bone-searching box-bed.

In the early hours of morning, Jacinto arrived, and after another refreshing swim in the river, we got away by daybreak.

The soft tones of the dawn of a fine morning fell alike upon field and flood, and tinged all creation with its rosy hues. The richly-coloured banks glowed with the warm light, that made the dripping leaves of forest, the ferns and flowers of the shore all flash and sparkle like jewels. On the river, here and there, patches of rising vapour partly obscured its sheets of gleaming gold, until a gentle breeze carried away the mist in the faintest of clouds. The fish splashed in the smoking waters, gay blue-bronze kingfishers darted from their perches on the bleached skeleton trunks of stranded snags, white herons skimmed the waters with wide outstretched wing; clouds of noisy, chattering parroquets flew by, numerous small birds twittered and chirruped, and in the woods the roars of *guaribas* or howling monkeys echoed and re-echoed from cliff to cliff of the banks. It was a picture, that even in the absence of personal comfort, one could gaze upon

---

[3] This is the only occasion in all my journeys that was likely to be productive of a jaguar adventure.

with delight, and all nature seemed to welcome the rosy dawn and pure fresh air, after the boisterous darksome night.

The scenery of the banks is ever changing, for the country inland, (mainly campos,) is a series of undulations, the valleys terminate in wooded lowlands by the river-side, and the spurs, or ridges, form cliffs sixty to eighty feet high. These cliffs show an extremely picturesque and wonderfully diversified appearance. Often their perpendicular faces are covered with long hanging masses of flowering vines and creepers, and their clefts filled with masses of ferns and mosses, watered by the moisture of dropping water; sometimes streamlets form little jets of water, and fall in a sheet of sparkling spray from the tops of banks; at other times the cliffs present bare smooth surfaces of variously-coloured rocks, on which a very curious structure often attracted my attention: in a full view, it resembles a dark bullock's hide stretched and nailed to the wall of rock, averaging eight by six feet in length and width, sideways it appears inflated and distended, and culminates in a hanging point, or apex, near its lower side. These curious formations are the nests of the *shupé*, a bee that produces great quantities of excellent honey, but are terrible stingers, and from the positions the nests are in, half-way up the smooth surface of the rocks, are difficult of access, unless the gatherer is enveloped in leather, and lowered down by ropes from above, which is sometimes done.

Altogether, the Somno, is thus far, a beautiful stream in a lovely country and climate. As we drift along, we hear many a heavy body splash into the water, generally a *capy-vara*, and on one occasion sight a tapir, that disappears before we can get within range.

At mid-day, the mouth of the Riberão de Espingada is passed, a stream that flows from the highlands of the boundaries of Maranhão and Goyaz, about forty miles to the north-east. It is some 100 feet broad, is navigable for about twenty miles, and traverses a totally uninhabited country.

Beyond this stream, the right bank forms exceptionally

lofty cliffs, crowned with all the luxuriance of dense tropical vegetation, and few yards are passed, but we hear the music of dropping water trickling down the rocky sandstone cliffs, amid such varieties and forms of vegetation, delicate ferns and flowers below, giant trees above, wreathed in festoons of vines, a veritable paradise of beauty, all mirrored in the clear waters below. The south bank is much lower, and capped only by the dwarfed vegetation of the adjoining campos; here we sighted the second tapir seen that day, and I got a shot, but the *bixo* treated the small grains of lead with the supremest contempt, and leisurely soused into the water; later on I bagged a fine *motum*,[4] or *currasow*, perched on some branches overhanging the water. There was a flock of some seven or eight on the boughs, but this one fine handsome bird was a prize in itself, for it is as large and heavy as a small turkey, and its flesh is quite as delicate and nutritious. The bird is well-known, and its description is needless, beyond mentioning that its Indian name, *motum*,[5] is an exact imitation of the hooting sounds it makes. These birds are easily tamed, and readily associate with poultry in Brazil, but attempts to breed them in England have hitherto not met with success.

During the course of the day we safely passed several *pancadas*, where there ensued much shouting, and rapid handling of poles to sheer off, here and there, from rocks. These little spurts were thorough awakeners, or rather "eye-openers," and a rare sight in this land of lethargy, to see the way the men's eyes dilate and flash with the excitement, and hear their shouts echo above the roar of water; and see how their splendid muscles move in their powerful arms, chests and shoulders, with their violent exertion; for these cumbersome rafts cannot be steered like a canoe, we drift almost where the current wills, and when it bears us on towards a rock

---

[4] *Crax alector.*
[5] Pronounce with a sharp accent on the *t*—*Moo-t'oeng.*

ahead, the only remedy, especially if the current is strong and the water deep, is to lower the poles at a charge, and immediately the rock comes within reach, to heave away, to right or left, with might and main ; the shock is great, and a tremendous effort, and cool skill and nerve, is required to act in one direction simultaneously, the stout poles arch up into bows with the struggle, as the heavy ponderous craft stopped in its course, finally sways away in the right direction, rolling and pitching amidst the dancing waves and rush of waters. I quaked to think what the *Apertada Hora* would be.

In the afternoon a squall of wind and rain drove us to seek shelter on shore, for on these occasions the men cannot see the signs of submerged rocks, and it is necessary to wait until the squall has passed. An hour afterwards the storm subsided and we drifted onwards again. Feroz, who was as fond of a swim as a Newfoundland dog, often amused himself with a plunge into the water, and a swim ashore whenever he heard any doubtful sounds in the woods, and where the banks were sufficiently low to permit him to scramble up. Sometimes he disappeared in this way for two or three hours at a time, when finally his black muzzle appears in sight up stream a long way behind, rapidly overhauling us.

At 6 p.m. we anchored by the edge of a small sandbank for the night : the two *balseiros* having occasion to go into the woods to cut spare poles for poling, I followed with my gun. Out in the *geraes* we came upon a clump of *pindahibas*, where the men pointed out to me a small *ocelot*[6] or tiger-cat, up a tree. A shot brought her down ; what a picture her death-throes presented of wild furious feline rage, how she gnashed her teeth, spitted and snarled and clawed ! but Feroz watching his opportunity, dashed at her, a grip, some bones cracked and pussy was quiet ; but the dog carried away the marks of her claws.

Just as darkness came on, more rain fell, much to the in-

[6] *Felis Pardalis.*

convenience of cooking operations, but Bob stuck manfully to his post and spread his *poncho* on some sticks over the fire to keep off the wet; although he of course got thoroughly soaked, he succeeded in more or less roasting the *motum*. It rained all night, and the men fared but badly under a rough shelter of boughs, as there was not space sufficient to raise the tent amidst the thick underwood of the banks.

Fortunately, thus far we had found no torturing insects at night, not a mosquito had we heard or seen, but occasionally some sand-flies attacked us in the day-time when we passed cerrado lands.

The next morning opened bright and clear, and Jesuino was seen looking at the water in a very pensive mood, and of course scratching his head, as all *matutos* do when thinking. I inquired the cause of his cogitations.

"It is the deuce, the river is neither full nor low, and we have to pass the Apertada Hora to day," he replies.

"Cannot we make a portage by land, or at least go by the shore, and have a look at things?"

"*Qual!* The banks are there walls of rock, and wide dense forests cover the adjoining country."

"Well, shall we chance it?"

"If the Senor Doutor likes to do so, we are ready."

"*Então, vamos embora* (Then let us away)."

As we progressed down the stream, it became evident that we were approaching a more rugged and stony country. Right ahead we could perceive, some miles away, a blue outline of hills intersecting the direction of the river, and the surface of the land became much more irregular, more and more forested, and considerable boulders of some dark-coloured rocks littered the shores, in place of the silvery sand-banks up-stream. *Pancadas* became frequent, and almost at every bend we had some excitement, especially at one place, the Pancada da Espingada, where the wavelets formed curling crested breakers three feet high, and swept the decks fore and aft, giving us all a thorough ducking, and made the raft dance and whirl as though it was a cork on the water; but the channel was deep and fairly free from rocks, and we dashed by the shore at a furious rate, and beyond the wetting, no damage was done. The *pancadas* appeared so rapidly one after the other, that taking notes and bearings, and sketching the river course were carried out under great difficulties.

The next lively moments were passed at the passage of *O Funil*, (the funnel,) where the river passes through two huge masses of hard, black rocks, about fifty feet apart. Their surfaces are worn smooth and regular by the action of the water, that probably once occupied a much higher level, for the upper parts of these rocks, carved into regular horizontal ridges, are now overgrown with thick vines and shrubs.

It was enough to startle a timid person to see, as we approached these huge gates, the water literally squirting through the narrow passage, and as soon as we entered the vortex, it seemed as though I was being bodily hurled along, and the raft appeared to be running away,—a moment only, and it is over; but not quite, for we are sent into a seething mass of whirlpools at the exit of the pass, where we spin round and round, and where only the grand nerve and strength displayed by the crew, saved us from capsizing in the cauldrons of water.

After this spurt of excitement we get a breather, but we are imprisoned in a deep gorge between cliffs high and unscaleable, whence we cannot return if we would, and a little further on the current will seize us, and carry us away to the Apertada. Well, we are in for it, and must take our chance. The dreaded rapids are four to five miles beyond the *Funil*. All the way through a deep ravine, worn out of the soil by the action of the water, we drift on at about three miles an hour, a speed that perceptibly increases as we progress.

The scenery is extremely wild and weird, in many places the cliffs are more than 100 feet high, and above their edges, like a delicate tracery against the blue ether, is a fringe of the feathery foliage of the tall and slender *bacaba*,[7] and the *tucum*,[8] palms,[9] (both equally new to me,) feathery bamboos, and the infinite variety of tropical vegetation. From the verge of the cliffs the land rises into considerable hills.

Meanwhile our speed increases to quite six miles an hour. The crew stand in the bows like statues of mahogany, with poles at the charge, ready for the enemy, and occasionally make long sweeps in the water to keep us head on, and as near as possible in the main current. Bob has offered his services, but they are declined with thanks, as the men have to depend upon each other for simultaneous action.

A sharp bend of the river now appears before us, to which we speed on with ever increased velocity, the raft pitches like a ship in a head-sea on the long wave-like rushing waters, a dull roar becomes perceptible—the speed still increases—the bend is reached and turned—the cataracts are before us. At the sight of the state of the rapids, the crew shout despairingly, "*Cruz! Ave Maria! Virgem Nossa Senhora! Estamos perdidos!*" (We are lost). Certainly the prospect was not a place to select for a day's boating. Down a perceptible incline, the river, more or less 250 feet broad, hurls its foaming seething waters, a mass of whirlpools, sheets of foam, and dashes of spray, amidst innumerable black rocks that dot the surface in all directions. At the furthest extremity a wall of rock crosses the stream, and shuts from view any visible outlet from the gorge. To me no channel is perceptible, it seems all one wide expanse of tearing boiling waters, foam and rocks, and that we are rushing on to inevitable destruction, for the strongest swimmer in that race of water would be helpless and must be dashed to pieces. But my plucky fellows despair not, and manfully pull themselves together for the approaching struggle.

I remember seeing them with dilated eyes, clenched teeth, and crouching bodies, gripping their poles with a vice-like

---

[9] This latter palm is largely utilized by the Amazonian Indians. From its materials they weave their fine grass cloth hammock, cords, mats, fringes to hammocks, shoes, baskets, &c.

grip, thrusting swiftly at, to me, I knew not what; the raft lurches and plunges and whirls around, at times totally submerged, at others rising out of the waves only to plunge again to the right, to the left, to all directions, it is with difficulty I hold on to the roof of the state-room, but the men have magnificent sea-legs, for no matter how the raft may roll or what seas may dash over them, the men's bodies appear to work on swivels from their waists upwards—a sudden stoppage, followed by a grinding crash—the raft heels over, and great masses of seething waters sweep it from end

In the rapids of the Apertada Hora.

to end—everything that is light is carried away, trunks and cooking utensils, *adeos!* many a treasured curiosity—the raft appears to be breaking up, for great fragments of the *burity* stems are torn away as it chafes upon the rocks, and the roof of the saloon oscillates and threatens to pitch forward, Bob is up to his waist in rushing waters, but grips the sloping sides of the roof. Still the crew are cool in nerve, and shoulder to shoulder wield their poles and thrust with Herculean strength at a rock near by, in an effort to get free from the rock that is grinding the raft to pieces, the stout poles are bowed with the severe struggle, and I pray that they will bear the strain. All around is a hurly-burly of rushing seething waters, that break over us in great clouds of spray. Suddenly the raft swings round, is heaved up—we move—we are off, and again careering wildly onwards—now we appear hurrying on only to be dashed against the cliff that seems to cut off all outlet at the end of the rapids. Again the raft strikes hard upon the rocks, but is instantly whirled round—we are free again—on once more plunging, leaping, and whirling swiftly onwards, rocking from side to side; as we near the cliffs, away to the right, a cleft appears—the crew struggle like madmen to gain it—and succeed, and in a moment we shoot into a narrow channel where, to my great astonishment, peace and quietness reign, and we glide along an almost currentless channel, less than twenty feet wide, between lofty walls of black rocks, covered with mosses, and ferns, and moisture. Where are those rushing waters? Where have they disappeared to? for we came out by the only apparent exit? There is only one solution, they have gone by some subterranean outlet under these rocks to our left, for hastily dropping a line with a weight attached, it quickly sinks some twenty feet, where a powerful undercurrent carries it forwards, a fact that sufficiently demonstrated the probability of my supposition.[1]

[1] Such disappearances of large bodies of water by subterranean outlets like the Apertada Hora are by no means uncommon in Brazil, where they are known as *sumidouros* (sinks), and Gardner described a very interesting example in the Rio São Bernardo, a tributary of the Rio Paranan, near the western slopes of the São Francisco-Tocantins watershed. In page 382 of his "Travels in Brazil," after mentioning that several streams that rise in the Serra Geral, lose themselves under a parallel range of limestone, and emerge twelve miles away, united in one body of water, known as the Rio São Bernardo, he describes the scene of the disappearance of one of the streams.

"I found that it did not enter by an open cave, but by an aperture far below the surface of the water. The current here runs with considerable velocity, strikes against the nearly perpendicular face of limestone rock, and forming a few whirlpools, is lost in the gulf below."

This narrow channel extends about 100 yards, and then terminates in the ordinary broad expanse of placid water of the river.

Now, in the quiet and shade of this peaceful haven, with dripping brows, and breasts heaving with the past excitement, we can fully realize the risk we have perhaps so foolishly incurred, but withal so happily terminated. The men take off their hats, and fervently express a grateful *Graças á Deos*, (Thanks to God), for a miraculous escape, and when I recalled the whole scene to my mind's eye, it was indeed wonderful how we had got through with our lives. Probably not a minute was consumed in the descent, but every second was fraught with danger. Had the men not been so well acquainted with the channels, the position of the rocks, so well practised in the manipulation of their poles, and gifted with such strength and cool nerve, we must have smashed up altogether on the rocks, and once in the water, *Adeos! até outra vista.*

The raft was not only much shattered, and the saloon all caved in, but many things had been lost, sacks of provisions, a trunk with clothes, many collections of curiosities, samples of minerals, many drawings, and, by no means the least, our invaluable frying-pan, all "*foisembored.*"

We had to travel a good mile before we found a place to land and repair. I wanted the crew to climb the cliffs, and return to the rapids, to look out for the lost articles, but they point-blank refused, on the plea that the intervening ground was so high rugged and so covered with dense forest, that it would require a long time to reach the scene, where everything that is thrown into the waters disappears immediately, as they had already found out by former experience. The only chance of finding any flotsam was to remain where we were and watch if anything floated by, but although a bright look-out was kept until sunset, nothing appeared.

We had escaped sound in body and limb, and it would be ungrateful to bewail a little loss of articles, no matter how valuable they might be. I did, however, feel a little sorrowful at the loss of so many sketches; fortunately my treasured drawings were not all in the lost trunk.

As far as I was able, I closely examined the composition of the walls of the narrow channel, but could not classify the material other than a rock of a very close and fine grain, extremely hard, a dark, neutral tint in colour, and altogether very similar to the rocks of Pirapora, that a well-known author described as, "*Grauwacker sanstein gres traumatico.*"

The melancholy dilapidated remains of the raft, as it lay alongside a bank, gave it an appearance of having been in a collision, or in a free fight; the bundles of leaf-stems had opened out, the stems stuck up in all directions, the saloon was "nohow," a very little more and it would all have been scattered, when we must certainly have perished. The baggage was all brought ashore, and the work of reconstruction absorbed the rest of the day.

The locality was a wild still solitude, surrounded by densely forested hills, for apparently a ridge here traverses the country, of a formation very different to what is generally found between the São Francisco and Tocantins, excepting perhaps the materials of the serra that crosses the Rio Grande at Boqueirão. The river Somno at this point is about 400 feet wide, enclosed between cliff-like banks, a deep placidly-flowing stream, seeming as it were, in the light of the setting sun a sheet of gold, bordered by the inverted reflections of cliffs and forests as in a mirror; not the slightest puff of wind marred the glassy look of its waters, or disturbed the silent leaves of its bordering forest; amidst the great stillness that prevailed, the splash of a fish, or the occasional cry of a bird, and the voices of the men sounded strange and hollow, and startled one with their strange distinctness.

Another wet night made our quarters again not desirable apartments, but the fatigues and excitement of the day blessed us with such a power of slumber that pelting rain and gusts of wind were unconsidered trifles; although we could not put up the tent, its folds of canvas spread on boughs gave a little shelter, and prevented the men from getting quite wet through.

A heavy mist on the river prevailed in the early morning, that made our chilled limbs feel all the chillier, and despite the men's previous assurances of there being no more rocks ahead, they would not start until the mist had cleared away, but 7 a.m. saw us again on our voyage.

The shores here show signs of *cascalho* and diamond formation. Probably diamonds do exist, for this river has only been navigated by my crew and one or two others, who like them, are utterly ignorant of the nature and characteristics of gold or diamond indications. I wanted much to closely examine the gravel, but time was precious; I had to hurry on, on the possible chance of catching the last trading *bote* descending the Tocantins to Para, it was already late in the season, but there was yet a possible chance. We saw during the morning a *lontra*, (otter), *capyvaras*, an all'gator, tapir No. 3, and in the trees of the banks, numerous monkeys about a foot high, with light brown bodies and limbs and black faces, and in these forests are also numerous herds of peccaries. I found we had not left all the rocks behind, for we passed during the day several *pancadas* caused by submerged rocks, all of which we passed safely.

As we progress down stream the banks become much lower, and the forest often extends to the water's edge on gently sloping ground.

In the afternoon, Feroz pricked up his stumps of ears and barked, and we soon after heard the grunt of peccaries in the woods; such an opportunity for a "square meal" could not be resisted, and all hands work together to pole the raft to the shore, but we drift down a half-mile before we gain a hold upon the trees and chain up. It reminded me of the men on the Thames barges, going down the river with the tide, and trying to sweep their cumbersome craft nearer the shore. Feroz had just had his rations served out, but as we spring ashore I tell him to lie down and keep watch; much as he would like to join us, he will remain there unfastened till we return. These forests are certainly charming to behold in their immensely varied and luxuriant vegetation, but to scramble through them is a work of difficulty; they form such a maze of brambles and vines, of tall straight tree-trunks, giant buttressed trees and slender saplings, trailing creepers and great roots, and thorns and spines that scratch one and sting like a wasp.

It requires a good half-hour's work before we arrive, hot and perspiring, scratched and sticky with broken dead leaves, at the first signs of the peccaries, in the disturbed soil where they had turned over the ground in pursuit of roots, and soon after their presence is detected by their *catinga* (odour); now a cautious advance is made from tree to tree, crawling under bushes, stopping, listening, ever disentangling the feet catching vines, and forcing aside the branches. I have just left the friendly asylum of a very handy little tree, and when proceeding in search of another, suddenly, crack-crack-crack, like file-firing, sounds with startling distinctness in the silence of the woods. Ye Gods! where is my tree, it's all thick bush and vines, anything for a tree, would that I were "up a tree" indeed. I plunge through vines and thorns, regardless of torn clothes and scratches, and reach a slender palmitto palm; I never climbed so quickly before—it was like being assisted up by a pitchfork; the men comfortably ensconced in a forked tree hard by, laughed heartily at my precipitation and ridiculous position—but I have no desire to meet these valiant animals amidst such tangled underwood. They seem, however, to content themselves with their defiance, for they do not appear in sight, and are again silent. I gingerly descend from my scaffold-pole and climb a more comfortable perch. Bob now imitates the barking of a dog, when the peccaries immediately reply by volleys of snapping and cracking of teeth; the thick jungle seems to swarm with them, but still they will not show themselves, and soon, by the sounds of their movements amongst the bushes, they are evidently retreating.

Jacinto and Bob then descend, and disappear cautiously and noiselessly into the underwood—some time passes—we wait listening—no sounds are heard but the ripple of the waters hard by, the murmur of the breeze amidst the rustling leaves of the tree-tops, and the buzz of passing insects, that makes the otherwise stillness all the more profound. Suddenly, two reports are heard in quick succession, some distance away, followed by squeals grunts and snapping of teeth ; the sounds approach nearer and nearer, the bushes rustle—and a number of brown peccaries rush by ; we fire, one animal falls, the rest disappear. Now we recognize them to be, not the warrior boars of the Sapão, but only the common and comparatively harmless *Caetatu*, or ordinary brown peccary. Jacinto and Bob return, each one carrying a pig, that with ours, or rather Jesuino's, made three killed.

The forest is barely more than 100 yards wide, for beyond that width, the land extends in long slopes covered with tall *capim agreste crua*, indicating at once an uninhabited locality. When we regained the raft, poor Feroz was found half drowned in a flood of saliva. His dinner was close to his nose, but as he had received orders to lie down and watch, he evidently thought they included his food also. He looked at me wistfully, but still waited patiently for a welcome order to *come*[2] (eat) ; few dogs would have carried out instructions so literally under such temptations.

About mid-day we passed the mouth of the Rio das Balsas, a considerable stream, about 160 feet wide. It is reported to be navigable, but traverses an uninhabited country, except near its source, where there is said to be a tribe of *indios brabos*, that may or may not be. Below this stream, the Somno widens out to about 500 feet in width.

Amidst the woods that day appeared for the first time the wild banana, *Bananeira do Matto*,[3] and a palm new to my

---

[2] Pronounce *komey*.

[3] It is a much disputed question amongst botanists whether the banana was ever indigenous to Brazil. Humboldt, in his " *Essai Politique*,'

experiences, the *Inaja*;[4] many of the trees were also densely covered with the vines of a large mauve-coloured convolvulus, amidst whose festoons great numbers of monkeys gamboled. The grunts of peccaries were frequently heard, but no more time could be spared for another hunt. On one occasion we heard in the depths of the forests, sounds like a number of knocks given in unison; I was told that the noise was produced by monkeys breaking nuts by pounding them with stones.

No more *pancadas* are now met with, and the river flows onwards like a well-behaved stream.

Late in the afternoon a heavy squall of wind and rain burst upon us, and drove us to seek shelter at the mouth of a small stream; as we rounded the bushes that partly hid its entrance, we disturbed quite a family of *capyvaras* luxuriating in the shallow water, they one and all dived at sight of us, and we saw them no more.

This life on the Somno is decidedly pleasant, it is quite like a long picnic, rough certainly, and unpleasant as all picnics are when it rains, and exciting enough on the Apertada Hora, a place that I should not care to pass again on a *balsa*. The climate is pleasant and very healthy, and the scenery beautiful and varied beyond description, and there are no mosquitos.

In the morning Jesuino put his head into the saloon and called my attention to Bob. I could not help laughing at the sight; he had gone to sleep on the sloping wet sand-bank by the side of his fire, but his long legs had rolled him down hill, and there he lay with them immersed in the warm river up to his knees, and still he slept on; he had made a bait of himself for alligators and *piranhas*, fortunately for him neither appeared, and not even a sneeze resulted from his damp bed.

A long quiet hot day passed in slowly drifting along the now oily-looking surface of the stream, verily the hottest day

---

vol. iii. p. 22, states that the plant is a native of Brazil. Possibly he may have had in view the *bananeira do Matto*, that is in relation to the cultivated banana what a crab apple tree is to its developed brethren.

[4] *Cocas plumosa*, Mart. *Maximiliana regia*.

I had experienced for a long time, for not a breath of wind tempered the scorching rays of the sun. In the shade of the saloon the temperature appeared even hotter than outside, the thermometer registered 96°, the heat was really sweltering, and we drifted, oh! so slowly. Amidst the woods the thermometer indicated 86°. We all, men and dog, had many a swim alongside as the craft drifted onwards, and thereby managed to keep a little cool.

One or two habitations now began to appear. I stopped at one, a poor little fazenda, such a scene of wretchedness.

The owner, a ragged brown unkempt fellow, about forty years of age, told me he had lived there some six years, having immigrated from up the Tocantins with several head of cattle, but was thoroughly disheartened with the results of his enterprise; his farm was a long way from a market for cattle, and at Pedro Affonso he could only sell hides, as he could not afford to buy salt to make dried beef, and moreover the jaguars played such havoc with his herds that their increase was very small. I bought some fine jaguar skins at one milreis each. He remarked that the day was exceptionally hot, for generally he could not complain of the district on the score of climate, salubrity, or soil. This man was so hopelessly lazy or despondent, that he had let everything "slide," and eked out a miserable existence on the barest necessities. His roça was a perfect wilderness of mingled jungle and vegetables. His house of sticks and grass, once well built, was almost uninhabitable; ants had destroyed the principal parts of the framework, and the hut seemed ready to topple forward at any moment; the grass roof was full of holes and hung in ragged bundles of decayed matter, only kept together by the roots of plants that vegetated luxuriantly in its rottenness.

The walls had partly disappeared, the rest were supported by props. In the interior were a few broken-down benches, a few hides, several old ragged dirty hammocks, and dust, dirt and disorder reigned supreme. The women were only half clad in extremely dirty ragged cotton skirts and parts of chemises, their hair was ragged and uncombed, and their skins grimed with dirt ; several children of various ages and colours waddled about perfectly naked, their faces sallow and pallid, their arms and legs miserably thin, pot-bellied, yet showing their ribs like skeletons. Bah! such squalor makes one feel bad, and I hurried away sick at heart, accustomed as I was to scenes of Brazilian poverty. I expostulated with the proprietor on his way of life, and tried to encourage him to do better things, to pull himself together and be a man, but I might just as well have tried to induce that personification of laziness, the *preguiça* or Brazilian sloth, to run a race. The only reply I received was a drawling, "*Não posso, não estou accostumado, não é nosso costume,*" &c. (I can't, I am not accustomed to it, it is not our way, &c.). Nothing could I buy except the skins, there were no fowls, pigs, goats, not even farinha the national bread, only water-melons, pumpkins, yams, and sweet mandioca, and none of these would they part with.

Yet considering that these people are thoroughly habituated to the solitudes of a wild country, if they would only exert themselves to do a reasonable amount of daily labour they might live in, what could easily be made to appear to them, a veritable paradise. It is a painful sight to witness the depths of degradation that apparently civilized beings will sometimes descend to. In this case, there was not even the excuse of the vice of drink to explain such woeful want. Nothing but irreclaimable constitutional indolence.

Early in the afternoon we passed the mouth of the Rio Perdido,[5] about 150 feet broad. Its margins are uninhabited, its waters are reported to be navigable, and the country it traverses is said to be rich in woods and grass-lands.

The woods hereabouts are full of noisy animal life, especially birds that welcomed with whistles, screeches, screams and chatterings, the advent of a fresh breeze in the afternoon : there were flocks of noisy *passos pretos*, very much resembling both in song form and colour our own blackbirds, harshly

[5] The lost river.

screeching *calind.'s* (large purple macaws), flocks of parroquets and love-birds, graceful white herons ; were heard also the loud cries of *serenhemas*, the sharp sudden cries of the *araponga* or anvil-bird, like the striking of a bar of iron, the grunting of *peccaries*, and the splashing plunges of the *capyvaras*. It must not be imagined that all these emanate from any one given locality like a menagerie or a zoological garden, that is a mistake that is often created in describing tropical scenes, for the traveller cannot well mention the different birds, animals, or strange cries, as he meets or hears them at different times during his day's journey.

We landed to pass the night for the last time on the Somno, on a broad bank of sand and shingle, a little below a Riberão de Lagedo on the north bank, where we enjoyed the soft balmy air of the clear starlight night, such a luxury after the late stormy evenings.

The next morning saw us bound Westward Ho for the last time ; for on the Tocantins we shall turn to the north, and sideways to " Orion's belt," which constellation, then due west, had so long been my direction by night, and how often I longed to turn my back upon it and go in the opposite direction. Now in after years I rarely see it, without recaling the old memories of those rough wild days and nights.

The latter part of the Somno's banks are very low, and much of the adjoining land is subject to inundations, the shores are slimy with the deposited humus of the river that here flows so very slowly, or may be the flooded waters of the Tocantins there back up and meeting the flow of the Somno become stagnant and deposit the matters they carry in solution, for certainly there is no soft soil up this stream to generate this mud ; the soil is too gritty and sandy.

Although the day's voyage was only some ten miles, it required seven hours to cover the distance ; at last a final bend of the river that had taken an hour to reach, opened out to some 600 feet wide, divided in the middle by an island, and then joined the broad brown waters of the Tocantins.

CHAPTER XII.

FROM PEDRO AFFONSO TO CAROLINA DOWN THE RIO TOCANTINS.

Arrival at Pedro Affonso—An indifferent host—Too late for the last "bote"—The botes and traders of the Rio Tocantins—An old Indian settlement—Indian boys—The Montaria—The new crew—Frae Rafael and his mission—The Coroado Indians—The country around the village—A tender craft—My tent is sacrificed—Adeos, Pedro Affonso—Cramped accommodation—Paddles of the Tocantins *v.* São Francisco—The shores of the Tocantins—A murderous rascal and his home—Persecution of the Indians and unpunished crimes of the interior of Brazil—Well-watered lands—Bico de Toucano and his resources—On the river Tocantins—A woeful loss—Uselessness of the inhabitants—Arrival at Carolina—Advised to abandon the voyage to Para—The city and its inhabitants—Disappointment in obtaining a troop for the journey overland—Scarcity of game—A hilly neighbourhood—Gold and copper districts—A church festival—A negro festival.

ON the 30th of April, after the voyage of five days, we landed at the south side of the river on a slippery muddy bank, amidst the *débris* of defunct *burity balsas*, to which our brave craft will now be added to rot, or drift away down the river.

It was quite time that the voyage ended, for the pores of the leaf-stems had become thoroughly impregnated with moisture, and the raft became more and more water-logged every day, so much so that the deck was just awash with the water.

The banks, fifty feet above the level of ordinary water, are fringed by a narrow belt of trees, at their rear extends a flat plain, covered with grass, scattered bushes, and clumps of trees.

Some 500 yards distant is the village of Pedro Affonso, consisting of the ordinary type of habitations, adobe wall and tiled-roof houses, and grass huts, scattered irregularly without any apparent arrangement, amidst groups of large and small trees and thick bushes; the narrow paths pass by the back of one house and the front of the next.

I went to the house of a Senhor L., to whom m kind friends at Porto Franco had given me a letter of introduction. I was directed to a half-closed venda, where I found a big sleepy apathetic young white man, dozing on the counter. He is too somnolent to express any surprise at my arrival, for he merely languidly turns his head as though I had been an every-day visitor, and an awful bore. He reads my letter, and with many an "*Ai! meo Deos!*" and with groans, and much tribulation, succeeds in raising himself to a sitting posture, and then drawls out the usual pertinent questions. "What is your name?" "Where do you come from?" "Where are you going to?" "What is your business?" "How much is your salary?" "How much are you worth?" &c. I suggested that if he was to ask, "What I would like for breakfast?" and, "When I would have it?" it would be more to the point, for we had not stopped at our usual breakfast-hour, and it was then two o'clock.

But, alas! the senhor is dull of comprehension and weary, and threatens to relapse again to his counter, and assume a masterly inactivity. So with a *com licensa*, I unceremoniously rummage his venda, and discover some farinha, eggs, a tin of sardines, some *cachaça*, a cup, water, sugar, and a spoon. He watches me curiously beat up eggs, and add *cachaça*, sugar, and water; never before had he seen such a mixture.

With the help of a more active neighbour, an empty hut was obtained, and the baggage duly housed. The men received their stipulated price of ten milreis each, and a couple more as a gratuity, then went their way for a few days' relaxation in the village, happy and contented with their trifling wages. If they had been paid three or four times the amount, they would not have said *obrigado* (thank you); it would only have given them a little longer spell of dissipation, like a " Jack ashore."

To my sorrow and great disappointment, I learned that the last trading *bote* had passed down the river only two days previously, and that there was not another above stream. This was doubly disappointing, for the chance was gone of being able to secure a passage to Para in a comparatively commodious cabined barge.

In after years, when on the lower Tocantins, I saw these large comfortable boats, called *botes;* they are somewhat similar to the *barcas* of the Rio São Francisco, but although not so smart in appearance, are very much larger, some being fifteen feet in beam, and seventy feet in length, with a large and commodious cabin amidship, and manned with a crew of twenty to forty Indians. This large number is carried to make the numerous portages at the many rapids on the lower Tocantins, below and a little above the Araguaya, where all the cargo has to be taken out and carried above the rapids, and the empty *bote* dragged up by ropes. In descending the river the *bote* shoots the falls. Twelve months are consumed in a trading trip from Para to the city of Palma on the upper Tocantins, ten in ascending, and two in descending the river. I was told that if a trader can make two successful trips without shipwreck, he is enabled to retire with a competence. The goods that are brought up are cotton prints, shawls, fancy goods, hardware, salt, gunpowder, cheap guns, Birmingham jewellery, dried Newfoundland codfish, flour, coffee, *cachaça*, and various trifles; these are bartered at the river-side villages and settlements for raw hides, gold dust, dried beef, *copahiba* oil, medicinal plants, tobacco, jaguar and other skins, beans, farinha, toucinho, &c. If a man can earn a moderate fortune in two years in such a life, he well deserves it, for it is arduous, unhealthy, and full of insect tortures; there is, moreover, the great risk he incurs of shipwreck of a whole year's work, which more often happens than not. To be a successful trader a man must have capital to start with, be "smart" in quite the American sense, be strong and healthy, and have an iron constitution, great patience, and be thoroughly acquainted with his trade, the people, and the river, and be, moreover, blessed with good luck.

I had expected to find Pedro Affonso a semi-Indian village, and was much surprised to meet only an ordinary Brazilian hamlet, although there were many pure Indians in the settlement, Cherentes and Coroados, who only differ in appearance from the ordinary Matuto in their stout *physique*, their features, and long straight black hair; amongst them were several Indian lads from the Rio Araguaya, who could barely speak Portuguese.

The lads came to my hut in the evening with an Indian who understood Portuguese, and after much persuasion they performed some of their native dances; they were merry sturdy fellows, and laughed with great glee when I read out to them a short vocabulary of words I had written from the explanations of their companion. They were working for a man, practically as slaves, but apparently well treated, after the rough country fashion, and were evidently happy and contented, and much better off than in their former savage state.

For the voyage down the Tocantins, the only means that offered was a *montaria*, or small river boat, that I purchased for *fifty milreis* (5*l.*); a broad shallow boat, built of thin narrow planks of cedro, with a little round thatched roof at the long pointed stern, where the name of the craft, "Sussu-

Apara" was painted. It was inconveniently small, being only 3 feet 6 inches beam in the middle, and 14 feet long, but it was a case of Hobson's choice, that or nothing.

A crew of two men were shipped as A.B. paddlers, Pacifico Dias Ribeiro, and Evaristo Santos Oliveira, the former contracted to go as far as the mouth of the Araguaya for 25$000, and the latter to Boa Vista for 6$000; both had the most villainous and rascally of faces, and both had been soldiers and convicts. Although there was little doubt of their being thorough scoundrels, I trusted myself with them, with much less hesitation than I would have with a London rough, in similar circumstances.

The next day was consumed in obtaining provisions for the voyage; a quarter of a bullock was bought for 3$500 (seven shillings), cut up into strips, rubbed with salt, and suspended in the sun to dry. This appears to be a rough method of preserving meat, but when it is done properly and effectively, it is complete,[1] and after a week or ten days, when roasted on a spit over a fire, its flavour is exceedingly palatable, even admitting the healthy relish for anything that the camp fire develops. It must not be confounded with the *Carne Secca*, that is such a great article of merchandise in the coast towns, that is truly abominable, impregnated as it is with the odours of the close holds of ships, and all kinds of undesirable flavours.

By the little information that could be gleaned of Pedro Affonso and its history, I learned that it was originally a village of cannibal Coroado Indians. In 1848, an Italian monk from Bahia, named Frae Rafael, arrived amongst them, he met with a rough reception at first, and was for a long time in daily danger of losing his life, but his tact, patience, and kind and gentle nature, gradually so gained the obedience and good-will of these wild sons of the forest, that he was enabled to baptize them in the Roman Catholic faith, and teach them a

---

[1] In the table-lands of Ceara and Piauhy the atmosphere is so dry that the meat can be preserved by simply drying it in the sun without any salt whatever.

few habits of industry, agriculture, and to provide for the coming morrow, yet still they wear only their natural garments, i.e., their skin, and a few feathers stuck in their hair on State occasions; possibly the poor *Frade* has nothing to dress them with, and wisely sees no shame where none exists.

In 1850, the first Brazilian settlers appeared amongst the Indians, who two years afterwards, accompanied by their beloved pastor, sought a more congenial existence in the wilderness on the borders of the Rio do Manoel Alves Pequeno. A few months ago (1875), the aged monk, reduced to helplessness by a stroke of paralysis, was visited by Frae Antonio (a brother, missionary monk), who carried the invalid with him to his home with the Cherente Indians, on the Rio Ipiabanha, 72 miles up the Tocantins. Every one spoke of these self-sacrificing men in terms of affection and respect. No reward on this earth can they expect, except that satisfaction and contentment, that an abnegation of self to the dictates of duty and conscience, must and does confer. I regretted immensely that time would not permit of witnessing the result of their labours, and forming an acquaintance of these wonderfully unselfish men. In about 1870, the chief of the Cherentes, known as Capitão Gabrielle, with a small following of his tribe, made a long journey to Rio de Janeiro, to visit the Emperor. They returned pleased with their visit, and loaded with presents.

The population of Pedro Affonso is variously estimated at 300 to 500 souls; the habitations are very scattered, and cover a considerable area of ground, yet the former number is probably the more correct.

The hamlet contains a little church of whitewashed adobe walls and tiled roof, extremely plain, and as unpretentious as a white box. Around it are scattered the greater number of houses. There was then no *Padre*, for no one had taken the place of Frae Rafael.

The inhabitants are extremely indolent, and their homes decrepit and dirty; the principal occupations, apparently are smoking, sleeping and gambling, in the considerable off time of rearing cattle, and a petty agriculture for the supply of local wants. Yet, even so, the place manages to support five *vendas* or stores, whose owners lead frightfully monotonous lives; it is not to be wondered at, that Senhor L. exists in such an utter state of collapse and limpness; such a life would drive any decent European into a lunatic asylum in a very short time.

The site of the village was well chosen by the aborigines, as it is far above any possible river floods.

On the opposite side of the river, the banks of the Tocantins rise into yet higher ground and form considerable bluffs, in one place cleaved by the exit of the rushing waters of a stream, that will furnish excellent water-power for the mills in the very very distant future, when these luxuriant pastoral and agricultural lands are colonized and developed.[2]

May 3rd.—This morning the *montaria* "Sussu-Apara," is brought alongside the muddy landing-place of the village to receive its cargo, but unfortunately it cannot carry all the crew, passengers and baggage, and some part of the latter must be left behind, and in consequence I regretfully have to part with my useful tent. At the last moment, Pacifico, who had been for some time uneasily twirling his hat and scratching his head, and evidently hesitating to make some request, demands an advance of 20$000 out of his 25$000.[3] A long and windy argument ensues, that finally ends, with the help of a Senhor Leoncio, in the man accepting 5$000. When we are all aboard, the gunwale of the craft is only three inches above the water, and it is so "tender," that any careless movement

---

[2] On old maps of Brazil a S. Lorenço is marked in front of the Somno. The oldest inhabitant could give me no information of its existence anywhere or at any time.

[3] This is a very objectionable but almost universal custom of the *camaradas* to obtain an advance of wages. As a rule they keep faith with their *patrão*, and abide by their agreements; but the *patrão* is nevertheless liable to have his crew desert him at any riverside place, where he may fail to obtain a substitute.

of the crew must certainly capsize us. Some dozen or so of people witness our departure, but the weary Senhor L. is not capable of the exertion of walking the intervening 200 yards. I stroll to his venda to bid him farewell. He lays coiled up in a hammock smoking a cigarette, and without raising himself, he wearily extends his flabby moist cold hand, yawns a *boa viagem*, and turns his heavy head to sleep a little more, grateful doubtless, for my departure. He told me once that I was always in such a hurry, and always so hot and red, that it made him *incommodado* (ill) to see me. How he managed to obtain a livelihood, would appear to be a curious problem, for no customers are to be met with in his half-closed store; his principal business consists in collecting the little local produce, and exchanging or selling it to the river traders, and as the trading season only lasts during three or four months of the year, he apparently sleeps away the other nine, like the animals in an Arctic winter.

With much shouts of "*Vom' embora rapaziada'! Vom' embora! Adeos, Pedro Affonso! Adeos, adeos gente! Adeos, Mariquinha! Adeos, raparigas gordas e bonitas! Vom' para o rio abaixo*," etc. (Let us be off, boys! Let us be off! Adeos, Pedro Affonso! Adeos, adeos, you people! Adeos, little Mary! Adeos, lasses fat and pretty. Let us away to the river below, etc.), we start off with a spurt of furious paddling that results in but little speed, and warns the men by the craft shipping water, that they must go quieter, and have no sky-larking, in fact, so tender is the boat that any change of position, or movement by any of us, has to be made by pre-concerted signals; even a sneeze has to be done with all due care. The prospect of a journey to Para in such a cramped space, and in such a frail craft, is not by any means enjoyable.

The paddles the men use are very different to the great heavy paddles of the Rio São Francisco, these are small and of light cedar wood, not more than three feet long, the blade is quite flat and circular, eight inches in diameter, the men are seated and paddle with short quick strokes, forty to the minute; on the São Francisco, the paddlers stand up and give long powerful strokes, not more than twenty-two to the minute.

As we pass down-stream, the sight of numerous huts on the banks recalls the riverside of the São Francisco, but there the resemblance ends, for this river is everywhere clothed with dense thick vegetation down to the water's edge, no matter how high the banks, their slopes are all green with dense foliage. The appearance of the Tocantins woods is rather mean, for the verdure appears to consist principally of compact masses of bushes of low growth, covered and bound together with flowering vines. Possibly the long *tiros* or straight reaches, that terminate in horizons of sky and water, tend to diminish and dwarf the appearance of the green banks, and the effect is really deceptive, for behind those walls of leaves are many trees of considerable magnitude that are not noticeable from the water.

Evaristo having asked permission to land at a little farm for a few moments, I accompanied him, and was rewarded by meeting a character. The path led for about half a mile away from the belt of bush and forest of the river, across undulating grass-land, and brought us to an adobe wall and tiled house, outbuildings and cattle currals, rather prettily situated by the side of a thicket of trees, close to a small stream of good water splashing over a roughly-made overshot water-wheel that worked the wooden rollers of a cane-mill. In one of the sheds some five or six young white women were at work drying farinha in a large open shallow pan over a small furnace constructed of adobe bricks; they were but partly clad in skirts only, and had they been well-cleansed, their skins would have been practically white; they all had good features, and were it not for their coarse expressions, they would have made quite handsome women; but their foul ragged skirts, dirty skins, and wild tangled hair, made them appear repulsively objectionable. They were the slaves of the Capitão, possibly his own daughters.

This individual now approaches, such a capitão, truly a veritable ogre; the being that now shouts a salutation to us, is tall and strongly built, in age apparently between sixty and seventy. A battered straw hat covers his long dirty white hair, that hangs over his brows and on his shoulders in unkempt tangled locks. Enormously bushy grey eyebrows almost meet together in a deep scowl over a long hooked nose, and nearly hide from view his small deeply sunk keen eyes, that peer at one with a look of mingled cunning and savagery; his long beard and moustache that should be white, are yellow with dirt and snuff, the beard covers his face to the verge of the puffy circles around his eyes. His garments comprise a very dirty ragged shirt, girdled around his waist by a cord, in which is stuck a sheathed *faca de ponta* (a pointed knife), his trousers, once white cotton, are brown with dirt; one ragged portion reaches to an ancle, the other barely to his knee, both frayed to rags and tatters and daubed with mud; his shirt is open to his waist, and exposes a rough grey hairy chest, more like a monkey's than a human being's. His broad powerful hands are covered with long grey hairs, his broad bare feet are caked with mud. Altogether he looks the most diabolical scoundrel that I had ever had the pleasure to sketch. As a model he would be invaluable.

On the way, Evaristo had acquainted me with his history. It is doubtful where he first hailed from, but he was known to have been once a large planter in Piauhy, then a trader on the river, and the proprietor of stores in different riverside towns and villages, and was for the interior of Brazil, then considered to be very rich, but an insatiable desire for killing got him into such trouble, and provided such opportunities to local authorities to turn an honest penny, that his property was consumed in the course of twenty-two trials for murder in as many years, each of which he had apparently escaped from by gradually parting with his wealth. Evaristo said he was rather proud of his exploits, and that he would be pleased to have a chat about them; accordingly I took an opportunity to broach the subject to the ogre. His eyes gleamed in their cavernous sockets at my questions, and he replied with a chuckle, that after all he was only credited with twenty-two *mortes* (deaths), *E' o reste ? E' o reste ?* (And the rest ? and the rest ?) he said, bending forward his head with a jerk, and peering into my face, at the same time giving me a dig in my side with his clawlike fingers, like a man driving into another the point of a good joke. He wanted to be affable and hospitable, but it was impossible to resist a feeling of loathing at the repulsive figure and murderous rascal, and I made a hasty retreat, for he might be seized with a desire to flesh his knife, for an experiment, on a Britisher. I believed he was a madman, and the strange look of his eyes rather confirmed the impression.

On the way back I notice a few young naked Indians about the premises, and inquiring of Evaristo where they came from, he tells me that the *Capitão* is in the habit of making raids on the wandering tribes of Indians in the wild districts between the Tocantins and Araguaya, when he and a few congenial natures slaughter them like beasts of prey, and bring away the children as captives.[4] The laws and constitution of Brazil

---

[4] As a proof that this story is probably no exaggeration, I quote the following extract from the official report of the Minister of Justice for the year 1883. The incident referred to occurred in the Amazons district. "In an official communication of the 27th January last of the President of the Province, forwarded during a voyage that he made up the Rio Purus as far as the Rio Acre, I was informed of the horrible crimes committed there, and yet unpunished for want of means for the effective repression of the criminals, and by the difficulty of meeting in these regions with a person of ability to exercise without remuneration the functions of a police agent.

"Conspicuous amidst these crimes are those of the barbarous persecutions by Leonel Antonio do Sacramento of the Indians of the Upper Purus, which have resulted in the destruction of more than five villages, and the assassination of more than 200 men, women, and children. In these circumstances the presidente promptly ordered a gunboat to proceed at once to the Purus, carrying the municipal judge, public prosecutor, and the notary. With these functionaries went ten soldiers of the line under the command of a sergeant for want of an officer. A person worthy

are undoubtedly on paper fairly reasonable and just, but in practice, red tape will often suit the convenience of the longest purse, more especially in the far interior of Brazil, where any local magnate can commit with impunity the grossest crime, provided he has influence and can afford to pay.

We continued the journey without incident, but the heat was considerable, 86°, and our limbs were horribly cramped by being confined within the limited space of the boat.

Numerous little streams join the river, as a glance at the map will show, and indicate how well watered are the margins of this river. We landed at a small sugar-cane field bordering the banks, to obtain shelter for the night at the squatter's farm, comprising a little adobe house and an open shed containing a rude mill, worked by cattle. The tenants stared at us stolidly, and in answer to our request for a roof, showed us the open shed, where we were permitted to sling hammocks, in company with pigs revelling in the delights of chewing the newly-crushed canes.[5]

During the next day I was much amused by the volume of stories, anecdotes and jokes, that flowed unceasingly from Evaristo (or *Bico de Toucano*, Toucan's beak, as the other men called him, on account of his long hooked nose).

Our stores of *carne secca* bought at Pedro Affonso, had been laid out like blankets on the roof of the little cabin to dry in the sun, but an undoubtedly high flavour becomes perceptible, the meat assumes a decidedly blue complexion, and sundry plump maggots are frisking about it. I give directions to

---

of all confidence was nominated as Delegate of Police." This little extract is sufficient to show what difficulties the government has to encounter to keep order in its vast domains. Its efforts are worthy of esteem, but for one such case as the above (that only by the casual accident of the President of the province travelling there, became thus officially communicated), there are scores of similar, or even worse, crimes that happen and pass away unheard of.

[5] Sugar-planters have told me that if any apparatus could be made as effective as a pig's jaws for extracting the greatest quantity of juice from a cane, it would excel the most modern contrivance for that purpose.

throw it overboard, but Evaristo expostulates, and asks "What shall we get to eat then, if you do that?" "Oh, buy some fowls, or something else at these riverside houses." "They will not sell you a thing, you just try," he replies. Accordingly, at the next house I went ashore, and discovered some fowls, and offered to purchase them. The people at once declined to sell them, or anything else, and I had to return empty handed. "Now," said Evaristo, "if you will give me that meat, I will feed you on the fat of the land for the rest of the voyage, That was a proposal I could not refuse. He took the folds of meat, and set to work at washing them in the river, the same as a wash-woman will soap and rub together soiled linen, then he proceeded to souse and slap it repeatedly in the water, begged some salt, which he rubbed in, and hung the meat in the sun to dry; "it will be all *podre* (rotten) to-morrow," he said, "but it will serve for to-day, you wait and see." In an hour or two the sun had dried the meat, and it looked quite wholesome. Evaristo had meanwhile been watching with a critical eye the various huts on the banks, and at last he found one to his satisfaction, when we paddled ashore. Taking the long strips of meat over his shoulder like one carries a rug, he climbed the muddy bank and disappeared from view. We waited a quarter of an hour, when he reappeared, and called for Pacifico. A little later on they returned loaded with six fat fowls, a bunch of bananas, a sack of oranges, several roots of sweet mandioca, sweet potatoes, yams, and rolls of tobacco, and both breathed an odour of *cachaça*, and said Evaristo with glee, showing some coppers, "there is the change out." I felt a pricking of conscience, but as the people would not sell, and the cravings of nature must be satisfied, well—well—paddle away quickly with our bargains.

A little later on, I had occasion to open a trunk, when a small home-made English Union Jack of my old comrade C—, became exposed to view. Evaristo at once observed, "What a pretty saint's flag; do lend it to me, I can make a young fortune out of it." "What do you mean?" "Why, with such a lovely flag as that, I could go to every house on the river, and get coppers by simply asking for "*Esmolas* (alms) *para o Divino Espirito Santo*."[6] O Evaristo, Evaristo, you bad wicked man. His consummate impudence was so comical, that I had a wee little desire to see the effect of his experiment. But dignity and propriety must be duly studied, so the flag was restored to its abiding-place. Evaristo then delivered a long discourse on the absurd punctiliousness of some people.

I must now have a little mercy on the long-tried patience of the reader in following the commonplace incidents of these journeys, and with a few paragraphs more I will land him at Carolina. I regret for his sake, that events have not been more "blood curdling," that are so nice to read about by a winter fireside at home.

The map will perhaps show better than a long description, the general configuration of the country. The banks are muddy and often composed of soft slime, black in colour and offensive in smell, yet the riverside is healthy, and mosquitos are absent, the best indication of the absence of malaria. In the river, the fresh water dolphins (*Bótus*), constantly rise to the surface, and with a deep sigh-like sound return to their watery depths. They are reported to give large quantities of oil, but are not utilized in any form whatever.

A little above the Rio do Manoel Alves a chain of hills crosses the river, and judging by the smallness of most of the streams that join the Tocantins on the east side between the Somno and the Manoel Alves, these hills are probably a continuation of the range that crosses the Somno at the Apertada da Hora. It is a feasible theory, and is entitled to exist until it is proved wrong. Otherwise the lands bordering the river are gently undulating, and everywhere covered with the grass and scrub of the sandy campos, excepting on the banks and up the many

---

[6] It is customary for the lay brethren of any church, when collecting alms for church expenses, to carry a small flag, either of plain colours or with emblems of the saint.

little valleys of the tributary streams where long narrow belts of forest prevail. I failed to notice any of the low marshy ground that is so characteristic of the Rio São Francisco, and also any highlands like the bluffs of the table-lands that follow that river almost throughout its course, for the valley of the Tocantins is a wide shallow depression that appears to be scooped out and to extend from its watersheds on the east and west.

The voyage was extremely monotonous; there was little to attract attention; very little bird-life is met with in the long reaches of water, bounded in the far distance by an horizon of sky and water, and right and left by long lines of dense bush; the sun beat pitilessly on us, and reflected its brazen rays from the shimmering surface of the water, and withal, the cramped space and the care required in making any movements, created great discomfort and an intense feeling of *ennui*, and throughout the voyage we did not sight a craft of any kind.

To simply say that the banks of the Tocantins are inhabited would create an erroneous impression, although every few miles huts do appear, but inland there are no habitations whatever, yet the riverside might just as well be quite unpopulated for what benefits or utility these people confer on the world, or their fellow-creatures. They lead entirely selfish lives, working just sufficient to eke out a wretched existence; they cannot be happy, for their dull listless physiognomies prove otherwise, it is a sort of penal servitude for life, at least so they make it. Much might be done on this river by industry, combination, and enterprise, but combination is a thing utterly absent from the Brazilian *matutos*' conception, and so they exist like the plants around them, each living for himself, sleeping away their lives, until death relieves them of their wearisome burdens. Still there is latent a good solid material in these people, what is indispensable is a century of good example and *new European blood* especially, and then these twelve millions of Brazilians will add their proper quota to the world's supplies; as it is, if a good half were wiped out the world would be none the worse, and yet the cry in Brazil is for more *braços* (arms).

One night an irreparable disaster occurred, that to this day I deplore. I had been making a sketch of the river when I was called away to the evening meal, and leaving the sketch and note-book in the stern of the boat, I adjourned to "dress for dinner." On my return the wretched Feroz was found occupying the place where my treasures had been left; alas! they had disappeared into the water, never more to be seen. The sketch-book alone, contained some 200 sketches, and the note-book contained many invaluable notes. I felt much disposed to grief; fortunately my diaries were yet safe in my trunk.

On the 7th May we reached Carolina. On the summit of a lofty bank of a red sandy loam, a little bushy flat leads to a few scattered huts, half hidden from view by tall bushes and trees, and following a narrow path for about 300 yards, I entered an oblong grass-grown sandy square, surrounded by houses. It looks silent and deserted in the bright glare and heat of the afternoon sun, and only one or two people are to be seen moving about. Not having any letters of introduction to any one, I called upon the *Juiz de Direito* (District Judge), and sent in my card by the hands of a *moleque* who had responded to the clap of my hands. The nigger boy took the pasteboard very gingerly, looked at it, smelt it, and ran away holding it at arm's length; he soon returned and in a patronizing manner told me I might enter. The judge was a handsome intelligent-looking white gentleman, polished courteous and "*très distingué*" in appearance despite his dressing-gown, ceroulas and slippers. In the conversation that followed he earnestly advised me to abandon the idea of going down the river to Para, not only on account of the late season of the year, and the consequent increased difficulties of passing the many rapids and falls, but also because of reports that had arrived of an exceedingly bad epidemic of malignant fevers and small pox that was raging on the river below the Araguaya and that it would be far preferable to go overland through the province of Maranhão, to its capital on the coast. Considering that the juiz was in a position to judge of the merits or disadvantages of either route, and at the time not knowing what motive he could have for dissuading me to abandon the Tocantins, and as either route was immaterial to me, I accepted his advice.

At the suggestion of the juiz, I sought and found the *Promotor Publico* (Public Prosecutor), a fair-haired young man, at whose house I obtained an accommodation until I could obtain a troop of animals to convey me to Chapada.

Carolina was created a township in 1831, and a city in 1859. It contains one mean little whitewashed church, two well-stocked stores, and five small *vendas*, a jail, a public school, and a police force of ten men, then commanded by a sub-lieutenant, the Senhor Commandante. It is reported to have a population of 1500 inhabitants; its chief inhabitants consist of the local authorities, the Juiz de Direito, the *Padre*, the Juiz Municipal, the Public Prosecutor, the Delegado de Policia, a lawyer, the schoolmaster, two principal *negociantes* (shopkeepers), and a few *fazendeiros*, who own town-houses. There are a few fairly comfortable houses of two stories, rejoicing in the unusual luxury of glazed windows, and in one house there is actually a piano. The accompanying sketch will convey an idea of the appearance of the praça of this sleepy city at mid-day.

The silence of the grass-grown square, and the absence of movement is remarkable even for an inland town, no country carts, no mule nor horse troops break the grim monotony; even on the shore of the landing-place, no *balsas*, nor canoes, nor other craft are to be seen.

A purchaser was found for the *montaria*, and the crew were dismissed, but had there been reason to anticipate the long delay of three weeks I was eventually subjected to in obtaining transport across country, I should certainly have rather preferred to take my chance of the fevers and dangerous rapids of the lower Tocantins, and have gone on to Para in the *montaria*, although it was perhaps advisable that I did not do so, for eventually, during my stay in Carolina, several way-worn boatmen arrived from the lower river, and stated that smallpox and malignant fevers were making such ravages there, that many homeward-bound boats were abandoned by the crews, and the unfortunate traders were left alone in the little towns and villages, to wait perhaps months for a cessation of the epidemic.

My efforts to obtain animals were a succession of disappointments, many a time a troop would be promised, but

The city of Carolina, Rio Tocantins.

when the day came, excuses were sent me instead of the expected animals, either that the owner was ill, or his animals were found to be unfit for work, or he suddenly wanted them for other purposes, or his wife, or mother, or child, or somebody was ill; it was most perplexing. At last I heard that the Juiz de Direito would be soon returning to Maranhão, and it suggested itself to me, that a companion to share his travelling expenses would be desirable, and the many excuses given me by the owners of horses and mules for not fulfilling their engagements were perhaps explained; whether it was so or not, at any rate I could not get away until the *Doutor* made his departure with me.

The inhabitants of Carolina and its neighbourhood, are an extremely quiet and peaceable set of people, even the petty jealousies and the rancorousness generated by politics, that so often render these little towns hot-beds of factions and intrigues, appear to be absent from this sleepy city. The advocate makes only a precarious livelihood, and were it not for the police, there would be no work for the sessions, the guardians of the peace thus having no other occupation than drinking, gambling and smoking, have themselves to provide work for their official duties, for during my residence the majority of them occupied the interior of the *calabuça* (lock up).

Such limited commerce as exists with the outer world, is transacted with Para by means of the trading craft of the Rio Tocantins. From what I could learn, the only exports appear to be hides and dried beef, and those only in insignificant quantities, but a much larger importation comes from Para, chiefly of cotton goods, hardware, and salt.

Although the river abounds with fish, no attempt is made to trap or net them. The following are some of the commonest fish of the river :—

FISH WITH SCALES.

Name of fish.	Length in inches.	Observations.
Pirarucu	60 to 80	Generally used for salting.
Piabanha	36 to 40	A good palatable fish.
Bicudo	30 to 36	Species of sword-fish, dangerous to bathers ; full of spines.
Caranha	20 to 24	Almost round ; good flesh.
Curamata	20 to 24	A fly-feeder.
Aruana	20 to 24	Long and thin ; no good for table.
Piranha	12 to 24	Ferocious fish ; full of spines.
Curupité	20 to 24	A good, palatable fish.
Curvina	16 to 20	No good.
Piau	12 to 18	A good, palatable fish.
Pirambeba	12 to 15	,, ,, flat body.
Mandubim	10 to 14	,, ,,

Some Varieties of Fish.

Fish without Scales.

Name of Fish.	Length in inches.	Observations.
Pirahyba or Piratinga	60 to 80	A species of fresh-water porpoise; eatable.
Dourado	50 to 60	An excellent fish.
Pintada	50 to 60	Similar to the *surubim* of the São Francisco.
Botu	50 to 80	Resembles the *pyrahiba*, but the flat of the tail is horizontal.
Pirahuna	50 to 60	Very thick body; palatable.
Jahú	40 to 50	Great thick body; not eatable.
Chicote	40 to 50	A large eel; palatable.
Para-que	35 to 45	Electric eel.
Caranha	30 to 36	20 inches wide.
Surubim	20 to 30	A good fish.
Barbado	20 to 30	A poor fish.
Cachorro	20 to 30	A good fish.
Candirú	18 to 22	Thick body; uneatable.
Mandim or Armado	20 to 26	A good fish.
Fidalgo	14 to 18	,,
Bico de Pato	12 to 15	,,

Many of these fish of the Tocantins bear names similar to those of the São Francisco, where often there is no identity of species. For instance, the *dourado* of the latter river is a scale-fish, with long sharp teeth; on the Tocantins it is a toothless scaleless mud fish. The *surubim* of the São Francisco, is enormous in size, here it is comparatively small, and the *curumata, curvina, piau*, are all different to their namesakes of the 'Frisco.

Of these scaleless fishes, there are only two that have large teeth, the *cachorro* and *caranha*.

But how insignificant is the mention of these few names of even the largest fish of these rivers, when it is remembered that there are already classified thirteen hundred species of fish of the Amazons.

Apart from the exasperation created by my inability to get away, there was no other reason to regret the long delay in Carolina, for there were several very nice families with whom

I associated with much pleasure, and to them I owe many a debt for their frank hospitality and many kind actions, that so softened the tedium of my stay amongst them. My chief resource for killing time, was by exploring the neighbourhood on foot, and in sketching.

From the high banks of the river, the land everywhere rises in long rolling hills of grass and scrub, that extend to groups of considerable hills, two, three, and four miles to the rear of the city.

Many streams intersect the country, and form it into undulating hills and vales, in the bottoms there is much wood, and the banks of the Tocantins are everywhere fringed with narrow forests. There was nothing to shoot beyond a few birds, chiefly pigeons, parrots, and a few toucans, and the many smaller manikins and finches of the roças, and hawks, *alma de gatos*, black anus, etc., of the campos.

The soil of the campos is everywhere sandy, the hills are sandstone and clay slate, and hard sandstone usually forms the bottoms of the watercourses.

On the western side of the river, several miles inland is a long range of hills, probably 1000 feet above the river level, they are reported to contain gold and copper, but very little is known of the neighbourhood, and the adjoining districts are practically uninhabited.

The river is nearly 1200 feet wide, and from the Somno to Carolina not a rock, rapid, or shallow exists to impede navigation.

There happened two festivals during my stay, one being the *Novennas* (nine days' celebration) and final feast-day of the *Divino Espirito Santo*, the other being the negros *Novennas*, and feast of their pet saint the black *Santa Rosaria*. The occasions brought many of the country people into the town, who, however, kept well within doors during the glare and heat of the daytime. Every day there was an incessant ringing of the church-bell, and firing of rockets, otherwise the usual sleepy appearance of the city was but little disturbed. In the evening large bonfires were lighted in the square, and the labourers and country folk assembled to dance *tamboa* and *batuque* dances to the rub-a-dub-dub accompaniment played with the hands on the skin-covered extremity of a hollow tree, and to the tum-thum of *violas*. The juiz and juiza, or patron and patroness of the Festival, one of the leading shopkeepers and his wife, kept open house, and regaled visitors with green tea, coffee, sweets and cakes.

The Negro festival was a more noisy and gorgeous affair. I was conducted to a small door and window house, the palace of the Emperor and Empress of the Feast, a big black negro, and a bigger and fatter negro lady, both pure Africans; they were solemnly seated in chairs on a raised daïs of boards, under a canopy of green and yellow cloth; each one wore a massive crown of solid silver on the head, and chains of gold were around their necks. The man wore the uniform of a captain in the Brazilian Army, the Empress was clad in a yellow-coloured muslin dress, and a long train of crimson cloth; two Negros in cavalry uniform, with drawn sabres in their hands, served as guards of honour; and several black damsels dressed in white muslin, and freely decorated with massive gold ornaments, attended the Empress; these girls were slaves belonging to various ladies of the city, who had apparently crowded on to the dark houris all their bracelets, rings, brooches, and necklaces. I was much surprised to see such a display of jewellery, especially when informed of its sterling quality. In an adjoining and larger room, a long table covered with a white table-cloth, was spread with a most liberal supply of comestibles for the use of the stream of visitors, who after making an obeisance to their Imperial Majesties, retired to this room. It was amusing to watch the ravenous despatch of the good things, none of the visitors wasted time on ceremony, or were particular in their choice, each seized whatever was nearest. Bottles of *cachaça* supplied the place of drinkables.

About 8 p.m their Majesties retired from their throne-room and all adjourned to the open square, where bonfires were blazing, and rockets banging. Then ensued dances that were kept up the whole of the long night. One, evidently an Indian dance, called the *cacuriha*, altogether eclipsed the *can-can*, that in comparison is innocence itself; there were other less "warm" dances, such as the *tamboa*, the *onça*, and the *batuque*. There was a strange weirdness in the moonlit scene, the blazing fire, the bounding agile figures, the strangely inspiring yet withal

A midnight festival at Carolina.

monotonous measures and chanting songs, mingled with loud laughter and shouts from several inebriated individuals, and overhead the white moonlit clouds drifting calmly and slowly across the dark still heavens, wafted along by the gentle breeze of the calm night, in solemn contrast to the little pandemonium on mother earth. The movements of the dancers were anything but modest, the turmoil was great, and many of the revellers were intoxicated, yet good-humour and hilarity only prevailed, and there was not the slightest approach to a quarrel.

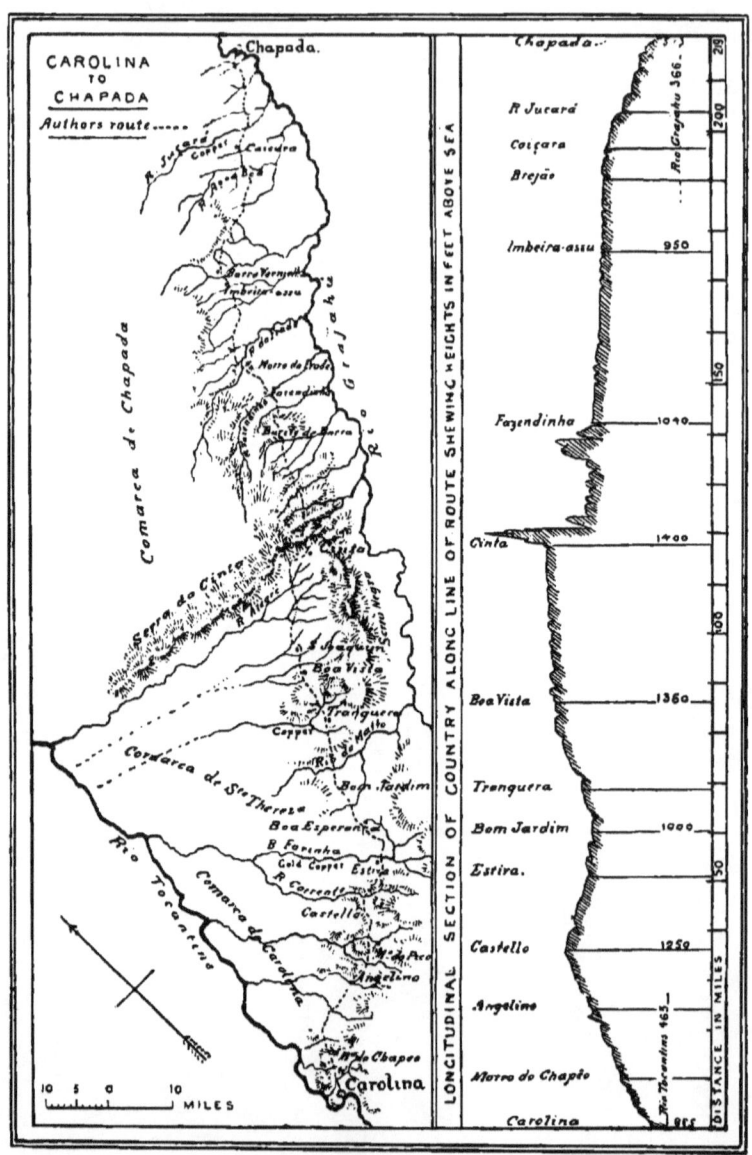

ROUTE MAP—CAROLINA TO CHAPADA.

CHAPTER XIII.

FROM CAROLINA TO CHAPADA.

Departure from Carolina—Poor means of land travelling in North Brazil—Chasing cattle—A complimentary escort—A merry camp—A hilly, elevated country—Picturesque hills—Angelino—An industrious negro—Castle Hill—A curious formation—My fellow-traveller—A thinly-inhabited country—Rough tracks—In the woods in the darkness—A scramble in the dark—João Nogueira—A copper region—Our wretched pack-horses—Dewy nights in camp—A march on foot—Scarcity of game—A charming camp—A strange tree—The Serra da Cinta an important range—A mountain path—A rattlesnake—Misery of travelling with poor animals—A tiring tramp—A palm forest—Morro do Frade—Timidity of countrywomen—A welcome rest—An untidy farm—Good news: a fresh horse—Flat plains and deep valleys—In a butcher's shop for the night—Copper indications—Trezedellas—Arrive at Chapada.

May 26.—The long-waited-for day of departure at last arrives, for the *doutor* is ready for his journey, and the many obstacles that had hitherto prevented my getting away all suddenly disappear, a curious coincidence certainly, and however unpleasant my surmises may be, I am only too glad to move on any conditions, and consider it advisable not to be too inquisitive as to the reality of certain conjectures I may have formed.

On this day, the usually quiet city appears quite animated. Farmers and country-people come trooping in from the neighbourhood on foot and on horseback, and join the townspeople assembled in great numbers around the house of the judge, to wish him a "*boa viagem.*" Every horse of the neighbourhood is requisitioned by the townsfolk to add to the procession of mounted *cavalheiros,* the complimentary escort of *o primeiro autoridade da comarca* (the first authority of the district), on his departure. My new troop now appears, two saddle and two pack-horses; fortunately I still have my old saddle and bridle, for the harness and cattle are mean indeed; gaunt knock-kneed sorry-looking steeds, pensive in attitude, and thoroughly dejected in appearance; the pack-harness is old dilapidated patched with cotton cloth, and mended with ropes; the stuffing of the packs is hard and "raws"-producing. What a difference to the smart mule troops of Minas! but the further north one goes, the more are the inconveniences of travel increased, there are no more roadside '*otels* or *hospedarias,* no bridges over the streams, mules are scarce in number and poor in quality, and the *tropeiros* do not understand their business so well as those of the south. The cause of this is not only due to the greater poverty of the inhabitants of these inland northern provinces, but chiefly to the existence of so many navigable rivers, that largely dispense with a land traffic.

The popularity of the judge is now evidenced by the sounds of many *vivas* from the people who salute him as, mounted on horseback, he makes a final tour through the precincts of the city, accompanied by a mounted following of some sixty of the principal inhabitants and farmers of the neighbourhood. The doors and windows of each house are lined with their inmates, who cheer the judge as he passes, hat in hand, bowing his farewell to his townsmen. The little cavalcade finally wends its way out of the town, when I soon after join it, after bidding good-bye to my friends.

We are soon amidst the many hills and undulating country that surrounds the city like a great amphitheatre. The higher levels of these undulations occasionally spread out in considerable extents of flat grassy tracts, the pasture-lands of numerous herds of cattle. The young "bloods" of the party, who have hitherto been practising upon one another the very mild, and not very funny, practical joking peculiar to young Brazil, now turn their attention to the browsing cattle, by chasing them wherever the ground is level and free from anything requiring a jump; one of them is evidently a true *sertanejo*, for he rides free as a *guacho*, and dashing alongside a galloping bull, seizes its outstretched tail with his hand, and lo! the astonished animal is capsized on the ground amidst the *vivas* of his comrades. I had often heard of this trick of the *sertanejos* (natives of cattle-districts), but had never before seen it performed. Here in the north, and in the central provinces of Brazil, it substitutes the use of the lasso and the bala of the south, and of the Argentine States.

As we progress the surface of the ridges of the undulations becomes more sandy and sterile, and my wretched hack sinks deeply in the loose soil, and heavily plods onwards with many a deep sigh, but every step is now a step towards the coast, and I rejoice thereat, callous to all other matters.

Every mile or so, we pass by groups of prominent hills, rounded or rugged, none are peaked, and all have more or less flat summits, the sources of numerous little streams that have worked out wide valleys from the sandy soil, and by the percolation of the water, have turned these hollows into fertile wooded lands.

Our start had been made late in the afternoon, and it was 7 p.m. before we reached a small habitation at the foot of the Morro do Chapêo (Hat Hill), a high rounded hill with a flat top and perpendicular sides, visible from Carolina, ten miles away. There not being room for ourselves and the numerous escort that had accompanied the judge thus far, and the night being fine, a huge fire is soon blazing in the yard in front of the house; where hides, mats, ponchos, and rugs are collected and laid on the ground for beds. It is a noisy camp, and the songs and laughs and jokes, are kept up till a late hour; but the next morning some of the youngsters look very sad and quiet, and are evidently repenting of a too free indulgence in *cachaça*, late hours, and too much hilarity, followed by a night in the open air and the chill mists of daybreak; one or two show very woebegone faces, tied up with handkerchiefs, that tell a tale of headaches and "sixpences."

The judge's friends now return to their homes, after bestowing upon both of us loving embraces and such fervently expressed, "Deos permit that you may have a good journey, Senhor Doutor! Deos permit that you may be happy, &c." All so flippantly uttered, and like their "*Seu criado está a seus ordens, minha casa, meos servicos a seu disposição*" (Your servant is at your orders, my house, my services at your disposition), is, at least in Carolina, utterly meaningless. For such apparently kind declarations had been constantly made to me during my stay in Carolina, but despite them all I had been kept a prisoner for nineteen days, and only at the departure of the judge could I obtain the sorry animals that now formed my troop. The fact diminished my love for the Carolinensas, and I shall not take away that respect and pleasant memories I should like to have done, for the otherwise kind treatment I received.

During the morning's ride the aneroid showed a continual increase in the altitude of the land, that became more and more irregular, and so cut up by deep narrow valleys and abruptly rising hills, that travelling was very laborious work.

Amongst the woods of the hollows, palm-trees of various species form the chief features of the vegetation; two were entirely new to me, the *pati*[1] and the *junçerera*, as was also a tree locally named *Moleque* that is conspicuous by a tall straight trunk, bright yellow ochre in colour, exceedingly brilliant green leaves and crimson flowers; there was yet an old Minas acquaintance, the *imbeira-assu*,[2] with its scarlet flowers and sap-green trunk, seamed with light yellow veins extending up and down the bark. The bark of this tree is largely used for binding purposes, for it parts easily in long strips, and forms tough pliable ropes. We sighted some deer in the open lands, (but they were very wild,) and in the soft black soil of the woods numerous traces of *porcos de matto* were seen.

At mid-day we reached Angelino, a small farm, situated amidst a group of hills rising 300 to 400 feet in height, many of them are very picturesque, for their fronts are scarped and rugged, and worn by time and weather into fantastic forms, towers, columns, pinnacles, flying buttresses and deep cavities, rich in colours all aglow in the bright sunshine; tall cactuses, thorny bamboos and matted bush clothe the lower slopes, grass and cerrados cover the intervening rolling ground between the hills.

Angelino is another good example of what can be done in the interior of Brazil by energy and hard work. The owner, a negro, was in his younger days a slave, but on the death of his master he received his freedom. He then left the scenes of his bondage and journeyed in search of a place to make a home for himself and his wife, and finally chose the place where he now still lives, in what was then a perfect wilderness; in the course of thirty years of an evidently industrious life he has acquired independence and comfort for his old age.

The farm included a rough mill for grinding sugar-cane and making *rapadura*, a comfortable house, fairly neat and clean, numerous sheds, bullock-carts and bullock-teams, con-

---

[1] Cocos Weddellii. The Indians make some of their bows from this palm.
[2] *Xylopia frutescens*.

siderable roças and sugar-fields, and a herd of 1200 cattle. He was asisted by two sons, fine healthy honest black fellows, and occasionally by a little hired labour. *These are the kind of men that Brazil wants.* Yet this man commenced life in the worst of conditions, penniless, uneducated, without friends and far in the interior away from all resources; but he had the advantage over a European emigrant in a rough knowledge of the soil, of what to grow and how to grow it, a robust health, a climate suited to his nature, a knowledge of the Portuguese language, and of the people with whom he comes in contact.

In the afternoon we left our laborious host and the hills of Angelino, and soon after emerged on to an undulating uninhabited treeless plain of *campinas*, intersected with occasional *brejos* (swamps), and extending for ten miles where we entered on more hilly and wooded ground. At sunset we reached Castello another small farm, situated at the foot of Morro do Castello (Castle Hill), so named apparently, from a fancied resemblance to a round tower. The aneroid showed that we were 712 feet above the level of Carolina; the summit of hill is about 400 feet more.

At Castello we met with indifferent treatment, the people would neither give nor sell anything, not even a bottle of milk, although several cows were in a curral hard by; possibly the owner had had an unpleasant acquaintance with the courts of the judge, for I noticed that the man appeared anything but delighted at sight of my companion.

From Castello to Estiva is sixteen miles, the road passes amidst hills, where it is rough and strewn with boulders, and over plains heavy with sand ; the vegetation comprises strips of woods in the valleys, *cerrados* on the hills, and scattered tufts of thin grass on the flats ; very few birds were seen, and no quadrupeds whatever.

The mid-day halt was made by the side of the Rio Farinha, a stream about forty feet wide, flowing towards the Tocantins. Its clear waters pass over, or under, flat slabs of ironstone rocks, that apparently form the sub-soil of the adjoining land. In some places the stream completely disappears from sight, but occasional crevices in the rocks show the waters underneath, sometimes over twenty feet deep; the owner of an adjoining hut informed me that gold and copper had been found in the neighbourhood, but had never been worked.

The mid-day rest was passed by my fellow-traveller in a hammock, in the enjoyment of the luxuries of a siesta, for he was already greatly fatigued with the journey, and prodigious were the yawns and groans with which, by a final effort, he got up and prepared for the road by re-assuming his comfortable vestments of a white cotton suit, white cotton gloves, long and wide light brown boots, broad-brimmed straw hat, blue spectacles, and white umbrella [3] lined with green.

It is late in the afternoon before we commence the sixteen miles to the proposed camp for the night, and already much too late to start on such a distance, but the road proves fairly good, over long dusty parched-up plains, passing on the way two habitations and the Rio do Matto, one of the sources of the Rio Grajahú.

As the sun disappears we enter a forest district, where, in reply to inquiries for our destination, our guide says, "*É perto, mais um bocadinho*" (it is close by, a little bit more), words that may and do imply anything, or any distance. As we proceed, the darkness falls apace, the woods become thicker, the path narrower and more obstructed, and the horses stumble over tree-roots and into holes; twigs, branches, thorns and hanging vines slap and scratch our faces and hands, knock off our hats and tear our clothes, and the darkness at last becomes complete; occasional efforts are made to light the way with matches or impromptu torches, that only serve to make the surrounding darkness darker, yet the animals, with many

---

[3] In after years, in travelling in Brazil, I adopted the same comfortable costume, minus the umbrella, and can strongly recommend their use with the addition of flannel belt.

a halt, squeeze through bushes, and still move onwards somewhere, where, it is impossible to tell; after what seems an interminable time, the voice of the guide is heard ahead calling out, "Look out! the descent," and then follows the noise of a scramble somewhere. How is any one able to look out for anything in this impenetrable gloom. A lighted match only faintly shows the ears of my horse and the thick foliage around us; suddenly the animal disappears from under me, and rolls down somewhere, and throwing myself from the saddle, I find myself shooting through bushes without any apparent foundation, but finally land, much scratched and with torn clothes, on all fours in the soft muddy bed of a stream, close to the horse, that is upside down and bestowing on me a shower of mud and water. The noise of the tumble and shouts to stop, prevent in time my companion following on top of me. The days of that guide must surely be shortened in consequence of the chorus of dreadful language that salutes him, but he is no better off than I, for he and his horse have similarly rolled down the bank into the muddy ravine. The men on the bank light a candle and pass it down, and with the addition of the light of an improvised torch of a few dried palm-leaves, hastily gathered, we discover we are in the bed of a narrow muddy stream, about twenty feet wide, and bordered by perpendicular banks, twelve feet high. But no harm is done beyond a shaking, a few bruises and scratches, and clothes torn wet and muddy. At first sight it appears difficult to see how the others can avoid descending except by my route, but a little time and patience shows an easier descent close by, and finally an exit out of the stream. It is a strange sight in the surrounding obscurity to see us huddled together in the water of the stream, faintly illumined by the light of the torch, some slipping down the sharp descent and tumbling into the stream, others struggling up the steep banks opposite; the gloom, the faint light, the noise of struggling animals and splashing of water, the shouts of the men echoing in this dark vault, formed certainly a weird scene, but cold wet muddy clothes, are very unromantic. We push on through the dark forest beyond, for a long half-hour, that seems an eternity, and finally emerge with a hearty feeling of thankfulness out into the starlight night of the open *campos*, but where the tracks are so faintly perceptible in the grass, that the guide loses loses all sense of his whereabouts; fortunately we discover a little stream of good water, and there camp for the night.

We get away with the first lights of dawn, and traverse at first, considerable tracts of flat marshy land, then undulating land, covered with *cerrado* and patches of forest, and at 10 a.m. reach Tranquero, a small farm belonging to a Senhor João Nogueiro, whom I can recommend to all future travellers on this road as a genial good fellow.

In the immediate neighbourhood of this place are considerable indications of copper, and the metal has been found in its native state, a rich specimen of which Senhor João showed me and kindly allowed me to keep. He had taken it, he told me, from a ridge of rocks cropping out of the surface of the ground about two miles away, for several miles around the land is of a very rocky character, chiefly ferruginous materials.

Our stock of corn being exhausted, we have to wait while Senhor João sends to his *roça* to fetch some; but good fellow as he undoubtedly is, it is past two o'clock before it arrives. It is an unfortunate thing for any traveller to be dependent on these country-people for any service, for time is so little appreciated by them, that to-morrow is just as good as to-day; even in answer to my requests to hasten the production of the corn, Senhor João mildly replies, "Have patience, friend, you can go on to-morrow, if not to-day."

At 3 p.m. we finally get away and proceed through a very diversified country, alternating between sharp-ridged hills, deep wooded valleys, and long plains of *campos*. The trail in many places is execrable, passing over rugged rocky roads, strewn with boulders and outcrops of stone, or through quagmires, thickly covered with tangled bushes, through which we have to hew a way with knife and billhook, finally the day's journey ended by traversing a long deep sandy flat, dotted with scattered thickets of the wild-orchard-like *cerrado*, by the side of one of which we camped; the ground was free from underwood, and the trees were most conveniently arranged for slinging hammocks.

This day's journey was twenty miles. So far the animals had held out much better than their forlorn appearance allowed me to hope for.[1] The only one that had failed was the one my man Bob had ridden, and he had to walk in consequence.

May 30.—A gloriously cool fresh breeze, 66° (F.), awakened us at early dawn and turned us out briskly from the dew-saturated hammocks. The night dews of these high-lands are very heavy, for in the morning one's beard is as full of moisture as a saturated sponge; little pools of water form in the hollows of the mackintosh sheet, and the rugs and coverings are as wet as though they had been out in the rain, and on this occasion chilled feet and cold noses created eager inquiries for hot coffee.

The next morning we traversed long flat sandy tracts and belts of thick forest, in passing through some of the latter, where the path is so little used and overgrown, much time was consumed by the men in cutting and hewing the thick obstructing boughs and branches; eventually a long flat treeless waterless sandy plain was reached, where the horses sunk over their fetlocks in the loose dry soil, it was hard laborious work,

[1] It is, however, astonishing to see what great loads these wretched cargo-horses of the north can carry, and what great distances they will travel. In Pernambuco it is a sight to see the trains of country horses arriving, with a huge bale of cotton on each side, many having come 200 to 300 miles from the *sertao*, and yet to see them one would only imagine them fit for the knacker, so bony and gaunt and spiritless do they appear.

and my man, who had run a venomous spine into his foot, hobbled along with great difficulty and pain. I gave him a lift on my horse whilst I walked, much to the surprise of the judge, who could neither understand my motive nor appreciate my taste. I walked half the morning's journey of sixteen miles, and although struggling through such heavy and hot ground under a burning sun is not very pleasant, yet the fresh breeze that sweeps over these open plains, created a sensation of exhilaration that made me rather enjoy the walk than otherwise.

These plains are singularly devoid of the usual sights and sounds of animal life, for the birds are very few both in variety and number, and not a vestige of a quadruped is to be seen. The wide far-extending plains are silent solitudes, disturbed only by the rustle of foliage, the gentle murmurs of the wind, and the soft tramp of our animals' hoofs.

At eleven o'clock we reached the margins of a most charming little stream, flowing through a shallow dip in the plain, its banks are gently sloping bright green grass swards, with here and there a tree or a detached bush, or a clump of Pindahibas, or other trees and palms, each surrounded by beds of bright flowers, chiefly arums and lilies; from the branches of the trees hang long festoons of passion-flowers and convolvuli; humming-birds of several species (especially a long scissor-tailed variety) are numerous, and dart with a swift flight from flower to flower, stopping instantaneously to dip their long sharp bills into the convolvulus cups as calmly as though they were seated on a perch instead of being poised motionless in mid-air by the extremely rapid action of their wings. Their brilliant plumage gleams and scintillates in the sunshine with flashing rays of colour like the gleams of a diamond. On the shaded margins of the stream, amidst the grasses of the banks and the moss-covered boulders, are great numbers and varieties of ferns, that add their graceful delicate foliage to the charms of the scene.

We had spread our rugs for the morning picnic under the grateful shade of a large tree standing alone on the green slopes of the stream, and noticing that it was a stranger to my experiences, I hacked off a piece of its very thick hard corrugated bark, and immediately a very volatile sap issued from the gash and the piece in my hand appeared saturated with it as though it had been dipped into kerosene, its odour was very similar, and in the fire it proved equally inflammable. I took away several pieces, and some days afterwards the odour had changed to the delicate perfume of violets. I could only find that the tree is known as *Merim*,[5] (an Indian diminutive term applied to anything,) although this tree was anything but small, for its lower branches were about twenty feet from the ground, and its trunk nearly five feet in circumference; its leaves were small and pinnated, and of a dark dull green colour. The thermometer registered 83° in the shade of this tree.

At 3.30 we left this very pretty camp, and travelled till 6.30, again across long sandy plains, lying between the wooded valleys of streams flowing to the west towards the Rio Tocantins. Soon after leaving we sighted ahead of us, the ridges of the Serra da Cinta, the most important watershed of Maranhão.

The journey terminated near the foot of the Serra at the Fazenda da Cinta, the abode of three families living in so many palm-frond houses. There the judge was amongst friends, who were evidently gratified to receive under their roof so important a personage as a *juiz de direito*.

There is one great advantage in travelling with such a *muito distincto pessoa* (very distinguished person), for he is such a focus of attraction that the passing *estrangeiro* is comparatively unnoticed, and consequently I am saved a load of weary

---

[5] This tree may possibly be the *sapucainha* (*Corpotroche brasiliensis*), which gives an excellent oil of a peculiar and very agreeable odour, and which must not be confounded with the *sapucainha* (*Mainea brasiliensis* of Velloso).

talkee and left in peace, as the Doutor replies to the usual impertinent inquiries as to my business, &c., especially the never-failing *Quanto ganha?* (how much does he earn?).

In front of the fazenda, the serra trends away in a W.N.W. direction towards Sta. Thereza on the Tocantins, (a three days' journey,) in a series of rounded elevations, with occasional peaks of apparently sandstone rocks, with rugged, scarped sides, or long slopes covered with tall rank brown grass and little bush; in the ravines and hollows, thick woods extend far up towards the ridges.

I calculated that the highest elevation is not more than 500 feet above the fazenda, that my aneroid indicated to be 862 feet above the level of Carolina, and 1400 feet above the sea-level.

On the road that afternoon the judge's horse had broken down, when its rider took possession of the horse of his *camarada*, who then had to join my man Bob in *batendo a areia* (beating the sand, i.e. walking). A fine spirited little horse was lent to the judge by his friends. I also sought for one for my man, but without success.

Monday, May 31.—A fairly early start was made at 6.30, on a bright clear cool morning, and shortly afterwards we were scrambling amidst the hills of the serra, by breakneck paths that wind around steep grassy slopes strewn with boulders, large and small (mostly of a coarse semi-decomposed grit, much stained with iron oxides), and deep chasms border the narrow way. On one of these dangerous paths a horse slipped, and down the steep slope he went, head over heels, the fastening of his pack broke, and away that went also. Fortunately, some trees and bushes stopped them before they had gone far, and after very considerable trouble both were hauled up to the path again, the horse quivering with fright, but beyond a few knocks he did not appear much hurt. The stiff climbs and rough roads now began to tell upon the animals, and several sunk down exhausted, and laid with panting sides and heaving nostrils, and only by means of many long rests could we get them along.

From the summit of the range there is an immense view to the north, over land mainly consisting of long sandy plains and undulating hills covered with *cerrado*, and deep wooded valleys.

The descent is much greater than the ascent, for the land on the north side is much lower than that we have left behind. The serra evidently acts as a huge retaining wall to that high plateau, and has prevented denudation to the

Crossing the Serra da Cinta.

extent of that of the north side, where the fall of the waters is greater, and has made the valleys narrow and deeply furrowed.

On reaching this low land the aneroid showed a difference of about 500 feet between the average levels of the two plateaux, giving the serra an approximate altitude of 1000 feet above its northern, and 500 above its southern base.

Many of its spurs could be seen stretching away for many miles in the form of ridges, winding in and out according to the sinuosities of their valleys, all trending to the east, and in places intersecting our direction, and will yet give us many a scramble. As we descended, the slopes became more rugged, in many places showing faces of variously coloured earths and rocks, reds, yellows and dark purples.

On the way the men killed a rattlesnake, 5 feet 3 inches in length. Its rattle of eight rings, was added to my other trophies.

On arriving at the lower plateau, after a little breather for the weary panting animals, we proceeded slowly over heavy roads deep in sand, until 11.30, when we reached a *vaqueiros* rancho called São José, twelve miles from Cinta. The march had been exceptionally slow and tedious, and we formed a long and widely-scattered party, for several of the horses had broken down, and even after their loads were shifted to the saddle-horses of the men, (who now all marched on foot,) they wearily lagged behind. A day's journey in Brazil with a good troop of mules, is, at the best of times, but a long wearisome ride even when all goes well, for one's limbs become stiff and cramped, the hot sun dries and parches the skin, the head aches, and the body is tired; it is, however, doubly so when the animals are tired and done up and require incessant urging onwards, and it is painful to witness the efforts of the poor beasts struggling against their failing strength, the perspiration streaming down their flanks, their parched tongues hanging out, their glaring eyes forcibly expressing their agonies.

I tried again at S. José to get an exchange of animals at any cost, but again met with *non-success*.

After a long rest, we departed in the afternoon, and went on pretty well until the latter part, when one of the last of the far-stretching spurs of the Serra da Cinta had to be crossed, a rough steep rocky road, that was the last straw to the animals, for, with the exception of the judge's horse, that was young and fresh, they repeatedly laid down, after stumbling and falling, one after the other, through sheer inability to do more,

It was only by continually taking off their packs and resting them, and going on little by little, that we were at last, after a most wearying time, finally enabled to reach the foot of the descent just as the sun set, and where fortunately, was a stream of water in an open *campos*. I had had to walk the last few miles, and the rugged road, and stiff climb, and hot sun, made me welcome the camp as much as the animals.

A fine cool night, with the thermometer at 64°, and a well-earned night's repose, refreshed man and beast. My horse, that was not so much done up as some of the pack-horses, had then to take a turn at carrying a cargo, that otherwise must have been left behind, and all started on foot, excepting the judge, who was good enough to offer me his horse and take his turn at *batendo a areia*, but a Brazilian gentleman on foot in the country would feel as comfortable as a fish out of water, and as I was in excellent training, and could well support the fatigue of walking, I did not accept his offer.

Soon after leaving camp the track entered a palm forest, as different to the forests of more southern latitudes as those are to an European wood. I confess, that then I had had such a surfeit of the beauties of the Brazilian flora, that I felt little disposed to appreciate the charms of these essentially tropical forms of vegetation, yet a traveller must be callous indeed to fail to notice the wondrous delicacy of such growths, for there seemed to be there collected, all that was graceful in the vegetable world: there were dwarfed ground-palms like the *Ubussu*,[6] growing in form like a clump of huge ostrich-feathers, tall palms, with soft feathery leaves like the *Jupati*,[7] or the spiny trunk and purple fruit clusters of the *Maraja*,[8] palms with drooping follicles like the *Inaja*,[9] palms with smooth stems, palms with spiny stems, tall and short tree ferns, and ferns of many other varieties, and scattered about were here and there large trees of various species, the huge buttressed

[6] *Manicaria saccifera.*
[7] *Raphia tedigera.*
[8] *Bactris maraja.*
[9] *Maximiliana regia.*

gammeleira,[1] the bulging *barrigudo*,[2] the tall straight yellow trunk of the *Moleque*, and the light-green small feathery foliaged mimosas; each tree-trunk spotted with lichens, pearly grey or brilliant crimson, and bearing a wealth of parasites (chiefly blue-banded *bromelias*, and the pendent *barba velha*), and ferns and mosses, little gardens in themselves; many shrubs of *Myrtaceæ* order helped to fill up the spaces between the trees; the vines, some in leaf, some in flower, some like the cordage of a ship, swung their graceful lines from tree to tree, or hung in long straight lines. The vegetation was not by any means dense and compact, like the forest of the Amazon's, for the sun's rays freely streamed into the open glades between the larger trees, and enabled the sunlight to fleck the glistening polished palm-leaves with its golden light, in beautiful contrast to the parts in shade. Many birds frequent these lovely dells, gorgeous in colour and in harmony with such scenes. There were the crimson and the blue and gold *araras*, green parrots, brilliant humming-birds, long yellow-beaked and purple and white-bodied toucans, chattering blue-green parroquets, red-headed woodpeckers tapping the trees with quick sharp taps in pursuit of grubs and insects, and the nests of the Japim birds[3] hung suspended in clusters of woven twigs. On the ground, large blue and green *cameleoēs*,[4] (lizards) startle one with their rustle as they run over the dry leaves, making one prepare for a possible snake; and one does not fail to appear, a glistening vermilion purple and cream coral snake, that gleams so brilliantly that there is nothing in nature to compare with it when a ray of sunlight falls upon the wonderfully soft yet metallic sheen of its colours. The wood, about four miles in extent, fills a low flat hollow between higher grass-lands, on to which we eventually emerged, a long deep sandy campos of scattered tufts of thin wiry grass. Two miles of soft sand brought us to another herdsman's

[1] *Urostigma doliaria.*
[2] *Echytes*, sp.
[3] *Cassicus icteronotus.*
[4] *Agama picta.*

rancho, called *Fazendinha*, where I yet failed to get fresh animals.[5] We pushed on again, and after traversing more sandy flats and belts of woods bordering the streams, all flowing into the Rio Grajahu to the east, we reached a picturesque stream near a considerable hill, called Morro do Frade, a huge square mass of dark variously-coloured rock, resembling a huge plum cake in appearance; its sides are precipitous and devoid of vegetation, its evidently once flat top is worn into irregular points, pinnacles and ridges, and green with vegetation, the character of which the distance would not allow me to distinguish. I had walked fifteen miles before we sat down to breakfast, (as usual at mid-day,) and I confess that I felt a longing to send for a hansom to do the rest. Fortunately, in the afternoon the animals recovered a little, and my Rozinante gave me a lift for a few miles, until he again broke down, and I had to foot it again. At 6 p.m. we reached a group of three houses with an *engenho* (mill-house) and outbuildings, all partly hidden amidst a tangle of trees and bush, known as Imbeira-assu. Voices were heard on our approach, then women were seen hurrying indoors. On our arrival all doors and windows were closed, and no answer was made to our calls, so without further ceremony we took possession of the mill-house for the night's quarters.

The night proved much warmer than usual, 76°, and we were much disturbed by the squealing of inquisitive pigs, pounced upon and worried by Feroz, and my old enemies, the mosquitos, also played a high-pitched concert, and pricked and stung us freely, but I was soon oblivious to all torments, for I was thoroughly tired out with my day's walk.

June 2.—My companion rode away early in the morning to see if he could procure another horse for me at some houses further on; then the male inhabitants of Imbeira-assu at last shyly approached and had a good stare at us, but they

---

[5] Although we had passed cattle-farms, we had rarely sighted any cattle on the way, for the grazing-grounds are often many miles away.

either could not, or would not, understand me, replying either with an interrogative grunt or a *Não entendo n'hor não*, to my expressed desires to purchase a horse, or vegetables, or fruits, or milk. The female portion we only saw at a distance, peeping at us from behind half-closed doors and window-shutters. The whole place, that might so easily have been made beautiful, was dingy dirty and dilapidated, and I was glad to get away from it.

We marched fourteen miles, nearly all the way over sandy plains, with a few small streams crossing the route ; now that the judge was away, his men grumbled loud and frequently at his *viagem braba* (forced march), and commenced to vent their anger by thwacking the poor animals. I happened to be behind one of the boys when he cruelly thrust a pointed stick into the nostrils of a horse ; he was considerably astonished to receive a smart blow of my staff across his shoulders, and an information that it would be repeated if he again tortured the animals. It was evidently beyond his comprehension why he was thrashed, he sulked for awhile, but a few sharp admonitions made him civil, much more so than he had been at any time, even the grumblings ceased when I was near.[6]

At Brejão I found the judge waiting for me, and, "O ! be joyful," he had obtained a fresh animal for me. I had had quite enough of *batendo a areia*. Fourteen miles does not seem much of a walk, but it is quite enough before breakfast over those hot sandy plains of Maranhão, but if any one wishes to taste delicious nectar, let him there walk a few miles, sinking into the hot sand at every stride, the clothes saturated with perspiration, the limbs stiff and aching, the mouth dry

---

[6] A great deal of judgment is required by the traveller in Brazil in dealing with the country-people. Justice and firmness is usually all that is necessary, and harsh measures are at best dangerous, and the traveller will risk a knifing ; but some characters, like mules and dogs, are better for a thrashing, and think all the better of their *patrão*.

and parched, and then arrive at a little stream of crystal water bubbling over rocks, through banks of flowers and ferns and grasses, and lay himself down and drink and drink the delicious grateful fluid ; for when one is really thirsty, all fluids will be refused for Nature's natural assuager of thirst.

From Brejão the land changes considerably, the previous long sandy tracts giving place to a more gravelly soil, covered with dwarf trees and shrubs, the latter chiefly consisting of the order of *Myrtaceæ*. The ground is fairly level, but intersected by very deep valleys, difficult of descent and ascent, with little turbulent streams in their bottoms. We reached at nightfall, Caiçara, a palm-frond hut, where we obtained the luxury of fresh beef at the price of eighty reis per pound, (about twopence). Like Embira-assu, the place was repulsive in its squalor and dirt. The judge elected to sleep in the house, but I preferred the fresh open air to the combined smells of freshly-slaughtered meat and various other odours, generated by refuse and the rubbish of the interior of the hut. At sunrise the thermometer indicated 72°.

June 3.—Being now within twenty miles of Chapada, the Doutor and I decided to go on together, and leave our men to bring on the baggage and animals at their leisure. The sharper pace we travelled at, was a welcome change to the slow walk at which we had made the journey hitherto, and decidedly preferable to " footing it." A few miles out we passed the Riberão de Juçará, where again are indications of copper, in the appearance of the rocks that crop out in many places in the form of dykes. The bed and banks of the Riberão are composed entirely of dark green rocks, of a fine close grain like basalt ; these rocks extend all the way to Chapada. The land is everywhere covered with *cerrado* and scrub, and the valleys are narrow and very deep. After a short halt for breakfast in a picturesque glade on a soft sward under the shade of a large Carahyba tree, and a dip in the pellucid waters of a stream, we pushed on again, and soon after mid-day we reached the valley of the Rio Grajahu, and descended 200 feet or more, by a precipitous path, to the village of Trezedellas, on the west bank of the river, and immediately opposite the villa (town) of Chapada, 188 miles, I estimated, from Carolina.

We crossed the river in a *montaria*[7] and the water was sufficiently shallow to allow the animals to wade across; the bed and banks are dark green rock, the soil of the higher ground is red clay, and gravel with outcrops of stone, and the surface is sand and gravel.

Chapada is somewhat like the city of Bahia in one respect, in having a lower and an upper town. The first consists of

The " praça " of the town of Chapada.

a street along the banks, parallel to the course of the river. A long straggling ascent up a very steep incline, freely obstructed by outcrops of rock and deep holes, brings us to the main portion of the town, built upon a high far-extending flat plateau, sparsely covered with a scrubby vegetation and a dry gravelly soil. There is a square with detached houses around it, and the conventional old unfinished church, with scaffolding that has been there for years, so peculiar to all these northern

[7] A small canoe-shaped boat.

towns and villages. Many of the houses look comfortable and pretentious (at least from a national point of view), gaudily painted in distemper, green, blue, chocolate, yellow, red, white, utterly regardless of combination or harmony of colours; the windows are latticed, and the tiled roofs project in wide eaves, forming almost verandahs over the brick *trottoirs* in front. Branching away from the square are several irregular streets of houses, some in rows, some detached and divided from each other by their *hortas* (gardens) of fruit-trees. There are several vendas, general stores, and open sheds of smithies, tinmen, carpenters, masons, &c. There is more life and movement than in Carolina, but even so it is not much. The streets are heavy with a soft deep sand that rises in clouds with every puff of wind, or are overgrown with grass and bushes where the soil is firmer, or almost like a rough rocky stone staircase, like the ascent from the riverside; the sun pours down its fierce rays on the shadeless streets, and all who can, keep within doors and doze in their hammocks.

My companion invited me to the house of his friend, colleague, and college chum, Dr. Candido Pereira Lemos, the Juiz de Direito of the Comarca of Chapada.[8]

[8] This word signifies a wide flat, and hence the name of this town on the borders of the table-land.

CHAPTER XIV.

FROM CHAPADA, DOWN THE RIO GRAJAHU, TO VICTORIA ON THE RIO MEARIM.

A pleasant family—Chapada children—A rich copper region—The sessions at Chapada—Trade—A white Indian—We charter an *igarite*—A grand departure from Chapada—Our new craft and its crew—The river Grajahu and its beauties—A camp by the forest—Howling monkeys—A quiet solitude—Mosquitos again—Animal life of the river-side—A mountain of whetstones—A hill of satin spar—A foul place—A night voyage—Snags—Buried alive—A night of torment—*Botes* of the river—In the forest—Ferocious fish; the piranhas—A race—A tortuous river—Morro do Oratorio—Fishing—Vegetation of the shores—Gammella Indians—First habitations since leaving Chapada—Hidden beauties—Pium sand-flies—Snags—An Indian anecdote—An exchange of compliments—The effect of a revolver—A morning mist—Torments of sand-flies—A day's journey to gain 600 yards—A useful parasite—An evening scene—A collision with a snag—Boarded by fire-ants—Amidst the bush in the darkness—A perfect inferno—Continual torments—The Director of Indians—Valuable natural productions of the forest—Indian village—*Sobradinho* and its tenants—A landslip—Itambeira Indians—Fever appears—A grand forest—Brown river-water—Untiring paddlers—An alligator and the Piranhas—A Penelope—A lost dinner—A dense bush—An Indian alarm—A noisy night with frogs—Dangers of a sleep on a sand-bank—Mournful tokens—The deadly climate of the river in certain seasons—More copper indications—A grand copper region—Ingativas—A diver bird—A farm abandoned through mosquitos—A long day's work—Asleep in a cattle-trough—A weary night—Inhabited lands—Brilliant distinctness of tropical scenery—An industrious couple—A *capoeira de palmerias*—A haunted lake—The submerged lands of the mouth of the Grajahu—A steaming-hot locality—On the Rio Mearim—No land to camp on—A slow and fatiguing journey—Arrive at Victoria—Rough quarters.

Manoel the pilot.

I PASSED three days with Dr. Candido and his family, pending the preparations for the voyage down the Rio Grajahu.

Soon after our arrival, all the principal inhabitants called to visit my fellow-traveller. The visits were conducted with much ceremony and bowing on either side, and exchanges of fulsome and meaningless compliments, but apart from their love of form, (that soon disappears after the ice of introduction has thawed,) many of the farmers and traders are bluff active fellows, and had they not been so long habituated to such indolent habits and conservative customs as exists amongst them, they would doubtless be a more practical people. One of them, a Capitão Antonio José dos Mattos, brought me samples of native copper and plumbago, found in an outcrop of rocks some four miles away, and as he pressed me very much to go and see the place, I went with him to it.

The district is extremely stony, and rocks appear above the soil in all directions. Where the samples of native copper were obtained was in a reef of rocks that runs N.E. and S.W.; its course could be traced for several hundred yards, and in several places I secured good examples of copper, both in a native state and in other forms. The plumbago is in another district to the east, that I did not go to see.

Being pressed by several of the inhabitants to pay them a visit, I proceed upon a round of calls. The men are full of gossip, and eager to know all about me, my salary being the never-failing topic of interest. The elder women folk are garrulous old dames, always considerably *en déshabillé*, the younger mothers are sickly and weary with the cares of household and a nearly always numerous progeny. The girls are seldom pretty (except when very young), and although a flower often decorates their black hair, they are as untidy and as slipshod as their mothers and aunts. But the children, especially the little ones, were my horror; even in the more well-to-do families they are sallow wizened and endowed with prominent "corporations," nearly always naked, and often infested, like their mothers, with the "pulex capital," and thoroughly grubby; their little cheeks show contoured layers of grime, where the hourly tide of tears has washed the soil into successive ridges. They are horribly spoiled, squall at the slightest provocation, and bite, scratch, and even swear at the patient blacks who attend them. Even when their howls prohibit all conversation, the mother only mildly protests by saying, "*Ai! Meo Deos! O que menino! Não faça isto, meo bem. Não chora, bemzinho. Ah! Meo Deos!*" (What a child! Don't do that, my dear. Don't cry, my darling). Observations that of course only result in redoubled noise, when the child is carried away screaming, kicking, and biting. At sight of me some will howl at once, others will advance in quite a friendly way and smear me with hands sticky and odorous, and swarm up my knees and there seat their little naked selves, looking more fit to be picked up with a pair of tongs and dropped into a congenial pig-sty. Certainly they are not what are considered kissable children.

The sessions were then on, and the local judge left us every morning at eleven o'clock, in his war-paint of black frock-coat, top hat, patent leather shoes, and umbrella (the thermometer at 88°), to descend to the lower town, where the trials were held in a little crowded room of a small door and window house. All the cases were for cutting and wounding, with generally fatal terminations; women, cards and *cachaça* being the primary causes of the troubles; and however great or horrible the crime may be, the criminal never suffers capital punishment, but is sentenced to the "galleys" for life, or a number of years, that may be either in the convict settlement of Fernando de Noronha, or the provincial gaol, or even the local lock-up. The judge departs with much groaning and sighing, as though he is the most overworked being, and returns about 2 p.m., faint and exhausted with his labours. Every evening the town band marches up the hill and serenades my fellow-traveller. It consists of two cornets, a trombone, a fife, two violins, and a big drum; the big drum and the trombone are especially effective, the other instruments are "nowhere." The compliment would not be complete without a few rockets, which are duly set off at intervals.

Chapada (in former times, like Carolina, an Indian village) has a population of more or less 1500 inhabitants. It is difficult to obtain any reliable information on this point, as no census is kept or made, I can only estimate by the number of houses. A considerable trade is carried on with the interior, both in export and import, for there is uninterrupted navigation from hence to the coast. Salt, hardware, cotton goods, guns, powder and shot, are the chief items of import, and hides, dried beef, sarsaparilla, balsam of copaiba, tobacco, piassaba,[1] and *cachaça*, those of export. No statistics whatever were obtainable as to the quantities, and although these are doubtless considerable for a little town like Chapada, the traffic would not recompense any costly outlay in improving the route, neither do I see in the absence of immigration any reason to hope for any perceptible immediate improvement. There is a railway proposed to be built from Barra da Corda to Carolina, that under present conditions of traffic is really childish. It would be expensive to build, and considerable sums would have to be yearly expended to work it. Barra da Corda is a small town on the Rio Mearim, about 70 miles to the East of Chapada. The river is navigable, and steamers run up as far as Barra da Corda

[1] *Attalea funifera*.

from the city of Maranhão. Unfortunately, I only found out this fact after I had left Chapada, otherwise I would have avoided the unpleasant journey down the Grajahu by going on to Barra da Corda.

At Dr. Candido's house I noticed a female servant, slatternly as might be expected, in contrast to whom, a London lodging-house general servant in the early stage of her day's work, would appear neat and clean. This particular woman being practically white, with long straight brown hair and grey eyes, yet with an undoubtedly flat Indian face, made me inquire whence she came; I was informed that she was a pure Indian, of a race known as the *Indios Brancos*, from the lower Tocantins. I saw also a fine athletic young fellow, but a little darker than many Spaniards, a Guajajara Indian from the Rio Pinaré. Although both man and woman, especially the woman, might well pass in Brazil for "white folks," if only their colour was considered, yet both had the unmistakable chief Indian characteristics. The large head with high cheek-bones, and wide flat face, small eyes, small nose, and prominent yet not thick lips, small chin and narrow forehead, short neck, broad deep chest, long arms, small hips, hands and feet, and short stature.[2]

I received a visit one day from a young man, who on learning that I was an "*engenheiro*," came to request me to be so good as to make his watch go. He seemed surprised when I told him I did not understand the repairs of a watch, but seeing that his Geneva was apparently only very dirty, I recommended him to "boil" it, as I had heard that had proved efficacious. He promised to try the experiment.

---

[2] The Baccahiris Indians, who formerly inhabited the region of the Rio dos Mortes, in the province of Matto Grosso, were said to be of a white complexion, and a branch of the Paracis, the chief Indian race of Matto Grosso. Henderson mentions in his work, the Manajos, or white Indians of Maranhão, as inhabiting the neighbourhood of the Tocantins, below the Rio Araguaya. This race is also known by the name of *Anambeios*.

We succeeded in chartering an *igarite*, with the services of a pilot and three paddlers. The boat had been offered to us, placed at our service in fact, by one of the most affectionate of my companion's very loving friends, who charged us just double what I afterwards found to be the proper price. The following were the prices we paid for the voyage to Arary:—

Hire of *igarite*	60$ 000.
Pilot's wages	60$ 000.
Three paddlers	150$ 000.
Provisions	26$ 660.
	296$ 660.

Say, roughly, £30 for 12 days' voyage for our two selves, three servants, and the four men composing the crew, nine persons in all, and considering that the craft would obtain a cargo on its return, it was dear enough.

Amongst the stores I laid in, I purchased in Chapada, Tennant's ale, Huntley and Palmer's biscuits, Bryant and May's matches, French sardines and bottled fruits, Portuguese wine, American kerosine, and Carnahuba candles, but beans, farinha, dried beef, salted pork, salt, sugar, coffee, and *cachaça* formed the chief substance of the provisions.

June 6th came at last, a joyful day, for it was our day of departure. All the *gente graúda* (magnates) of the place, the Coronels, the Majors, the *Capitões*, the Tenentes, and the Alferes, assembled at the house of Dr. Candido, duly arrayed in their best, (some in black coats and top hats,) to form a procession of honour to escort my companion to our ship. The preliminary *adeos* were made with much embracing and exchanges of all kinds of wishes for everlasting happiness and fortune and good health, and then bidding good-bye to my kind friend Dr. Candido and his amiable Senhora, Donna Maria, I joined the tail of the procession that increased as we proceeded. At the port were a crowd of men, women, and

ON THE RIO GRAJAHÚ.

Frontispiece to Vol. I.　　　　See Vol. II. pp. 265 to 295.

children, and several negro girls bearing baskets of bread, cakes, preserves, cheeses, honey and eggs, all presents to my companion; three large *botes* were on the river to receive the escort of friends, on one was the drum and trombone band, which immediately commenced its noisy operations, accompanied by the reports of exploding rockets and bombs, shouts and *vivas*, anything to make the din and noise that the *matuto* so dearly loves.

More embracing, and speeches inaudible amidst the racket, ensue as we go aboard our craft; finally we get under weigh, followed by the convoy of *botes* loaded with the band and all who could crowd aboard. For several hundred yards the banks are lined with townspeople, who shout and *viva* their utmost, rockets are sent up from banks and barges, bombs explode with loud reports, the noisy band and the shouts, echo and re-echo amidst the rocky cliffs of the shore, a perfect hurly-burly of noise. We proceed for about a mile when the Doutor's friends disembark and meet him on shore to have another loving cuddle, with arms entwined around his neck, and lovingly and gently pat his back. He makes an excellent speech in reply, as almost any educated Brazilian can do, and do well, and after more cuddles, he tears himself away, we cast off, and the men paddle us quickly beyond the last echoing *viva*. The Doutor said he was very vexed at such a demonstration, as it was evidently intended as a rebuff to his colleague, who is not popular in his district.

Now that we are left to the quiet solitudes of the forest and the river, one can look about the new craft. The *igarite* is a broad flush-decked shallow boat, twenty feet long and six feet beam, and only two inches above the water amidship; it has a shallow draught and is keelless, the bows and stern are rounded raised and pointed like a spoon; and a rudder is substituted by a long broad paddle, that works in a notch at the point of the stern; amidships a rounded roof hut, made of palm-fronds, and thatched with the same, and covered with hides, serves as cabin and saloon, and is just big enough to hold the stores, baggage, and a couch; the ends are open, and another entrance is through a small opening in the side, like the entrance to a dog-kennel. The pilot, Manoel, is a mild-eyed very quiet brown-skinned countryman, that nothing apparently, will excite, hurry, or render nervous; he is slow in speech and slow in his movements, he is clad in a leather jacket and hat, and a coarse cotton shirt and trousers. The crew are not very attractive in appearance, one is an oldish brown fellow, with a very long hairless face and drooping under lip, another is a wild rollicking irrepressible fellow, with a great mass of thick curly hair, he shouts, he sings, and shows his filed teeth, he laughs all the time, and cracks jokes and chaffs his solemn-faced companion; the third is a younger brown gentleman, with a sullen sulky face. *Camisolas* (sleeveless cotton shirts) and trousers are their only garments. The judge and two attendant negro lads, my man Bob, and myself, complete the party.

At the port of Chapada I measured the river, and found it to be 109 feet in width, with varying depths of three to six feet, in what was then a dry month. The current flows at the rate of about one mile per hour. The water is clear and tepid. The ordinary water-level is 366 feet above the sea, 72 feet below the Tocantins at Carolina, and 150 below the upper town of Chapada. This river is wonderfully beautiful, cliffs of dark green rock, ten to thirty feet high, form the banks, down whose face hang the huge roots of great trees growing in the soil above, water drips and trickles at every few yards and the moisture generates ferns and mosses in every ledge and cranny, and in the narrower parts of the stream the great trees spread their boughs overhead from either side and mingle one with the other in a lovely green arcade of verdure, the leaves golden green, and the tracery of boughs dark and opaque against the blue sky, that here and there sends a flood of sunshine upon the shaded waters of the river.

First Night on the Grajahu. 267

The most conspicuous trees are broad-leaved, and fantastically formed trunks of Gammeleiras; bulging Barrigudas or Samaumas;[3] purple flowering Bignonia Páu d' Arco[4] de Flor Roxa, and the green trunk of the Páu de Embira.[5] The underwood comprises shrubs of the *Myrtaceæ* family, great clumps of bamboos of various varieties (some attaining a height of fifty feet), and the white *gravata*,[6] whose remarkable fibres can be made into the finest tissues. Palms of any species are rare in these woods.

The *bote* makes a fair progress of nearly four miles the hour, propelled by four paddles (for Bob had joined the crew). The men stand up and row by pulling the long paddles like sweeps. The rowlocks are each formed by the ribs of the boat being continued two feet above the deck, to whose extremities the paddles are secured. As it was near four o'clock before we started, we make but a short journey, and land at sunset on the rocky banks, at a point where the roots of a great *gammeleira* above had spread a network of ramifications, leaving holes and crannies partly filled with earth and *débris*, just the places a snake loves to coil away in. We climb the bank, and clear a space in the woods, the fire is made, dinner prepared and despatched, hammocks suspended wherever a convenient place is found, (I prefer my box bed on deck,) and then the long dark evening is before us. As the sun sets the forest resounds with the deep hoarse roars of the *guaribas*[7] (howling monkey), resembling more the roar of a bull than of so small an animal; but as the short twilight changes to dark night they cease their din, and a deep silence follows disturbed only by the faint droning hum of mosquitos, and the occasional splash of a fish. The night is warm and close (82°), thick coverings are insupportable, and the mosquitos have grand times, and I already begin to regret the cool fresh

---

[3] Genus *Echytes*, that furnishes the vegetable silk.
[4] *Tecoma curialis*.   [5] *Xilopia frutecens*.
[6] *Bilbergia tinctoria*.   [7] *Myctis Beelzebub*.

nights of the open highlands we had so lately traversed. But confound these mosquitos—slap—slap—if there is anything to make a man feel unkind, it is to be a helpless prey to crowds of these bloodthirsty insects.

We are all astir at 4 a.m., and after a splash in the river that somewhat refreshes one fevered from a night of mosquitos, we get under weigh whilst it is yet dark, and drift slowly with the stream so as to avoid a violent collision with snags. In due time the grey dawn appears, and the mist rolls away from the surface of the warm water; as the shadows disappear and the warm light of daybreak glows on the trees and water, the woods become lively with sounds, the sonorous bell-bird twangs its orisons, a pretty red and gold and purple-black *corrupião*[8] warbles its sweet notes (probably the only tropical bird of brilliant plumage that can utter melodious notes). The *guaribas* howl again in the distance, a group of brown monkeys in some trees chatter and grin at us as we pass onwards. On a muddy bank ahead we sight a *pavão* (the wild peacock of Maranhão) chasing the flies and mosquitos. (Why it is called a *pavão* I cannot tell, unless the similarity of its cry has originated the name.) It is a dark purple in colour and a delicately formed bird, the size of an ordinary fowl. An alligator, small in size, and several lumbering *capyvaras* next appear.

At a part of the river called Sta. Luzia, the *porto* of a neighbouring fazenda, there is a considerable hill, composed almost entirely of *Pedras d' Amolar*[9] (whetstones) of the finest quality.

At mid-day we pass a high cliff of white stone, that glistens and sparkles in the sunshine, its base is worn away by the river, and its summit considerably overhangs the water; its substance is the fibrous variety of gypsum known as satin-spar.

[8] Belonging to the genus *Xanthornus*.
[9] This species of sandstone belongs to the Carboniferous or Devonian series.

The cliff is about sixty feet high, and extends into the woods in a greater elevation.

After passing this cliff, the banks gradually give place to low mossy slopes, or to low land, that is so covered with dense bushes and trees and flowering creepers that the soil is invisible.

We land at sunset on ground not two feet above the river, and as floods have been known to rise at Chapada twenty to thirty feet above the then level, an idea may be formed of the malaria and mosquitos that are generated by the subsidence of the waters from these flooded lands. The soil is soft, and deep in rotting leaves, through which our feet sink like in a sponge. The air is close and musty, a warm humid heat, like that of a closed hot-house; the mosquitos are in such crowds that their united notes create a roar like the sound of a distant waterfall, we have to keep continually moving, or stand to leeward of the fire, amidst its smoke. No time is lost over dinner that evening, and as soon as possible we push off again into the darkness of the night; the moon is new, the light is faint, and the dark shadows are intense.

We have not travelled far before we run into a submerged snag, and the craft heels over, and one side sinks under water, if the boat had not been decked it must have filled and gone down. As the river is not more than four feet deep, the men enter the water, and with axes and bills release the boat from the log.

About 8 p.m. we land on a sand-bank, where we are again so persecuted by mosquitos, that the men dig graves in the sand, and bury themselves in the holes, leaving only their heads above ground, covered with a cloth. They had been rowing from 5 a.m. to 8 p m., and being well tired out, they are soon asleep in their novel beds, that form a curious sight to see by the light of the fire, the row of heads sticking out of the sand. The judge had wisely provided himself with a mosquito-curtain, through which he passes the hammock strings; mine, unfortunately, I had left at Formosa. I try all manner of means to escape my tormentors, but in vain; the night is close and warm, and I pass it slowly and horribly in pacing to and fro on the sand-bank, for to attempt to lie down to sleep is to choose between being half-stifled by the heat of coverings, or stung by the venomous insects.

I turn out everybody at 4 a.m., and soon after we are under weigh in the darkness and mist; then, regardless of snags or shipwreck, I obtain a welcome sleep.

About 8 a.m. we pass a *bote* (that had left Chapada the day before we did), loaded with hides and balsam of copaiba, bound for Maranhão, the crew of eight naked Indians are breakfasting on shore, their tough hides apparently impervious to mosquito bites, for the men sit as quietly as though none of the insects are about.

At breakfast-time I enter the adjoining forest, that in this place is remarkably free from underwood, and even the usual *cipos* (vines) are few in number and variety. It is a novel sight to see this maze of tall straight trunks (from the massive tree with a girt of twelve or fifteen feet, to the lofty slender sapling, whose crown of branches is so high above the ground that it looks quite top-heavy), all supporting a great canopy of dark foliage, almost impervious to a gleam of sunshine. One can glance down great colonnades of these trees, where the farthest columns appear to merge into the blue haze of the sombre shade. Under foot, the soil is soft with the accumulations of fallen leaves, all rotting amidst the black soil and moisture of the ground. The air is cool and damp, but it smells faint and sickly, like that of a charnel-house. As the floor of the forest is only a few feet above the low water of the river, it must be deeply covered by the annual floods, that have probably swept away or drowned the underwood, and the deep shade prevents its reproduction.

I do not return without a subscription to the stock-pot, for hearing the sounds of a low whistling amongst the foliage high up above, I there perceive a number of monkeys, eagerly scanning my movements with evident curiosity. A shot brings one down, a pretty brown fellow, with a fringe of grey hairs around his face.

I now return to the shore, with the intention of taking a swim, but the sight that meets me effectually dispels such an intention. The judge is seated on the boat with a stick in his hand, dangling a line with a piece of meat tied to its end, and hauling in *piranhas* as fast as he can pull them aboard, no hook or float is necessary, for immediately the bait enters the water, great numbers of the fish struggle and fight with one another to seize it, when, (as they hold on firmly to the meat,) they are easily jerked aboard. The deck is quite alive with numbers of them leaping about and snapping their serrated sharp teeth.

These small but ferocious fish[10] are one of the dangers of many Brazilian rivers (in the Rio Grajahu, exceptionally abundant), and are said to be able to reduce to a skeleton in comparatively few minutes, any horse or bullock that enters the water. In the Grajahu they vary in size from four to fourteen inches in length, their proportions are about a third of their length in depth from back to under fin, and about one-sixth of their length in thickness. The face is quite that of a pug dog, and the mouth is armed with a most formidable array of keen-edged, sharp-pointed, serrated teeth, so sharp that one of the fish, flapping about the deck, easily bit in two a stick that I inserted in its mouth. The colour is a dark bluish purple on the back, graduating down the sides into light green and deep red, and terminating in a yellow ochre underneath. They are similar to the *piranhas* of the Rio São Francisco, of which a sketch is given on page 343, vol. i.

The *bote* we had passed in the early morning now goes by whilst we are breakfasting, but at mid-day we again come up to it and a capital race ensues, eight rowers against four. Both

[10] *Serra Salmo Piraya;* Cuvier. The Caribe of the Oronoco.

crews exert themselves to their utmost, even our phlegmatic Manoel bestirs himself a little, and mildly tells his men to *puxa! rapaziada! puxa!* (pull! boys! pull!) They shout and struggle their hardest, their eyes sparkle, and the perspiration streams down their faces and chests. Finally we forge ahead amid the shouts of derision from our crew, who offer a cable to tow the *bote velho* (old barge). *Vom' embora! vom' embora rapaziada! adeos! adeos! bote velho* (Let's away! let's away, boys! *adeos! adeos!* old barge). The *Bote velho* is ignominiously defeated, and never more overtakes us.

The high banks of the river have now quite disappeared, and all day we pass by forests of tall straight trunks with scarcely any undergrowth, an appearance that more resembles a pine-wood than the typical Brazilian *floresta*.

I had started from Chapada with the intention of roughly mapping the course of the stream, but it is so extremely tortuous that the operation of approximately determining the direction is well-nigh impossible, unless by such a process that time and means would not admit of. So far there had not appeared a straight piece of the river longer than 100 yards. I tried patiently to roughly calculate the length of the ever-varying bearings, that comprised the four quarters of the compass, but when plotted, the course evolved such a jumble, and the bends got so mixed up, and the river crossed and re-crossed itself so repeatedly, that I almost gave it up in despair.

Several small *jacares* (caymen) are lazily floating on the water like logs, but dive under the water with a wriggle as we approach; and a large brown *Socco*[1] (Brazilian bittern) is seen on the banks of a little tributary streamlet, watching for fish, with his long neck doubled up out of sight amidst the feathers of the shoulders, and often the beautiful white herons[2] swoop down ahead of us, almost skimming the surface of the waters with their outstretched, snowy wings. By the light of

[1] *Ardea exilis* (?).   [2] *Ardea candidissima*.

the moon the voyage is continued far into the night. The men row quietly, and sing in low voices their river songs, accompanied by the regular splash of the paddles, and the ripple and wash of the waters alongside, sounds that create a strange and weird effect in the impressive silence of the night and the intense shadows of the forest, while the heavy dew forms light filmy clouds of mist in the cool damp air.

At about 8 p.m. an isolated rounded hill is sighted, some little distance inland on the right, known as the Morro do Oratorio (Oratory Hill), from a deep wide cavity that appears half-way up its face. By the bright moonlight a large white patch could be discerned on the hill-side, the rest of the hill being covered with vegetation. The *padres* of this district are evidently not enterprising, or they would have established another São Bom Jesus da Lapa in such an evidently natural receptacle for a saintly troglodyte.

We land at 9.30 on a sandy shore bordered by forest, where we pass a blissful night without mosquitos. Manoel baited a line on arrival and caught too fat *surubim*, each weighing about five or six pounds. These fish are somewhat similar in form and in texture of skin to their relations of the São Francisco, but are marked by longitudinal *bands* of dark neutral tint upon a light buff-coloured ground instead of by *spots*.

The morning appears fresh and cool with the morning mists, thermometer showing 70°. We get away by daybreak, for these early mornings, although chilly and damp, are far preferable to the heat of day. To-day's voyage shows a change in the character of the forest, for not only does the major part of the vegetation consist of a great variety of palms, but the general disposition is very different to any of the forests up-stream. The underwood is dense, but above it there is no dark canopy of leaves supported by colonnades of tall tree-trunks, for here in these palm-forests the loftier trees and palms form groups, or stand alone and separated from the next group, or isolated tree or palm, by a growth of more dwarfed vegetation. Each of these clusters is immensely different one to the other, and every few yards present an ever-varying change in the composition and arrangement of the plants. For instance, from amidst bushes clothed with flowering parasites, a *Marajar* palm rears its huge fronds like a gigantic shuttle-cock, or a tall and stately Bacaba palm appears enveloped in the Python-like folds of a huge vine that near the feathery head of its supporter ramifies into the branches of a great tree, that will eventually crush and destroy the palm, and then appear like an immense corkscrew. Next comes a glade filled with dwarfed bamboos, plumed *Najar* palms, and *Cana braba*[3] (wild sugar-cane), mingled with thorny bushes and parasitic plants, all gleaming and glistening in the sunshine. Now a huge *Samauma* rears its huge bulging trunk high above its lowlier neighbours, and softens their brightness with the deep shade of its widespreading foliage. The next is perhaps a group of other tall palms, all entwined with parasitic pendent or festooned flowering vines, brilliant and vivid in colour, and so one might continue, and fill pages descriptive of these beautiful palmforests where the vegetation is so varied. In the bright glare of mid-day one sees alternately broad masses of foliage gleaming in the sunshine, and soft shadows thrown upon the lowlier verdure by the spreading boughs of huge umbrageous trees.

During the morning we meet two *botes* and an *igarite* proceeding up-stream from Maranhão to Chapada, the crews of polemen are naked Indians of the tribe of Gamellas,[4] stout

---

[3] The Indians fabricate their best arrows from this reed, that is straight, light, and tough.

[4] These Gamellas have been so named by the Brazilians, from a custom that they have when in a savage state, of wearing a slightly concave round piece of wood in a slit in their lower lips, that bears some resemblance to a *gamella*, i.e. a bowl, an adornment common to the chief aboriginal races.

strongly-built fellows; they pole their way slowly and with difficulty against the current. What a labour of patient hard work it is, and already they have been forty-one, forty-three, and forty-six days respectively, on the voyage from Arary on the Rio Mearim.

Further on, I shoot a *jacu* (Penelope), perched on a branch overhanging the river, the bird falls into the water fluttering; but before we can reach it, it is dragged out of sight by the *piranhas*, that splash and agitate the surface of the water as they struggle with each other over their prey.

At 10.30 we land at the Porto of Tenente Coronel Marianno Bandeira, a *fazendeiro*. Hitherto we had passed no riverside habitations since leaving Chapada. In this neighbourhood the slopes of the Geraes or highlands, approach within a mile of the river, and on their open grassy *campos* are a few cattle-farms, five, ten, or even twenty miles apart.

The colonel's house is built with adobe walls and tiled roof, the centre is open to the front and surrounded at sides and rear by the various rooms of the house; this open space under the roof serves as an accommodation for passing travellers, and is liberally supplied with hooks to suspend their hammocks.

An old black informs us that the "colonel" and his sons are away *campiando o gado* (driving the cattle to new pastures), and that the females of the establishment are *occupado* (occupied, or in other words too shy to appear), but we feel we are being surveyed, by the sounds of giggles and the rustles of gowns that are heard behind the nearly closed door.

During the rest of the day a fresh breeze serves to temper the scorching rays of the sun; but the judge says he cannot support the glare and heat any longer, and now lays extended under the shade of the *tolda* or cabin hut, but not by any means in undisturbed repose, for a new torture has now come aboard in the form of *pium*,[5] a black sand-fly, small as a grain

[5] *Trombidium*, sp. (?)

of fine gunpowder; and as they prefer shade to sunshine, they are making things unpleasant for my companion. He is surrounded by clouds of the insects, and as he rubs his smarting flesh, he anathematizes them heartily, still he will not leave the stewy shade of the *tolda*, and is being rapidly covered on face and hands with innumerable minute red spots. At every bite the insects draw blood, the skin rapidly inflames and causes a most irritating smart, and the puncture forms a minute black spot that will remain for many days.

Apparently the only obstacle to the navigation of the Grajahu besides its quadrupled length of twists and turns and long *détours*, is the prevalence of snags. Two years ago (in 1873), the province paid 10,000$000 (1000*l*. about), to clear them all away, but as the banks consist chiefly of soft alluvial soil, trees continually fall into the river, obstruct the passage of boats, and render the navigation dangerous, for in some places the current is so strong, that in suddenly turning any one of the sharp bends, a boat is liable to be driven on to a log before there is time to avoid it, and then capsize. At one place a great *Jatoba* tree [6] has fallen into the river, and barely allows sufficient space to pass between its branches and the bush of the opposite bank; as it is, the boughs carry away part of the palm-thatch of the cabin.

Late in the afternoon we pass a high bluff of reddish earth, capped by bush and forest, that Manoel tells me is the scene of an adventure he had with the Indians in 1863. The following is, as near as I can translate, the story he related of a romantic tale of Indian magnanimity, although it is as impossible to convey the pilot's quaint terms and expressions, as it would be to render broad Scotch into idiomatic French.

"Since a young man I have lived upon this river, for many years as a poleman and paddler, and now as a *practico* (pilot). Some few years ago the Itambeira Indians were all wild, and often ravaged the outlying farms in vengeance for their slaugh-

[6] *Hymenæa courbaril*, a *leguminosa*.

tered comrades, for whenever we saw an Indian in those days we used to shoot him, but many a time *botes* were surprised and the crew killed in retaliation. Ah! those were wild times! Well, in the year 1863, I was a poleman on a boat returning from Maranhão, we were all chanting a song as we poled slowly up-stream, when, as we neared that bluff and rounded the corner, *Ave Maria!* a great number of the wild Indians

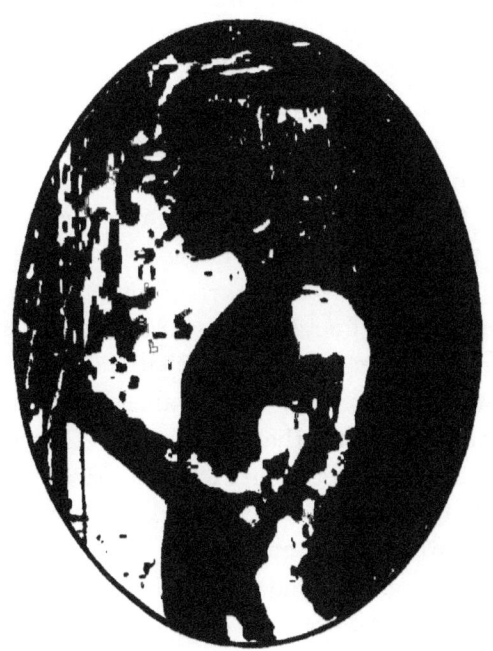

An Indian.

appeared from amidst the bushes with bended bows pointed at us; we were quite taken by surprise, and before we could get our guns ready, a great number of them jumped into the water, and swam or waded off to our craft, for we were close to the shore. Resistance was useless, for a dozen arrows were pointed at every man. The *indios* came aboard, and despite our struggles we were borne down by weight of numbers and overpowered, and clubs and spears were handled threateningly.

At that moment the *capitão* of the tribe appeared on the edge of the bluff, dressed in robes of feathers, and at a signal from him, the *indios* became quiet although they held us securely. The *capitão* spoke a little Portuguese, enough for us to understand him, and said, 'It is Curuxé that speaks, let the *Christão* listen. The *Christões* kill the *Itambeiras* like they kill the snakes, and Curuxé has killed the *Christões*; good! but Curuxé has seen the good men[7] that teach the *Guajajaras*, and they tell him not to kill the *Christões*; why do they then persecute the Indians who want to be their friends? Curuxé can kill you all and take your stores, but he remembers the good white men, therefore he says, go thy ways in peace to thy brothers, and tell them not to kill the poor *indio* when they again see him on the shore.' At another signal from the chief the *indios* left us in peace without taking a thing. The story was told throughout the river, and the boatmen for a long time left the *indios* alone; but, Senhor Doutor, some men are such *diabos* that they must kill something, and after awhile the old troubles recommenced, and arrived at such a state, that finally the Government sent troops into the disturbed districts to occupy the Indian villages, after this the warfare ceased, and now those same *indios* chiefly furnish the crews for the *botes* of the river."

At sunset we stop alongside a sand-bank bordered by forest. Soon after lighting the fire a large *bote* with twelve polemen, mostly mulattos and negros, arrives from down-stream, and the crew land on the opposite shore for their supper. After a short time they commence to amuse themselves with shouting obscene remarks, and hoot and yell and jeer at our smaller party. Our men are not slow to respond, and both sides become excited, and there is every appearance of a nice little scrimmage. But the judge now comes forward and calls to both sides, *Calla boca, tu brutos* (Shut up, you brutes). Our men quietly obey, but the opposite party only renew their yelling and

[7] Italian missionaries probably.

hooting with redoubled vigour. "Give the *canalha* a ball or two, Senhor Shammes; never mind killing such vermin," is now quietly suggested to me. I discharge three shots from my revolver over the heads of the disturbers of the peace. The effect is comical. A silence follows the first shot, yells and a scramble for cover, the second, and after the third they implore, "*Por amor de Deos, não atira mais*" (For the love of God, do not shoot any more). "Then hold thy peace and go away immediately." They hesitate not a moment, and get their craft under weigh, and are soon poling up-stream in silence; when they imagine they are well out of range, they again break out into curses, abuse, and vile language, but another shot, and the dropping of a ball into the water close by them expedites their departure.

We soon clear away in the opposite direction, and put some miles between ourselves and our unruly neighbours. A growl and fierce barking of Feroz rather scares us during the night, with a possibility of the enemy trying on a night attack, but the morning light shows the fresh tracks of a tapir that had passed near us in the darkness and caused the alarm of the dog.

June 10.—A dense white mist shrouds the river and forest at daybreak, so thick that objects ten yards away are undiscernible, nevertheless we push off and drift down-stream with the current, and an hour or so afterwards the mist rises and floats away.

This day the *piums* board us with full battalions; to see us with heads wrapped in handkerchiefs, with just nose and eyes visible, and hands in pockets, one would think we were suffering from cold weather. At breakfast time, it is necessary for each one to swing a branch about the head and hands of the other, whilst that one hastily swallows his breakfast, and afterwards returns the service. To attempt to endure these onslaughts with complacency would be to assume a smiling face like São Sebastião when he served as an archery target, for the stings of these *piums* resemble a shower of hot needles, our hands and faces are red and swollen, and covered with minute black spots as though they have been peppered with gunpowder. On the water the pest is not so bad, but still quite sufficient to make things unpleasant. All day is passed winding to the right, to the left, to all points of the compass in fact, and imagine one's dissatisfaction when, late in the afternoon, Manoel pointed out to me a part of the wood where, within 600 yards inland, we had breakfasted that morning, a day's rowing in fact to gain 600 yards. The intervening ground appears, as Manoel assured me it is, perfectly flat, and without rock, and a narrow canal could easily be cut through, and yet these many *bote* owners send their fleets down the river year after year, and never attempt any combination of efforts to make these slight improvements; for such tremendous *voltas* occur several times in the course of the river. Everything, no matter how trivial the work, or the cost, is cast upon O *Governo* (the Government), and yet these impracticable people, all classes alike, will assure you, "Oh, yes; we are *muito atrazado* (much behind the times), *nosso povo são gente muito preguisozo* (our people are very lazy fellows)," the speakers apparently not remembering that they themselves are units in the *povo*. All day we wind our way through the beautiful palm-forests, often through arcades of greenery, from whence swing long vines and horsehair-like *barba velha*,[8] and hanging balls of woven-stick birds'-nests.

I find the following in my diary. The scene is the hour of evening Ave Maria, the atmosphere is still and warm, there is

---

[8] This parasite is likely to prove an useful production, as an English firm in Rio has experimented with it, and finds it gives an excellent substance exceedingly similar to horsehair. The long, slender hanging parasite, like a very fine twine, is collected and dried in the sun; the bark then becomes dry and brittle, and is easily rubbed off, leaving exposed a long black glistening thread similar to, and quite as strong as, horsehair. The parasite has a wide range all over tropical Brazil, and gives an essentially tropical appearance to the trees.

a hum of heat and insects on the shore close by. The warm glows of departing day tinge the top branches and leaves of the trees of the opposite bank with ruby and golden colours, and spread a soft light around. Close by, fringing the sandy shore, huge trees tower above and cast deep shadows upon us, the fringe of night's dark pall; the river moves by slowly, without a murmur, without a ripple, reflecting like a mirror, every branch and leaf and twig of its wooded banks. The blue smoke of the fire curls upward in a straight column and fades away amidst the foliage. Bob is alternately attending to cooking and slapping his limbs, the men lie or sit upon the deck slapping their faces, their bare bodies and legs, and cursing the *piums*. Manoel is forward fishing *piranhas* in the intervals of slapping. I am seated on the deck writing, with head enveloped in a towel and a pair of the judge's gloves on my hands, and surrounding myself with tobacco smoke. The judge sits upon a fallen log near the fire, hurrying the movements of Bob, and wrapped from head to foot in a sheet. Thermometer 84°. "*Andar gentes! andar! andar! vamos embora! ja está moite! vamos jantar Senhor Shammes, deixe está seu livro*" (Hurry up, men! hurry up! hurry up! let us be off! it is already night! Let us dine, Senhor Shammes, leave off writing), he impatiently calls, for the departing *pium* are being succeeded by the first sing-sing of mosquitos that have come to take their places for the night, until the early morning, when the *piums* will then relieve guard for their operations for the day.

The pale moonlight mingles with the last pearly gleams of departing day, as the men, refreshed with rest and the evening meal, splash their paddles in the dark waters and move on once again amidst the black shadows, or out in the glistening moonlit stream, singing and keeping time with their strokes. It is a pleasant hour of peaceful quiet and refreshing coolness, that compensates somewhat for the heat of the day.

But as we proceed we get into terrible trouble, first we run into three snags, the first two we get free of with some difficulty, but in the third we are hard and fast in the fork of a submerged tree, and the men are so scared of the *piranhas* (and with reason) that they will not venture into the water, and have to set to work sawing and chopping at the obstacle; suddenly they surprise us with strong ejaculations and general anathemas, and on going forward to see what the trouble is, we very soon find out, for we have taken aboard a swarm of large black ants that the men at first unanimously dub *formigos do diabo*, and really they are not far wrong, for the ants are the formidable *formigos de fogo* (fire-ants), whose venomous stings are like a severe burn. What a time we are having! there is no escape, candles are lighted, and we smash, caper, and bless alternately, but more and more swarm aboard at every instant, and despite the pain (for the ants cover us), all lend a hand, some at destroying the enemy, others at trying to push off, by poling, chopping, and sawing, and after infinite trouble, that must be realized to be conceived, we again float. Now every one's attention is so devoted to smashing the ants, and we are so absorbed in that occupation, that no one notices a rather strong current round a bend that carries us before we know where we are, right into a jungle of thorny bushes of the banks, where besides the sharp scratches the men receive, we take on board a mingled cloud of mosquitos and hornets. The water is deep and the current strong, and sets us in right amidst the bushes, it is pitch dark in their deep shadows, and it is only after much trouble and vexation of spirit that we get away, feeling really desperate with the acute pain and smart of such a complication of tortures. Mark Tapley might perhaps have chuckled at so much jollity, but we didn't.

A little further on, we pass a bote moored for the night, our men shout a "*Boa noite, rapaziada*," (Good night, lads), but the only responses are sulky answers and foul language.

An "Inferno."

A little below, we land on a sand bank, and there terminates the unpleasant evening.

Every one complained of the acute pains of the ants and hornets, and the almost naked bodies of the men must have caused them to suffer greatly, for the few stings that I received were extremely painful.

Mosquitos again tortured us all night. Truly on this Grajahu there is no escape from such an "inferno," in the water *piranhas* and electric eels; on the water *piums* and ants, and *motúca* flies; and on land mosquitos and hornets. I felt in a raging fever from the pain and irritation of so many inflictions, and yet this is the best season for travelling on the Grajahu, when it is free from fever, and insect pests are fewer. What, indeed, must the months of March and April be like, when malignant fevers of a fatal type prevail, and when, as the men say, the mosquitos are *muito;* I could well consider them as very *muito* (many) indeed even then.

June 11.—Every one is only too glad to get away early despite the thick chilly mist, but progress is difficult on account of numerous snags, many of which we strike, and, were it not that the deck completely covers the *bote*, we should long since have foundered.

Dense clouds of *piums* again persecute us at breakfast-time, and later on the *motúca* flies [9] add their contingents to our enemies. This is also a bloodthirsty fly that leaves a small drop of blood on one's skin if he is allowed to take his fill. One can almost feel inclined to apologize for the cruelty of the old boatmen of the river when they shot down the defenceless *indios* on shore, for under such a process of incessant torture a feeling is generated of a mad desire to smash or damage something or anything. In the afternoon we meet a *bote*, commanded by Capitão Dias, manned entirely by his nude Itambeira Indians. They are all powerful athletic young fellows, dark olive in colour, and by no means unpleasing

[9] *Hadrus lepidotus.*

faces. The *capitão* is the director, or superintendent, appointed by the Government to "catechise" them, i.e., to take charge of them, and get them to work; the results are supposed to be entirely given to the use of the tribe, but I am told the *capitão* has a good business, for the labours of some 200 Indians engaged in collecting balsam of copaiba, sarsaparilla, Sapucaia nuts, besides the produce of their *roça*, should amount to a considerable sum per annum.

The reader must picture to himself the glories of the forest and our continual miseries for the rest of the day and night.

On the morning of the next day we passed the Porto dos Indios, or landing-place of the *aldeia* or village, situated about two miles inland, on the high plateau of the *campos* above the wooded valley. I regretted to learn that the *meninos* were not at home, as I should like to have left my card.

A few miles further on, a little bluff juts out into the river, where, as Manoel informs me, his *bote* was menaced in 1868 by some Indians on the shore, that he knew not whence they came or who they were, happily he passed on without exchanging shots. In the afternoon we land at a riverside farm, called Sobradinho, the residence of a middle-aged couple, a white man and a white woman. Their house of palm-leaves is fairly clean and comfortable, they own a cow, fowls, pigs, and some tame birds of the woods, toucans and macaws, and it is pleasant to see the affection between the couple and their pets, that are extremely tame. The man, who is evidently superior to the general run of these country-people, informs me that he was brought up on the coast, where, having met with reverses, he had retired to these solitudes with his *velha*, (old woman), to support himself by cultivating a small *roça*, breeding fowls, and collecting balsam of copaiba, which he exchanges with passing *botes* for such necessaries and luxuries as he requires. "But, my friend, how do you exist amidst these *piums* and mosquitos?" With a shrug of the shoulders he replies, "*Aguento, meo amigo*" (put up with it, my friend). The couple are by no means thriftless or indolent, for there is always plenty of work for willing hands, even in such a solitary abode. Between the house and the river are thriving groves of oranges, limes, bananas, plantains, pine-apples, *araças*, and a few flowers, all bordered by the lovely vegetation of the palm-forests. There is excellent fishing in the river, and good shooting in the woods and in the *campos* lands at the rear, but the locality is too warm to be pleasant (then 86° inside the house), and the *piums* are enough to drive one mad, although the tenants of the house do not appear to be much inconvenienced by them, they are either accustomed to them, or perhaps the insects have temporarily left them in peace for a change of pasture on ourselves.

Some few miles down the river, we come on to a troublesome passage, caused by a late landslip from a sandstone cliff on the banks of the stream ; the *débris* has filled up the river, that passes over it in a series of tortuous swift-running channels, that give us many a bump, and much trouble to get through.

During the evening, the camp fires of Capitão Dias' Itambeira Indians are seen glinting through the trees and bush. The Indians are on one of their migratory expeditions in quest of the balsam of copaiba (*copaifera*, sp. var.) ; some of the men are on the shore fishing, but make no response to our greetings as we pass by.

June 13.—This morning one of the paddlers, he with the long face, is shivering with an attack of ague ; it is only surprising that more of us have not been attacked with it before.

Early in the day, we pass on the west bank the mouth of the Rio Marajá, a stream of clear, light brown water ; it is about 120 feet broad, and probably rises in the Serra da Cinta. Its margins are reported to be uninhabited, except by *indios brabos*, and have not yet been explored.

At breakfast-time, taking my gun I retreat from the *piums* into the forest. Near the river the undergrowth of the forest is a mass of brambles, creepers, and small myrtle bushes, all bound together by the vines and mingled branches, and covered with the dried slime of past floods; but hewing me a way through the tangled jungle, I eventually come on to gently-rising ground, where the forest is freer from bush, and soon resolves itself into grand colonnades of tall, straight column-like trees; progress is only made inconvenient by projections of huge roots, and the masses of vines hanging down like a string of fine twine, or as huge colossi, thick as a man's body, entwined around great trunks; others of varied sizes, forms, and species, extend along the ground in coils, or in masses like a tangled bundle of string, or form natural swings from tree to tree, a perfect maze of almost leafless cordage, for there no flowers are seen, and even a green leaf is rare. High up above, is a dark roof of foliage, through which the daylight appears here and there in dots, like the stars of night. Under-foot is a deep soil of black humus, thickly covered with the *débris* of rotting trees, decayed leaves, and the slime of many floods. The atmosphere feels cool, and damp, and fresh, after the fierce glare of the river, but it is pregnant with many indescribable odours, that vary in different places; either a pungent peppery smell, or an odour of garlic, or a damp earthy smell, or a sweet aromatic perfume. The silence is intense, even increased by a singsing of a passing steel-blue mosquito, or a buzzing fly or beetle. Eventually I come across a little stream of cool crystal water, bubbling over rocks and masses of rotten leaves, between sloping banks thickly covered with mosses and ferns, where my attention being attracted by a movement among the latter, I perceive a beautiful bird of dark glossy greenish purple plumage, and nearly as large as a fowl, strutting along and uttering occasionally a low melancholy note. I feel like a brute as I knock it over with a shot, but our commissariat is indeed limited in variety, and necessity hardens my heart. The bird, a new acquaintance, I learn afterwards is a *jacamine*, and its flesh is much esteemed.[1]

Continuing my voyage at 11 a.m., an uneventful day is passed in gliding by the eternal forest, where not a sign of human life is seen, and barely a sound is heard, for very little animal life disturbs the solitudes this day.

The river is perceptibly rising, and the colour of the water is now a deep brown, like weak coffee; the waters are *represada* (backed up) from probably a flood in the Mearim river.

In the afternoon we meet another *bote*, manned by twelve nude Indians; what hides these fellows must have to withstand the scorching heat of the sun and the stings of insects. In the evening, the moon being bright and the river clear, (now about 200 feet wide), and the men being in a good humour, they open their lungs in loud songs, that are duly encouraged by us, for then they forget fatigue and the time of night, and pull well together with rhythmic strokes, listening with childish glee to the sounds of voices and oars echoing amidst the black gloomy shadows of the trees. They are really wonderful fellows for this work, they have been rowing this day from 6 a.m. until 10 p.m., with only two short rests for meals; in fact, since leaving Chapada, they have done daily, on the average, at least twelve hours' actual rowing, that, I calculate, is equal to forty or fifty miles per day.

The night-camp is warm close and mosquitery, but the morning appears bright, clear and cool, bringing with it, of course, the *piums* to relieve guard with the mosquitos. The temperature of the water is 80°, and the air 70°, that soon increases, as the sun gets up, to 84°. The sick man has apparently benefited from a dose of castor oil followed by quinine, (then my only medicines), and has joined his comrades at work.

[1] Probably the Paradise Jacamar (*Galbula paradisea*).

On the way, passing close to a small *jacaré* (alligator) basking in the sun on a muddy sandy bank, I plant a bullet in him from my heavy navy revolver; he wriggles away to the water, where he splashes and gasps, opening and shutting his jaws with sounding snaps; he is evidently badly hit, and the *piranhas* seem to recognize the fact, for the water for several yards around becomes violently disturbed, as they swarm on to their prey, for even an alligator's tough hide will not protect him, if wounded, from their sharp teeth. The men shout with delight, "*Ai! jacaré, agora as piranhas tu mordes*" (Ha, ha! you alligator, now the *piranhas* have you).

At breakfast-time, hearing the notes of a *Jahu*[2] close by in the forest, I go in quest of it, imitating its cry as I proceed; it advances towards me, now and then stopping and listening with upraised foot. The game is bagged, but after all I reap no benefit by my slaughter, for whilst Bob was lazily cleansing the bird in the river, and not minding what he was about, the *piranhas* suddenly seize and snatch it away. We eat the bird however in an indirect form, by catching a heap of the fish that stole the bird, and have them for breakfast.

After leaving this place there appears again a considerable change in the vegetation on shore, for the grand virgin and the palm-forests are no longer met with; now is seen a much denser, but dwarfed growth of thick bushes, in many places the whole surface of them is covered with a network of flowering and other kinds of parasites; one variety is especially conspicuous, in its quantity, form and colour, it consists of great masses of very soft, leafless filaments, bright gold in colour, and covers considerable extents of bushes, that it apparently destroys by excluding air and light from them. The ground, too, is in many places low flat and inundated, a perfect hotbed of miasma, that is perceptible in the puffs of hot humid air that reach us, accompanied with clouds of sand-flies.

In the afternoon I shot another alligator and also a *Magury*,

[2] Penelope.

a slate-coloured heron, that unfortunately struggled away into the swamps.

We have to row on till nearly 7 p.m. before we find a place to land at, so low and swampy are the margins of the river. At this stopping-place the crew of an *igarite* are bivouacked for the night, and in a state of alarm on account of having seen some wild Indians on the banks that afternoon, and on our continuing the voyage by the light of the moon, they strongly recommend us to keep alert at night, and camp on the east bank, the side of the river opposite to which they had seen the *meninos*.

The voyage is continued until 9 p.m., when a landing is made for the night on a point of *terra firma* bordered by trees and surrounded inland by swamp, where frogs and toads are making a noisy concert. The boatmen, tired out with the close heat and fatigues of the day, are soon asleep, regardless alike of noises, insects, Indians, or anything else, the judge suspends his hammock and soon turns in, leaving me alone by the fire and the darkness and many strange noises of the night.

The light of the moon is strong and clear, the trees, some gleaming in the pale light, others lost in the blackness of unlighted night, assume strange and fantastic forms, and cast intensely black shadows upon the waters of the river, that glistens like a silver mirror in the moon's cold white beams. The night is not so quiet as usual, for the frogs in the adjoining swamp make a clatter like the mixed sounds of some huge cotton factory, whirring, baaing like a sheep, whistling, croaking, hooting, shouting hi! hi! roaring, a perfect babel of noises, that rise and fall as the voice of one or another species predominates. Then there is the booming of the *Soccó Boi* (a large bittern), like the bellow of a bullock, *ciganas* utter harsh screeches, owls hoot, *bacuris* (a species of night-jar) call out in treble notes, bark-oo-ree, bark-oo-ree, the *mandim* croak under water like a grunting pig, and other fish splash; yet all these sounds only render the grim solitude the more impressive. The mosquitos, fortunately, have not found us out, and the atmosphere is cool and pleasant.

It is a queer feeling to recall in such circumstances as these old scenes and old memories, and contrast them with the present weird and uncanny sights and sounds, but whilst thinking and musing, Indians, friends, London streets and Grajahu swamps gradually resolve themselves into chaos and dreamland, and the sentry sleeps.

June 15.—A cool morning with thermometer at 65° sees us all astir at daybreak, and I congratulate myself that another night has passed without trouble, for however callous and indifferent a traveller may philosophically become to possible or even probable risks, there is always, especially that night, a contingency of a *jacaré* taking a snap at one whilst asleep on the ground, or a huge anaconda might like to put himself outside of an Englishman, or a prowling jaguar might like to pick a bone or two, let alone such small fry as any of the choice varieties of venomous snakes that Brazil can produce, that really one does feel inclined to think that it is just as well that the time of doubt has passed.

On several occasions on the previous days I had noticed many rough wooden crosses protruding from amidst the bushes on the banks, and this morning I counted nearly 100 within a length of a few miles, the indications chiefly of the graves of men who have fallen victims to the deadly fevers that at certain seasons of the year (March and April) prevail upon this river; some, however, are the results of a squabble, or a free fight, and also of Indian ambuscades.

The vegetation now becomes if possible more bushy dense and compact, and the land to far away appears inundated; but amidst this low land, gently sloping spurs from the highlands here and there stretch out, where the forest again appears in all its grim and grand luxuriance.

At eleven o'clock we reach one of these spurs that terminates in a bluff on the river-side. On the summit is a small clearing and a palm-leaf hut, called Matto dos Bois (the Bullock's Wood). The ground is here very rocky, the stone being very similar to that of Chapada, a close-grained hard dark greenstone. The owner of the hut, Senhor Antonio Henrique Maciel, tells me that copper had been found close by, and to substantiate his statement he shows me some specimens of copper ore that he kindly allows me to take away. Undoubtedly this must be a great copper region, for I have traced its indications over some 500 miles of my journey.[3] I believe the higher lands of the plateaus, even in the neighbourhood of Matto dos Bois, to be quite healthy, and there is no want of Indian hands, or even of native Brazilian labour, and the water-carriage is free and uninterrupted to the city of Maranhão. It should necessarily be a place of great enterprise, when perhaps the future New Zealander surveys the ruins of Old London.

There is an *aldeia* of semi-civilized Itambeira Indians on the Rio Pinaré, distant twenty-four miles from Senhor Antonio's, who informs me that the land more inland is fairly well occupied by cattle farms, five or ten miles apart from each other.

All the rest of the day we pass by monotonous low-lying lands, where *Inga* trees [4] grow in prominent numbers. This tree produces an edible fruit, having a hard kernel, with a thin covering of a light fluffy nature, sweet and fresh to the palate, the outer rind is crisp and brittle. Owing to the prevalence of these trees in great numbers this class of bush is known as *Ingativas*.

During the afternoon the pilot shot a *mergulhão* (diver) as large as a partridge; plumage glossy black, the neck long and slender, the eyes a brilliant green, the beak long straight and strong, with the extremity of the upper mandible overlapping the lower one.

---

[3] It even extends to the neighbourhood of Para.
[4] Family of *Leguminosæ*.

At about 5 p.m. we land at some deserted houses to prepare dinner; no explanation is necessary to account for the abandonment of the homestead, for the mosquitos are *impagavel*,[5] and when we hurry away they accompany us in swarms as gnats will follow one on a summer's eve at home.

The moonlight later on shows another tract of the grand forest, and during the evening we pass several riverside habitations and clearings, the former all built of palm-leaves. With the hope of buying some *cachaça* (for the store is exhausted), the men are induced to row on until near midnight, when finding there is no prospect of obtaining the desired *manipoeira*, we land at a riverside habitation to pass the rest of the night. The tenants have naturally long since retired, but an open shed offers a shield from the heavy night-dews. The men lie down anywhere and anyhow, for they are thoroughly tired with their long day of rowing, from 6 a.m. to 12 p.m. The judge is snug in his hammock, and protected from the mosquitos by the net, and soon the sounds of slumber indicate the peaceful repose of every one. But I am restless and feverish, and in these circumstances one mosquito is enough to work one into a state of intense nervous irritation, let alone when one is surrounded by the droning roar of myriads. Finally, the long hours are passed in tramping to and fro in a semi-somnolescent state, with throbbing head, parched and inflamed skin, and the nerves in a state of tension, when every sound startles one unnaturally, and the glare of the moonlight, the black shadows, the surrounding discomfort, and the humid damp earthy-smelling air, all seem so unearthly and strange, as though one is losing his senses.

At 4 a.m. I turn out every one, and as we drift down the stream in the cool of dawn and the absence of mosquitos, I obtain a welcome relief, and get a good nap.

[5] Literally, unpayable, but it is a common Brazilian term, and comprises a variety of meanings, insupportable, "*uma coisa impagavel*," an incomprehensible thing, something extraordinary.

On awakening, the sun is high and hot, and the air from great tracts of inundated forest we are passing, comes in puffs of steamy atmosphere, loaded with the odours of swamps and rotting vegetation. Occasionally we pass tracts of higher lands, all still covered with dense forest, and showing several habitations built upon piles, the floors being six or eight feet above the ground. Many of these huts are wonderfully picturesque, surrounded as they are by grand trees and beautiful tropical vegetation, places to thrill an artist's heart with delight, yet to picture them faithfully what minute delineation of details is absolutely indispensable, where in the sunlight every leaf and branch is so clearly defined by its underlying black shadows, for here one sees that a vivid brightness and sharpness of outline can only be obtained by an extremely dark contrast of colour, consequently any faithful sketches of tropical scenes show an effect that those who have not seen the tropics fail to comprehend, and are ready to condemn the picture they cannot realize, as harsh in tone and unnatural.

On the way some *cachaça* is bought for the craving souls of the hard-worked crew, and they well deserve such a small recompense for their good behaviour and untiring exertions, and the little "drop of comfort" makes them happy after their fashion. At the same time I obtain for a few coppers from some men in a canoe, sufficient fish of varied, but all of excellent qualities, to provide enough breakfast for all on board.

At mid-day we land at a quite new house and clearing, called Rego, belonging to a young married man, not more than twenty-two or twenty-three years of age, who with his young wife, and a negro slave, show a rather rare example of industry in the debilitating climate of this lower river-side. The young fellow, bright active and intelligent, owns a few head of cattle, and a square mile or two of pasture-lands on the *campos* at the rear of the forest, that with the produce of a small *roça*, enables him to lead a free and independent life, laborious certainly, but blessed with the privilege of independence, and the satisfaction and contentment derived from an industrious life.

The house is situated on the crest of a little knoll, pleasantly exposed to the breezes of the trade-winds, it is cool clean and comfortable, and the owner says he is, as he really appears to be, happy and contented.

Close to the house is a so-called *capoeira de palmeiras*, nature's covering of a worked-out clearing, that in Minas Geraes, or Bahia, becomes a bramble of bracken, *capim de cheiro*, bamboos, young palms, saplings and bushes; here it is different, for a growth of young palms have spontaneously taken possession of the ground; they are all practically of the same height, fifteen or eighteen feet high, the foliage resembles groups of great ostrich-feathers, whose extremities mingle one with another, and form delightfully shady natural avenues; it is really a wonderfully graceful retreat, fashioned by nature's gardening.

To the east, about twelve miles away, there is a considerable inland lake, called Lagoa-assu, about four miles in diameter, its waters are deep clear and pellucid, its margins are bordered by a rich soil and vegetation, and by many homesteads. Like most of the lakes, or any large pool of water in Brazil, it is peopled with hobgoblins and superstition; houses are said to have been observed at the bottom in the transparent water, and sounds have come therefrom as of singing and dancing, and it boasts of an enchanted snake and mermaid (*Cobra encantada e mae d'agoa*), possibly originated by the spiritual effects of full charges of *cachaça* on the imagination of some belated countryman, when his brain was singing, and he saw all the trees dancing and whirling about him.

After leaving Rego, we soon lose sight not only of houses and forest, but also of *terra firma*, and the water becomes almost stagnant, and progress is made by rowing only, unaided by any current; the river spreads itself out into a number of channels, divided only by low bushes, or sometimes into a series of lakelets, covered by floating aquatic plants. No particular channel is visible, and we might easily become lost for a time in such a watery maze, and now is really the only occasion on which we have required the services of a pilot.

The air is very hot and oppressive, not a breath ruffles the glassy surface of the water, that reflects like a mirror, the inverted images of every twig and leaf of the bushes. Many small alligators are seen floating like logs, and in many places the water is disturbed by the fighting of the *piranhas* that when hard up for food, demolish one another. On the bushes are great numbers of *Cigana* birds, that fly lazily from bush to bush, or hop tamely on the branches as we pass close by, regardless of our presence; they are as large as a pheasant, and much resemble it in appearance, but their heads are decorated with a crest of feathers like a cockatoo; as their flesh is considered uneatable, they consequently enjoy an immunity from persecution by the passing boatmen.

About 5 p.m., after a long tedious winding in and out of the channels, we enter the broad waters of the Rio Mearim.[6] It is assuredly with no feeling of regret that I thus emerge from the Grajahu, and leave behind me its many undeniable beauties and charms, with also its abominable insects. But the memories of its glorious scenery, like all other things that are pleasant, will and do survive the reminiscences of those days and nights of torture. I have traversed it, and am glad that I have done so, but should be very, very sorry indeed to have to do it again.

The Rio Mearim now stretches away before us on a long straight course some 600 feet in width, and bordered by low inundated wooded banks. The water flows so slowly, oh!

---

[6] I estimate the distance from Chapada to the mouth of the Grajahu, following the course of the river, to be at least 450 miles, and as the mouth is only thirty-five feet above mean sea-level, the fall of the river averages nine inches per mile. In a straight line the distance does not exceed 240 miles.

so slowly, for my impatience is great indeed to see once more the open sea and civilized humanity.

As the sun sets with a golden glory upon sky and water, the mosquitos board us in *corps d'armées*, even here out in the open river; to stop anywhere is out of the question, for no dry land is visible. The men row on wearily but manfully until midnight, when we reach the *praia* (shore) of the town of Victoria. The men are overcome with sleep and fatigue, and as soon as the craft is secured, they lay themselves down on some logs of timber on the muddy shore, and in a few moments a chorus of snores announce their indifference alike to mosquitos or hard beds. For the first time I feel really sick and unwell, and I parade the shore for a long time with fevered body and aching head.

CHAPTER XV.

FROM VICTORIA TO MARANHÃO.

S. Antonio's day at Victoria—The town and its Padre—Good-bye to my companion—On to Arary—A bustling port—An influential trader—Portuguese hospitality—Passage booked to Maranhão—An evening thunder-storm—An unusual scene—A return from the Wilderness—A gossip with a frank young lady—A marshy country—A considerable proprietor—The navigation of the lower river and its trade—A crowded craft—Kindness of mine host—Rough accommodation—A dreary scene—A tidal wave—A river steamer—In the bay of São Marcos—Land at Maranhão—A return to civilization—Difficulties in leaving the port—A helpless countryman and a kind and useful Brazilian official—On board the *Bahia*—An attack of fever at sea—Bob's disgust and departure to his home—Adieu to poor Feroz—Lost, stolen, or strayed.

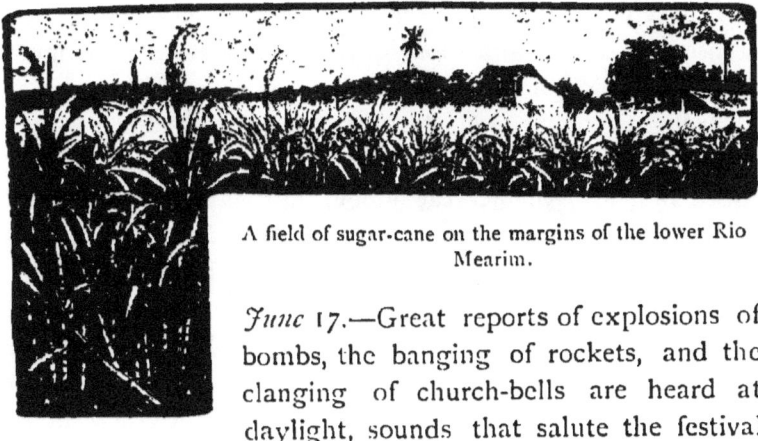

A field of sugar-cane on the margins of the lower Rio Mearim.

June 17.—Great reports of explosions of bombs, the banging of rockets, and the clanging of church-bells are heard at daylight, sounds that salute the festival day of São Antonio.

The muddy shore is strewn with *débris* and refuse, and with huge logs of cedar that have been brought down the rivers for sale; there are several *botes*, *igarites*, and canoes, all, like the shore, unpeopled; for the crews are in the town for the festival.

I accompany the judge to the town, where his first visit is to a church to offer thanksgiving for his safe arrival.

As it is yet early we stroll through the untidy grass-grown sandy streets, and a *praca* or square bordered by houses (all more or less dilapidated) and also a fairly well-built old church, but much in want of repair; the streets branch out of the square at right angles. There are a few two-storied houses with verandahs and glazed windows, but the generality of the tenements are small door and window adobe houses, and wattle and dab huts. Some half-dozen *vendas* and stores appear fairly well stocked with goods. We eventually call upon the Padre, a bluff jolly fellow, who is, I am told, a great favourite with the townspeople, although his housekeeper is young and pretty, and his house resounds with the shouts and cries of his numerous offspring, hardly two of whom show similar tints in their complexions. The town presents, even late in the morning and on such a grand festival day, a decidedly sleepy appearance, few people are seen in the streets, and those only move in a listless languid manner, as though life is a weary burden.

Owing to the flooded state of the river, the town is surrounded by water and cut off from all communication with the mainland. In fact the judge, who leaves me here, will cross country in a canoe, to his home amidst the lakes and large sugar estates at Vianna, beyond the Rio Pinaré.

We part with mutual expressions of regret, for after all we have endured together many severe trials of patience on our journey, and no hasty word or action has once marrèd our good relations. I doubt if any two average Englishmen would have got on so well together.

This long and tedious narrative is now drawing to a close, (What a blessing! I can fancy the reader saying, and he would say it all the more fervently if he had had to compile it), and we will hurry away from Victoria after my short visit and remarks, for it is like any other country town in North Brazil, there is much of a muchness in them all, all are dilapidated, some more so than others, and Victoria is one of the " more so."

About eight miles down the river, passing by low flat marshy lands, that much resemble the flat country below Plumstead on the lower reaches of the Thames, we arrive at

Arary, Rio Mearim.

Arary on the south side of the river, amidst quite a little fleet of small river-craft and large schooners from the city of Maranhão.

The port is lively and bustling with men discharging or loading the vessels. The one main street skirts the river, and is only two or three feet above the level of the water; it comprises several large warehouses, and the *sobrado* residence of Capitão José Antonio Soares (a Portuguese trader of considerable wealth and influence); at the west end of the street is a fairly large and well-built church, another *sobrado*, some smaller houses, and another large warehouse; at the rear of these buildings the land stretches away in perfectly flat marshy ground, covered with grass and a very few scattered clumps of trees and bushes, the grazing-ground of considerable herds of cattle.

Having a letter of introduction to the Capitão, I duly call upon that gentleman, and find him in his large store, odorous with the mingled smells of Newfoundland cod-fish, dried beef, wet sugar, toucinho, kerosene, dirt and grease. The Capitão tenders me a frank and hearty reception, invites me upstairs, produces refreshments, and tells me to "make myself at home," and *nao faça ceremonia* (make no ceremony). After a short chat I learn that the Mearim steamer is not due for ten days, but that a *hiate* (a sailing-craft) is about to proceed to Maranhão in a day or so. I find out, and soon come to terms with, the owner, who refuses however to let me have the use of the little cabin on deck, as he has to fill it with cargo, so I must content myself with an *alfresco* voyage, and such accommodation as can be obtained on the top of the cargo. Well, better that than nothing, and I am not likely to object to yet a little more exposure to sun and night-dews, and anything will do, so long as I can reach the coast. A violent storm from the south-east, of wind, rain, thunder and lightning, sweeps over the place in the afternoon, and clears the air from the previous hot stifling heat, and leaves a delightful freshness.

The view from the Capitão's verandah is extensive and varied, and after the squall the sky has cleared, and as the sun sinks below the horizon of the far-extending flat marshy meadow-lands on the opposite side of the river, the sky is all aglow with the softest of tones, and tinges with its warm hues the surface of the broad gently-rippling river, the trees of its banks, the houses, the rude quays, and the masts and forms of the various river-craft. In the street below gangs of men pass at a trot to and from the vessels, with bags of sugar or other goods on their heads. Up river, a *barca* is hauled on shore, and the clatter of caulking mingles with the songs of the bargemen unmooring a large schooner ; a number of men in an open shed are gambling, their looks intent upon their game, and insensible to all surroundings ; in the street, boys are playing at shuttlecock, and the Capitão is negotiating the purchase of a canoe-load of produce that lays alongside his quays. Black and brown women in gaudy shawls and prints pass to and fro, and exchange in passing many a *repartee* with the idlers and workers. It is a return from the solitudes of the wilderness to the busy striving world, and causes me to experience an indescribable exhilaration and feeling of contentment that I am thus far, so well out of the glorious vegetation of the interior, with its hardships and pleasures, torturing insects and lovely scenes.

During my stay in Arary, I had a rather amusing conversation with a young woman that I feel I must relate, as it will serve to somewhat portray the opinions and character of a Brazilian country girl. The fair one was an only daughter of a trader generally reported to be very well-to-do.

I had been to visit the father, whose acquaintance I had made, and he had left me in the verandah for a time whilst he attended to his store below.

Whilst ruminating on things in general, I hear a soft ahem ! ahem ! from close by, and then I perceive in the balcony of an adjoining room that a young woman has meanwhile appeared. I notice that she has beautiful hair and beautiful eyes fringed with long eye-lashes, her complexion is pale but clear, her features are good, and she is altogether decidedly good-looking. She is peering very demurely down into the street below, but the corners of her mouth move suggestive of smiles, and sundry other softly-pronounced ahems are heard. In my best Portuguese I say, "*Boa tarde, minha Senhora*" (Good evening, my lady). "*Boa tarde, Senhor*," she replies. The ice thus broken, I am at once plied with questions.

"What is your name ? "

"James."

"What did you say?"

"James."

"*Nosso Senhor!* I can never pronounce that. I do not believe it is a name. Please do tell me properly; say it slowly."

I pronounce my full name. She laughs heartily, taps her feet, and claps her hands, and continues,—

"What funny sounds! Imagine any one with such a curious name! But you are a foreigner, I know, so it may be all right, but I shall never be able to pronounce it. Do say it all again. Ha! ha! how very funny. But why do not you foreigners have nice names like us Brazilians? You are French, are you not?"

"No, I am an Englishman."

"Yes, yes, I know, it is all the same."

"But do you not know that the English are as different to the French as your people are to mine."

"Well, that is strange. I thought all foreigners were alike, for they are all so different to us Brazilians, and none of them can speak Portuguese properly. Have you any padres in your country, or any churches? Are you baptized?"

"Certainly."

"Now, would you believe it, I really thought you were all pagans, but I cannot believe that you have any real padres."

"I can assure you that they are really padres, but in my country they are permitted to marry."

"To marry? A married padre!"

This appeared so thoroughly comical, and tickled her risible faculties so much, that she fairly screamed with laughter and danced with merriment, and made so much noise that it attracted the attention of her father in his store below, who came out and inquired, "What is it, my daughter?"

"Oh! it is nothing, my father, only this foreigner is telling me some funny stories about his country. You go away."

The indulgent father thereupon retired to his bags and barrels.

"But now, tell me honestly, have you actually churches?"

"Certainly, and some of them are very fine and beautiful structures."

"Really? Are they like ours?"

"Well, not exactly; they are a little larger and a little cleaner, and some people might consider them perhaps a little more elegant."

"There now, when you say that I am sure you are telling stories, I will not believe another word you say. I am sure there is not a prettier or grander church in all the world than ours at Victoria. But are you married?" she suddenly inquires after a pause.

"No, I am a bachelor."

"Why do you not get married?"

"I cannot find any one to have me."

After a pause, and heaving a little sigh, she continues,—

"I am going to be married."

"When?"

"On the 30th of this month."

"Allow me to congratulate you upon the near approach of such a happy event."

She stamps her foot, and says, "It is not soon, it is quite a long time to wait. I do so want to get married." (After another pause and a repetition of the sigh), "But, perhaps, after all, I shall not marry even then."

"How is that?"

"Because it is very likely that I may find some one else that I like better. I have already been nearly married lots of times, but when the time comes I refuse. The last occasion was because my lover told me that he did not like me to talk to other young men; did you ever hear of such impudence? I sent him off immediately, for I am not going to be shut up in a house all day with only stupid slaves to talk to. But papa gets dreadfully angry on these occasions and scolds me, then I cry very much, which he does not like, and then gets angry with my lover and sends him away, and then I am so sorry, for I am always thinking of young men, as young men are always thinking of young women, as is quite natural. Do you not think so? But I am sure you are a pagan, and if our padre was here I would get him to baptize you."

" You think then there is no chance for us poor foreigners?"

" Most decidedly there is not, but I will mention you in my prayers, and that may be of some benefit to you."

The father now enters the room, evidently thinking that the interview has lasted quite long enough. But the young woman shows her discontent by bouncing indoors with a very pouting face.

I could not resist a feeling of commiseration for the young man who runs so probable a chance of being wedded to the spoiled girl.

Nearly all Arary belongs to mine host, the Capitão, who practically monopolizes all the inland provincial trade, for the various craft that navigate the river cannot proceed further than this place, from whence larger and stouter vessels are required for the navigation to the city of São Louis de Maranhão; and as these large sailing-vessels cannot, or do not, ascend the various streams up country, the Capitão thus occupies the position of a middleman or broker, between the importers and exporters of the interior and those of the capital; but the long credits (twelve months) to the up-country traders, render his operations very precarious, and the then late introduction of steam navigation on the Rios Pindaré and Mearim had considerably lessened his business, by bringing producer and buyer into direct communication, and obviating the necessity of Arary as an intermediate market.

June 20.—In the afternoon the *barca* comes alongside the quay to take in the rest of its cargo, and at sunset we leave for Maranhão. The vessel is inconveniently crowded with freight, the cabin is filled, and the deck piled high with baskets of fowls and turkeys, bags of oranges, bales of dried beef, rolls of salted pork, bunches of plantains and bananas, and bags of *farinha*, and barely enables one to find a precarious footing, and no place to repose upon except the knobby surface of the cargo, all points and hollows.

I bade good-bye to mine host, who accompanied me to the *barca*, where some blacks were waiting for me with a case of port wine, and sundry roasted fowls, sweets, bread, etc., a gift of the generous Capitão. I never saw this kind man again, and neither did he expect to meet me any more, and yet I could not have been treated kinder if I had been a member of his family. A stranger I came, and left as an old friend.

June 21.—My bone-aching and uncomfortable bed upon the sacks, bales and baskets of cargo, offers no inducement for indulging in late rising, and the chilly dawn finds me on foot, stiff in limb and wet with dew, for the rugs are as damp as though they have been dipped in water.

The tide is out, and shows the river-bed in great shoals of soft black mud; there is no wind, and with the aid of sweeps only, we make but slow progress in the currentless stream. The banks are low and muddy, lined with mangroves, and team with countless numbers of small red crabs,[1] and several light-rose coloured *culheireiros* (spoonbills).[2] As the sun mounts higher and higher, the fierce heat becomes almost insupportable, and the harsh glare shows a dreary scene of flat grey-green marshes, and shores and shoals of mud. Suddenly, in a moment as it were, the turn of the tide comes with a mighty rush of waters, that forces the skipper to anchor, for the craft is violently heaved up, and the waters rush up stream at six or seven miles the hour.

Eventually we get under weigh, but all day the wind blows

---

[1] The *Gelasimus*, a species of the genus *Ocypoda*.
[2] *Platerhynchus* or *Platalia ajaja*.

only in light cats'-paws. I am already pretty well sun-dried, but the shadeless exposure on such a broad expanse of grey muddy water, without a breath of wind to alleviate the glare and sweltering heat, is by no means pleasant in a latitude only three degrees south of the Equator.

At 4 p.m. the river again shallows, and becomes unnavigable, when the skipper anchors in a little cove behind a point of land, where we wait sheltered from the force of the *piraroca*,[3] (a bore, or tidal wave,) that here accompanies the turn of the tide. By the moonlight I see it advancing, a line of curling crested waves, that reaches from shore to shore (here a mile apart); it passes by with a rush and a roar, and makes our craft spin and dance round her cable and rock violently in the eddying waters, but the cove is a harbour of refuge, where the force of the waves is somewhat broken by the adjoining promontory. Later on, the paddle-wheel steamer from the capital, with a tail of barges in tow, passes by, puffing splashing and gleaming with her row of lights in the darkness of night.

There was much grumbling on the river at the high, and almost prohibitive rates charged by the company, (that enjoys a monopoly, and a heavy provincial subsidy,) and a general opinion prevailed that the directors and the authorities were a happy family, and did not care a straw for the interests of the farmers they were supposed to cater for.

The mosquitos boarded us with their armies, and made us active and watchful until 10 p.m., when the tide permitted our departure.

Eventually, on the night of the 24th June, we anchored in the bay of St. Mark's, at the rear of the city of Maranhão, where incessant reports of rockets and bombs announced the keeping of St. John's Eve, the Brazilian 5th November. The rest of the voyage proved so uneventful and monotonous that there was little to specify; there were occasional delightful hours, when we sailed along merrily with brisk

---

[3] The word is derived from the Indian *piroca*, bald.

favourable winds, that cooled and refreshed one's too, too warmed up body, stung to irritation by mosquitos at night, and scorched by the sun by day. The river is broad, in some places extending to two miles in width, but everywhere the low slimey banks, topped by thin grasses, or lined by mangroves, create indescribable scenes of desolation, such a change from the scenery of the Grajahu, yet near the river there are extensive sugar estates, and all the wealth of the province. Many of these plantations are very extensive, and have been worked for a hundred years or more, for the rich black soil of these flats is well adapted to the growth of sugar-cane. In these districts, intermittent fevers and agues are said to be very prevalent at certain seasons of the year, as the sight of the flat marshes, sweltering in the heat of such a torrid climate at once suggests, and were it not for the fresh, healthful breezes of the trade-winds that sweep over the shores and highlands of Brazil, these and similar localities would be as untenable as the worst parts of the West Coast of Africa.

On going ashore early on a Sunday morning, amidst the houses of an important city, with tramcars and gas lamps, well dressed people moving about the paved streets, and all the many scenes and movement inherent to civilized humanity, I feel as if I have stepped down upon mother earth from another planet, so strange and unusual is the bustle after the quiet scenes of the interior, but paramount above all is an intense feeling of satisfaction and gratitude that the long journey is over.

I commenced my travels full of enthusiasm and delight at the prospect of "roughing it" in the distant little-known wilds, but I terminated them with a far greater pleasure, and a grateful feeling of relief, as though I had awakened from a nightmare. Yet now, in after years, as time rolls on, the memories of those old days assume an ever-softening aspect, for the many pleasurable incidents and scenes seem to lose their accompanying drawbacks, and stand out bright and salient in one's thoughts as the evil side of the picture fades away into the dark shadows of forgetfulness. The camp fire, the breezy *campos* and hill top, the shaded forest, the brilliant sunshine, the wonderful vegetation, those moonlight nights on the São Francisco, the Somno and the Grajahu, how different all now appear, when divested of insect pests, discomfort, and hard fare.

Hearing that a National steamer, the *Bahia*, was in port, and would that day sail to the south, I hastened to the office of the company to secure a passage to the city of Bahia, but as I could not produce a passport, (having foolishly sent it with some baggage overland to Bahia, from the city of Barra do Rio Grande,) I was point-blank refused a ticket. Declarations, protests, expostulations, were all unavailing, but being advised to go and see the Consul, I called on that individual and had to wait a long time before he awoke from his slumbers, and then only to refuse me any help or assistance, although I offered to produce papers to substantiate my story; at last he suggested that I should see the Chief of Police. Upon inquiring for that gentleman at his residence, I was shown up stairs, where from an adjoining room I was invited by a loud frank voice to "come in and have some breakfast." I found the chief with his family at their morning meal, and having apologized for my early intrusion, I briefly explained the necessity of seeking his assistance. "Sit down, my friend; have some breakfast, and talk afterwards." During the meal I recounted a slight sketch of my journey; the "chief" expressed great interest thereat, and unhesitatingly gave me a permit to leave the port. So my first acquaintance with my countrymen was not a pleasant episode.

At mid-day I embarked on board the *Bahia* with my follower, Bob, who was evidently dazed with all he saw, for he had never yet seen the sea, let alone a steamer. I felt such a relief, such a rest, that a reaction followed the long struggle against difficulties and privations, and I fairly collapsed into a substantial attack of fever, but happily recovered before I reached the city of Bahia.

Some three weeks after arriving in Bahia, Mr. J. B., who had descended the Rio São Francisco, arrived with all the camp equipage of the expedition, and the next day, the 30th July, 1875, I returned to England by the magnificent yacht-like *Britannia*, a large steamer of the Pacific Steam Navigation Company, to enjoy a holiday at home after seven years work in Brazil.

Before leaving Bahia I had obtained for Bob employment in an iron foundry, where he could find an opportunity to utilize his great strength, but the same evening I met him on the stairs of the hotel, crying like a big baby, apparently because the workmen had been playing practical jokes with him. He would return no more, and the next day I put him aboard a steamer going to Cachoeira at the end of the bay, whence he will go on foot to his distant home in Minas Geraes.

A sorrowful incident terminated my wanderings. In passing down the coast I left my dog Feroz at Pernambuco in charge of a friend, to take care of until I returned. When homeward-bound, I went ashore at this city, when I learned to my great grief that my faithful comrade was lost. He had once run away from the house of my friend, and was found at the landing-place of the seashore, gazing anxiously on the open ocean, seated on his haunches, and howling dismally for his absent master, while surrounded by a semi-circle of people, all afraid to venture near such a fierce-looking animal; my friend induced the dog to return with him, but he again got loose, and despite of strenuous efforts to discover his whereabouts, he was never afterwards seen. Poor Feroz! Adeos, my trusty friend!

THE END.

APPENDIX A.

SURVEY OF THE RIOS PARÃOPEBA AND UPPER RIO SÃO FRANCISCO.

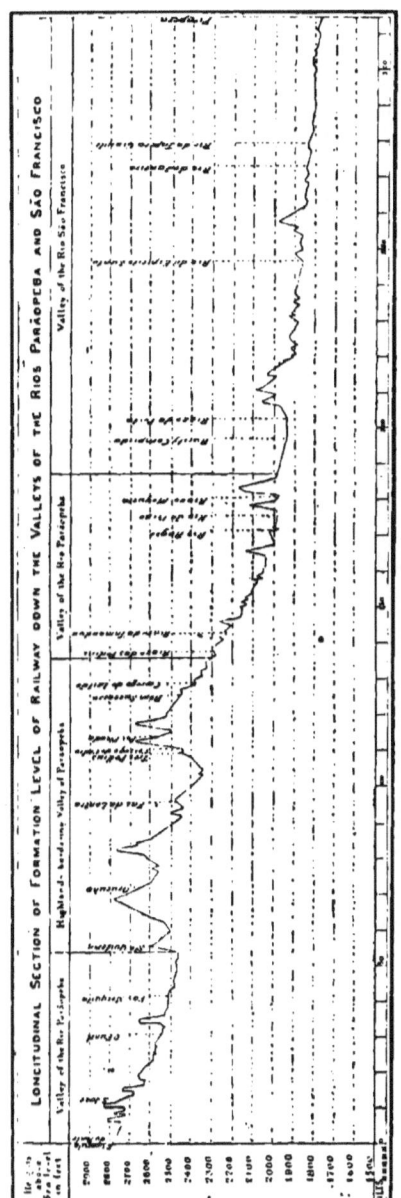

The total length surveyed from São Gonçalo da Ponte to Pirapora was more or less 315 miles, or 190 in the Parãopeba, and 125 in the São Francisco valley. On the map the total distance scales only 210 miles. The length of the course of the river Parãopeba in the extension surveyed is approximately 320 miles; the fall is 813 feet, equivalent to an average per mile of 2 ft. 6.50 in. The course of the Upper São Francisco, comprised in the survey, is more or less 150 miles; the fall is 190 feet, or 0 ft. 9.48 in. per mile.

The construction of the railway would be very expensive, as the following particulars will show:—

6,220,766 cubic yards of excavation.
647 culverts.

199 bridges, with an accumulated length of 8607 feet.
3 viaducts, each of four spans of 100 feet.
17 tunnels, of a total length of 14,635 feet.

The first 38 miles, from São Gonçalo da Ponte, is by far the roughest part of the line, as this section requires 1,359,848 cubic yards of excavation, the three viaducts, and eleven tunnels, besides numerous bridges and culverts.

Eight engineers were engaged on the survey that occupied twenty months of outdoor work and three months of office work.

DISTANCE FROM SÃO GONÇALO DA PONTE OF CHIEF PLACES OF NOTE.

Miles.	
14	Village of São José.
31	The pass in the Serra de Tres Irmãos, "O Funil."
44	Village of Capella Nova do Bitim.
62	Ditto Santa Quiteria.
73	Oracuhá.
89	Village of Inhaúma.
110	Hamlet of Tres Pedras.
114	Village of Taboleiro Grande.
127	Hamlet of Bom Successo.
173	Village of Bagré.
195	Burity Comprido.
315	Pirapora.
335	Mouth of the Rio das Velhas.

APPENDIX B.

EXPLORATION OF THE TOCANTINS—SÃO FRANCISCO WATERSHED; FROM CARINHANHA TO THE VALLEY OF THE PARANAN.

IT will be seen by examining the map that accompanies this work, that Januaria offers a much shorter road to the Tocantins than Carinhanha; but the latter had to be the starting-point of the expedition, in accordance with instructions. The course followed in the exploration was by Cocos, up the valley of the Rio Formosa to Sitio, São Pedro, and Posse. The result shows that there are four alternative routes to the Tocantins :—

1st. From Januaria, in the direction of the sources of the Rios Carinhanha and Correntes.

2nd. From the city of Carinhanha, by following the valley of the river of this name to the source of the Correntes.

3rd. By the valley of the Rio Carinhanha, to the mouth of the Rio Itaguary, then up this valley to the source of the Correntes.

4th. By the Rios Carinhanha, Itaguary, then across the desert to the Rio Formosa, and up this valley to the Correntes. In either of these routes the valley of the latter river offers an easy and favourable course to its junction with the Rio Paranan, seventeen miles below Flores. Canoes and light craft can descend thence to the town of Palma, the starting-point of the large *botes* that descend the Tocantins to Para. In fact, all that and the surrounding district sends its exports to, and receives its imports from, Para.

The watershed is a wide arid sandy table-land, perfectly flat in places, in others very undulating. The eastern slopes are very gentle and regular, but the soil is of such a sterile sandy nature, that from Burity Torto, sixteen miles west of Cocos, quite a houseless desert (*travessia*), extends for 165 miles to Sitio, where, before the traveller enters it, it is necessary to provide everything necessary for himself and animals; food, forage, and water. Throughout the course followed of the Rio Formosa, not one single tributary stream was met with in a distance of eighty-three miles. The rain-water filters through the sandy soil into the Rio Formosa, whose waters are extraordinarily clear and limpid, hence its name, Beautiful river. The whole of this desert is valueless for either agriculture or pasture; but in places, the margins of the Rios Carinhanha, and Itaguary, are lined with belts of fairly sized timber, and occasional clumps of woods are met with in the hollows of the land and of the dividing plateau. The Carinhanha could easily be made navigable with perfect safety; but its waters are now rarely used as a means of transport, on account of its extremely tortuous course; there is one great bend that requires a day to traverse it, and where the traveller can prepare his supper in the same place that he breakfasted.

But it must not be imagined that the *travessia* is an African desert, on the contrary, a rich and curious field for the botanist exists amongst the pindahibas, the mangabeiras, the tree lilies, the ground cactus, the burity, carnahuba, and the dwarf palms, the mimosas, and all the many varieties of strangely dwarfed and distorted gnarled trees, hardy shrubs, grey wiry grasses and brilliant flowers peculiar to the sandy *campos* of Brazil. The atmosphere is wonderfully clear and pure, seeming, as it were, a reflex of the bright blue sky and its drifting snow-white clouds, and the soil, the grass, the bright flowers, all gleam and scintillate in the fierce rays of a scorching sun.

The west side of the watershed is quite different to the east; for the Tocantins being so very much lower than the São Francisco, the fall of its tributaries from their eastern sources is necessarily greater than the São Francisco feeders, consequently the western slopes of the divide are often abrupt and precipitous; the land is much better watered by quick-flowing streams, and the soil is more fertile. The valley of the Rio Paranan is fairly well inhabited, and stocked with numerous cattle-farms. Here immense herds are raised, and sent by the great land journey of 1100 miles, *viâ* Januaria and Curvello, to Rio de Janeiro. This district is well watered, and the pasture is excellent. It is a beautiful country of rolling hills and grassy plains, dotted with *capões* (forest islands, in the Guarany language) in the hollows, and by belts of forests on the margins of the streams. But there is one drawback, in the prevalence of much marshy land, that generates a considerable amount of intermittent fever. Several of the members of the expedition suffered some sharp attacks during their progress through this otherwise vale of Paradise.

In the distant future, when the necessity may exist for a railway to connect the São Francisco and Tocantins, the engineer will find most favourable conditions for his work, for there are no hills to tunnel or climb over, no deep valleys to span, and the gradients will be everywhere gentle, and the curves easy. At present there would be nothing but a cattle traffic, and no railway would be able to lower its fares sufficiently to compete successfully with the countrymen who send their cattle to market by road, and to whom time represents no value. A *matuto* (peasant) will refuse to undertake a day's journey for pay, but will willingly make a day's journey to purchase some requirement some few pence cheaper than in his home neighbourhood, for he loves to hoard what he declines to earn.

APPENDIX C.

CLIMATE.

The following results are obtained from temperature statistics published by the assistant calculator of the Imperial Observatory at Rio de Janeiro:—

MAXIMUM AND MINIMUM ANNUAL SHADE TEMPERATURES.

Year.	Maximum.	Minimum.
	deg. F.	deg. F.
1880	27th January, 99.50	1st July, 56.66
1881	9th December, 94.46	6th August, 56.66
1882	27th November, 98.06	1st September, 50.36
1883	25th November, 99.50	19th August, 55.22
1884	12th January, 98.96	16th September, } 58.10 7th October,

```
                           deg. F.
  1851—67  mean temperature  74.48
  1868—78       ,,      ,,   75.02
  1879—84       ,,      ,,   73.04
```

The months May—October, comprise the dry, and November—April, the rainy season.

There is naturally a very considerable difference between the temperatures of the low-lying city and the elevated suburbs on the hills surrounding it. On 10th December, 1885, the temperature of the day and night of the city on that date was respectively 91°.0 and 73°.0, whereas at the hotel at Paineiras, on the Corcovado railway, the thermometer registered on the same occasion 75°.2 in the day and 64°.4 at night.

When the Fluminenses find capital and courage to construct a railway to the highlands at the rear of the city, now so difficult of access, they will realize a most profitable enterprise, and confer a great boon upon themselves.

OBSERVATIONS taken at Pirapora, Rio São Francisco, the thermometer being suspended inside a grass-thatched hut, built upon a slight eminence (the coolest place in the neighbourhood):—

1874.	Minimum.	Maximum.	Daily Range.	
			Minimum.	Maximum.
January	63	93	71—82	64—93
February	64	95	69—85	64—95
March	63	94	68—89	65—92
April	64	91	67—84	68—95
May	63	93	70—78	66 83
June	49	81	64—71	57—91
July	45	93	48—76	47—93
August	46	98	54—73	46—81
September	61	88	64—89	64—94
October	64	90	69—74	64—90
November	67	88	71—75	67—88
December	67	97	76—83	70—97

OBSERVATIONS at Carinhanha, Rio São Francisco. Thermometer suspended in corridor of a house in the main square of the city:—

Date. 1875.	Time of Observations.				Remarks.
	7 a.m.	10 a.m.	1 p.m.	4 p.m.	
March 5	78	82	85	88	
6	76	82	92	92	
7	79	86	88	89	
8	78	81	87	88	Thunder in the west.
9	75	85	89	78	Thunderstorm 2·30 to 3·30 p.m.
10	76	80	81	80	
11	75	79	84	84	Shower mid-day. Thunder and strong shower in evening.

TEMPERATURE.

Date. 1875.	Time of Observations.				Remarks.
	7 a.m	10 a.m.	1 p.m.	4 p.m.	
March 12	76	81	86	78	Rain 2 to 3 p.m. and at midnight.
13	76	80	82	81	Rain 2 to 3 p.m. Thunder and rain 10 p.m.
14	78	80	79	77	Rain mid-day and in evening.
15	74	77	79	79	Rain 2 to 3 p.m. Heavy thunderstorm 5 to 6 p.m.
16	72	76	78	80	Fine weather.
17	73	76	78	79	The river rose 11 inches and rapidly fell 9.
18	74	79	82	86	
19	76	78	86	88	
20	77	82	86	88	
21	77	82	85	86	
22	78	88	85	84	
23	78	80	82	81	Rain 7 a.m.
24	79	80	82	84	Strong showers in the S.E.
25	79	80	85	84	
26	78	81	82	85	Strong tempest in the N.E.
27	76	83	86	85	
28	76	80	82	80	
29	72	79	81	81	Heavy black cumuli clouds all day, passing rapidly to N.
30	72	76	78	82	
31	70	78	82	81	
April 1	70	74	80	80	
2	68	75	80	80	
3	69	79	81	82	
4	71	80	81	84	
5	72	82	81	84	
6	71	80	83	86	
7	72	80	84	88	Signs of rain in the N.E.
8	76	80	91	87	Sharp shower 7 a.m.
9	76	83	86	85	Two sharp showers in afternoon.
10	77	82	85	82	
11	74	84	83	83	Two light showers during day. Heavy rain for one hour at midnight.
12	78	79	85	83	
13	78	82	81	83	
14	77	80	83	84	Heavy clouds. At 4 p.m. a thunderstorm passed by at some distance.
15	73	81	85	84	
16	76	84	84	86	
17	74	82	87	84	Heavy rain for two hours at 2 a.m.
18	75	82	84	84	Two light showers during day.
19	72	78	82	82	Heavy rain 9 to 1 at night.
20	73	75	78	80	Rain from 6 p.m. to 9 a.m.
21	68	72	76	76	Rain at midnight.
22	68	71	72	74	
23	68	76	78	76	
24	70	76	78	77	
25	69	72	84	82	
26	72	82	86	84	
27	73	78	82	80	

TEMPERATURE.

Date. 1875.	Time of Observations.				Remarks.
	7 a.m.	10 a.m.	1 p.m.	4 p.m.	
April 28	69	74	81	82	
29	66	71	82	82	
30	70	80	80	82	
May 1	72	80	86	87	
2	71	78	81	84	
3	72	79	81	84	
4	70	78	81	82	
5	73	79	82	79	Heavy rain to E. at 4 p.m., wind then veered to S.E. Heavy rain in S.S.E.
6	74	81	84	86	Night of 6th strong gale from E. brought storm of rain and thunder that passed to N.
7	70	77	80	80	
8	68	71	78	78	
9	64	72	78	80	
10	66	74	80	78	
11	64	76	79	78	
12	66	78	80	79	
13	66	70	79	81	
14	68	71	76	82	
15	70	79	81	80	
16	69	75	82	81	

TEMPERATURES observed during the exploration of the route from Carinhanha to the Rio Paranan, Rio Tocantins. N.B. These readings, especially the one and four p.m., are higher than actual shade temperatures, owing to the difficulty of obtaining a shady resort on a journey through *campos* lands:—

Date.	Name of Locality.	Distance in miles from Carinhanha.	Hours of Observations.				Height above sea level in feet.
			7 a.m.	10 a.m.	1 p.m.	4 p.m.	
March 5	Lagoa do Peixe	10	72	88	100	82	1534
6	,, ,,	,,	66	95	94	96	,,
7	,, ,,	,,	75	108	103	91	,,
8	,, ,,	,,	84	...	...	...	,,
,,	Curral Falso	33	...	...	...	92	,,
9	,, ,,	,,	74	...	...	...	,,
,,	Burity	45	...	...	...	82	,,
10	,,	,,	73	...	...	...	,,
,,	Rio Itaguary	,,	...	85	...	...	1599
,,	Carahybas	66	...	...	92	80	1853

TEMPERATURE.

Date.	Name of Locality.	Distance in miles from Carinhanha.	7 a.m.	10 a.m.	1 p.m.	4 p.m.	Height above sea level in feet.
March 11	Carahybas	66	75	...	...	...	1902
,,	Cocos	74	...	85	...	...	1852
12	,,	,,	73	...	...	...	1839
13	,,	,,	76	...	...	...	1873
14	,,	,,	73	77	82	83	1892
15	,,	,,	74	...	...	...	1880
16	,,	,,	74	...	...	...	1869
,,	Rio S. Antonio	82	...	83	...	...	1811
,,	Burity Torto	90	...	...	80	...	1891
17	,,	,,	74	...	...	...	,,
,,	Rio das Pedras	111	...	...	...	83	2037
18	,,	,,	73	...	...	...	,,
,,	Rancho Calande	120	...	...	88	76	2200
19	,,	,,	71	...	...	...	...
,,	Burity Pintado	140	...	...	...	88	2417
20	,,	,,	73	...	...	...	,,
,,	Rio Formosa	152	...	...	88	...	2464
21	,,	,,	74	...	...	...	,,
,,	,,	165	...	...	78	73	2577
22	,,	,,	70	...	...	82	,,
23	,,	180	72	...	...	82	2614
24	,,	190	74	...	...	79	2624
25	,,	200	72	80	84	82	2714
26	,,	,,	71	...	...	...	...
27	,,	206	74	78	...	...	2753
28	,,	219	70	...	...	88	2814
29	,,	227	68	84	86	94	2858
30	,,	,,	69	...	...	...	,,
,,	Summit of divide	233	...	77	...	...	2935
,,	Burity	243	...	...	85	...	2637
31	Rio Correntes	250	...	82	85	...	2521
April 1	,,	,,	66	...	...	...	,,
,,	Sitio	255	...	...	...	82	2425
2	,,	,,	70	...	76	...	,,
3	,,	,,	...	75	...	...	,,
4	,,	,,	68	...	...	...	,,
5	,,	,,	68	...	...	...	,,
6	Rio Correntes	263	...	86	...	...	2398
,,	S. Vidalgo	274	...	...	...	87	,,
7	,,	,,	60	...	...	...	,,
,,	Ribeirão	,,	...	...	92	...	2334
8	,,	290	74	...	...	...	,,
9	Dores	309	70	...	...	...	2444
,,	S. Pedro	325	...	...	...	88	2694
11	Posse	342	73	...	...	...	2629
15	Fazenda do Poco	348	72	...	82	...	2714
16	Trombo	360	72	...	90	...	2058
17	Boa Vista	383	73	...	90	...	1922
,,	Valley of Paranan	...	75	...	...	...	1766
,,	Flores	425	...	...	...	...	...

TEMPERATURES observed on the journey from Barra do Rio Grande, on the Rio São Francisco, to the city of Maranhão :—

Dates		Locality.	Hours of Observation.		Distances from Barra do Rio Grande in miles.	Heights above sea in feet.
			7 a.m.			
February	23	Barra do Rio Grande	77	...	...	1312
March	3	Boqueirão	76	...	66	1412
	5	Tamandua	76	...	80	1430
	6	Estreita	74	...	100	1475
	7	Galinheira	70	...	121	1480
	8	Santa Rita	78	...	140	1500
	11	Gato	76	...	157	1512
	13	Formosa	72	...	210	1670
April	4	Vao	70	...	225	1700
	5	Santa Maria	73	...	251	1732
	9	Brejo Escuro	73	...	298	1880
	12	Batalha	65	2 p.m.	336	2090
	13	Varjem Bonito	70	...	342	2140
	,,	Summit of hills	...	79	...	2320
	14	Source Rio Diogo	72	...	350	2070
	15	Camp	71	...	358	1705
	16	,,	73	12 a.m.	...	1630
	,,	Mouth of Brejão	...	82	369	1605
	19	Source Somninho	...	83	373	1682
	21	Passage ,, No. 1	76	...	379	1485
	24	,, ,, No. 2	76	...	424	1060
	28	Mouth Rio Preto	...	84	435	907
	29	Porto Franco	76	...	457	815
May	1	Rio do Somno	76	...	...	740
	4	,,	77	...	...	670
	5	,,	75	...	...	645
	6	,,	76	...	...	622
	8	Mouth Rio do Somno	76	...	...	610
	,,	Pedro Affonso	76	...	584	663

Great as is the vast extent of Brazil, the climate of north and south does not show any very great extremes of heat or cold. Egypt is hotter in the summer, and Spain is always colder in the winter. The Amazons, which traverses the region of the equator, is not by any means such a torrid zone as its position would leave one to suppose. A two years' residence at S. Antonio, on the Rio Madeira, one of the most unhealthy regions of the Amazons basin, showed a general highest average by day, of 82°—88°, and lowest at night 69°—75°, but on one or two exceptional occasions in daytime the thermometer registered 95°.

At Pernambuco, about 8° south latitude, the thermometer rarely exceeds 84°, or descends lower than 65°.

In the south, in Rio Grande do Sul and Parana, the range of temperature is much greater than in the central and northern regions. Here slight frosts occur in the winter nights, whereas in the summer daytime the thermometer will reach as high, or even a higher degree of temperature than any part of the tropical sections of Brazil.

The equable and comparative mildness of temperature of the Brazilian coast, and of the elevated table-lands of the interior, is due to the trade-winds that so unfailingly sweep the land with their pure and refreshing breezes, and carry away and dissipate the malaria generated by the swamps of the low shores of the northern coast, that otherwise would probably be as unhealthy as the West Coast of Africa. It is only in deep valleys, or where localities are shut out from the winds of the ocean by surrounding highlands like Rio de Janeiro, that the thermometer occasionally shows a high degree of temperature.

PUBLIC HEALTH OF RIO DE JANEIRO.

STATISTICS OF THE MORTALITY OF RIO DE JANEIRO AND ITS SUBURBS, OBTAINED FROM OFFICIAL PUBLICATIONS.

Unfortunately there is no certain data to accurately determine the number of the present population of this area, but I believe that 400,000 will fairly represent it, although such an estimate will perhaps be considered by many, to be quite a maximum amount.

During the last year (1885) the total mortality was 10,182, distributed as follows :—

Sex.		Condition.		Nationality.	
Masculine	6332	Free	9881	Brazilians	7112
Feminine	3850	Slaves	301	Foreigners	3070

Ages.		Localities.	
0 to 7 years	2363	Private houses	6847
7 to 25 ,,	1494	Hospitals	3358
25 to 40 ,,	2026	Highways	4
40 to 55 ,,	1678	The sea	23
Above 55 ,,	1811		
Unknown	810		

1st half of year 5201.
2nd ,, 4981.

Causes of Mortality.

Consumption	1754	Various fevers	193
Various causes	1624	Violent deaths	196
Heart	1232	Lockjaw of newborn	
Stillborn	793	children	178
Bronchitis, &c.	654	Convulsions	131
Digestive organs	581	Lymphatic diseases	131
Cerebro-spinal	555	Consumption of the	
Pernicious fever	545	bowels	130
Apoplexy	480	Diarrhœa	55
Yellow fever	374	Dysentery	41
Liver	289	Erysipelas	39
Typhoid fever	206	Smallpox	4

Mortality from various Fevers from 1877 to 1885.

	1878.	1879.	1880.	1881.	1882.	1883.	1884.	1885.
Yellow fever	1174	974	1433	912	95	1336	618	374
Pernicious fever	668	552	555	472	...	600	426	545
Typhoid fever	208	168	178	186	...	160	157	206
Other fevers	285	214	208	170	749	352	135	193
Measles	52	42	14	4	...	149	15	...
Smallpox	2175	197	27	127	937	1366	89	4
	4562	2147	2415	1871	1781	3963	1440	1322

As will be seen by the table of fever mortality during the past eight years, Rio de Janeiro has considerably improved its sanitary condition.[1] The deaths from yellow fever average in different

---

[1] Since the foregoing observations were written, this year (1886) having proved to have been an unusually hot season, yellow fever has been again very prevalent, still despite the high temperature of the first months of the year, not to such an extent as in former years; it has however extended the area of its ravages, for

years from about 1 to 10 per cent. of the total mortality. The victims of yellow fever are generally newly arrived foreigners (chiefly young men, who are often careless in their habits, or in the exercise of precautions indispensable to an unacclimatized stranger), the countryman fresh from the interior; jack-ashore, or working in the sun, and sleeping in the dews of night; and the inhabitant debilitated by a general bad state of health, from too long a residence in a tropical climate ; but sometimes the disease will, despite all precautions, seize a quiet-living old resident, or a lady who may have come from a healthy suburb into the infected city for a little shopping.

The several varieties of marsh fevers that are prevalent in many parts of the interior require conditions to promote an attack quite the reverse of those of yellow fever, for a healthy newly-arrived foreigner can generally travel through a malarious district with comparative impunity, even when the local inhabitants are one and all suffering from the endemical fevers, and even if the stranger becomes a resident he will be less liable to an attack than the natives. But in some of the tributaries of the Amazons, these fevers will sometimes assume an extremely malignant form, and of the india-rubber gatherers that yearly proceed up the river, thousands never return. The Rio Purus especially, has a notable reputation for the occasionally deadly character of its climate.

many inland towns, and many cities of the coast, have this year been visited for the first time by the fell disease. As usual the epidemic ceased with the approach of the cool season in May to September.

APPENDIX D.

GOLD AND DIAMOND MINING IN BRAZIL.

PROBABLY there is no other part of the world where gold has been scattered so broadcast over so large an area as in Brazil; from north to south, east to west, it is met with, either in quartz or alluvial, and there is hardly a single province in which it is not found. A certain Antonio Rodrigues, a native of Taubaté, in São Paulo, is credited with having discovered it in 1693. In those days, what are now provinces were then called *capitanias*, each one under a governor, and practically independent of each other.[1] When the Paulistas of Taubaté made the gold discovery, they endeavoured to exclude new arrivals from Europe and the neighbouring *capitanias* from sharing their find, and finally, in 1708, under the leadership of a Manoel de Borba Gato, they sought to expel all intruders; thus commenced the wars of the Caboclos and Emboabas, that after many skirmishes ended in the party of Paulistas being treacherously betrayed and killed to a man. The scene of the massacre was near São João del Rey, and thus was originated the name of the Rio dos Mortes (River of the Dead) that passes near the city.

This is only one of the many recorded instances of the anarchy and ruffianism that existed in those early days in the wild interior of the country, but despite all difficulties and privations, the old colonists, evidently full of "go" and a spirit of enterprise, spread themselves over the face of the land, and penetrated to distant localities in Goyaz and Matto Grosso, where the existing vestiges

---

[1] This may perhaps have originated the plural of "The Brazils," as it is stil occasionally spoken of in the foreign correspondence section of newspapers.

of the old workings show that an immense amount of work was done, hills were bored or levelled, whole valleys and districts were turned over. Sluicing was largely employed, and water was conducted in open channels, sometimes for thirty or forty miles, over generally most rugged country, and an immense number of labourers must have been engaged in the operations.

In 1713 the Colonial government exacted a royalty of one-fifth (Quinta Real) from the gross proceeds of all mines, but despite its jealous care it must have been extremely difficult to prevent smuggling, or operations in distant localities far away from official inspection; yet even so, it is marvellous to read in the archives of Ouro Preto of the fabulous sums received in payment of the royalty, much of which helped to rebuild Lisbon after the earthquake of 1755.

All this vast mining interest practically ceased about seventy to eighty years ago, probably owing to the exhaustion of the old workings, or the increased cost and dearth of slave and Indian labour; still I cannot but help having the opinion that Brazil will yet be a great gold and diamond mining country; there are many reasons both for and against such a belief.

Against.

1st. That hitherto most of the efforts made by foreigners and natives to re-develop some of the old abandoned workings have ended in failure, for the old miners did their work most effectually and often scientifically, and picked the bone thoroughly clean.

2nd. That practical Californian miners have prospected parts of the country and have met with no prizes.

3rd. That at present there is no individual prospecting by natives that corresponds to that of the old Californian who trudges into the recesses of the Rockies, to hunt for himself, and toils, and suffers privations that he would never endure for any wages, no matter how great.

For.

That taking into consideration the enormous area of Brazil, and especially of the vast tracts that yet have never been trodden by man, except by the wandering Indian,[2] it is only feasible to suppose that there are yet as "good fish in the sea as ever were caught," or in other words, it is impossible to believe that the few pin's-points on the map of Brazil that represent the position of old and present mines can possibly be the only auriferous deposits that exist. It is contrary to one's reason to suppose so. The trouble is to find out the prizes; it may be like searching for a needle in a haystack, but the needle is there, and many more besides. I should like to get a half-dozen practical, hardy Californians or Australians, and direct them where to go in Brazil. I feel convinced I could put them on the right road, by prospecting unexplored regions in a continuation of the now easily-traced lines of gold-bearing country.

Of late years there has been a considerably increased national interest shown towards gold-mining, and the minister of Agriculture is constantly receiving applications for concessions to explore alleged auriferous lands, but many of these concessions are required, not so much for a *bonâ fide* exploration, but as something to sell to promoters of companies, certainly at present the most lucrative system of gold-mining in Brazil. One very 'cute, but apparently simple-minded *Mineiro*, succeeded in disposing of a concession to an American company; the capital was raised, and costly machinery sent by a long and arduous journey to the interior of Minas Geraes, but on commencing operations the land was proved goldless; it had been cleverly "salted." The well-known American mining engineer who had been sent to report upon the property, was accompanied in his prospecting operations by the simple-looking countryman, the *concessionaire*, who declared that gold was everywhere, and lovingly tapped with his walking-stick every pan the engineer personally tested, and made some apparently casual remarks upon its riches. This walking-stick was hollow, and filled with gold dust, and ingeniously contrived to let a little fall out when required. Not bad for a *matuto*.

Near São João d' El Rey I have panned gold really from the dust of the highway, and all the country round about is literally peppered with gold, still it would not pay to work, as it is very minutely

[2] There are many perfectly unknown regions within 100 miles of the coast.

scattered. The land is above the water-level, and there is no place to "dump" the washings. The old miners have pretty effectually cleaned out the workable placers of this district, even to deviating the course of a river.

In vol. i., page 328, I quoted an example of what one man can do alone with pick and pan in favourable districts such as the Rio Paracatu; and in the district of Diamantina there is still a very considerable amount of diamond-mining carried on, of which the outside world knows absolutely nothing.

Brazil has largely supplied the world with diamonds, and still continues to do so, but no one ever reads in any Brazilian newspaper of any account of these mines or workings. They are possibly so profitable that the miners may consider it is just as well to keep their results of working only known to their good selves.

The English have made many attempts at quartz mining in Brazil, and out of many failures, only one, the São João d'El Rey Company has proved a success, this mine has returned its capital over and over again. It is now the deepest mine in Brazil,[3] and a most substantial undertaking, conducted at very great expense. There is no evidence to fear that it may be soon exhausted, but whether it will ever again recover its once palmy days will largely depend upon the administration, for the peculiar conditions of the mine require special treatment. The name of the company is misleading as to the present situation of the mine; originally a shaft was sunk at the city of São João d'El Rey, that was eventually abandoned, and the company commenced their present operations at Morro Velho near the Rio das Velhas. Captain Burton, in his "Highlands of the Brazil," gives most complete and minute details of this and the other English mines in the neighbourhood.

The present condition of the mining laws in Brazil is very unsatisfactory, mainly on account of the uncertainty that prevails, for it has never been definitely decided whether mineral deposits belong to the State, to the owner of the property, or to the finder, consequently a concession of rights to mine is often worded differently by different ministers, according to the construction that they or their advisers may put upon the law.

[3] The shafts are inclined planes about 2000 fathoms in length.

There is no difficulty in obtaining from the Government a sole right to explore a given district within a given area, that secures to the prospector a monopoly of the district for two years; to afterwards make good his right to mine, he has to present to the Government, before the expiration of this period, topographical and geological maps of the district, with various items of information. Then he must be prepared to satisfy the landowner, although he may be told that the owner has no right to compensation for the minerals in his land, but the Brazilian *matuto* has a very inconvenient way of settling such legal questions, and it is just as well to have everything satisfactorily adjusted with the owner, or trouble will sure to ensue.

If the *concessionaire* has fulfilled all his obligations in carrying out his explorations, he will be granted a right to select, within the limits of the area indicated in his preliminary concession, fifty *datas* or squares of 827 metres. Having selected which his rights over the rest of the ground explored will cease.

STATISTICS OF BRAZILIAN RAILWAYS IN TRAFFIC, CONSTRUCTION, AND PROJECT, TO END OF 1884.

The LARGE TYPE indicates the lines belonging to the State, the smaller type the National Companies, the *italics* the English Companies.

N.B.—1:000$ = a conto ; or 1:000 milreis at the par value of 27 pence = £112 10s. 0d.; or 1:000:000$ = £112,500 0s. 0d.

Province.	Name of Railway.	Length.			Gauge in metres.	Ruling Gradient.	Capital.			Price per kilometer.	Percentage Guaranteed.	Traffic results in 1884.			
		In traffic.	In construction.	In survey or projected.			Guaranteed or subventioned.	Not guaranteed.	Total.			Receipts.	Expenses.	Balance.	Deficit.
		kilom metres	kilom metres	kilom metres		%	$	$	$	$	%	$	$	$	$
Para	Braganza	109:482	...	141:000	1·0	2%	5:656:000$	...	5:656:000$	...	7	299:508	261:157	38:350	...
Ceará {	BATURITE	128:920	61:000	84:200	1·1	1·8%	...	...	6:519:241	...	...	63:997	150:150	...	86:153
	CAMOCIM AND SOBRAL ...				1·1	1·8 ,,	...	...	2:464:904	...	...				
RioGrande do Norte }	*Imperial Brazilian* Natal e Nova Cruz	121:000	...	...	1·	2·5 ,,	5:496:052	1:615:058	7:111:111	58:769	7	69:871	229:316	...	159:445
Parahyba do Norte	Conde d'Eu	121:519	...	...	1·	2· ,,	6:000:000	...	6:000:000	49:586	7	148:056	179:602	...	31:545
Pernambuco	*Recife and São Francisco*	124:739	85:943	...	1·6	1·25,	{10:666:666 4:316:997}	2:192:037	17:175:681	137:000	{7 5}	1:090:224	677:156	413:067	...
	Ditto (EXTENSI N)	58:982				1·8 ,,						79:376	137:567	...	58:190
	RECIFE AND CARUARÚ ...	...	90:500	20:474	1·	1·8 ,,	...	...	5:735:590	...	...				
	Great Western... ...	96:300	...	46:000	1·	2· ,,	5:000:000	2:537:590	27:272:562	54:075	7	573:618	519:390	54:228	...
	Ilrazilian Street Railway	18:625	...	9:000	1·2	1·3 ,,	...	1:277:771	7:537:500	39:897	...	193:825	140:494	52:331	...
	Recife and Olinda	12:500	...	...	1·4	3·5 ,,	...	500:000	1:277:771	...	...	58:128	269:862	...	213:007
	PAULO AFFONSO... ...	115:853	...	...	1·	3·0 ,,	...	...	500:000	...	...				
Alagoas ...	*Alagoas...*	88:000	...	...	1·	2·0 ,,	4:553:000	...	4:553:000	51:738	7	14:497	9:761	4:736	...
Sergipe ...	Aracaju to Simão Dias	...	176:000	...	...	...	1:250:000	...	1:250:000	...	7				
Bahia	*B.hia and São Francisco*	123:340	82:600	...	1·6	1·25,	16:000:000	...	16:000:000	129:724	7	591:826	529:998	61:828	...
	Ditto (Timbo branch)	...	141:776	131:089	1·	1·66 ,,	2:050:200	...	2:050:200	...	6				
	Ditto (EXTENSION)	180:568	77:000	350:000	1·	1·8 ,,	...	...	...	...	(EXTENSION)	80:136	227:432	...	147:295
	Brazilian Imperial Central	225:000	...	...	1·	3· ,,	13:000:000	2:400:000	13:000:000	66:6820	7	439:729	365:546	:54:182	...
	Santo Amaro	36:020	...	94:000	1·	3· ,,	...	201:000	2:400:000	...	...				
	Nazareth	34:000	...	237:000	1·	2·5 ,,	1:049:500	1:200:000:000†	1:250:000	...	7	80:932	175:382	...	85:449
	Bahia and Minas ...	142:000	30:000		1·	2·5 ,,			1:200:000:000						
Espirito Santo }	Cachoeira to Itapemirim	...	72:000	...	1·	3· ,,	1:250:000	...	1:250:000	...	7				
Rio de Janeiro	Petropolis	25:030	63:000	...	1·1	1·5 ,,	...	3:100:000	3:100:000	...	...	574:506	292:750	281:856	...
	Cantagallo and Rio Bonito	209:413	...	120:000	1·1	1·8 ,,	...	10:873:133	10:873:133	...	...				
	Ditto (branch)	61:319	4:766	19:600	1·1	2·5 ,,	...	...	...	...	...	1:405:1019	1:226:087	179:811	...
	Macahé and Campos ...	96:500	...	...	0·96	1·5 ,,	8:000:000	8:000:000	8:000:000	...	...	1:535:002	858:216	676:386	...
	Barão de Araruama ...	40:500	...	...	0·96	1·5 ,,	...	800:000	800:000	...	...	128:027	71:477	56:600	...
	Quissaman	35:000	...	...	0·96	1·5 ,,	...	...	...	...	...				
	Campos and São Sebastião	18:200	...	...	1·	1·5 ,,	...	...	...	32:067	...				
	S. Antonio de Padua ...	188:000	15:000	135:881	1·	1·5 ,,	6:000:000	600:000	6:000:000	29:000	7	343:689	247:242		
	S. Fidelis	92:852	...	61:000	1·	2·2 ,,	...	...	...	...	...				

		Kilom. Meters	Miles.										
Rio de Janeiro	Vasourias	6·000	...	...	0·99	3·5 ,,						70·227	4·040
	Uniãs Valenciana	63·350	...	1·1	2·75 ,,							51·455
	Pirahyense	38·700	22·000	58·976	1·	3 ,,			12·00·000	12·00·000	27·280	241·333	171·506	
	Rezende and Areas	28·336	...	31·000	1·	1·23 ,,					43·597	60·759	64·800	
	Rio Bonito	8·000	21·000	26·000	1·						...	533·933	105·307	
	Banalense	...	23·000	...	1·	2·7 ,,			300·000	300·000	...			
	Porto Novo to Paquequer	...	6·000	45·800	1·	6·0 ,,			840·000	840·000	...			
	Theresopolis	724·908	61·428	239·146	1·60	1·8 ,,			...	...	130·296	1·1355·1959	6·591·350	4·1999·533
	D. PEDRO SEGUNDO	58·056	...	18·120	1·00	1·8 ,,			94·453·201	94·453·201				
	Rio do Ouro	3·789	...	...	1·00	30·0 ,,			1·164·832	1·164·832				
	Corcovado	...	48·800	25·000	1·	2·0 ,,			700·000	700·000				
	Rio de Janeiro to Magé								2·000·000	2·000·000				
São Paulo	S. Paulo and Rio de Janeiro	231·020	...	...	1·	2·0 ,,			10·665·000	10·665·000	46·169	1·191·599	1·0263·655	127·943
	São Paulo	139·450	...	...	1·6	2·5 ,,			23·555·850	23·555·850	169·466	5·812·432	1·521·299	4·291·136
	Jundiahy to Campinas	241·500	80·000	35·000	1·0	11·0 ,,			20·00·000	20·00·000	67·100	1·118·183	525·075	593·108*
	Ituna	160·000	...	...	1·0	2·0 ,,			2·052·696	2·052·696	33·273	330·413	104·476	1·355·937†
	Bragantina	52·000	127·098	87·518	1·0	1·8 ,,			2·300·000	2·300·000	44·165	15·683	36·635	20·952
	S. Carlos de Pinhal	368·000	46·800		1·0	2·5 ,,			3·000·000	3·000·000	18·096	310·500	149·033	161·407
	Mogyana	186·000	270·600	188·000	1·0	2·0 ,,			3·250·000	3·250·000	226·30	1·020·784	852·781	768·000
	Mogyana extension		20·000		1·0	2·5 ,,			5·100·000	5·100·000				
	Sorocabana				1·0	3·0 ,,			7·000·000	7·000·000	43·000	322·639	202·511	120·128
Parana	Parana to Curitiba	41·000	69·400	...	1·0	2·25 ,,			5·500·000	5·500·000				
Santa Catharina	*Donna Thereza Christina*	116·620	...	...	1·0	3·00 ,,			111·492·043	111·492·043	30·084	141·273	...	111·273
						2·0 ,,			5·451·209	5·451·209	8·650	63·472		54·822
Rio Grande do Sul	Southern Brazilian Rio Grande do Sul													
	Caccequay to Uruguayana	...	280·500	...	1·0	3·0 ,,			13·521·453	13·521·453	48·241			
	Brazil Great Southern	...	...	261·000	1·0	1·8 ,,			13·300·849	13·300·849	50·000			
	Porto Alegre to Novo Hamburgo	42·851	...	183·500	1·0	...			6·000·000	6·000·000	32·698	238·946	400·036	161·091
	Porto Alegre to CACEQUAY	179·597	189·208	...	1·0	2·0 ,,			1·800·000	1·800·000	82·580			
	S. Jeronymo	13·000	...	11·920	1·	1·0 ,,			1·738·635	1·738·635	64·900			
	S. João do Monte-Negro			200·000		1·5 ,,			292·400	292·400	...			
Minas Geraes	*Minas and Rio*	170·000	...	373·000	1·0	3·0 ,,			15·495·253	15·495·253	91·149	263·410	339·977	23·442
	Leopoldina	400·000	168·920	120·000	1·0	2·5 ,,			20·000·000	20·000·000	...	1·467·300	765·430	37·627
	West of Minas	99·000	...	...	0·76	2·0 ,,			...	...	222·751	139·386	101·754	
	Ditto (extension)	...	...	128·000	1·0	2·5 ,,			11·200·000†	11·200·000†				
	Minas Central	...	56·000	164·000	1·0	...			4·000·000	4·000·000	...			
	Pitanguy to Patos	37·000	3·000	300·000	1·0	...			9·000·000	9·000·000	...	191·152	31·594	12·332
	Piau			36·000		2·0 ,,			8·000·000	8·000·000	...			
	Italiano to Cachoeira das Panellas					...			400·000	400·000	...			
	Ponte Nova to Natividade	...	...	195·000	...	...			2·000·000	2·000·000	...			
	Lavras to Sta. Rita	...	...	350·000	...	...			10·000·000	10·000·000	...			
				200·000					4·000·000	4·000·000				

Resumé.   Kilom. Meters   Miles.   In 1835, Miles.
In traffic ... 6·115·343   3800   4414
,, construction 1·990·935   1248   1411
,, project ... 5·472·224   3400   3138

The above statistics are taken from the Annual Report of the Minister of Agriculture for the year 1885.

* For six months ending June 30, 1884.
† Cost of construction partly paid for by Provincial subvention.
‡ French Company.

APPENDIX E.

RAILWAYS.

Brazilian State Railways.

The Dom Pedro Segundo. This is the most important railway in the empire, in its length, its traffic, and its cost. It is admirably situated, for it receives the whole of the exports and imports of Minas Geraes, and the rich coffee districts of the valley of the Rio Parahyba. The main line extends to beyond Queluz, and a long length is now in course of construction to extend the line finally to the neighbourhood of Sabará on the Rio das Velhas. Another branch to Ouro Preto, the capital of Minas Geraes, is also under construction. These two last sections will for many years greatly diminish the profits of the railway, for the insignificant traffic will have to be carried on with a very considerable excess of expense over receipts. Immigration to these districts is practically *nil*, and a very large proportion of the land is only fit for a meagre pasturage for cattle; still there are scattered amidst the hills and mountains many valleys and hollows, where a very fair soil exists, sufficient to yield abundant produce, even with the present number of inhabitants, if they were only fairly industrious, but I fear that even the presence of the railway in their midst will fail to stir them up to more vigorous action.

DOM PEDRO SEGUNDO RAILWAY.

PASSENGER AND TRAFFIC RETURNS AND EXPENSES
IN VARIOUS YEARS.

Year.	Miles open.	Passenger and goods traffic. Amounts in milreis.			Number of Passengers.	
		Receipts.	Expenses.	Balance.	Suburbs.	Main line.
1858	38	295:845$	172:092$	123:753$	...	115,112
1861	43	1:099:815$	697:836$	401:979$	136,559	279,380
1863	55	1:001:997$	854:109$	147:888$	160,122	304,766
1866	117	1:858:076$	847:845$	1:010:231$	233,246	405,529
1869	126	4:325:817$	1:845:662$	2:480:159$	531,068	778,543
1871	147	5:434:984$	2:387:677$	3:047:307$	583,201	903,470
1874	233	7:604:032$	3:381:894$	4:222:438$	785,413	1,230,114
1878	348	9:970:500$	5:447:794$	4:522:706$	1,474,089	2,193,357
1881	403	13:067:911$	5:605:765$	7:462:145$	1,852,970	2,755,487
1884	453	11:502:561$	6:503:029$	4:909:533$	2,170,206	3,125,127
1885	453	12:212:955$	6:368:496$	5:844:458$	2,475,269	2,489,225

The table of the number of passengers and the traffic returns tells a very eloquent story of the wonderful progress of this section of the empire. The suburban passenger traffic is indicative of the growth of the city; that of the main line shows the increased movement, or travelling of the people, for it has become augmented out of all proportion to the increase of population. The last fifty miles of the railway passes through comparatively unproductive land, where the sparse traffic has run up the working expenses, and the total receipts have even diminished from 1881 to 1885. Still, although the railway may not be able to look for greater profits in this direction, it may reasonably expect an improvement from the further development of its twelve tributary railways actually in traffic, many of which are prolonging their lengths, so as the good prospects will balance the evil ones of the future, there is every reason to believe that the Dom Pedro II. railway will still continue to be an important contributor to the revenue of the State, and well it is so, in order to balance the appalling deficiencies of the eight other State railways, only one of which, the Baturite, gives a small profit. This railway and the Sobral, both in the northern province of Ceará, and the Paulo Affonso, on the margins of the lower Rio São Francisco, were built by the State in order to get some return, or work done, for the food it supplied to the starving thousands during the great famine in the north of Brazil in 1877, 1878, 1879.

The prolongation by the State, of the Bahia and São Francisco railway is a gigantic error, save for perhaps strategic purposes, as is also the extension of the Recife and São Francisco. Both of these new lines traverse a wild and chiefly sterile country; that of the Bahia especially, is a howling desert practically devoid of streams, good soil, or inhabitants. The object of both of these lines is to reach the Rio São Francisco, where the present traffic and the utter absence of immigrants is far below being able to provide remunerative returns for the costly outlay on the long lines of either one of the railways, much less for both. There are more hopeful prospects for the Caruarú line, in Pernambuco, for it traverses an old agricultural district, fairly well stocked with sugar estates. The Porto Alegre and Cacequay, in Rio Grande do Sul, will also probably soon prove remunerative, for it is in one of the few provinces to which immigrants are now flocking.[1]

Cantagallo. This railway is owned by the Provincial Government of Rio de Janeiro. A part of the line, between seven and eight miles, is constructed with the "Fell" system of central rail, in order to make the sharp ascent from the plains to the elevated highlands of Novo Friburgo. Since 1878 the line has always earned a small profit, and last year, 1885, owing chiefly to a more economical administration, the profits of the year's working reached a little over five per cent. of capital. It traverses coffee and sugar regions, and a country that is being steadily, if slowly developed. The climate of the highlands is delightful, and although the soil generally is poor, there is yet considerable tracts, or rather patches of excellent land waiting for development. The future of the line is secure and very promising.

[1] The extention (1885) of railways in traffic built and owned by the State, is 1067 miles, the cost of which at the par value of the milreis has been about 17,193,224*l*., and the nett receipts of all these lines produce about 3½ per cent on the capital employed.

THE NATIONAL COMPANIES' LINES.

Mogyana. This São Paulo railway is the most successful national line in Brazil, not only owing to the fertile district it traverses, but also to the economy of cost of construction and the able management of its administrators. For some time past, it has been earning progressively increasing dividends, and is already paying to the province amounts received during its earlier days for guarantees of interest. The last half-year showed a profit of sixteen per cent. on main line and Amparo branch, and seven per cent. on Rio Preto branch. Although coffee forms a large item in its traffic, yet the line is not dependent on this production alone for its goods traffic. Its five per cent. debentures are quoted on the London Stock Exchange, and offer as sound an investment as any one need desire. Its ordinary shares are quoted in Rio at 50 per cent. premium. The company is extending its line to the navigable waters and fertile regions of the Rio Grande, under a guarantee of 7 per cent. from the general Government.

West of São Paulo or *Paulista railway.* This is a continuation of the English São Paulo line, from Jundiahy to Campinas. The concession was originally offered to the São Paulo Company, but being unwisely refused, a national company was at once formed, and the capital raised in São Paulo. The Province originally guaranteed 7 per cent. on a quarter of present capital, it is a most prosperous line, and its profits are steadily increasing. It now pays dividends of 11.2 per cent., and the shares are 25 per cent. premium.

São Carlos and Rio Claro. This is another successful São Paulo railway. The capital was raised without any guarantee, and the cost of its construction is the cheapest of any 1.00 $m.$ guage railway in Brazil. Its traffic is increasing rapidly. It pays 10 per cent., and its shares are 5 per cent. premium.

The Grão Para or *Petropolis line*, in Rio de Janeiro, is a continuation of the first railway built in Brazil, the old Mauá railway. It is now a decided success, and pays 9 per cent. dividends. The shares are 25 per cent. premium.

These four railways are the only ones whose ordinary shares realize a premium on the Rio Stock Exchange.

The Leopoldina is the chief tributary line of the Dom Pedro II.

railway. The company is most enterprising and energetic, and the line is now one of the most important railways in the empire. As yet, its traffic does not earn the dividends, that have to be made up by the help of guarantees, but as the line traverses a rich and fertile zone (much of it hitherto undeveloped), and the inhabitants display an unusual degree of "go" and enterprise, there is a good future before it. At present it pays 7 per cent. dividends on the ordinary shares that are quoted at .28 per cent. discount. The capital is 30,969,600$ in ordinary shares, and 500,000*l*. in 6 per cent. debentures. The expenses are approximately 50 per cent. of receipts, and the profits are about equal to 2 per cent. of capital.

Campos and Carangola is a progressively improving line. In the first half of 1884, it received 139,902$ from the general Government to make up dividends, but in the similar period of 1885, it only required 84,448$. The traffic now earns a profit equal to 3 per cent. of capital. The ordinary shares, at 35 per cent. discount, receive 5 per cent. dividends on nominal value, the $5\frac{1}{2}$ per cent. debentures are not quoted.

Macahe and Campos traverses almost entirely, one of the most important sugar-producing regions of Brazil. A company without any guaranteed interest, it has during the last few years worked its way from almost bankruptcy to a prosperous condition. The shares, once 80 per cent. discount, attained 20 per cent. premium, but since the amalgamation with the S. Antonio de Padua railway they have suffered another relapse of 50 per cent., but the line is prosperous. The profits increased from 645,349$ in 1882, to 697,067$ in 1884, the latter being equivalent to 8.7 per cent. of capital, but this balance is now absorbed in settling temporary obligations acquired in its amalgamation with the S. Antonio de Padua.

An inspection of the accompanying tables will show the capital and traffic results of the other national lines whose dividends are all dependent on guarantees on the whole or part of their capitals. There is one unfortunate line, the Bahia and Minas, constructed by the aid of a provincial contribution of 9000$ per kilometre, that is a "white elephant" to its proprietors the builders, for in 1884 the traffic was insignificant and the expenses more than double the amount of receipts, and there is no guaranteed interest to help it to wait for better times.

The English Railway Companies.

The São Paulo,[1] from Campos to Jundiahy. This successful line is intrinsically superior to any other English railway in Brazil, and there are very few in any part of the world that have proved such a financial success, although its cost of construction per mile is greater than any other railway in the country. This great expense was caused by the abrupt ascent from the coast to the high level of the table-land of São Paulo. Part of the line consists of inclined planes with stationary engines. To end of financial year, 1883-4, the company had returned to the State, from profits of traffic, the sum of 334,091*l.*, derived from the half of net revenue exceeding 8 per cent. There is no reason to fear any permanent drop in the present high quotations of the shares on the London Stock Exchange, for the extension of railways in the province of São Paulo is making great strides, and the whole of their traffic must pass through the toll-gate of the São Paulo railway, and whatever changes may occur in the Government or the country, this traffic should be always increasing.

It is a "far cry" from the prosperity of the São Paulo to the financial conditions of the other English railways, all of which are, without exception, dependent on the State for their dividends. I will mention them in their present order of merit, or ratio of expenses to receipts as existed at the end of 1884.

Recife and São Francisco. This is the oldest English line in Brazil, and in 1884, after over a quarter of a century of existence, its expenses were 62.1 per cent. of its receipts, and its profits equal to nearly $2\frac{1}{2}$ per cent. of capital. It serves a rich sugar region, where the traffic, like most of the lines in North Brazil, is entirely influenced by the good or bad crops. From 1873 to 1882 the passenger traffic showed practically no difference, the goods traffic increased barely 30 per cent. In 1884 the receipts were much the same, but expenses diminished 15 per cent. The Company has paid $5\frac{1}{2}$ per cent. dividends on its capital stock since 1876.

Bahia and São Francisco. This railway, opened to traffic in 1860, has ever since shown the most deplorable results. From 1860 to 1882 there were seventeen annual deficits and six annual small

---

[1] Commonly called San Paulo, a title that is neither English nor Portuguese.

balances to the good; and in the last six months, ending December 31st, 1885, the railway barely cleared its working expenses. It has been all this long time a most crucial test of the value of the State guarantees, for more than 150 % of the whole cost of the line has been paid to the company for guaranteed interest. A branch line to Timbó is now in course of construction. This branch traverses a fertile region, fairly populated, and yielding a considerable amount of produce. Great hopes are built upon the prospects of an improved traffic by the contributions of this tributary.

Brazilian Imperial Central of Bahia. This line, the first of the modern section of English lines, was in part, opened to traffic in 1882. Like all of the later companies, its traffic was estimated to yield 4 per cent. profit, an estimate accepted by the State as feasible, for it endorsed its belief by granting the 7 per cent. guarantee. The line trends in the direction of the Rio São Francisco, to be eventually probably another competitor with the other Bahia, the Pernambuco, and the Paulo Affonso lines, but as it accompanies mainly the old road route to the river, traversing districts more populated and fertile than either of those of these three lines, its prospects are more hopeful than those chimerical undertakings. The expenses for 1884 were 87.37 per cent. of receipts, and profits were under half per cent. of capital. In 1885 the traffic increased 63.5 per cent., but the expenses absorbed 94.5 per cent. of receipts.

Great Western of Brazil. This Pernambuco line, with the high-sounding name, makes but a very small step into the far-west of Brazil. Opened to traffic in 1881, under most hopeful auspices, it produced until lately, small profits. In 1881 and 1882, they were about half per cent. of guaranteed capital, in 1883 about two, in 1884 they dropped to 1 per cent.; 1885 ended in a small loss. This railway should be a fairly successful line, for a very considerable traffic from the interior passes it on the main road that runs more or less parallel with it. But its previously high freights proved to the country people that it was cheaper to continue their long journey from the distant west by the road rather than over the remaining comparatively short distance of sixty miles covered by the railway. The remedy is to extend the line about 100 miles,[2]

[2] To Campina Grande in Parahyba do Norte.

lower the freight, run the horses off the road, and then it should pay, for there is apparently sufficient goods traffic, even in bad times, to earn a fair dividend, and the proposed extension of the line into the fertile region of Timbauba is very desirable.[3] As the traffic is dependent mainly on the sugar crops, its returns must always vacillate with the good and bad seasons, and the last year or two have been exceptionally bad, owing to poor crops and the present unremunerative prices of sugar.

Minas and Rio. This line joins the Dom Pedro II. railway at about 156 miles from Rio de Janeiro, and runs into Minas Geraes, so its connection with Rio exists only in its title. It is the most costly of the modern group of English-built railways in Brazil. It has been alternately condemned as a "railway to the clouds," and praised as a most promising undertaking. Its shares have always hitherto been quoted at a premium, why? in comparison with other railways in Brazil; well, let the question remain simply, why? Its traffic produced in 1885 a small balance to the good, but the gross receipts were less than 3 per cent. of the capital. It is likely to pay its way, and consequently so long as the Brazilian Government 5 per cent. bonds are at or near par, the 7 per cent. interest guaranteed shares of this and *similar* working-expense-covered lines are worthy of a premium. There will probably be a prosperous if remote future for this line, for it traverses a land fitted for agriculture and pasture, the traffic is not dependent on special crops, and the climate is admirable, but it must wait awhile for the long-expected inroad of immigration, and even then its exceptional amount of capital will require large returns to earn small dividends.

Southern Brazilian Rio Grande do Sul. This railway cost per mile a little more than half that of the last-mentioned line. It is in its first year of traffic, and so far the line has demonstrated that it can pay its way, for its receipts in 1885 equalled over 4 per cent. of capital, and left a small profit. Its best feature is, that it is situated in a progressing section of Rio Grande do Sul, a province that, like São Paulo, absorbs a large proportion of the immigrants who come to Brazil to really work.

[3] The company have now commenced the construction of this branch, about 26 miles in length.

There is very considerable reason to believe that this railway is likely to earn its dividends in the course of a very few years, when if such an event occurs, its irredeemable 6 per cent. debentures will command a very high premium.

Alagoas. All the foregoing lines now make or have made small profits, or more or less cover working expenses; this line, opened to traffic at the latter end of 1884, showed at the end of the year 1885 a small loss, the gross receipts being about 3 per cent. of capital. But a good sugar season would show a very much more favourable result.

Conde d'Eu. The loss on the results of the working of this line absorbs a considerable fraction of the amounts received for guaranteed interest. It is unfortunately hemmed in between two considerable markets that are fed from the interior. Its terminus is also at Parahyba, fourteen miles up the river of this name, the navigation of which is yearly becoming more and more difficult, and until the railway is continued to the end of this intervening fourteen miles, to the mouth of the river, (where there is an excellent port,) and thereby augment the shipping facilities, and improve the state of the local market, there is absolutely no prospect of improvement in traffic returns. It would also be advisable (in case the Great Western does not prolong its lines) to extend another 100 miles to the west, and there tap the important road traffic from the interior that now goes to Pernambuco in the south, and Mamanguape in the north. When the line was first opened, it received a most unexpected flood of local goods traffic, the whole of the rolling-stock being fully occupied, but the farmers soon realized the difference between the cost of cheap transport by road and the high freights of railway, and this favourable spurt quickly disappeared, not only owing to high freights, but also to the fact that the poor market prices of Parahyba, have caused the farmers to send their produce by road to Penambuco, even with the payment of the provincial import duties.

Donna Thereza Christiana. This line was constructed especially for carrying the produce of coal-mines at the extremity of the railway, but as it was opened to traffic long before the capital was raised for working the coal, the traffic returns were rather startling.

The expenses in 1885 were about 4⅘5 per cent. of the receipts, that only amounted to about 1 per cent. of capital. Now, whatever may be the fortune of the coal-mines, they will at any rate provide a certain amount of traffic, and as there is in Santa Catharina a magnificent climate, a fair soil, and the commencement of immigration, let alone the eventuality of a great success in the coal industry, there is some ground to hope for better times.

Imperial Brazilian Natal and Nova Cruz. The results of the working of this line are unique in the history of railways. The ratio of receipts to expenses was, in 1884, 70 to 229 ; in first half of 1885, 22 to 118 ; in the last half of same year, 50 to 109 ; consequently a great portion of the guarantees are required to make good losses on working expenses. There never existed the slightest prospect of a paying traffic, and it would be interesting to examine the estimates on which were based the calculations of 4 per cent. profit on capital that are required by the Government regulations to be demonstrated before a guarantee is conceded. The gross receipts are about 1¼ per cent. of guaranteed, and under 1 per cent. of total, capital.

The accompanying table of receipts and expenses for the year 1885 was furnished to me by the kind courtesy of the London managers of the various railway companies. The receipts are those derived from actual earnings, independent of any amounts received from the Brazilian Government for guaranteed interest. I find it, however, extremely difficult to reduce to a common basis the expenses of the various lines, for nearly each one of the companies treats differently to the other, the division of expenses in London and in Brazil; for instance, I was informed by the Natal and Nova Cruz Company that the given expenses include all and everything both in London and in Brazil,[4] whereas those of the other lines show only the cost in Brazil, some of these latter including in this, the cost of management, loss on exchange, insurance, accidents, &c. ; others excluding some of these last items. Again, in the older lines appear items that in England would be debited to capital account, such as new buildings for the increase of station accommodation, &c. In the Recife and São Francisco this constitutes a

[4] The London expenses of each company vary from 3000*l*. to 6000*l*. per annum.

large amount, and a difference appears in the amount of expenses as returned by this company, and that sanctioned by the Brazilian Government owing to a disagreement as to the periods over which this unusual cost should be distributed.

Still, despite this want of unison in common data, the amounts in question are not sufficient to materially affect the financial aspect of these lines, and consequently the tables will serve to enable the reader to approximately judge of the relative merits of the various railways, and my necessarily brief observations, to roughly estimate the probabilities, as to which of these lines may in a near or distant future be able, like the São Paulo, to earn its own dividends.

STATISTICS OF TRAFFIC RECEIPTS AND WORKING EXPENSES OF ENGLISH RAILWAYS IN B[RAZIL]

Periods.	Recife and S. Francisco.		Bahia and S. Francisco.		Brazilian Imperial Central Bahia.		Minas and Rio.		Great Western.	
	Receipts.	Expenses.	Receipts.	Expenses.	Receipts.	Expenses.	Receipts.	Expenses.	Receipts.	Expenses.
Year 1884.	1:090:224$	677:157$	597:827$	529:299$	439:779$	385:547$	262:832$	183:530$	573:619$	519
Half-year ending June 1885.	530:121	376:533	254:123	259:123	249:790	217:660	191:984	167:157	180:178	196
1885										
July...	38:922	43:597			32:289	37:023			13:607	28
August	35:139	40:119			27:918	35:261			22:472	33
September ...	44:710	38:386			27:142	34:421			15:064	26
October	65:537	41:391			30:926	37:100			35:381	33
November ...	118:248	50:214			34:403	34:314			51:593	31
December ...	158:439	18:659			41:717	35:787			41:095	28
Total of six months	446:995	295:366	230:637	228:637	194:395	213:906	254:823	266:173	179:212	192

Periods.	São Paulo.		Dª. Thereza Christina.		Alagoas.		Imperial Brazilian Natal and Nova Cruz.		Southern Brazilian Grand do Su.	
	Receipts.	Expenses.	Receipts.	Expenses.	Receipts.	Expenses.	Receipts.	Expenses.	Receipts.	Expe
Year 1884.	5:812:700$	1:886:276$	8:649$	63:472$	144:978	97:761$	69:871$	229:347$	305:777	271
Half-year ending June 1885.	3:021:810	980:943	23:780	139:593	67:925	68:796	22:593	117:930		
1885										
July...			2:899	17:040	8:784	12:165	2:562	17:854	36:230	44
August			4:018	16:910	7:194	11:221	2:667	17:716	37:645	41
September ...			6:046	15:569	9:747	11:293	7:406	18:598	45:190	42
October			7:416	17:334	7:787	10:307	13:216	18:931	60:225	44
November ...			3:739	15:669	8:696	11:095	11:259	18:205	52:381	48
December ...			5:159	20:244	14:402	14:032	8:879	19:320	61:981	46
Total of six months	3:111:274	949:714	29:257	102:766	56:610	70:103	45:989	110:624	293:652	269

N.B.—1:000$ or one thousand milreis at par value or 27 pence = £112 10s. 0d.

APPENDIX F.

CENTRAL SUGAR FACTORIES IN BRAZIL.

This must be a painful subject to many readers, for it forms an enterprise that has been bitterly disappointing to nearly every one connected with the business, the only exceptions probably being the promoters, who realized a "good thing" and left the unfortunate shareholders to take care of their own interests. Probably no one has been more deceived over these undertakings than the Brazilian Government, for, at the period when it was resolved to grant the guaranteed concessions, sugar realized a comparatively high price in the foreign market, and there existed an imperious necessity to provide the great sugar estates with new and improved machinery, so that the planters might profitably compete with the West Indian and Demerara growers, and at that time there was no reason to anticipate the eventually great and ruinous decline in the price of this commodity, or that the guarantees would be other than a normal obligation upon the Government. But the whole history of this business presents a series of errors and mismanagement by the companies, and corresponding sharp practice by the State in order to cancel the concessions.

The successful *concessionaires* profitably disposed of their rights and privileges to London promoters, by whom many of the ruling principles that should guide and influence the peculiar management of such undertakings were quite ignored. The capital was all absorbed in preliminary expenses, purchase of concession, and the contract for building, and no margin was left for working expenses, in itself an unpardonable commercial omission. Many of the contractors, experienced in railway work truly, were utterly in the dark as to the cost of erecting these factories, and where they expected to realize a handsome profit, only a dead loss resulted. If this business had been administered otherwise than it has been, by the perhaps well-meaning but costly misinformed London boards of direction, there need not have been so deplorable a state of affairs as actually exists, for in Brazil there are identically similar national sugar factory companies, formed on precisely similar guaranteed concessions. On the whole these are successful, and some of their shares have realized considerable premiums, and now they show a most favourable contrast to the English companies; of course a good or a bad season in either case affects the result of each year's working. One of the main causes of difference of results of the English and national companies is that the latter altogether supply higher-priced local or home demands than what is offered by the foreign market to which the English companies have hitherto sent their produce. But there are considerable hopes that after the companies have so bitterly paid for their experience, and the price of sugar improves, which it must do, in view of the now diminished "beet" supplies, there should be hopes that this section of British investments will improve, and even a little more common sense and inquiry by the administrators into what is wanted, should even now very much improve the state of affairs; *for there are large home demands where the prices realize double the prices of the English market*, a fact that the boards are apparently unaware of. The disappointing results of these undertakings have been very great to the State, and has caused it to exercise not only the sharpest control, but also to issue the most vexatious and irritating (because unnecessary and useless) regulations, and to avail itself of any trifling non-fulfilment of the strict letter of contract, (no matter how important to the general interest of the locality it was destined to serve,) and so evade its obligations by cancelling the concession, or contract, which it really is. I will quote an example.

One of the concessions was brought to London at a time when the present companies were all floated, and their shares had already depreciated, but as the locality that this particular concession represented, offered (and even now in these bad times still offers) most exceptionally favourable conditions, the new company was organized after some nine months of tedious work, no plunder was allowed to any one connected with it, and from the capital guaranteed a fund for working expenses was put by. The plans were sent to Rio in September, but March came, and nothing decisive was done by the Government except to raise trifling objections that only served as excuses to delay the effective acceptance of Imperial responsibilities.

Finally, the agent of the *concessionaire* went to Rio, where at last plans were approved, and a telegram sent by the Government to the Minister in London to authorize the company to call up its capital and go to work. Some ten days afterwards, as the agent was about to go to the site of the factory to start preliminary work, he learned to his astonishment that the Minister of Agriculture had, without warning or notice, arbitrarily cancelled the concession, on the plea that the contracts made with planters to supply cane did not state weight, but only quantity, of cane undertaken to be supplied. Even if this plea held good (the same contracts had been verbally accepted by the previous minister), the *concessionaire* was still entitled, by the terms of his concession, to about two months longer to reform this clause, if necessary, which it really was not. As a proof of the soundness of this undertaking, the local planters had subscribed 15,000*l*., and the chairman and his friends another 15,000*l*., towards the capital of the company. Thus, by an arbitrary stroke of the pen, a sterling enterprise was destroyed, and a twelve months' labour and anxiety, and several thousand pounds, all lost, for the concession and land had been paid for in cash, and practical men had been sent out to Brazil to report, besides the many legal and personal expenses incidental to the organization of such an enterprise, all of which were incurred on the faith of an Imperial Brazilian Government guarantee. Altogether this action, so inconsiderate, so utterly regardless of all sense of right or law, is utterly unworthy of the dignity of a great country, and is **a great blot on the hitherto untarnished honour of Imperial Brazil.**

APPENDIX G.

THE PAST, PRESENT, AND FUTURE OF BRAZIL.

IN the brief space that can only be allowed for this subject (that to do it justice requires so much to be said), I must confine myself to chiefly abstract matters and a few statistics.

The past of Brazil affords an interesting picture of what changes time creates in a country; one of the main results of which in Brazil, has been a transference from the interior to the seaboard of its wealth-producing centres, a temporary loss to a permanent gain, an exchange of the evanescent riches obtained by mining to the more stable results produced by agriculture, commerce, and industries. Had the discovery of gold in Brazil been contemporary with that in Australia and California, when the land was governed by a more liberal and enlightened policy than in the days when it was a Portuguese colony, it would have attracted to its vast interior thousands of the hardy races of North America and Northern Europe; but the discovery was made when the land was a veritable *terra-incognita*, before the day of foreign correspondents and telegraphs, and its virgin stores of diamonds, gold, and silver, served only to profitlessly enrich the old colonists, and become a curse to the country. This mineral wealth built the great monasteries, convents, and churches, (whose massive time and weather-worn walls a traveller notices in the principal old cities of the coast, and in parts of the interior); the grand old fazenda buildings; even towns like Villa Rica, in Parana (now a ruin in the wilderness), and numerous once prosperous towns and villages of Minas Geraes, Goyaz, Matto Grosso, Bahia, and other provinces, now all so ruinous, dilapidated, and so decadent. When it is remembered that in the old time the commerce of Brazil was confined to Portugal, and under certain conditions, to a limited extent, to Great Britain, it does cause one at first sight to marvel much at seeing so many evidences of a former national spirit of activity and energy so vastly different to what now exists amongst the inhabitants of the interior. There are many feasible reasons to account for the change. It may be admitted that the old race of Portuguese, (whatever they may be now,) once possessed an indomitable energy, and a great spirit of adventure, that long after the first colonization of Brazil, were fostered and strengthened by the struggles inherent to settlers in a new land, combating with warlike aborigines and great natural difficulties. Then came the discovery of gold and diamonds; shiploads of negros were imported from Africa, the aborigines were probably also conquered and pressed into the service, the cost of labour was a mere bagatelle, and abundant, and probably enabled mines to be worked with a great profit, that now, even with the present high perfection of mining science and appliances, could only be worked at a loss, in consequence of the actual scarcity and cost of labour. Great, indeed, must have been the mineral wealth extracted under these conditions, and equally great must have been the profits obtained by those, who by agriculture, supplied the necessities of the mining population, for the demand for provisions must have been considerable, the supply small, and gold and labour cheap and plentiful. But what were the natural results? There followed an age of luxury, when the succeeding generations became habituated to more indolent lives by a too-easily acquired wealth; and a tropical climate wrought its baneful influences upon the grand old race. In due time, the old mines and placers became exhausted, or insurmountable difficulties were met with, and the old energy of the people had become vitiated and demoralized, for no more explorations were attempted, and finally the whole of the population turned their attention to stock-raising and agriculture, even in the far distant districts of the interior; but thus all being producers, the demand is lessened, and the supply increased, and a market on the coast is too far away to pay for transport. Then followed years of inactivity and unproductiveness, lives unanimated by ambition or hope of change, consuming what was produced, even to the accumulated wealth of their forefathers, divided and subdivided between the ever-increasing descendants, and so was engendered the horrible state of thriftlessness, lethargy, indolence, and moral degradation that exists so often amongst the greater part of the country people of the distant interior of Brazil, a state that will exist yet for many,

many years to come, for what is the use of railways and communications to such people as these, unless they are reanimated by the example of hard-working, thrifty immigrants?

But on the seaboard a far more hopeful state of affairs exists. By the seaboard I mean a fringe of land along the coast, extending from 50 to 300 or 400 miles inland. This narrow belt, with also the valley of the Amazons, produces nearly all the exports of Brazil. Here foreigners and foreign capital have done much to resuscitate the race that is now realizing that there are other paths to follow besides the old ones trodden by their fathers. When one glances back only a few years, and compares the then utter want of national public enterprise with the present actual state of affairs, it is marvellous to see what has been done by national capital, science, and work in railways, steamship companies, tramways, telephones, telegraphs, commercial and industrial undertakings, besides the institution of scientific and art societies. It is an awakening from the great relapse that followed the evanescent and fictitious national prosperity of the old days, a recovery from the crisis that in comparison, that of the slave and financial questions are mere bagatelles, for it was a crisis that temporarily ruined the country, body and soul. Now look at the long list of native companies, and at the railways built with native capital by native engineers and builders, and by means of the increased facilities for communication and travelling the people go further away from the narrow circle of their villages, and their ideas become enlarged. See the thousands that yearly pass to and fro from the often drought-smitten and arid Northern Provinces to the marvellous forests of the Amazons, in quest of the valuable india-rubber, where they brave peril from fevers, and suffer great privations, for the prize is great to any of these poor coloured folk to be able to earn 10 to 20 milreis per day.

This modern initiation of public enterprise by the inhabitants of the seaboard is like a revival of a latent spirit of adventure, and is the most favourable feature of a sterling national progress, both in enlightenment and welfare, that tends to counterbalance the very unsatisfactory national accounts, and the stagnant state of the interior.

The ordinary revenue of the country is usually sufficient to meet ordinary expenses; but so many obligations have been rashly incurred without a practical inquiry into the merits of the guaranteed undertakings, or a duly serious consideration of the responsibilities in the possible eventuality of the non-realization of the always rose-coloured statements and estimates, that the State now finds itself struggling with a huge burden of indebtedness, much of which is even indirectly unremunerative, the result is a serious disequilibrium of its finances.

For many years past, even since the cessation of the Paraguayan war, not one single year can show a balance on the right side. Unfortunately, there is no conveniently elastic remedy to make up for deficient revenue like our own "income tax," in fact, hardly any direct taxes worth mentioning, exist; they are all to be raised, and form one of the resources that the State must depend upon, if it is eventually "cornered." The deficits, and (despite the paying off of old loans) the ever-increasing national debt, has been hitherto met by continual borrowing, both external and internal. Still, although the Brazilians themselves are thoroughly acquainted with the national finances, and the *Jornal do Commercio* (the *Times* of Brazil), is ever recalling serious attention to the trouble, the internal six per cent. bonds command a nine per cent. premium, and form the investments of the greater part of the reserve funds of the national public companies.

For the last twenty years the British investor in Brazilian enterprises and bonds has threatened the "thunders of his vatican," the London Stock Exchange; still, despite of all, the country progresses steadily and surely, and the credit of the State is very high. One thing, however, must be borne in mind, namely, that the national financial state of any country cannot be considered in the light of a commercial house, for there are very few, if any, existing governments, that if their actual assets were realized, would be able to meet present obligations. The credit of Brazil, despite of all that has been said against it, ranks very high both with Brazilians and foreigners, and it must also be remembered that so far as is publicly known, it has no mortgage on its revenue, property, or resources; neither is the country taxed to the extent it might be, even, in one case (a land tax), with very great national advantage. Its capacity for borrowing is undoubtedly great, but so are its resources. The following tables show the revenue returns, expenditure, and national debt for each year from 1875 to 1883-4.

NATIONAL FINANCES.

Year.	Revenue.	Expenditure.	National Debt.		
			Year.	Foreign.	Internal.
1874-5	113,887:185$	133,252:048$	1875	177,166:222$	487,573:173$
1875-6	109,957:377	133,441:856	1876	169,217:777	514,577:411
1876-7	108,747:079	143,691:511	1877		510,269:504
1877-8	120,632:606	161,579:170	1878	160,320:000	588,850:150
1878-9	125,144:878	190,153:455	1879	158,283:555	623,813:466
1879-80	137,587:677	166,957:238	1880	151,077:333	608,283:246
1880-1	145,216:449	152,524:588	1881	141,072:000	672,958:728
1881-2	149,265:862	156,749:546	1882	133,355:555	675,030:532
1882-3	145,080:089	165,652:707	1883	169,213:333	691,979:562
			1884	163,732:444	690,515:604

It will thus be seen that during these years, the revenue has increased 28 per cent. and expenditure 24½ per cent.; the foreign debt has diminished 8 per cent., and the internal has increased 41 per cent. Against the debt in 1884 must be credited as assets,—

Owing by the Republic of Uruguay .	16,607:298$
„ „ Paraguay . .	256:049
Unpaid taxes	12,550:033
Total	29,413:380$

The foreign debt, as indicated in above tables, is calculated at the par value of the milreis, 27 pence. The amount in 1884, 163,732,444$, is equivalent to 18,419,900*l*., since which date it has been further considerably reduced by amortization, but the 1886 loan of 6,000,000*l*. has run it up again to over 24,000,000*l*. The internal debt comprised,—

4, 5, and 6% Internal currency bonds . .	338,111:9900$
6% „ gold loan, 1868[1] . .	22,800:000
4½% „ „ 1879[1] . .	44,203:640
Paper currency	187,936:661
Treasury notes	46,548:500
Savings' banks	18,848:946

[1] A large proportion of these loans are now held in Europe, and are quoted on the London Stock Exchange, apparently figuring as a Brazilian external debt.

Orphans, &c., deposits	.	.	18,668:623$
Sundries	.	.	13,389:334
			690,515:604$

This amount, calculated at the par value of the milreis, is equivalent to 77,683,005*l*., thus the total debt of Brazil, in 1884, was 96,102,905*l*., a large amount for a country whose annual exports are about 1*l*. 7*s*. 6*d*. per head of population, and about 18% of its national debt.

The following table of Rio de Janeiro exports and imports is indicative of the progress of national industries, for in the year 1884-5, the imports decreased from the average of the years 1879-84, 8 per cent., whereas the exports increased 10½ per cent. A large proportion of this decrease is owing to the establishment, during the last few years of more than sixty cotton factories, all of which are most prosperous.

OFFICIAL VALUE IN MILREIS, OF IMPORTS AND EXPORTS AT RIO DE JANEIRO.

Countries.	1884—1885.		Yearly average of 1879—1884.	
	Imports.	Exports.	Imports.	Exports.
Great Britain	36,265:211$	6,464:052$	39,199:555$	10,397:737$
France	12,514:654	6,645:542	16,370:151	10,291:995
Germany	9,009:121	10,367:758	8,795:632	9,538:315
United States	7,731:273	67,946:143	8,024:875	53,922:974
Uruguay	7,263:546	1,538:331	7,161:365	2,079:956
Portugal	5,544:637	463:869	6,337:716	3,136:236
Belgium	4,062:767	2,869:701	4,415:932	3,000:581
Argentine Republic	2,723:887	2,014:826	3,462:888	1,335:659
Various	2,002:943	2:678	549:310	858:901
Italy	689:653	1,357:210	805:804	394:340
Austria	243:137	5,396:510	116:417	1,217:865
Sweden and Norway	173:040	1:225	191:861	52:829
Spain	114:746	10:832	333:608	36:326
Holland	86:859	4:855	130:451	2:568
Chilé	62:194	87:115	241:304	45:931
Russia	32:221	622:621	51:467	13:042
Cape of Good Hope	1:192	2,008:119	442	1,367:627
Mediterranean	... ...	1.337:727	... ...	854:379
Denmark	... ...	5:910	4:018	249:785
	88,521:101$	109,145:024$	96,192:796$	98,797:046$
Total for the whole of the Empire	162,970:402$	223,864:731$		
Value in sterling at 19 pence per milreis	£12,901,393	£17,722,033		

It will be seen that the United States and Germany are now the largest purchasers of Brazilian produce, and Great Britain, France, Germany, the United States, and Uruguay, constitute in this order of rotation, the largest suppliers of the Brazilian market. The United States is Brazil's best customer for coffee and india-rubber, and Germany second best for coffee and tobacco.

The following immigration statistics will indicate the countries that are supplying Brazil with new blood and muscle, and also the provinces that chiefly attract the new arrivals, and show how São Paulo and Rio Grande do Sul, are attracting the working immigrants, for Rio de Janeiro largely absorbs a great proportion of the Portuguese, who remain there as labourers, mechanics, and traders.

IMMIGRANTS IN 1884.

Arrived in Rio de Janeiro.		Left Rio de Janeiro.	
Nationality.	Number.	Left Rio de Janiero for various Provinces.	Number.
Portuguese	8683	São Paulo	4427
Italians	5933	Rio Grande } do Sul }	1985
Germans	1240		
Austrians	598	Minas Geraes	1202
Spaniards	576	Rio de Janeiro	875
Poles	359	Sta. Catharina	611
French	155	Paraná	385
English	100	Espirito Santo	33
Russians	98	Amazonas	27
Uruguayans	90	Para	21
Swiss	70	Bahia	11
Argentines	29	Alagoas	11
Americans	24	Pernambuco	10
Belgians	19		
Turks	16		
Moors	8		
	17,999		
Passed Rio on way to Santos.	1609		
	19,608		9598

The immigration movement in 1884, was considerably less than in 1883 and in 1882, when 24,493 and 24,827 arrived in Rio in each of these years. The drop in the numbers to 19,608, was mainly caused by the ports of Brazil being practically closed during the greater part of the year against colonists from Europe, on account of the cholera.

The following statistics of Post Office receipts and expenditure in the various provinces of the empire in the years 1877 and 1884, will serve to show the relative commercial importance of each province, and also indicate the development of some, and the retrocession of others. Judging by the receipts of 1884, it will be seen that Minas Geraes and Rio Grande do Sul are now ahead of Pernambuco, whereas the distant interior provinces of Matto Grosso and Piauhy, have fallen to the bottom of the list in the order of amounts.

POST OFFICE RETURNS.

Name of Province.	Receipts.		Expenditure.	
	1877.	1884.	1877.	1884.
Rio de Janeiro	553,021$	673,045$	672,445$	865,761$
Sao Paulo	138,399	325,016	144,677	291,271
Pernambuco	80,692	105,959	80,741	90,460
Minas Geraes	72,768	175,062	170,286	312,298
Rio Grande do Sul	72,766	127,155	77,763	142,901
Bahia	63,414	83,798	84,546	132,106
Pará	30,141	63,179	23,334	52,622
Maranhão	18,433	24,868	39,655	45,839
Ceará	11,572	23,553	33,358	42,586
Paraná	11,502	24,316	27,687	41,414
Sta. Catharina	11,344	18,310	13,871	27,309
Alagôas	8,350	16,174	24,539	27,797
Espirito Santo	5,400	15,211	10,618	22,927
Amazonas	4,902	10,671	8,271	14,914
Sergipe	4,866	5,893	14,129	16,728
Matto Grosso	3,078	2,235	6,644	10,846
Rio Grande do Norte	2,960	5,269	18,029	21,349
Goyaz	2,797	6,071	20,916	44,572
Piauhy	2,220	3,735	16,232	21,352
Parahyba	1,802	6,334	22,417	25,620
Totals	1,100,400$	1,747,555$	1,507,077$	2,259,677$
Deficits	406,677$	512,122$		

In entering upon the probabilities of the future of Brazil, the caution occurs (I think it was Artemus Ward who gave it) of not prophesying unless you know, still there are many reasons, both favourable and adverse, upon which to base reasonable conjectures, at the same time many existing illusions must be destroyed in considering such a theme. The chief one is that Brazil is not by any means so universally fertile a country as is generally believed even by the Brazilians themselves, as the pages of this work will show; probably there is no similar area in the world that offers such a glorious field to the botanist, but even where he may find some of his greatest treasures, namely, on the wide and far-extending *campos*, there is a soil that is generally absolutely worthless for agriculture. The *campos* of Brazil, that covers perhaps three-fourths of its area, are the Dartmoors of the empire, consequently these large valueless tracts must be duly discounted when optimists ventilate their glowing accounts of "vast area," "unbounded resources," &c. But dismissing the subject of these "wastes" to take care of themselves in the dim distant future, there yet remains immense tracts of fertile lands to be populated and developed, and there is no necessity to go to the far-west to find them. I will only mention three, the fertile basin of the Rio Doce, the western boundaries of Espirite Santo, and even within a day's journey of the capital of the empire, amidst the highlands of Theresopolis, are excellent fields for new settlements. In the two first, much of the districts are not only uninhabited, but unexplored, owing to the difficulties of making way through their dense forests. In the third-mentioned district, there is glorious scenery and a magnificent climate, and occasional patches of soil capable of producing most European produce. Here any thrifty and hard-working immigrant with a moderate amount of capital, say 500*l*. and properly guided and directed by experienced friendly advice, would have a much better chance of success than if he followed the usual stream of immigrants to the Colonies or the United States.

But even these districts are not by any means so wonderfully fertile, for Brazil is deficient in two natural fertilizing elements, namely, winters and earth-worms. In the fall of the leaf, in the dry months of June, July, August, September, the *cerrados* and *campos* of the high-lands show great areas all covered with a sparse vegetation, dried up and parched, the boughs and branches all bare and leafless, and the soil baking in the dry heat, then the fallen leaves, dried hard and crisp, are scattered and broken by the wind, and their elements dissolve into gasses. It is only in the thick forests, where the soil is naturally damp and moist, that these sources of fertility are allowed to collect and enrich the soil.

However, to return to our subject. Brazil has now a population estimated at between twelve to thirteen millions, about one-tenth of which are slaves. The Post Office authorities estimate the population to be 12,899,691 (it is as well to express the last 1, as it suggests very great care in the estimate), but the major part of this number must be dismissed as a valueless factor in considering the productive powers in the near future progress of the empire, for so large a proportion of the inhabitants are scattered over so vast an area, that in the distant interior, where their productions are little in excess of local demands, it is impossible to make remunerative communications, neither does the necessity exist when so much is required on the border-lands of the coast. This popular idea of developing the interior without a stream of immigrants to occupy it, is an *Ignis fatuus*, in the pursuit of which the State has sadly crippled its finances. Even under the most favourable conditions, it will take years and years to occupy the waste fertile lands of the coast, consequently the tenants of the far-west may be left to take care of themselves, vegetate as the trees around them, increase and multiply until the time comes when the east will commence to crowd upon the west, then its numbers may have a value which at present does not exist.

Whether Brazil will ever be a popular field for immigrants like the Argentine Republic, is a question that only the future can answer. Brazil openly tenders a welcome to the foreigner, and the State has expended 4,000,000*l.* in trying to induce immigration, but there exists an insurmountable national jealousy, not to say antipathy, of foreigners that is apparently unconquerable. There are a very considerable number of thriving German colonies in the southern provinces, and the colonists become more Brazilian than the Brazilians themselves; they love their adopted country, are thrifty and industrious, and attain a prosperous condition that their less active Brazilian neighbours envy but cannot understand. The antipathy thus engendered is not so much directed against the individuals as against their success. As an example of the existing jealousy, I will quote that in 1882 a lottery was held in Porto Alegre, Rio Grande do Sul, in connection with an exhibition, the first prize of 200,000$ was drawn by a German living in Hamburg. This so incensed the Brazilians that they fired the building, and everything was destroyed. A further source of bad feeling is, that the Germans, with their shrewdness, have secured the best lands. But whatever trouble may ensue, all well-wishers of Brazil can only earnestly hope to see it populated by an energetic race, whatever may be the nationality. In the case of the Germans of the south, they may be temporarily an element of discord, but they are extremely loyal to the Government, and constitute a solid foundation for a future vigorous prosperity.

The fact of the Emperor having no immediate male heir to the throne, forms a great bugbear to the fearful ones, and serious ruptures are feared in the solidity of the empire on the much-to-be-regretted demise of the present ruler. But whatever changes may happen in the government of the country, there is good reason to believe that it will always faithfully fulfil its obligations, for once its credit is shattered what is to become of its great internal debt; the country itself without foreign aid could not meet its liabilities, consequently this internal debt is a bulwark of the stability of the State like our own National Debt; and come weal, come woe, it must pay up. The fact of Brazil being situated in South America very much detracts from the value of its bonds to many would-be investors who are rather misty in their geography, for to the greater part of the British public, Brazil is one of those South American republics, don't-yer-know, somewhere in South America, liable to revolutions, earthquakes, and yellow Jack, and all that sort of thing, yer-know, and somehow or other, there is an emperor who rises at unearthly hours in the morning, and the Brazilians are Spanish.

Finally, the near or remote future of Brazil will depend almost entirely upon whether the country becomes sooner or later a favourite with immigrants from crowded Europe. In the Argentine Republic, and in the growth of the United States, is witnessed the marvellous results produced by a flood of immigrants, and if the stream is eventually directed to Brazil, the prosperity of the country must increase by leaps and bounds. As it is, even with the present very moderate yearly accession of immigrants, the steady increase in the social prosperity of at least the southern seaboard areas is undeniable, and is likely to continue.

Distribution of British capital now invested in Brazilian Government Bonds and in various public enterprises in Brazil.

	£
Imperial Brazilian Bonds	29,241,844 [2]
Railway companies	18,850,258
Navigation companies	3,864,660
Submarine telegraph companies	3,432,049
Banking companies	2,000,000
Sugar factory companies	1,735,820
Gas companies	1,291,803
Mining companies	1,068,540
Water and Drainage companies	1,034,700
Tramway companies	124,200
	£62,643,874

[2] This amount includes £4,907,644 of the gold bonds of the *internal* loan of 1879, that are now mainly held in London, and quoted on the Stock Exchange.

APPENDIX H.

EXTRACTS FROM A PAPER, READ BY THE AUTHOR AT A MEETING OF THE ROYAL GEOGRAPHICAL SOCIETY, ON THE 8TH FEBRUARY, 1886, AND ENTITLED "A SKETCH OF THE PHYSICAL GEOGRAPHY OF BRAZIL."

I HAVE been induced to write this paper, not only so much on account of the extraordinary illusions that exist with regard to Brazil, but to the fact that nearly all maps (certainly all English ones), tend to create a most erroneous idea of the country, by representing it to be a very mountainous land, rather than what it is, chiefly a vast plateau, excavated into numerous valleys by denudations, with relatively few purely mountain chains, that is, true mountains of upheaved strata. It is much to be regretted, that English map-makers do not avail themselves more of the rich stores of geographical information yearly collected by travellers in all parts of the globe. For instance, it is now nearly ten years since I had the honour to present to this Society information and a sketch map of a considerable portion of unknown Brazil, wherein was shown the interesting fact, that north-east Brazil is practically an island, but in no English map of the country is yet indicated this fact, whereas both German and Brazilian map-makers have minutely followed my surveys.

A glance at the sketch-map[1] will show four main features in the physiognomy of the country. Firstly, the low-lying vast flat plains

[1] See Physical Map of Brazil at end of volume.

of the Amazons, as Humboldt called that great hollow; and the flat grassy plains of the Rio Paraguay. Secondly, the elevated highlands that extend over the major part of the empire north and south of the Amazons. Thirdly, the yet higher lands that constitute the watersheds of the principal rivers. Fourthly, the groups of mountain ranges consisting of primitive rocks of purely upheaved strata.

This vast area contains naturally so many varying constituent elements, that to deal with them in the short compass of this paper, I am necessarily compelled to treat the subject in the broadest manner possible, commensurate with a facile comprehension of my purpose. With this view, I have divided the whole area into three great hydrographic sections, or systems, and if the positions of their watersheds are retained upon the memory, it will greatly help to a lasting impression of the configuration of the country. I will now trace the course of these divides.

It will be seen that a line of elevation bisects the centre of the South American continent, rising gradually from west to east. Its western section, although such a prominent watershed, consists of a series of groups of wide undulating table-lands, intersected by the numerous sources of the streams that run to the north and to the south. The separation between many of these waters, flowing parallel to each other, yet in opposite directions, is so slight, that in many cases, the basin of the Amazons could with facility be connected with that of the Plate rivers by canals, and communication by water rendered complete from one system to the other. For instance, near the city of Matto Grosso, the Rio Alegre, a feeder of the Amazonian Rio Guaporé, rises in a small elevation jointly with the Rio Agoapehy, a tributary of the Rio Paraguay. These two baby sources of mighty rivers flow eastward a few miles apart side by side, for twenty to thirty miles, through undulating grassy country, and many of their own branches are divided from each other by only a few hundred yards, and canoes have been dragged from one stream to the other over the intervening lowland. There are other similar near connections of opposite flowing rivers, separated only by low-lying land; the head-waters of the Tapajos nearly join those of the Rio Sararé, another tributary of the Guaporé, and the Rios Xingu and Araguaya are nearly connected with those of the Paraguay. Near the borders of Matto Grosso and Goyaz the line of these table-lands bifurcates, one branch trending southward, still in the form of wide elevated flats, the other runs northeast, and assumes more the form of a series of ridges and isolated peaked hills, known as the Serra do Cayapó, and Serra das Divisões do Rio Claro. Near the city of Goyaz the divide becomes distinctly mountainous, and the ranges radiate in all directions; here are the Montes Pyreneos, that constitute, as far as is yet known, the second most elevated ridge in Brazil, attaining to heights variously estimated at 7700 and 9700 feet above the level of the sea. But beyond this point, as this watershed runs north, and forms the divide between the Tocantins and S. Francisco, it is no more in the form of mountains as is usually depicted on maps, but really as a wide sterile sandy plateau, thinly covered with small scrub and tufts of wiry grasses. In this wide flat ridge a traveller can often journey 100 miles without meeting water, or he can traverse it in a canoe from Barra do Rio Grande, on the Rio S. Francisco, to the mouth of the Rio de Somno, on the Tocantins. This high elevated plateau, known as the Chapada da Mangabeira, extends to latitude 10° south, where it joins a similar high flat plateau that forms a horseshoe in its course, and constitutes the watershed of the rivers of north-east Brazil. Now returning to the Montes Pyreneos, it will be seen that another continuation of the central ridge proceeds towards, and joins on to the Maritime range, and forms the divide between the S. Francisco and River Plate basins. This again cannot be considered as a mountain range as commonly represented, for the greater part of it consists of great rolling rounded hills, with occasional peaks and many flat-topped table-lands; but as it nears the Maritime range, it becomes more elevated, and terminates in distinct ranges of granitic gneiss, and in hills largely composed of exceedingly rich ironstone.

In this neighbourhood the surface of the land is extremely irregular and mountainous. One range, formerly known as the Serra de Deos te livre (meaning "The Lord deliver you Mountains"), is sufficiently expressive in its name of its rugged paths, deep defiles and precipices.

The point of intersection of the central watershed with the Maritime range is geographically a most interesting locality, for its lofty ridges constitute a divide of waters that flow to the four quarters of the compass. See how relatively near the coast are some of the sources of the S. Francisco and River Plate rivers, that flow in opposite directions through thousands of miles of valleys, to their distant outlets in the Atlantic, and probably, of the rains that fall on some of the dividing hills, one part is carried away to the north, the other to the south.

Let us now trace this great Maritime range, the great bulwark of the Brazilian plateau. It commences in the southern province of Rio Grande do Sul; starting from the western boundary of the province on the Rio Uruguay, it proceeds towards the coast in the form of a series of slopes facing the south, and constitutes the southern extremity of the Brazilian plateau; after approaching within a few miles of the coast it accompanies it northwards, sometimes hugging the shore, sometimes many miles inland, until it reaches Cape Frio.

From the summit of its seaward face, the surface of the ground and the rivers, slope with gentle gradients towards the River Plate basin. In many places where these great bluffs approach the shore, their varied outline, and serried walls covered with forest, their deep recesses, their crags and peaks, present some of the most charming mountainous coast scenery of the world. At Cape Frio it terminates in great scarped hills of granitic gneiss; hoary, time-worn and weather-beaten—defenders of the coast-line against the encroachments of the sea.

At Rio de Janeiro this grand line of rocky mountains culminates in the Serra des Orgãos in altitudes 7000 to 8000 feet above the sea. The land-locked bay of this city, surrounded as it is by scattered groups of mountains of this range, presents such marvels of scenery, that no port in the world, not even Naples, Sydney, San Francisco, or Constantinople, can compare with it in its manifold beauties, all must yield the palm to the lovely bay of Rio de Janeiro.

Now leaving the coast range, and proceeding northwards through the great coffee districts, we dip into the valley of the Parahyba, and again ascending, reach the most celebrated ridge in the country, the Serra da Mantequeira. It rises in S. Paulo, where a branch trends northwards and forms one of the walls of the basin of the Rio Grande; the main line continues up the western side of the Parahyba in the form of lofty precipitous wooded slopes, often rising to great boulder-strewn crags and pinnacles. It faces the south, exposed to the moisture-laden winds of the ocean, that are condensed into almost daily rains. Here is situated the Peak of Itatiaia-assu, the most lofty known elevation of Brazil, 10,040 feet above the sea, and only sixty miles from the coast in a straight line. As far as Ouro Preto, the range presents more or less the same character, a sharp rugged ascent from the south and south-east, and very gentle gradients to the north and west in the form of a great undulating grassy table-land. At, and a little beyond Ouro Preto, it gives birth to innumerable streams, that have excavated deep cavernous valleys, giving the intervening highlands the appearance of mountains that are often really denudation mountains. Some of these ridges of primitive rocks attain great altitudes, notably Itacolumi, near Ouro Preto, and the peak of Itambé further north. Beyond Ouro Preto the main range rapidly begins to assume the character of a high table-land, that widens as it advances into Bahia; it crosses this province in great wide sandy plateaux, with an occasional upheaved dyke-like ridge here and there or showing where a local mass of harder materials has resisted the disintegrating and denuding influences of time and weather. Its course is bisected by the Rio S. Francisco, that plunges into the lower seaward plateau at the great falls of the Paulo Affonso, the Niagara of Brazil. A little further on, in the province of Pernambuco, it joins the eastern arm of the north-eastern watershed, and together the plateaux extend to Cape S. Roque, another prominent advanced outpost of the shore-line.

Thus I have briefly traced the main framework of inland Brazil, the chief bones of the monster, and in following the course of these elevated lands, it will be seen that the rivers of Brazil are divided into three great systems:—the basin of the Amazons, the basin of the Plate rivers, and the many distinct and separate rivers running eastwardly into the Atlantic. Taking these riverine systems in the order mentioned, I will endeavour to say something of each, and point out their different prominent characteristics.

In the Amazons system, for the sake of brevity, I have included the Tocantins and Araguaya, yet, although they are not now tributaries of that great river, there is good reason to believe they were formerly, when the river Para, was once one of the true mouths of the Amazons.

This Amazons basin consists of the bottle-shaped low-lying forest of its upper valley, 1300 miles long, by 800 miles broad, and the circumscribing elevated table-lands, that near Obidos and Santarem, approach close to the banks of the main river, and constitute the neck of this stupendous bottle of vegetables. Throughout the length of this river, east and west of Obidos, the adjoining land is so low and flat that it is in many cases rather a series of more or less parallel streams than one great clearly defined stream. It is possible to go in a canoe up the whole of the valley in these lateral channels (locally termed Paranamerins), and also pass through the deep forests by natural canals, from one tributary to another, without once entering the main river.

It is a singular feature of the Amazons valley, lying as it does, such a mass of water in the Equatorial regions, that it is so healthy as it really is, although some of its tributaries are however very insalubrious, and where life in any condition is made a misery by the insect pests, yet I have never met any one who has had an experience of life on the Amazons, who has not become passionately fond of it. The glorious vegetation, the life free from conventionalities, the brilliant sunlight and warmth tempered by fresh breezes, contain some of the elements of making a paradise, and the numerous lines of river steamers now plying on these majestic waters afford means for rapid communication, and of obtaining the necessaries and luxuries of life for the settlers.

The vegetation of this great valley is essentially different to what is found in the other two riverine systems; it is vaster, purely tropical in character, and contains a growth and variety peculiar to itself. The rich low-lying lands, subject to annual inundations, frequent rains all the year, and the continual heat, produce a vast wealth of dense tropical verdure and a forest area greater than can be found in any other part of the globe, intersected by thousands of miles of immense navigable streams, that to the traveller appear more like grand inland seas rather than rivers.

Amongst the immense stores of valuable vegetable productions of this great forest, the indiarubber-tree figures pre-eminently. It exists in such vast quantities, and the collection of the juice is so very lucrative, that it has attracted to even the most remote rivers thousands of adventurous Brazilians from the adjoining provinces; and despite the hardships, perils, and privations of such a life, still flows on the tide of eager hunters. Rubber is doing to the Amazons what gold did for Australia and California; although most other industries on the Amazons are neglected and paralyzed, rubber has enabled Para, Manaos, and other riverine cities to make unprecedented progress, and it has covered thousands of miles of rivers with steamers, and spread a population over vast areas that otherwise would have remained dormant for many, many years.

So little relatively is as yet known of the river, that it is still a question of dispute amongst geographers, as to whether the Para river is one of the mouths of the Amazons or not. When, however, it is remembered, as can be proved, that the quantity of water passing the city of Para is relatively little in excess of what is found at the actual junction of the Tocantins with the waters of the Uanapú, Pacajas, Camaraipy, and Jacundá, there is very little room left for the Amazons water—in fact, the Amazons is only connected with the Para river by a number of narrow *furos* or channels, so narrow that steamers proceeding through them from Para to the Amazons almost graze the bushes on each side, and the volume of water that can flow through these furos is really insignificant in proportion to the volume of water of the Tocantins group; so I see no reason why the Para river should be considered as one of the mouths of the Amazons. Undoubtedly it was so formerly, but the meeting of the flow of water of the Tocantins group with the main river has evidently silted up the old wide channel, of which part still exists, but its western extremity is now closed, and the mass of water of the Amazons finds its way direct to the sea. This exit of the Amazons has not yet been surveyed. I feel convinced that a much better channel could be found here for Atlantic steamers proceeding up the river, rather than through the narrow tortuous channels between Para and that river.

To any one ascending the Amazons river, a most noticeable feature strikes his attention, namely the table-topped hills of the Serras de Ereré and Obidos, and the somewhat similar formation on the opposite bank, at the rear of Santarem. These opposite highlands form the walls of the valley through which the river, once probably a great inland lake, has excavated its way to the sea. It is really a mistake to call these heights Serras, for the word Serra implies a range of hills or mountains, and the so-called Serras of Ereré are no more entitled to be considered as a mountain range, than are our Dover cliffs. Their summits, instead of being ridges, extend in the form of undulating savannahs far inland, ever ascending, furrowed into hollows and valleys, by many a stream or watercourse. Strange and interesting as is the appearance of these cliffs of 1000 feet high, yet they are not exceptional to the basin of the Amazons; at its farthest western extremity in the Serra de Cupatí, bordering the banks of the Rio Japura, and also in the western face of the Chapada da Mangabeira, are encountered identical formations, and even to the north, in Roraima and its brother Kukenam, also exists a somewhat similar appearance. These great precipitous bluffs and isolated table-topped hills are indicative, or at least suggestive, of a great denudation that has either long since occurred or is yet happening. I rather am disposed to the latter supposition, especially in viewing the appearance of the western face of the Chapada da Mangabeira, the Tocantins S. Francisco watershed; from the S. Francisco it rises gradually and by regular gradients to the divide, where it appears as perpendicular walls of sandstone with flat summits, and presents an appearance, when viewed from the east, of gigantic fortresses. The base of these cliffs is composed of a natural earth slope of the modern débris of the fallen material of the walls. That this table-land extended yet further to the west twenty, thirty, or sixty miles, is evident by the detached groups of flat-topped hills that one meets with at these distances of identical formations, and many of whose summits are practically level with the main table-land. I have ascended to the top of one of these miniature Roraimas, and found a vegetation and soil precisely similar to that on the great plateau, whereas the vegetation of the surrounding lowlands was quite different in its character. Some of these isolated table-topped hills are split across, and the extremities appear ready at any moment to fall and add their elements to the adjoining lowlands. The sketch of the Morro do Munducurú,[2] a hill some sixty miles away from the main table-lands, will better indicate my suggestion of continual denudation that is so evidently apparent in the impending fall of one extremity.

The Amazons presents another peculiar characteristic, namely the absence of a delta, for although the exit of the river is amidst the channels of a great archipelago of islands, yet these islands are largely composed of a rocky basis. In fact, rather the reverse of a delta exists, as it can be proved that the sea is encroaching upon and eating away the land faster than the river can deposit its alluvial matter; yet so great is the force of this mighty monarch of rivers, that its discoloured waters can be sighted at sea 100 miles from land.

The Plate basin differs from the Amazons basin in the following features. The climate is more variable, the rainy and dry seasons are more distinct. The low plains, instead of being covered with forests, are often vast flat areas of grass and scrub, subject to inundations from the rivers; the vegetation is less tropical in character, in fact, on the Parana and adjoining rivers are considerable forests of the araucaria pine and other trees of temperate regions. The north-east section of this basin consists of part of the undulating great Brazilian plateau, with belts of forest existing only in *the valleys* of the rivers. The Rio Grande and Rio Parana traverse the great southern table-land of the Plate basin, the latter river *entering* the lower level of the plateau at the falls of the "Sete Quedas." This north-east section comprises admirable fields for future colonization, a fine climate and a good soil, both for grazing and for agriculture, but it requires development of communications; at present a colonist would find the value of his products absorbed in cost of transport. A considerable part of this basin is unpopulated, except by a few poor tribes of Indians; but on the Paraguay, and the extreme north-east, and the section in S. Paulo, Rio Grande, and Parana, near the

[2] See page 180, vol. ii.

coast range, there is a considerable population, principally devoted to cattle-raising and agriculture, and the modern railways in S. Paulo and Rio Grande, have undoubtedly given a great impetus to the progress of the country, aided as it has been by German and Italian immigrants.

The third division of the empire, containing the rivers flowing from the coast ranges and the central watershed, to the Atlantic, also possesses characteristics of its own, different to the Amazon and Plate basins. In the southern portion, from Rio Grande as far as Rio de Janeiro, the coast range, "Serra do Mar," gives rise to numerous precipitous streams falling into the Atlantic. The Rio S. Francisco, that might well be considered a distinct basin, as it really is, I have included in this section. It is accompanied during the greater part of its course by the bluffs of table-lands on each side of its valley; sometimes they approach near the banks and form healthy situations for townships; at other times the table-lands are only seen ten or twenty miles away from the river. In almost every case these bluffs or cliffs are designated as Serras, a very great mistake, for they should be called "Taboleiros" (table-lands). Near the village of Jacaré and at São Bom Jezus da Lapa, are some very curious limestone formations; they rise abruptly with perpendicular sides from a plain, their summits are weather-worn into pinnacles, points, and towers, with the interstices filled with the tall blue candelabra-like Munducurú cactus. Their fronts are stained and hoary with time, they look what I believe them to be, the ancient bones of the plateau that once filled the valley, their softer surrounding materials having long since been denuded and carried away to the distant Atlantic. The valley of the S. Francisco, is very different to that of the Amazons, in the absence of anything like the vast forest of the latter. The former only shows forest on the immediate banks of the stream, behind which are lower levels of lagoons, that accompany the river on its course, they vary in width from a few yards to a few miles, and often extend to the foot of the adjoining slopes of the table-land. The great part of the lowland of the valley, where not swampy, is covered with a dwarfed, scrubby vegetation, and tracts of grass-lands with occasional small extents of forest. This river, in many parts is extremely unhealthy, especially in the upper course. Yet with a little work, these malarious lagoons might easily be drained as the water of the river subsides, and these localities might be turned into extraordinarily rich and fertile lands, instead of being uninhabitable in many parts, as at present.

To the east and north of the S. Francisco valley, are the remaining riverine depressions that constitute the rest of the Atlantic river system. Here there are so many rivers, each containing its own basin distinct, that it is impossible in the compass of this paper to mention the numerous little groups; suffice to say that the north-east rivers rise in the elevated ridges of the north-east watershed, and flow by gentle gradients to the sea. The rivers Gurupy, Mearim, Itapucurú, and Parnahyba, are navigable for the greater part of their length, as are also many of the Atlantic rivers from the eastern divide of the S. Francisco. This region, although in many parts much broken up by isolated groups of hills and flat-topped elevations, is fairly regular. The Northern provinces of Ceará, Parahyba, Rio Grande do Norte, and Pernambuco are much subject to great and devastating droughts, that cause an immense amount of misery and suffering.

This third hydrographic division contains within itself the greater part of the population, wealth, and industry of the empire. Its climate varies from the genial climate of 32° south latitude to the damp heat of the Equator, and comprises an immense variety of soil and vegetation, from the forest-clad slopes of the Serra do Mar and Mantequeira; the woods and plains, of Rio de Janeiro; the virgin forests of the Rio Doce; the arid table-lands of Bahia, with their stores of mineral wealth; the rich mineral mountains of Minas Geraes; the sandy table-lands of the head-waters of the north-east division of the empire, and the intervening belt of forest at the foot of the coast slopes of the table-land, that terminates in low grassy plains, broken by occasional groups of hills.

In reviewing the subjects I have treated, it will be seen that the positions of the highest altitudes are practically in a straight line, for if a line is subtended from Roraima in the most northern extremity of the empire to the peak of Itatiaia-assu in the south, it will cut through the Montes Pyreneos in Goyaz, showing respective heights of 8600, 10,040, 9700 feet above the level of the sea, the highest being Itatiaia-assu, near the southern coast, and lowest Roraima in the north.

It is also interesting to note the great depression that extends through the centre of the South American continent, practically similar to what exists in the North American. For instance, a canoe can be navigated from the Rio Orinoco to the Rio Negro, thence to the Amazons, then up the Rios Maderia, Mamoré, Guaporé, and Alegré, here it will not be more than 500 or 600 feet above the sea; the canoe can then be hauled across a low grassy flat as is often done, to the Rio Agoapehy, then descend by the Rio Jaurú and Rio Paraguay, to Buenos Ayres. The distance from the Amazons to the Plate by this route is about 2500 miles, of which 1650 have already been traversed by steamers, leaving yet 850 miles to be navigated. But it must not be inferred, that, the whole of this route offers an almost uninterrupted course of navigable rivers; on the contrary, the remaining 850 miles that have not been explored by steamers, not only contain insurmountable obstacles to the passage of even the lightest draught steamer, but also in many places even to the ascent of a canoe. Yet this route will most probably be, in the more or less remote future, the main line of internal communication. By far the greater part of the lands of this natural way are as undeveloped as the Congo of Africa—in fact, more so, as the districts are only thinly populated by Indians and a very few settlers. There is also the connection between the Rio S. Francisco and Rio Tocantins. A canoe can leave the former river and go up the Rios Grande, Preto, and Sapão. The source of this last river is in a beautiful lake in a valley surrounded by fortress-looking table-topped hills; the margins of the lake are bordered by groves of grand Burity palms (*Mauritia vinifera ;*) on the west the lake drains out in a quick-flowing considerable stream, the Rio Diogo, joins a Rio Preto, and thence onwards by the Rio do Somno to the Tocantins. This journey could be made without once taking the canoe out of the water, except to descend with safety a few rough bits of water on the western outlet of the lake.

It will be seen on any map of Brazil that there are many spaces shown without rivers, and that many of the distances between the

DISTRIBUTION OF FOREST AND SCRUB.

indicated streams would scale many miles of apparently unwatered areas; still, I imagine that there is no country on the globe so well watered as Brazil, and my experience leads me to believe, that, it would be difficult to travel in any part of the country ten miles without meeting water, excepting on the arid table-lands of some of the watersheds. In a survey made down the Paraopeba and Upper S. Francisco, in a distance of 317 miles we passed seventy-seven streams, varying from at least fifteen feet wide to a much greater width, besides innumerable smaller streams and watercourses. But in N.E. Brazil, there occasionally occur great droughts that dry up all the streams, and even considerable rivers, and turn the country into a veritable desert.

It will be perceived that vast as is the Amazon forest, it occupies only about one-fourth of the area of the empire; the rest is taken up by the undulating table-lands 1000 to 3000 feet above the sea, mountain ranges rising to 5000 to 10,000 feet, and by the river valleys. In addition, however, to the forests of the Amazons there are the eastern slopes of the Maritime range, that as far as the meridian of Ouro Preto are, or were, primitively covered with indigenous forest growth. In the province of Parana are also considerable tracts of pines and other trees. In most of the valleys are also found long narrow belts of forest bordering the rivers; but the higher intervening ground between the valleys may safely be considered as what is known as *chapadas, taboleiros, geraes, campos, cerrados*, that is, flat ridged or undulating country covered with grass only in places, or in others by grass, bush, flowering plants, cacti and dwarf palms, or by the cerrados, a name that cannot be rendered into English as there is nothing in Europe to correspond to it; it practically means thick bush, having much the appearance of a wild neglected English orchard, overgrown with underwood, bushes, and grasses; the trees are small, extremely distorted and much scattered; they are of extremely hardy varieties, and resist equally heat and cold, wet and drought. These campos lands often extend over great areas; in Goyaz one can travel for several days through such lands without once sighting forest of any kind. The atmosphere of these elevations, especially of the campos, the savannahs, or prairies of Brazil, is most delightful and exhilarating. To thoroughly appreciate it, one must have resided for some time amidst the dark gloom of the forests, in their damp humid air impregnated with the myriad odours of fragrant or offensive plants, and of rotting vegetation; worried by the sting and the monotonous drone and hum of insects; bewildered by the maze and tangle of colossal trees and creeping twining festooned vines; and experience the sense of grim solitude, and the feeling of low depression that the shady gloom produces, and then emerge, like from night to day, on to these bright breezy uplands, sparkling with sunlight, gemmed with flowers, fragrant with sweet perfumes, and lively with the sounds of birds whistling, screaming, and warbling a noisy concert,—then how one will feel revived and take in the pure serene atmosphere, full of ozone, eagerly and with boyish inclinations to shout, to gallop your horse, anything to express your feeling of ecstasy and delight!

From the savannahs of Roraima, and the campos of the Amazons, right through Brazil to its southern provinces, is found on these uplands this glorious atmosphere. But delightful as it is, bright and extensive the far-spreading landscape, extending far away in great billowy earth-waves here and there shadowed by the passing clouds, and fading into the blue outlines of hills on the horizon, yet this campos land is considered, (north of the latitude of Ouro Preto,) unfit for anything but pastoral purposes. South of this division the soil improves in richness and moisture, and much of it can be adapted to the cultivation of cereals.

Another characteristic of these uplands, especially of the higher plateaux near the city of Barbacena, is the existence and appearance of numerous great rugged hollows in the sides and slopes of many of the great rolling grass-covered hills. These hollows are actually landslips, caused by the existence of springs of water. The aspect of these great natural excavations is picturesque in the extreme, both in form and colour; their sides are worn into every imaginable shape, pinnacles, domes and pointed towers, buttresses and cavities; ravines, narrow deep and precipitous, or wide open spaces surrounded by lofty perpendicular walls riven by cracks, and ready to fall, and add yet more to the chaos of boulders, and fantastic masses of earth that strew their floors. But it is in their colour that their great charm lies. The prevailing tint is a deep Indian red, that with the green of the hills and the blue sky above, flecked with glistening white clouds, constitute a charming combination of tones. Any one of these barrancas, as they are called, offers excellent opportunities to the geologist for the study of the soil, and truly the appearance is often extremely interesting. In many of them is found lying upon beds of sandstone near the floor of the hollow, extensive deposits of fine laminated clays, varying in thickness, but frequently divided into layers as thin as a sheet of paper, and consisting of an infinite variety of colours of the most opposite tint lying side by side—pink, blue, white, black, grey, orange, crimson, purple, and yellow. Professor Agassiz described precisely similar formations in the valley of the Amazons, and found them resting upon the sandstone beds of the lowest formation. Many of these barrancas especially in the neighbourhood of São João del Rey, show an upper stratum of white or yellow quartz gravel conglomerate, exceedingly rich in gold, and often gold can be procured from the surrounding earth from top to bottom of the sides, making the hill as it were literally peppered with grains of gold. In that district I have even procured it from the dust of the highways.

A characteristic of Brazil is a rich red highly fertile clay soil, that is found scattered over the whole of the country. I have been enabled to trace it in the valley of the Upper Paraopeba; in the neighbourhood of São João d'El Rey; the mouth of the Rio das Velhas; in the valley of Rio Preto, near Formosa; at Carolina on the Tocantins; and at Chapada in Maranhão. The substance and formation of this material, may be briefly described as a sheet of red unstratified clay, interspersed with pebbles and boulders overlying the rock in place. This stiff soft clay contains within itself all the mineralogical elements usually found in old metamorphic rock, such as granite, gneiss, mica, clay-slate, &c.; the boulders are usually masses of a kind of green stone, composed of an equal amount of greenish-black hornblende, and felspar, and they are entirely foreign to the rocks they often rest upon. It is well known that this formation originated Agassiz's theory of an ancient glacial age in Brazil, but I believe that his views have never been endorsed by any competent geologist, and have been ably and effectively controverted by Sir Charles Lyell. There yet remains a field for scientists to explore in definitely determining this curious phenomenon; but Mr. Buchanan, of the *Challenger*, directed his attention to it, and his theory of its formation is not only probable, but appeals to one's common sense without verging upon the marvellous.

THE END.

INDEX OF CONTENTS

AND

GLOSSARY

OF

BRAZILIAN WORDS AND IDIOMS USED IN THE BOOK.

ABAÊTÉ brilliant, the discovery of the, i. 329.
Abaête, the Rio, i. 329.
Abelha do cupim (bees that occupy the nests of the white ant), ii. 127.
Adventures with snakes, i. 331, 347, 394 ; ii. 181.
Ajojo, or raft, described, the, ii. 31.
Amador, village of Manga do, i. 16.
Anaconda of Brazil, the, i. 347 ; ii. 167, 172.
Animal life in palm forests, the ii. 253.
Ants, the fire- (formigos de fogo), ii. 282 ; a battle of, ii. 147 ; the Saúba, i. 147, ii. 58.
Ant-eater, the great, ii. 141.
Aranha d'agua (pr. *ar-ráhn-yah-dahg-oo-ah*), sting-ray, ii. 176.
Arary, the port of, ii. 299.
Araujo (*ar-rah-oó-shu*), the outlaw, ii. 155, 160.
Architecture, modern Brazilian, i. 12.
Armadillo, the, i. 153, 225.
Aroeiro-tree, the, i. 223.

Arráial (*ar-rah-ee-arl*), a village. The old Portuguese meaning of the word (now almost obsolete) is an encampment of a body of troops. The word was also formerly indicative of a semi-fortified village, and numbers of the old villages of Brazil still retain the name of arraíals, the same as many an old frontier fort or block-house in North America has left the title of fort to what is now a quiet country town or village, ii. 47.
Arriero (*ar-rey-air-o*) the chief muleteer of a mule troop, i. 55.
Art in Brazil, i. 24.
Arucaria pine, the, i. 68.

BACCAHIRIS Indians, the, ii. 263.
Bagre, the village of, i. 262.
Balsa, a raft, ii. 177, 190.
Balseiros (*bahl-say-rows*), raftsmen, ii. 190, 202, 205.
Bamboos, fodder for cattle, ii. 121.
Banana, the wild, ii. 209.
Baratas (*bar-ráh-tuz*), cockroaches, i. 181; ii. 175.

Barbacena, the city of, i. 71; its imports and exports, i. 79.

Barca of the Rio São Francisco, i. 407.

Barqueros (boatmen), i. 407; ii. 59; etiquette of, ii. 33; enormous appetites of, ii. 35; patience and endurance of the, ii. 65.

Barriguda, or vegetable silk-tree, the, i. 399.

Barro do Rio Grande, the city of, ii. 52.

Bat, the vampire, ii. 116, 122.

Batêa, a gold-washer's pan, i. 94.

Batuque dance, the (*bar-too-kee*), i. 190, 198, 334.

Bed, a convenient portable camp, ii. 61.

Bees, varieties of, i. 147, 201, 221; ii. 127, 197.

Beetles, i. 227.

Begging, ii. 28.

Bico de Toucano, the paddler, resources of, ii. 225.

Birni, the, an insect pest, i. 147, 158.

Bixo or bicho (*bee-shu*), a word that expresses any living thing or strange substance, an elephant, a foreigner, an insect, or a ghost, i. 50.

Boating, rafting, and canoeing experiences, i. 190, 335; ii. 31 to 52, 58 to 68, 193 to 213, 217 to 228, 265 to 296, 305 to 308.

Bode (a male goat), a slang term for mulattoes, ii. 16.

Bom Jardim, the town of, ii. 48.

Boqueirão, the Serra of (*bo-kay-roun*), ii. 69.

Bote, the traders' boat of the Rio Tocantins, ii. 216.

Bôtu, fresh-water dolphins, ii. 227.

Bracken, the Brazilian, i. 83; ii. 187.

Braços (arms) wanted in Brazil, ii. 229, 280.

Brazil, its state in the past, present, and future, ii. 346.

Brazilians, the upper classes of, i. 11, 28, 31, 39, 213, 247, 250; ii. 3, 26, 45, 54, 81, 229, 261, 298, 308; industrious, i. 184, 214, 251, 369; ii. 20, 50, 78, 100, 162, 174, 241, 284, 293; indolent, i. 12, 63, 88, 100, 107, 129, 134, 255, 263, 267, 297, 338, 374, 390, 396, 401; ii. 17, 23, 28, 71, 84, 101, 173, 211, 221, 228, 254; *enfans terribles*, i. 362, 363; ii. 261.

Brejos, (swamps or marshes,) of the Rio Paräopeba, i. 202; of the Rio São Francisco, i. 271, 273, 280, 291, 312, 322, 406; ii. 17, 24, 33, 56; of the Rio Grande, ii. 61, 63, 66; of the Rio Grajahu, ii. 288.

British products in Brazil, ii. 264.

British in Brazil, the, i. 33, 47, 75, 279, 308.

Buried alive, a refuge from mosquitoes, ii. 269.

Burity palm, the, i. 269; ii. 113, 121, 131, 139.

Burityzal, a cluster or grove of Burity palms growing in a morass, ii. 120, 129.

CABEÇA de frade, a dwarf cactus, ii. 125.

Caboclo, a Brazilian peasant; the term, however, implies an Indian descent, ii. 16.

Cabra (female goat), a term applied to the coloured lower classes of Brazilian peasants, ii. 16.

Cachaça, (*kah-shâh-sah*), a coarse spirit distilled from molasses. Restillo is the same spirit redistilled. Agoadente de cana is

INDEX.

a superior rum distilled from the juice of crushed sugar-cane, i. 197.

Cachoeira (*karsh-o-air-rah*) (a waterfall, cataract, or rapid) of the Apertada Hora, ii, 191, 200, 202; das Broacas, i. 326; de Formoza, i. 337; do Funil of the Parãopeba, i., 122; do Funil of the Somno, ii. 201; de Pirapora, i. 340; de Paulo Affonso, ii. 362; of the Tocantins, modes of passing, ii. 216.

Cactus peculiar to limestone rocks, ii. 11, 36.

Caëtatu, the common peccary, ii. 209.

Caju-trees, i. 255.

Camarada, literally a comrade, but in Minas Geraes, and in many other parts of Brazil, it is the name for travellers' attendants and for farm-labourers, for the free and independent Matuto objects to being called a "criado" (servant) in a slave-holding country, i. 49.

Campos or prairies, notes on the, i. 77, 173; exhilarating atmosphere of, i. 70, 173, 368; ii. 122, 371; vegetation of the, i. 68, 79, 253; ii. 314.

Camps and camp scenes, i. 267, 275, 277, 281, 288, 306, 314, 338; ii. 12, 124, 130, 153, 178, 195, 206, 267, 280, 289, 292.

Canal suggested to supply the northern provinces with water in time of drought, ii. 85.

Candles, wax, from the Carnahuba palm, ii. 47, 264.

Canga, a quartz conglomerate, one of the diamantine formations.

Canoeing, see *Boating*.

Capão, the Portuguese for capon, but in Brazil it is also an abbreviation of the Indian word "caü-poam," a island, or anything round, a term that well expresses the clumps and belts of woods that dot the open campos lands like islands of forest in a sea of grass, i. 79.

Capella Nova do Bitim, the village of, i. 128, 160.

Capim (*kah-peen*), grass. Capim melado or gordura, or de cheiro, a tall, velvety grass thickly impregnated with a viscid substance, and so highly perfumed that it scents the country-side, as new-mown hay will do in Europe; it is peculiar to the mountainous regions of Brazil and abandoned plantations, and is excellent fodder, i. 105.

Capitalists in the interior of Brazil, rarity of large, ii. 47.

Capoeiras of Rio, the (*kah-po-airas*), a class of vagabonds and assassins, i. 29.

Capoeiro, the second-growth forests of abandoned cultivations; according to its age it is known as capoeiro fino (saplings, bush, and shrub), or capoeiro (forest), or capoeiro grosso, or capoeirão (old forest, much resembling in appearance the virgin forest).

Capyvara or water-hog, the, i. 152; ii. 108.

Caraujos Indians, the, ii. 189.

Carinhanha, the city of (*kar-reen-yahn-yah*), ii. 25; the Rio de, ii. 25, 314.

Carnahuba palm, the products of the, ii. 47.

Carolina, the city of, ii. 229.

Carrapatos, ticks, i. 90, 147, 150.

Cascalho, a gravel belonging to

the diamantine formation, i. 330; ii. 207.
Cataracts (see *Cachoeira*).
Cattle districts, i. 219, 253, 301, 364; ii. 20, 83, 186, 211, 314.
Cattle, frantic desire of, for salt, i. 195, 272.
Cavalheiro d'industria, a, ii. 91.
Cecropia, candelabra or sloth-tree, i. 67; ii. 94.
Cedro, the cotton factory of, i. 214.
Central sugar factories, ii. 343.
Cerrados (*sair-rardos*), a class of vegetation that is found on all the uplands of Brazil, description of, i. 223.
Chacara(*shark'-ar-rah*), the grounds of a detached residence, as the "compound" in India. In North Brazil the word is substituted by "sitio," that is also a designation for small farms.
Chapadas, a term used in Brazil to designate any wide flat extent of land. The city of, ii. 257; da Mangabeira, ii. 144, 155.
Chapêo d'Uvas, the village of, i. 56.
Charming scenes and scenery, i. 3, 18, 33, 45, 68, 77, 96, 122, 253, 288, 312, 325, 334, 349; ii. 7, 50, 64, 76, 94, 116, 143, 196, 247, 252, 266, 274, 294.
Cherente Indians, ii. 162, 219.
Christão (a Christian), a name assumed by the Brazilian inhabitants of Indian border-lands, ii. 158.
Churches, i. 14, 23, 24, 92, 140, 216, 263, 390; ii. 36, 52, 82.
Clergy of inland Brazil, the, i. 112, 304, 391.
Climate of Brazil, ii. 316.
Climate of the campos, i. 70, 173.
Coaching, i. 44.

Coffee traffic in Rio, i. 21; districts, i. 44.
Coin, want of small, i. 297, 364.
Colonization, ii. 354.
Colour, tropical, i. 9, 33; ii. 293.
Comarca, an area of territory subject to the jurisdiction of a Juiz de Direito; it is divided into freguezias or parishes, and these into districtos (districts).
Comfort in Brazil, absence of, ii. 80.
Congonhas, cha de, a species of maté, i. 89.
Congonhas do Campos, the village of, i. 93.
Connection of the São Francisco and Tocantins rivers, ii, 141, 369.
Contendas, the village of, i. 387.
Copper regions, ii. 245, 260, 291.
Coração de Jezus, the village of, i. 373.
Coral-snake, the lovely colours of the, ii. 253.
Coroado Indians, ii. 161, 218.
Cost of travelling, i. 189; on the Rio São Francisco, ii. 29; on the Rio Grajahu, ii. 264.
Cotton cloth, native hand-woven, i. 100.
Cotton factories, i. 214; ii. 351.
Country fare, 58, 102, 239.
Crew, my, on the São Francisco, ii. 31, 34, 39; on the Rio Grande, ii. 59, 65; on the Rio do Somno, ii. 190, 198; on the Rio Tocantins, ii. 220; on the Rio Grajahu, ii. 266, 287.
Crimes in the interior often unpunished, ii. 225.
Cross, the village, i. 375.
Curassow, the, ii. 198.
Curiosity of the country people, i. 351, 374, 388; ii. 97.
Curioso, a jack-of-all-trades, i. 182.
Currupião bird, the, ii. 268.

INDEX. 379

DANCES, native, i. 198; ii. 236.
Debt of Brazil, the national, ii. 350.
Decadence of inland Brazil, i. 63, 92, 100, 125, 166, 197, 289, 361, 391; ii. 173, 346.
Deer-hunting, i. 111, 292; ii. 108, 126, 129; an adventure with a, ii. 182.
Diamond formation, the, i. 330; regions, i. 104, 207, 264, 329, 361; mines, ii. 328.
Disastrous loss, a, ii. 203, 229.
Discovery, an interesting, ii. 141.
Dissipation of the country folk, i. 200, 338, 387; ii. 17, 23, 39, 49, 234.
Diver-bird, the, ii. 292.
Dom Pedro Segundo Railway, i. 39; ii. 322; prospects of future extension of, i. 358; ii. 332.
Don Quixote, the hunter, ii. 111, 132, 135.
Donna Chiquinha, the monkey, i. 320; ii. 90, 103.
Dourado-fish, the, i. 318, 343; ii. 233.
Doutor, the, i. 298; ii. 45.
Ducks, and other water-fowl, varieties of, i. 324, 346; ii. 56, 64, 75, 109, 272, 295, 306.

EMA, or South American ostrich, i. 208.
Embira-assu, the bark of, ii. 241.
Entre Rios, the coffee district of, i. 44.
Esmolas (alms), ii. 28, 227.
Espingarda, the Riberão de, ii. 197.
Excursions in Rio, i. 18, 44, 73.
Expectoration, a national habit common to all classes of Brazilians, i. 74; ii. 97.
Expedition, the nature of the, i. 37; ii. 27.

FARINHA (*far-réen-yah*), a coarse-grained flour, made either by pounding maize (farinha de milho), or by grating the roots of mandioca (farinha de mandioca). Either one or the other of these farinhas is found upon almost every table of all classes of Brazilians throughout the Empire, i. 381.
Farms and farmers, i. 44, 61, 124, 161, 170, 202, 210, 219, 251, 266, 302, 315, 369; ii. 2, 12, 20, 50, 78, 100, 162, 174, 183, 186, 222, 228, 241, 245, 275, 293, 306.
Fazenda, a farm, or a plantation of coffee, sugar, tobacco, &c., but the great sugar estates of North Brazil are known as "engenhos," so named after "engenho," a mill; de Boa Esperança, ii. 174; de Mesquita, i. 161; de Mocombo, ii. 2; de Mottes, i. 124; de São Antonio, i. 202; de São Sebastião, i. 251; de Lontra, i. 210; de Picada, i. 219; de Porto Franco, ii. 186; de Tabua, ii. 21; d' Angelino, ii. 241; of Maranhão, 307.
Feroz (*fay-róss*) and his exploits, i. 285, 384; ii. 95, 199, 209.
Festa (or festival), a negro, ii. 235; a church, ii. 235, 297.
Fever districts, i. 267, 274, 280, 362; ii. 231, 290; varieties of intermittent, i. 291; ravages of, i. 273, 279, 283, 292, 308; attacked with, i. 290, 305, 309,; yellow, i. 28; ii. 324.
Finances, Brazilian, ii. 349.
Fish, of the Rio São Francisco, i. 343; of the Rio Tocantins, ii. 232; modes of catching, i. 260; shooting, i. 318; Indian mode of cooking, ii. 194; fishing, i.

114, 260; ii. 67, 194, 271; abundance of, i. 343; ii. 67, 271; the surubim, i. 260; ii. 233; the dourado, i. 318; ii. 233; the piranha, ii. 271; the curumatão, i. 312; the mandim, i. 260; the matrimxão, i. 260; the bótu, or fresh-water dolphin, ii. 227.

Flooded lands, ii. 10, 13, 24, 34, 40, 61, 294, 298.

Fogo, formigos de (fire-ants), ii. 282.

Fording streams, i. 263, 283, 357, 366, 385; ii. 152, 177, 178.

Forest scenes, i. 66, 118, 122, 145, 148, 157, 273, 295, 323, 325, 298; ii. 10, 94, 208, 243, 252, 270, 274, 286.

Formoza, village of, ii. 95.

Fortress-like hills (see *Chapada da Mangabeira*).

Frogs, nocturnal sounds of, i. 386; ii. 289.

Funeral, a peasant's (see *Wake*).

Funil, the rapids of (see *Cachoeira*)

GAMBLERS, ii. 49, 91.

Game, reasons for scarcity of, in inhabited districts, i. 397; districts, i. 123, 190; ii. 131, 165: partridges, i. 294; deer, peccaries, ii. 131, 165, 209; jaguars, ii. 131, 196, 211; pacas, i. 190.

Gamella Indians, ii. 274.

Gammeleira-tree, a wild fig, i. 205; ii. 267.

Gaols, country, ii. 26.

Gardner, the naturalist, ii. 114.

Garimpeiro (*gár-em-pear-o*), a diamond-digger.

Geraes, wild moorlands (*gee-rise*), ii. 112, 122.

Geralistas, inhabitants of the geraes, ii. 183.

Gipsies, Brazilian, i. 379.

Glacial theory of Brazil, ii. 372.

Goitre, i. 168, 265.

Gold, districts, i. 94, 258, 304, 361; ii. 173; mining, ii. 325.

Golfoẽs, (water-lilies), ii. 63.

Grass (see *Capim*) fires, i. 312.

Gravata, the wild pine-apple, ii. 267.

Guajajara Indians, ii. 263.

Guára (wolf), i. 292.

Guariba, the howling monkey, i. 320; ii. 267.

Guariroba palm, the, i. 288.

Guiacuhy, the village of, i. 358.

Gypsum deposits, ii. 268.

HALFED, M., survey of the Rio São Francisco, i. 49.

Hospitality, i. 184, 213, 220, 250, 317, 270; ii. 2, 20, 37, 44, 53, 81, 164, 184; churlish, i. 371; ii. 14.

Hotels and inns, Rio de Janeiro, i. 17; inland, i. 47, 56, 62, 72, 87.

Hunters, Brazilian, i. 293; ii. 111.

Hunting, i. 112, 109, 260.

IBIS, the, i. 345.

Igaritê, a decked river-boat (*e-gar-e-táy*), ii. 264.

Imbaûba (see *Cecoropia*).

Indian alarms, ii. 289; boys, ii. 217; border-lands, ii. 161; magnanimity, ii. 276; paddlers, ii. 274; raids and warfare, ii. 43, 114; persecution of, ii. 224, 277, 283; type of, ii. 148, 263, 277; the Baccahiris, ii. 263; Cherente, ii. 162, 219; Coroado, ii. 161, 218; Gamella, ii. 274; Guajajara, ii. 263; Itambeira, ii. 277, 283, 285; Anambeio, or white, ii. 263; primitive races of Rio de Janeiro, i. 19.

Ingativas, ii. 291.

INDEX.

Inns (see *Hotels*).
Insect plagues, i. 90, 147, 150, 221, 272; ii. 23, 32, 172, 175, 283: tortures of, i. 150; ii. 23, 283.
Ipey or Pau d'Arco tree, the, i. 67.
Iron mountains, i. 96.
Itacarambi, Morro de, ii. 11.
Itaipava, village of, i. 338.
Itambeira Indians, ii. 277, 283, 285.

JACARÉ (alligator), ii. 295; seized by piranhas, ii. 272; village of, ii. 8.
Jaguar, the, ii. 196.
Jalapão, the district of, ii. 160, 187.
Januaria, the city of, i. 406 to 410.
Japim bird, the, ii. 94.
Jararaca snake, the, i. 331, 348.
Jigger, the, bixo de pé, ii. 172.
Juiz de Fora, the city of, i. 46.
Jurubeba, the, i. 144.

KNIFING is killing, not murder, in Brazil, i. 199; ii. 93.

LABOURERS, i. 199, 267.
Lagoons, ii. 61.
Lakes, haunted, i. 280; ii. 294.
Land, large proprietors of, i. 44, 364; cheap price of, ii. 4; doubtful ownership of, i. 303; ii. 101; in Brazil not so fertile as is generally believed, ii. 354; sterile, ii. 370; rich, ii. 371.
Landslips of the campos, ii. 371.
Lapa (a cave), São Bom Jezus de, i. 36.
League, the Brazilian, i. 116.
Leather garments of the stock-raisers, i. 159.
Leather leggings, a Brazilian, ii. 111.
Life in Brazil, comparative safety of, i. 93; ii. 255.

Limestone rocks, fantastic appearance of, ii. 10, 36.
Lizards, i. 244, 340.
Lobo-homen (the wolf-man), i. 280.

MACAWS, ii. 123.
Magury heron, ii. 289.
Maize-leaf cigarettes, i. 121.
Mandim fish, the croaking, i. 289.
Mangabeira, Chapada de (see *Chapada*).
Mangabeira-tree, the, i. 254, 268.
Mantequeira, Serra de, i. 68; ii. 361.
Maracaja, or wild cat, i. 199.
Maranhão, the city of, ii. 306.
Marble deposits, i. 400.
Marimbondas, hornets, i. 151; ii. 283.
Marmosets, i. 226.
Marriage, a country, i. 234; not an indispensable ceremony in inland Brazil, i. 104.
Marsh (see *Brejo*) birds, i. 346; ii. 56, 75, 108.
Maté, or Paraguayan tea, i. 89.
Matuto, peasant, an inhabitant of woodlands in contradistinction to Sertanejo, an inhabitant of the campos-lands of cattle districts.
Mearim, the Rio, ii. 295, 299, 306.
Menu of a country inn, i. 58.
Minas Geraes, the name of this province is indicative of its mineral wealth; the literal translation is "mines in general," or the land of all kinds of minerals.
Mining (see *Gold*).
Misery in inland Brazil, i. 402; ii. 70, 211, 228.
Missionaries, Italian, ii. 219.
Mists, i. 34, 42, 94, 189.
Monkey, the howling, ii. 267.
Montaria, a small boat used on the

Amazons river and its tributaries, ii. 217.
Morality of the matuto, religious, i. 303.
Morro velho mine, ii. 328.
Mortes, Rio dos, origin of name of, ii. 325.
Mosquitos, i. 146, 272; ii. 22, 32, 41, 267; how to keep off, i. 272.
Motúca fly, the, ii. 90, 283.
Mountain peaks of Brazil, ii. 368.
Mules, i. 50, 60, 103, 119, 121, 387; ii. 95, 73, 150, 189; sufferings of, ii. 189; hire of, ii. 189.
Muleteers, i. 55, 133; ii. 238.
Munducuru, a candelabra cactus, Morro do, ii. 179.
Mutton, popular prejudice against, ii. 20.
Mutum, the curassow, ii. 198.

NATIONAL beer, i. 48, 124.
Native opinion of Englishmen, i. 135; ii. 302.
Natives, treatment of, by travellers, ii. 255.
Natividade, an old mining centre, ii. 173.
Negroes, industrious, i. 365; ii. 241.
Neotim, the hamlet of, i. 119.
Night scenes in camp, i. 257, 281, 306, 308, 334, 350, 386; ii. 12, 21, 124, 130, 133, 152, 194, 240; on the Rio São Francisco, ii. 32, 41, 50; on the Rio Grajahu, ii. 267, 269, 278, 281, 289, 292.

OGRE, a veritable, ii. 223.
Old age in Brazil, 49, 204.
Orchids, i. 49; ii. 19.
Ostrich, the South American, ii. 19.

PACA, or spotted cavy, the, i. 153, 190.

Pacuhy, the Rio, i. 385.
Paddles, varieties of, ii. 221.
Padres (priests), i. 391; ii. 6.
Palm forests, ii. 252, 273; the Burity, ii. 113, 121, 131, 139; the Bacaba, ii. 201; the Guariroba, i. 288; the Carnahuba, ii. 47; the Inaja, ii. 210; the Maraja, ii. 252, 274; the Tucum, ii. 201; the Ubussu, ii. 252.
Pancadas, a local name, used to designate strong currents of water on the Rio do Somno, i. 193, 198, 200.
Pantanal, a fen.
Para, the hamlet of, ii. 48.
Paracis Indians, the chief race of Matto Grosso, ii. 263.
Parahyba, the Rio, i. 43.
Parahybuna, the Rio, i. 45.
Paraopeba, the Rio, i. 114, 122, 166, 200.
Partridges, i. 293.
Passion-flower, the indigenous, ii. 19.
Pasto, a pasture, i. 60, 150.
Pau d' Arco, i. 67; great range of, ii. 94.
Pau Pereira tree, the, i. 274.
Paulo Affonso, the falls of, ii. 362.
Pavão, or wild peacock, ii. 268.
Peccaries, ii. 131, 165, 207; described, ii. 137; attacked by, ii. 133.
Pedra de fortaleza, i. 45.
Pedras de Maria da Cruz, village of, i. 401.
Pedro Affonso, the village of, ii. 215.
Penelopes, ii. 275.
Phosphorescent fungus, ii. 126.
Picada, a lane cut through the woods, either for the purpose of surveying, or for a path or a road, i. 144.

INDEX. 383

Pig-sticking, ii. 141, 150.
Pindahyba groves, i. 266; ii. 145.
Piranha fish, the, i. 343; ii. 271, 288, 295.
Pirapora (an Indian word implying a fish-leap), the rapids of, i. 340, 349; the village of, i. 341; excessive heat of the district of, i. 339, 344; the beautiful vegetation of, i. 350.
Pium, sand-flies, ii. 275, 279, 281.
Plumbago, deposits of, ii. 260.
Police, the country, ii. 232.
Porteira, the village of, i. 361.
Porto Franco, ii. 183.
Prairies (see *Campos*).
Precautions against fevers, i. 284; ii. 324.
Produce, prices of country, i. 297.
Productions of districts, i. 61, 80, 82, 111, 224, 297, 329, 343, 377; ii. 4, 56, 82, 173, 232, 260, 307.
Public gardens of Rio, i. 22.
Pulex penetrans, ii. 172.

QUEIMADOS, bush fires, i. 205.
Quilombeiros, a band of outlaws, fugitives slaves, &c., ii. 160.

RABBITS, i. 346.
Race, a, i. 259; ii. 272.
Raft, the Burity frond, ii. 190, 206.
Rafting, ii. 193 to 213.
Railways in Brazil, State, ii. 332; national, ii. 335; British, ii. 337; the Dom Pedro Segundo, i. 21, 38, 41, 358; ii. 332.
Rainy seasons, ii. 98, 178, 185, 188; depressing effects of, ii. 5, 13.
Rancho, a hut, i. 289.
Rapids (see *Cachoeira*), shooting, i. 337; ii. 193, 200, 203.
Rattlesnakes, i. 181, 394; ii. 251.
Restillo (see *Cachaça*).
Rhea Americana, i. 208.

Rio de Janeiro, the river of January, so named by the first discoverer on entering it the first time during this month, and imagining it to be the mouth of a great river instead of a bay.
Rio das Balsas, ii. 209; Diogo, ii. 147; Parahyba, i. 43; Parahybuna, i. 45; Grande, ii. 71; Grajahu, ii. 266; Carinhanha, ii. 314; Preto, ii. 74, 115; Somno, ii. 193; São Francisco, ii. 366; Tocantins, ii. 222; Mearim, ii. 305; Perdido, ii. 212; Sapão, ii. 117; das Mortes, ii. 325; das Velhas, i. 358; da Tapera Grande, i. 325; Paracatu, i. 328; Jiquitahy, i. 366; Maracaja, ii. 285.
Roads, macadamized, i. 45; want of, i. 401; natural, i. 83; sandy ii. 255; forest, i. 65, 400; mountain, i. 65, 98; ii. 249; bridgeless, i. 379; the União e Industria, i. 45.
Roça, a mixed plantation of maize, beans, manioc, potatoes, &c.
Rodrigues, the tropeiro, ii. 77, 80, 107, 116, 136, 189.

SAILING on the Rio São Francisco, ii. 33.
Saline properties deficient in Brazilian grasses, i. 195.
Salt, largely imported, ii. 188; licks, ii. 123; costliness of, ii. 123, 188, 211.
Samambaia bracken, the, ii. 166, 187.
Sand-flies, i. 279.
Sandy regions, ii. 245, 255; roads, ii. 239.
Santa Maria, the hamlet of, ii. 113.
Santa Quiteria, the town of, i. 173.
Santa Rita, the town of, ii. 81.

São Bom Jezus da Lapa, the cave, church, and village of, ii. 37.

São Francisco, Rio de, junction of, with the Rio das Velhas, i. 360; the valley of the, i. 311, 337; the climate of the, ii. 367; source of the, i. 340; fevers of the, i. 291; ii. 17; vegetation of the, ii. 367; the swamps of the, i. 312; ii. 55; diamond regions of the, i. 264, 329, 341; trade of the, ii. 334; railways to the, ii. 334; proposed new province of, ii. 43; the barca of the, i. 407; the barqueiro of the, ii. 35; fish of the, i. 343; a storm on the, ii. 41; nights on the, ii. 32, 41, 50; length of the, i. 340.

São Gonçalo da Ponte, the village of, i. 100.

São João d' El Rey, the city of, i. 73; the gold-mine of, ii. 328.

São José, the village of, i. 106.

Sapão, the Rio, ii. 117.

Sapucainha tree, the, ii. 248.

Satin spar, deposits of, ii. 268.

Saúba ant, the, ii. 53.

Saudades (*sah-oo-dahdys*), i. 247.

Schoolmaster, a country, ii. 70.

Serenhema, the, i. 207.

Serpents, i. 347.

Serra (*sáir-rah*), a mountain range; the term is, however, often applied in Brazil to the bluffs of table-lands; of the Apertada Hora, ii. 206; serras of Brazil, ii. 359; de Boas Mortes, i. 95; de Boqueirão, ii. 69; da Cinta, ii. 250; do Genipapo, i. 360; do Mar, ii. 361; de Mantequeira, i. 65; dos Orgãos, ii. 361; de Tres Irmãos, i. 122; do Tipy, ii. 85; Monte Marius, i. 77.

Sertão (*sair-tóun*), the name of many of the elevated campos-lands of Brazil, where the occupations of the inhabitants are mainly those of cattle-farmers, i. 219, 252.

Sertanejo (*sair-tarn-áye-shu*), an inhabitant of the Sertão, i. 240, 252.

Sessions of Chapada, the, ii. 261.

Shooting, i. 112, 190, 260; ii. 55, 108, 127, 129.

Shupé bee, curious nests of the, ii. 197.

Sitio de Matto, the town of, ii. 43.

Slaves, i. 161, 179, 196; ii. 187.

Snags, trunks and roots of fallen trees that obstruct the navigation of rivers, ii. 276.

Snakes, varieties of, i. 201, 244, 287, 331, 348; ii. 267; vitality of, i. 246; adventures with, i. 331, 347; ii. 181; poison of (a subcutaneous injection of permanganate of potash, is a most efficacious and the best antidote, and is largely used in Brazil with very great success).

Soil, varieties of, i. 54, 83, 86, 117, 133, 375; ii. 89, 99; peculiar to Brazil, ii. 372; of Brazil not so fertile as it is generally believed to be, ii. 354.

Soccó (bittern), ii. 272, 289.

Solitude, the doubtful pleasures of, i. 350; ii. 185.

Somno, the Rio do, ii. 193 to 213.

Spoonbills, ii. 43.

Sport (see *Hunting, Fishing, Shooting*).

Spotted cavy, the, i. 153, 190.

Sting-ray (Aranha d' agua), ii. 176.

Stock-raising, ii. 186.

Storms, i. 137, 169; ii. 7, 40, 177, 195, 300.

Students, Brazilian, ii. 45.

Succurihu (*Soo-koo-re-yoo*) boa, the,

i. 348; ii. 167; top-boots made from the skin of, ii. 171.

Sugar-mills, ii. 340; regions, ii. 307, 336, 337; the most effective crusher of cane, ii. 225.

Sumidouro, a sink, or places where a body of running water disappears by a subterranean channel, ii. 204.

Sunday travelling, the misfortunes of, i. 287; in country villages, i. 132, 216; at Fazenda Mesquita, i. 164.

Sunset effects, i. 349; ii. 76, 196, 206, 281.

Sunstroke, an attack of, i. 344.

Superstition, i. 264, 280, 287, 351; ii. 39, 74, 294.

Surubim fish, the, i. 261, 343; ii. 233, 273.

Surveying through marsh, forest, and prairie, i. 157, 220, 293, 323.

Sussu-apara, the largest species of deer in Brazil; adventure with a, ii. 182.

Swamps (see *Brejos*).

Swine, Brazilian, i. 342, 390.

TABLE-LANDS of Brazil, exhilarating climate of, i. 368; areas and characteristics of the, ii 370.

Taboleiro Grande, the village of, i. 215.

Taboleiro (*tah-bo-léy-ro*), a tray, a wide flat surface, the name also of the gently undulating plains of the summits of table-lands.

Tamanduá Bandeira, the great anteater, ii. 141.

Tapirs, i. 197.

Tapuyos (*tah-poó-yews*), wild Indians; the word "gentiho" is also used with a similar meaning (see *Indians*).

Tea, Brazilian, i. 89.

Temperature of Brazil, ii. 316.

Ticks, varieties of, i. 90, 150.

Timber, why it is so expensive in Brazil, i. 399.

Tin regions, i. 156.

Tocantins, the Rio; aspect of, 222, 228 voyaging on, ii. 228; trade and navigation of, 216; not a tributary of the Rio Amazons, ii. 364; the valley of, ii. 228.

Toucan, the, i. 345.

Trade and traders, ii. 69, 83, 216, 232, 255, 262, 299, 304; the commerce of Brazil, ii. 351.

Tramping on foot, ii. 216, 232.

Transport of goods and baggage, i. 106, 301, 320, 332.

Travelling in Brazil, comfortable costume for, ii. 243; safety of, ii. 93; arduous life of, ii. 251.

Travessia (*trahves-se-ah*), meaning of the word, ii 85.

Tropeiro (*tru-pay-row*), a muleteer, i. 121, 133, 359.

Tropical light and shade, i. 9. 118, 122, 160, 217, 362, 376; ii. 76, 293.

Toucinho (*too-séen-yo*). The outer fatty covering of the bodies of pigs is cut off from the flesh, in one sheet, it is then gashed with a knife, salt is sprinkled over and rubbed in, and finally the whole is made up into a roll, and constitutes the *toucinho* of commerce. The thickness varies according to the fatness of the animal, and a pig is classified as "two, three, four, or five fingered," the standard of the thickness of a finger being adopted for measuring the thickness of fat that the animal will show when killed. This product is used by all classes in Brazil as

the main basis of all culinary operations.
Tucum palm, the, ii. 202.
Turbulent districts, ii. 51.

VAMPIRE bats, ii. 116, 122.
Vanilla, wild, i. 268.
Velhas, Rio das, i. 357.
Vellozias, or tree-lilies, ii. 122.
Venda, a general store of groceries, hardware, dry and wet goods, i. 123.
Victoria, the town of, i. 297.
Villa Pastura, the barca, ii. 9.
Vulture, the urubu, i. 41.

UNDER canvas, i. 218, 257, 281 ; ii. 195.
União e Industria road, i. 44.

Urubu, the town of, ii. 43.

WAKE, a Brazilian, ii. 104.
War of the Guimarães, ii. 51.
Water in Brazil, abundance of, ii. 369.
Water-hog, a pest to farmers, i. 153 ; ii. 109.
Water-lilies, a river obstructed by, ii. 63.
Watersheds, i. 86 ; ii. 117, 141, 359.
White Indians ii. 263.
Whetstones, a hill of, ii. 268.
Wilderness, sighting strangers in the, ii. 155.
Wolf, the guàra, i. 226.

YELLOW fever, i. 28 ; ii. 324.

THE END.

www.ingramcontent.com/pod-product-compliance
Lightning Source LLC
Chambersburg PA
CBHW022118290426

44112CB00008B/716